The Middle Ages

VOLUME II

Readings in Medieval History

FIFTH EDITION

Brian Tierney
Cornell University

McGraw-Hill, Inc.
New York St. Louis San Francisco Auckland Bogotá
Caracas Lisbon London Madrid Mexico Milan
Montreal New Delhi Paris San Juan Singapore
Sydney Tokyo Toronto

McGraw-Hill College
A Division of The McGraw·Hill Companies

Editorial director: *Jane E. Vaicumas*
Sponsoring editor: *Lyn Uhl*
Editorial coordinator: *Rachel Morgan*
Senior marketing manager: *Suzanne Daghlian*
Project manager: *Cathy Ford Smith*
Production supervisor: *Sandy Ludovissy*
Cover designer: *Gino Cieslik*
Interior designer: *Maureen McCutcheon*
Compositor: *Shepherd, Inc.*
Typeface: *10/12 Palatino*
Printer: *R. R. Donnelley & Sons Company/Crawfordsville, IN*

The Library of Congress has cataloged the two-volume edition as follows

The Middle Ages / [edited by] Brian Tierney. — 5th ed.
    p. cm.
    Includes bibliographical references and index.
    Contents: v. 1. Sources in medieval history —
    ISBN 0–07–303290–1 (v. 1 : alk. paper)
    1. Middle Ages—History—Sources. 2. Middle Ages—History.
I. Tierney, Brian
D113.M49 1999   98–16808
909.07—dc21   CIP

www.mhhe.com

Contents

FEUDAL SOCIETY: PROBLEMS
AND APPROACHES

ECONOMIC LIFE AND SOCIAL CHANGE

HUMANISM AND "RENAISSANCE" IN THE TWELFTH CENTURY

WOMEN AND FAMILY

SPIRITUAL AND TEMPORAL POWER

ON THE MARGIN; VAGABONDS, OUTCASTS, AND JEWS

PROBLEMS OF LATE MEDIEVAL SOCIETY

About the Author

After serving in the Royal Air Force, Brian Tierney received his B.A. and Ph.D. from Cambridge University. He has taught at Catholic University, Washington, D.C., and at Cornell, where he is now Bryce and Edith M. Bowmar Professor in Humanistic Studies Emeritus. He has been the recipient of Guggenheim Fellowships and of fellowships from the American Council of Learned Societies and the National Endowment for the Humanities. Professor Tierney has been awarded the honorary degrees of Doctor of Theology by Uppsala University, Sweden, and Doctor of Humane Letters by Catholic University. A specialist in medieval church history, he has published many articles and several books, among them *Foundations of the Conciliar Theory; The Crisis of Church and State, 1050–1300;* and *Religion, Law, and the Growth of Constitutional Thought, 1150–1650.* He is the coeditor with Joan Scott of *Western Societies: A Documentary History.* His most recent book is *The Idea of Natural Rights: Studies on Natural Rights, Natural Law, and Church Law, 1150–1625.*

Note on the Fifth Edition

A book of *Readings* on medieval history should reflect the current concerns of scholars in the field. The problem for the editor of a new edition is that the range of scholarly interests is always expanding while the book has to stay roughly the same length. Nowadays many students want to know more about family history, women's roles, demographic trends, attitudes about the natural environment. But it remains true that, to understand the Middle Ages at all, we still need to know such things as how feudal institutions worked, what the claims of the medieval papacy were, and how Thomas Aquinas thought he could prove the existence of God. The new interests are a supplement to the old ones, not a substitute for them.

In this new edition I have again tried to maintain a balance between new themes and traditional ones. Some readings have been replaced by alternate ones and some additional readings included. The new readings in this edition are from Robert Bartlett, Antony Black, Elizabeth A. R. Brown, R. W. Carlyle and A. J. Carlyle, Patrick Geary, Bronislaw Geremek, Barbara Hanawalt, and Christiane Klapisch-Zuber.

Preface

This two-volume collection of *Sources of Medieval History* and *Readings in Medieval History* is intended for use in college history courses. The collection was prepared to accompany *Western Europe in the Middle Ages, 300–1475*, by Brian Tierney and Sidney Painter, but it can be used equally well with any of the popular textbooks in the field.

The purpose of the work has helped to determine its form. In particular, the amount of introductory, narrative material has been deliberately kept to a minimum. It seemed more useful to present the widest possible variety of medieval *Sources* and modern *Readings* in these volumes rather than to reproduce routine information that any teacher can supply or that the student can find for himself in any standard textbook. Again, while every anthology must reflect to some degree the taste and judgment of its compiler, I have tried not to emphasize unduly my own idiosyncrasies in making the selections. The *Sources* and *Readings* illustrate topics in the mainstream of medieval history, topics that most instructors will want to discuss with their classes.

The *Sources* are drawn from many different kinds of medieval materials. The *Readings* include essays on social, economic, political, religious, and intellectual history. One criterion that I have tried to keep constantly in mind is that of Johann Huizinga—"Unreadable history is no history at all."

Brian Tierney

THE END OF
THE ANCIENT WORLD

Why did the Roman empire "fall"? This is the first great problem that a historian of the Middle Ages encounters. The question is one of endless fascination; no simple, satisfactory answer to it has yet been found. We know that the empire was invaded by barbarians and that its people lacked the strength and nerve and will to defend their society effectively. Ever since the Renaissance period (when Machiavelli was much concerned with the problem), historians have tried to explain why this was so. Often the explanations tell us as much about the intellectual prejudices of the historian's own generation as about the affairs of ancient Rome. Each new movement of thought in the modern world gives rise to a new explanation for the decay of classical civilization. Thus, in the writings of the twentieth century, we can find social, economic, religious, racist, demographic, and ecological interpretations of the fall of Rome.

Edward Gibbon, unsurpassed among historians as a literary artist, viewed the late Roman empire from the standpoint of the eighteenth-century Enlightenment. In his day no single power dominated all of Europe, and Gibbon was well content with this state of affairs. He attributed the decline of Rome simply to ``immoderate greatness.'' Also he was inclined to think that the rise of Christianity had exercised a debilitating influence on ancient society. Rostovtzeff, a Russian historian, was a professor at the University of St. Petersburg when the Communist revolution broke out in 1918. In 1920 he emigrated to America. Rostovtzeff emphasized social conditions, especially class antagonisms, as the underlying cause of Rome's fall. Later historians have suggested that his interpretation, like Gibbon's, was much influenced by the circumstances of his own lifetime.

Some scholars have rejected the description of the fourth and fifth centuries as simply an age of ``decline and fall.'' If there was evident political disintegration, they argue, there was also enormous religious vitality. In the final reading, Peter Brown discusses the interplay of Christian and classical cultures in the late Roman world.

CHAPTER 1

General Observations on the Fall of the Roman Empire in the West

Edward Gibbon

The rise of a city, which swelled into an empire, may deserve, as a singular prodigy, the reflection of a philosophic mind. But the decline of Rome was the natural and inevitable effect of immoderate greatness. Prosperity ripened the principle of decay; the causes of destruction multiplied with the extent of conquest; and, as soon as time or accident had removed the artificial supports, the stupendous fabric yielded to the pressure of its own weight. The story of its ruin is simple and obvious; and, instead of inquiring why the Roman empire was destroyed, we should rather be surprised that it had subsisted so long. The victorious legions, who, in distant wars, acquired the vices of strangers and mercenaries, first oppressed the freedom of the republic, and afterwards violated the majesty of the purple. The emperors, anxious for their personal safety and the public peace, were reduced to the base expedient of corrupting the discipline which rendered them alike formidable to their sovereign and to the enemy; the vigour of the military government was relaxed, and finally dissolved, by the partial institutions of Constantine; and the Roman world was overwhelmed by a deluge of Barbarians.

The decay of Rome has been frequently ascribed to the translation of the seat of empire; but this history has already shown that the powers of government were *divided* rather than *removed*. The throne of Constantinople was erected in the East; while the West was still possessed by a series of emperors who held their residence in Italy and claimed their equal inheritance of the legions and provinces. This dangerous novelty impaired the strength, and fomented the vices, of a double reign; the instruments of an oppressive and arbitrary system were multiplied; and a vain emulation of luxury, not of merit, was introduced and supported between the degenerate successors of Theodosius. Extreme distress, which unites the virtue of a free people, embitters the

From Edward Gibbon, *The Decline and Fall of the Roman Empire*, J. B. Bury, ed., 2d ed. (London: Methuen, 1901), Vol. 4, pp. 161–169.

factions of a declining monarchy. The hostile favourites of Arcadius and Honorius betrayed the republic to its common enemies; and the Byzantine court beheld with indifference, perhaps with pleasure, the disgrace of Rome, the misfortunes of Italy, and the loss of the West. Under the succeeding reigns, the alliance of the two empires was restored; but the aid of the Oriental Romans was tardy, doubtful, and ineffectual; and the national schism of the Greeks and Latins was enlarged by the perpetual difference of language and manners, of interest, and even of religion. Yet the salutary event approved in some measure the judgment of Constantine. During a long period of decay, his impregnable city repelled the victorious armies of Barbarians, protected the wealth of Asia, and commanded, both in peace and war, the important straits which connect the Euxine and Mediterranean seas. The foundation of Constantinople more essentially contributed to the preservation of the East than to the ruin of the West.

As the happiness of a *future* life is the great object of religion, we may hear, without surprise or scandal, that the introduction, or at least the abuse, of Christianity had some influence on the decline and fall of the Roman empire. The clergy successfully preached the doctrines of patience and pusillanimity; the active virtues of society were discouraged; and the last remains of the military spirit were buried in the cloister; a large portion of public and private wealth was consecrated to the specious demands of charity and devotion; and the soldiers' pay was lavished on the useless multitudes of both sexes, who could only plead the merits of abstinence and chastity. Faith, zeal, curiosity, and the more earthly passions of malice and ambition kindled the flame of theological discord; the church, and even the state, were distracted by religious factions, whose conflicts were sometimes bloody, and always implacable; the attention of the emperors was diverted from camps to synods; the Roman world was oppressed by a new species of tyranny; and the persecuted sects became the secret enemies of their country. Yet party-spirit, however pernicious or absurd, is a principle of union as well as of dissension. The bishops, from eighteen hundred pulpits, inculcated the duty of passive obedience to a lawful and orthodox sovereign; their frequent assemblies, and perpetual correspondence, maintained the communion of distant churches: and the benevolent temper of the gospel was strengthened, though confined, by the spiritual alliance of the Catholics. The sacred indolence of the monks was devoutly embraced by a servile and effeminate age; but, if superstition had not afforded a decent retreat, the same vices would have tempted the unworthy Romans to desert, from baser motives, the standard of the republic. Religious precepts are easily obeyed, which indulge and sanctify the natural inclinations of their votaries; but the pure and genuine influence of Christianity may be traced in its beneficial, though imperfect, effects on the Barbarian proselytes of the North. If the decline of the Roman empire was hastened by the conversion of Constantine, his victorious religion broke the violence of the fall, and mollified the ferocious temper of the conquerors.

This awful revolution may be usefully applied to the instruction of the present age. It is the duty of a patriot to prefer and promote the exclusive interest and glory of his native country; but a philosopher may be permitted to enlarge his views, and to consider Europe as one great republic, whose various inhabitants have attained almost the same level of politeness and cultivation. The balance of power will continue to fluctuate, and the prosperity of our own or the neighbouring kingdoms may be alternately exalted or depressed; but these partial events cannot essentially injure our general state of happiness, the system of arts, and laws, and manners, which so advantageously distinguish, above the rest of mankind, the Europeans and their colonies. The savage nations of the globe are the common enemies of civilized society; and we may inquire with anxious curiosity, whether Europe is still threatened with the repetition of those calamities which formerly oppressed the arms and institutions of Rome. Perhaps the same reflections will illustrate the fall of that mighty empire, and explain the probable causes of our actual security.

I. The Romans were ignorant of the extent of their danger, and the number of their enemies. Beyond the Rhine and Danube, the northern countries of Europe and Asia were filled with innumerable tribes of hunters and shepherds, poor, voracious, and turbulent; bold in arms, and impatient to ravish the fruits of industry. The Barbarian world was agitated by the rapid impulse of war; and the peace of Gaul or Italy was shaken by the distant revolution of China. The Huns, who fled before a victorious enemy, directed their march towards the West; and the torrent was swelled by the gradual accession of captives and allies. The flying tribes who yielded to the Huns assumed in *their* turn the spirit of conquest; the endless column of Barbarians pressed on the Roman empire with accumulated weight; and, if the foremost were destroyed, the vacant space was instantly replenished by new assailants. Such formidable emigrations can no longer issue from the North; and the long repose, which has been imputed to the decrease of population, is the happy consequence of the progress of arts and agriculture. Instead of some rude villages, thinly scattered among its woods and morasses, Germany now produces a list of two thousand three hundred walled towns; the Christian kingdoms of Denmark, Sweden, and Poland, have been successively established; and the Hanse merchants, with the Teutonic knights, have extended their colonies along the coast of the Baltic, as far as the Gulf of Finland. From the Gulf of Finland to the Eastern Ocean, Russia now assumes the form of a powerful and civilized empire. The plough, the loom, and the forge, are introduced on the banks of the Volga, the Oby, and the Lena; and the fiercest of the Tartar hordes have been taught to tremble and obey. The reign of independent Barbarism is now contracted to a narrow span; and the remnant of Calmucks or Uzbecks, whose forces may be almost numbered, cannot seriously excite the apprehensions of the great republic of Europe. Yet this apparent security should not tempt us to forget that new enemies, and unknown dangers, may *possibly* arise from some obscure people, scarcely visible in the map of the world. The Arabs or Saracens, who spread their conquests from India to Spain, had languished in poverty and contempt, till Mahomet breathed into those savage bodies the soul of enthusiasm.

II. The empire of Rome was firmly established by the singular and perfect coalition of its members. The subject nations, resigning the hope, and even the wish, of independence, embraced the character of Roman citizens; and the provinces of the West were reluctantly torn by the Barbarians from the bosom of their mother-country. But this union was purchased by the loss of national freedom and military spirit; and the servile provinces, destitute of life and motion, expected their safety from the mercenary troops and governors, who were directed by the orders of a distant court. The happiness of an hundred millions depended on the personal merit of one or two men, perhaps children, whose minds were corrupted by education, luxury, and despotic power. The deepest wounds were inflicted on the empire during the minorities of the sons and grandsons of Theodosius; and, after those incapable princes seemed to attain the age of manhood, they abandoned the church to the bishops, the state to the eunuchs, and the provinces to the Barbarians. Europe is now divided into twelve powerful, though unequal, kingdoms, three respectable commonwealths, and a variety of smaller, though independent, states; the chances of royal and ministerial talents are multiplied, at least with the number of its rulers; and a Julian, or Semiramis, may reign in the North, while Arcadius and Honorius again slumber on the thrones of the South. The abuses of tyranny are restrained by the mutual influence of fear and shame; republics have acquired order and stability; monarchies have imbibed the principles of freedom, or, at least, of moderation; and some sense of honour and justice is introduced into the most defective constitutions by the general manners of the times. In peace, the progress of knowledge and industry is accelerated by the emulation of so many active rivals: in war, the European forces are exercised by temperate and undecisive contests. If a savage conqueror should issue from the deserts to Tartary, he must repeatedly vanquish the robust peasants of Russia, the numerous armies of Germany, the gallant nobles of France, and the intrepid freemen of Britain; who, perhaps, might confederate for their common defence. Should the victorious Barbarians carry slavery and desolation as far as the Atlantic Ocean, ten thousand vessels would transport beyond their pursuit the remains of civilized society; and Europe would revive and flourish in the American world, which is already filled with her colonies and institutions.

III. Cold, poverty, and a life of danger and fatigue, fortify the strength and courage of Barbarians. In every age they have oppressed the polite and peaceful nations of China, India, and Persia, who neglected, and still neglect, to counterbalance these natural powers by the resources of military art. The warlike states of antiquity, Greece, Macedonia, and Rome, educated a race of soldiers; exercised their bodies, disciplined their courage, multiplied their forces by regular evolutions, and converted the iron which they possessed, into strong and serviceable weapons. But this superiority insensibly declined with their laws and manners; and the feeble policy of Constantine and his successors armed and instructed, for the ruin of the empire, the rude valour of the Barbarian mercenaries. The military art has been changed by the invention of gunpowder; which enables man to command the two most powerful agents of nature, air, and fire. Mathematics, chymistry, mechanics, architecture, have been applied to the service of war; and the adverse parties oppose to each other the most elaborate modes of attack and of defence. Historians may indignantly observe that the preparations of a siege would found and maintain a flourishing colony; yet we cannot be displeased that the subversion of a city should be a work of cost and difficulty, or that an industrious people should be protected by those arts, which survive and supply the decay of military virtue. Cannon and fortifications now form an impregnable barrier against the Tartar horse; and Europe is secure from any future irruption of Barbarians; since, before they can conquer, they must cease to be barbarous. Their gradual advances in the science of war would always be accompanied, as we may learn from the example of Russia, with a proportionable improvement in the arts of peace and civil policy; and they themselves must deserve a place among the polished nations whom they subdue.

Should these speculations be found doubtful or fallacious, there still remains a more humble source of comfort and hope. The discoveries of ancient and modern navigators, and the domestic history, or tradition, of the most enlightened nations, represent the *human savage*, naked both in mind and body, and destitute of laws, of arts, of ideas, and almost of language. From this abject condition, perhaps the primitive and universal state of man, he has gradually arisen to command the animals, to fertilise the earth, to traverse the ocean, and to measure the heavens. His progress in the improvement and exercise of his mental and corporeal faculties has been irregular and various, infinitely slow in the beginning, and increasing by degrees with redoubled velocity; ages of laborious ascent have been followed by a moment of rapid downfall; and the several climates of the globe have felt the vicissitudes of light and darkness. Yet the experience of four thousand years should enlarge our hopes, and diminish our apprehensions; we cannot determine to what height the human species may aspire in their advances towards perfection; but it may safely be presumed that no people, unless the face of nature is changed, will relapse into their original barbarism. The improvements of society may be viewed under a threefold aspect. 1. The poet or philosopher illustrates his age and country by the efforts of a *single* mind; but these superior powers of reason or fancy are rare and spontaneous productions, and the genius of Homer, or Cicero, or Newton, would excite less admiration, if they could be created by the will of a prince or the lessons of a preceptor. 2. The benefits of law and policy, of trade and manufactures, of arts and sciences, are more solid and permanent; and *many* individuals may be qualified, by education and discipline, to promote, in their respective stations, the interest of the community. But this general order is the effect of skill and labour; and the complex machinery may be decayed by time or injured by violence. 3. Fortunately for mankind, the more useful, or, at least, more necessary arts can be performed without superior talents or national subordination; without the powers of *one* or the union of *many*. Each village, each family, each individual, must always possess both ability and inclination to perpetuate the use of fire and of metals; the propagation and service of domestic animals; the methods of hunting and fishing; the rudiments of navigation; the imperfect cultivation of corn or other nutritive grain; and the simple practice of the mechanic trades. Private genius and public industry may be extirpated; but these hardy plants survive the tempest, and strike an everlasting root into the most unfavourable soil. The splendid days of Augustus and Trajan were eclipsed by a cloud of ignorance; and the Barbarians subverted the laws and palaces of Rome. But the scythe, the invention or emblem of Saturn, still continued annually to mow the harvests of Italy: and the human feasts of the Laestrygons have never been renewed on the coast of Campania.

Since the first discovery of the arts, war, commerce, and religious zeal have diffused, among the savages of the Old and New World, those inestimable gifts: they have been successively propagated; they can never be lost. We may therefore acquiesce in the pleasing conclusion that every age of the world has increased, and still increases, the real wealth, the happiness, the knowledge, and perhaps the virtue, of the human race.

CHAPTER 2

The Decay of Ancient Civilization

Michael Rostovtzeff

Every reader of a volume devoted to the Roman Empire will expect the author to express his opinion on what is generally, since Gibbon, called the decline and fall of the Roman Empire, or rather of ancient civilization in general. I shall therefore briefly state my own view on this problem, after defining what I take the problem to be. The decline and fall of the Roman Empire, that is to say, of ancient civilization as a whole, has two aspects: the political, social, and economic on the one hand, and the intellectual and spiritual on the other. In the sphere of politics we witness a gradual barbarization of the Empire from within, especially in the West. The foreign, German, elements play the leading part both in the government and in the army, and settling in masses displace the Roman population, which disappears from the fields. A related phenomenon, which indeed was a necessary consequence of this barbarization from within, was the gradual disintegration of the Western Roman Empire; the ruling classes in the former Roman provinces were replaced first by Germans and Sarmatians, and later by Germans alone, either through peaceful penetration or by conquest. In the East we observe a gradual Orientalization of the Byzantine Empire, which leads ultimately to the establishment, on the ruins of the Roman Empire, of strong half-Oriental and purely Oriental states, the Caliphate of Arabia, and the Persian and Turkish empires. From the social and economic point of view, we mean by decline the gradual relapse of the ancient world to very primitive forms of economic life, into an almost pure "house-economy." The cities, which had created and sustained the higher forms of economic life, gradually decayed, and the majority of them practically disappeared from the face of the earth. A few, especially those that had been great centres of commerce and industry, still lingered on. The complicated and refined social system of the ancient Empire follows the same downward path and becomes reduced to its primitive elements: the king, his court and retinue, the big feudal landowners, the clergy, the mass of rural serfs, and small

From Michael Rostovtzeff, *The Social and Economic History of the Roman Empire*, 2d ed. (Oxford: Clarendon Press, 1957), Vol. 1, pp. 532–541. Reprinted by permission of the Clarendon Press, Oxford.

groups of artisans and merchants. Such is the political, social, and economic aspect of the problem. However, we must not generalize too much. The Byzantine Empire cannot be put on a level with the states of Western Europe or with the new Slavonic formations. But one thing is certain: on the ruins of the uniform economic life of the cities there began everywhere a special, locally differentiated, evolution.

From the intellectual and spiritual point of view the main phenomenon is the decline of ancient civilization, of the city civilization of the Greco-Roman world. The Oriental civilizations were more stable: blended with some elements of the Greek city civilization, they persisted and even witnessed a brilliant revival in the Caliphate of Arabia and in Persia, not to speak of India and China. Here again there are two aspects of the evolution. The first is the exhaustion of the creative forces of Greek civilization in the domains where its great triumphs had been achieved, in the exact sciences, in technique, in literature and art. The decline began as early as the second century B.C. There followed a temporary revival of creative forces in the cities of Italy, and later in those of the Eastern and Western provinces of the Empire. The progressive movement stopped almost completely in the second century A.D. and, after a period of stagnation, a steady and rapid decline set in again. Parallel to it, we notice a progressive weakening of the assimilative forces of Greco-Roman civilization. The cities no longer absorb—that is to say, no longer hellenize or romanize—the masses of the country population. The reverse is the case. The barbarism of the country begins to engulf the city population. Only small islands of civilized life are left, the senatorial aristocracy of the late Empire and the clergy; but both, save for a section of the clergy, are gradually swallowed up by the advancing tide of barbarism.

Another aspect of the same phenomenon is the development of a new mentality among the masses of the population. It was the mentality of the lower classes, based exclusively on religion and not only indifferent but hostile to the intellectual achievements of the higher classes. This new attitude of mind gradually dominated the upper classes, or at least the larger part of them. It is revealed by the spread among them of the various mystic religions, partly Oriental, partly Greek. The climax was reached in the triumph of Christianity. In this field the creative power of the ancient world was still alive, as is shown by such momentous achievements as the creation of the Christian church, the adaptation of Christian theology to the mental level of the higher classes, the creation of a powerful Christian literature and of a new Christian art. The new intellectual efforts aimed chiefly at influencing the mass of the population and therefore represented a lowering of the high standards of city-civilization, at least from the point of view of literary forms.

We may say, then, that there is one prominent feature in the development of the ancient world during the imperial age, alike in the political, social, and economic and in the intellectual field. It is a gradual absorption of the higher classes by the lower, accompanied by a gradual levelling down of standards. This levelling was accomplished in many ways. There was a slow penetration of the lower classes into the higher, which were unable to assimilate the new elements. There were violent outbreaks of civil strife: the lead was taken by the Greek cities, and there followed the civil war of the first century B.C. which involved the whole civilized world. In these struggles the upper classes and the city-civilization remained victorious on the whole. Two centuries later, a new outbreak of civil war ended in the victory of the lower classes and dealt a mortal blow to the Greco-Roman civilization of the cities. Finally, that civilization was completely engulfed by the inflow of barbarous elements from outside, partly by penetration, partly by conquest, and in its dying condition it was unable to assimilate even a small part of them.

The main problem, therefore, which we have to solve is this. Why was the city civilization of Greece and Italy unable to assimilate the masses, why did it remain a civilization of the *élite*, why was it incapable of creating conditions which should secure for the ancient world a continuous, uninterrupted movement along the same path of urban civilization? In other words: why had modern civilization to be built up laboriously as something new on the ruins of the old, instead of being a direct continuation of it? Various explanations have been suggested, and each of them claims to have finally solved the problem. Let us then review the most important of them. They may be divided into four classes.

(1) The political solution is advocated by many distinguished scholars. For Beloch the decay of ancient civilization was caused by the absorption of the Greek city-states by the Roman Empire, by the formation of a world-state which prevented the creative forces of Greece from developing and consolidating the great achievements of civilized life. There is some truth in this view. It is evident that the creation of the Roman Empire was a step forward in the process of levelling, and that it facilitated the final absorption of the higher classes. We must, however, take into consideration that class war was a common feature of Greek life, and that we have not the least justification for supposing that the Greek city-community would have found a solution of the social and economic problems which produced civil war in the various communities. Further, this view suggests that there was only one creative race in the ancient world, which is notoriously false. Another explanation, tending in the same direction, has been put forward by Kornemann. He regards as the main cause of the decay of the Roman Empire the fact that Augustus reduced the armed forces of the Empire, and that this reduction was maintained by his successors. The suggestion lays the whole emphasis on the military side of the problem, and is therefore a return to the antiquated idea that ancient civilization was destroyed by the barbarian invasions, an idea which should not be resuscitated. Besides, the maintenance of a comparatively small army was imperatively imposed by the economic weakness of the Empire, a fact which was understood by all the emperors. Still less convincing is the idea of Ferrero, that the collapse of the Empire was due to a disastrous event, to an accident which had the gravest consequences. He holds that by transmitting his power to his son Commodus instead of to a man chosen by the senate, M. Aurelius undermined the senate's authority on which the whole fabric of the Roman state rested; that the murder of Commodus led to the usurpation of Septimius and

to the civil war of the third century; and that the usurpation and the war destroyed the authority of the senate and deprived the imperial power of its only legitimacy in the eyes of the population which was its main support. Ferrero forgets that legally the power of the emperors in the third century was still derived from the senate and people of Rome, that it was so even in the time of Diocletian, and that the same idea still survived under Constantine and his successors. He also forgets that the subtle formula of Augustus, Vespasian, and the Antonines was incomprehensible to the mass of the people of the Empire, and was a creation of the upper classes, completely outside the range of popular conceptions. Finally, he fails to understand the true character of the crisis of the third century. The struggle was not between the senate and the emperor, but between the cities and the army—that is to say, the masses of peasants—as is shown by the fact that the lead in the fight was taken not by Rome but by the cities of the province of Africa. A deeper explanation is offered by Heitland. He suggests that the ancient world decayed because it was unable to give the masses a share in the government, and even gradually restricted the numbers of those who participated in the life of the state, ultimately reducing them to the emperor himself, his court, and the imperial bureaucracy. I regard this point as only one aspect of the great phenomenon which I have described above. Have we the right to suppose that the emperors would not have tried the plan of representative government if they had known of it and believed in it? They tried many other plans and failed. If the idea of representative government was foreign to the ancient world (and as a matter of fact it was not), why did the ancient world not evolve the idea, which is not a very difficult one? Moreover, the question arises, Can we be sure that representative government is the cause of the brilliant development of our civilization and not one of its aspects, just as was the Greek city-state? Have we the slightest reason to believe that modern democracy is a guarantee of continuous and uninterrupted progress, and is capable of preventing civil war from breaking out under the fostering influence of hatred and envy? Let us not forget that the most modern political and social theories suggest that democracy is an antiquated institution, that it is rotten and corrupt, being the offspring of capitalism, and that the only just form of government is the dictatorship of the proletariat, which means a complete destruction of civil liberty and imposes on one and all the single ideal of material welfare, and of equalitarianism founded on material welfare.

(2) The economic explanation of the decay of the ancient world must be rejected completely. In speaking of the development of industry in the ancient world, I have dealt with the theory of K. Bücher, accepted with modifications by M. Weber and G. Salvioli. If the theory fails to explain even this minor point, much less will it serve to explain the general phenomenon. Those who defend this theory forget that the ancient world went through many cycles of evolution, and that in these cycles there occur long periods of progress and other long periods of return to more primitive conditions, to the phase of economic life which is generally described as "house-economy." It is true that the ancient world never reached the economic stage in which we live. But in the

history of the ancient world we have many epochs of high economic development: certain periods in the history of many Oriental monarchies, particularly Egypt, Babylonia, and Persia; the age of the highest development of the city-states, especially the fourth century B.C.; the period of the Hellenistic monarchies, where the climax was reached in the third century B.C.; the period of the late Roman Republic and of the early Roman Empire. All these periods show different aspects of economic life and different aspects of capitalism. In none of them did the forms of house-economy prevail. We may compare the economic aspect of life during these periods to that of many European countries in the time of the Renaissance and later, although in no case would the comparison be perfect, as there is no identity between the economic development of the modern and that of the ancient world. According to the different economic conditions of these several periods in the history of the ancient world, the relations between house-economy and capitalistic economy varied, and they frequently varied not only in the different periods but also in different parts of the ancient world during the same period. The ancient world was in this respect not unlike the modern world. In the industrial countries of Europe, such as England and some parts of Germany and France, economic life nowadays is by no means the same as it is in the agricultural countries, like Russia and the Balkan peninsula and large parts of the Near East. The economic life of the United States of America is not in the least identical with the economic life of Europe or of the various parts of South America, not to speak of China, Japan, and India. So it was in the ancient world. While Egypt and Babylonia had a complex economic life, with a highly developed industry and wide commercial relations, other parts of the Near East lived a quite different and much more primitive life. While Athens, Corinth, Rhodes, Syracuse, Tyre, and Sidon in the fourth century B.C. were centres of a developed commercial capitalism, other Greek cities lived an almost purely agricultural life. In the Hellenistic and Roman periods it was just the same. The main fact which has to be explained is why capitalistic development, which started at many times and in many places, and prevailed in large portions of the ancient world for comparatively long periods, yielded ultimately to more primitive forms of economic life. Even in our own times it has not completely ousted those forms. It is evident that the problem cannot be solved by affirming that the ancient world lived throughout under the forms of primitive house-economy. The statement is manifestly wrong. We might say exactly the same of large areas of the modern world, and we are not at all sure that a violent catastrophe might not bring the modern capitalistic world back to the primitive phase of house-economy.

To sum up what I have said, the economic simplification of ancient life was not the cause of what we call the decline of the ancient world, but one of the aspects of the more general phenomenon which the theories mentioned above try to explain. Here, just as in the other spheres of human life, the political, social, intellectual, and religious, the more primitive forms of life among the masses were not absorbed by the higher forms but triumphed over them in the end. We may select one of these phenomena and declare it to be the ultimate cause; but it would be an arbitrary assumption which would not convince any one.

The problem remains. Why was the victorious advance of capitalism stopped? Why was machinery not invented? Why were the business systems not perfected? Why were the primal forces of primitive economy not overcome? They were gradually disappearing; why did they not disappear completely? To say that they were quantitatively stronger than in our own times does not help us to explain the main phenomenon. That is why many economists, who are aware that the usual explanation only touches the surface and does not probe the problem to the bottom, endeavour to save the economic explanation, and the materialistic conception of historical evolution in general, by producing some potent physical factor as the cause of the weakness of the higher forms of economic life in the ancient world. Such a factor has been found by some scholars in the general exhaustion of the soil all over the ancient world, which reached its climax in the late Roman Empire and ruined the ancient world. I have dealt with this theory above. There are no facts to support it. All the facts about the economic development of the ancient world speak against it. Agriculture decayed in the ancient world just in the same way and from the same causes as the other branches of economic life. As soon as the political and social conditions improved in the various parts of the Empire, the fields and gardens began to yield the same harvests as before. Witness the flourishing state of Gaul in the time of Ausonius and of Sidonius Apollinaris; witness the fact that in Egypt, where the soil is inexhaustible and those parts of it which are not flooded are very easily improved by the most primitive methods, agriculture decayed in the third and fourth centuries, just as in the other provinces. It is plain that the economic explanation does not help us, and that the investigations of the economists reveal, not the cause of the decline of the ancient world, but merely one of its aspects.

(3) The rapid progress of medicine and of biological science has had its influence on the problem of the decay of ancient civilization. A biological solution has been often suggested, and the theories of degeneration and race-suicide have been applied to the ancient world. The biological theory supplies us with an apparently exhaustive explanation of the decline of the assimilative forces of the civilized upper classes. They gradually degenerated and had not the power to assimilate the lower classes but were absorbed by them. According to Seeck, the cause of their degeneration and of their numerical decline was the "extermination of the best" by foreign and civil wars. Others, like Tenney Frank, think of the contamination of higher races by an admixture of the blood of inferior races. Others, again, regard degeneration as a natural process common to all civilized communities: the best are neither exterminated nor contaminated, but they commit systematic suicide by not reproducing and by letting the inferior type of mankind breed freely. I am not competent to sit in judgment on the problem of degeneration from the biological and physiological point of view. From the historical point of view, I venture to remark against Seeck that in wars and revolutions it is not only the best that are exterminated. On the other hand, revolutions do not always prevent the succeeding period from being a period of great bloom. Against Frank I may suggest that I see no criterion for distinguishing between inferior and superior races. Why are the Greek and Latin races considered the only superior races in the Roman

Empire? Some of the races which "contaminated" the ruling races, for instance, the pre-Indo-European and pre-Semitic race or races of the Mediterranean, had created great civilizations in the past (the Egyptian, the Minoan, the Iberian, the Etruscan, the civilizations of Asia Minor), and the same is true of the Semitic and of the Iranian civilizations. Why did the admixture of the blood of these races contaminate and deteriorate the blood of the Greeks and the Romans? On the other hand, the Celts and the Germans belonged to the same stock as the Greeks and the Romans. The Celts had a high material civilization of their own. The Germans were destined to develop a high civilized life in the future. Why did the admixture of their blood corrupt and not regenerate their fellow Aryans, the Greeks and the Romans? The theory of a natural decay of civilization by race-suicide states the same general phenomenon of which we have been speaking, and gradual absorption of the upper classes by the lower and the lack of assimilative power shown by the upper. It states the fact, but gives no explanation. The problem this theory has to solve is, Why do the best not reproduce their kind? It may be solved in different ways: we may suggest an economic, or a physiological, or a psychological explanation. But none of these explanations is convincing.

(4) Christianity is very often made responsible for the decay of ancient civilization. This is, of course, a very narrow point of view. Christianity is but one side of the general change in the mentality of the ancient world. Can we say that this change is the ultimate cause of the decay of ancient civilization? It is not easy to discriminate between causes and symptoms, and one of the urgent tasks in the field of ancient history is a further investigation of this change of mentality. The change, no doubt, was one of the most potent factors in the gradual decay of the civilization of the city-state and in the rise of a new conception of the world and of a new civilization. But how are we to explain the change? Is it a problem of individual and mass psychology?

None of the existing theories fully explains the problem of the decay of ancient civilization, if we can apply the word "decay" to the complex phenomenon which I have endeavoured to describe. Each of them, however, has contributed much to the clearing of the ground, and has helped us to perceive that the main phenomenon which underlies the process of decline is the gradual absorption of the educated classes by the masses and the consequent simplification of all the functions of political, social, economic, and intellectual life, which we call the barbarization of the ancient world.

The evolution of the ancient world has a lesson and a warning for us. Our civilization will not last unless it be a civilization not of one class, but of the masses. The Oriental civilizations were more stable and lasting than the Greco-Roman, because, being chiefly based on religion, they were nearer to the masses. Another lesson is that violent attempts at levelling have never helped to uplift the masses. They have destroyed the upper classes, and resulted in accelerating the process of barbarization. But the ultimate problem remains like a ghost, ever present and unlaid: Is it possible to extend a higher civilization to the lower classes without debasing its standard and diluting its quality to the vanishing point? Is not every civilization bound to decay as soon as it begins to penetrate the masses?

CHAPTER 3

The Impact of Christianity

Peter Brown

The expansion of Christianity was not a gradual, ineluctable process beginning with St Paul and ending with the conversion of Constantine in 312. Its expansion in the third century was impressive, because it had been totally unex-
pected. Very suddenly, the Christian Church became a force to be reckoned
with in the Mediterranean towns. The very seriousness of the measures taken
against the Church as a body, and not merely against individual Christians, in
the persecutions of 257 and after 303, shows that something was lacking in the
life of a Roman town, which Christianity was threatening to fulfil.

The Christian Church differed from the other oriental cults, which it resembled in so many other ways, through its intolerance of the outside world.
The cults were exclusive and, often, the jealously guarded preserve of foreigners; but they never set themselves up against the traditional religious obser-
vances of the society round them. They never enjoyed the publicity of intermittent persecution. While the oriental cults provided special means to
salvation in the next world, they took the position of their devotees in this
world for granted. The Christian Church offered a way of living in this world.
The skillful elaboration of the ecclesiastical hierarchy, the sense of belonging
to a distinctive group with carefully prescribed habits and increasing resources heightened the impression that the Christian Church made on the uncertain generations of the third century. Seldom has a small minority played
so successfully on the anxieties of society as did the Christians. They remained
a small group: but they succeeded in becoming a big problem.

Christian missionaries made most headway in just those areas where
Roman society was most fluid. The seedbeds of the Church were the raw new
provinces of the hinterland of Asia Minor. In a province such as Lycaonia, the
arrival of Greek civilization had virtually coincided with the arrival of St Paul.
The religious leader Marcion, who brought the Christian community in Rome
some 200,000 sesterces, was a contemporary from the same region as the Phry-
gian merchant who had made this journey seventy-two times.

It is part of the appeal of a religious group that it can be a little ahead of
social developments. It was possible to achieve in a small group, "among the

From Peter Brown, *The World of Late Antiquity* (London: Thames and Hudson, 1971), pp. 65–68,
82–89. Reprinted by permission of Thames and Hudson Ltd.

brethren," relationships that were being achieved in society at large at a heavy cost of conflict and uncertainty. As a member of a church, the Christian could cut some of the more painful Gordian knots of social living. He could, for instance, become a radical cosmopolitan. His literature, his beliefs, his art and his jargon were extraordinarily uniform, whether he lived in Rome, Lyons, Carthage or Smyrna. The Christians were immigrants at heart—ideological *déracinés*, separated from their environment by a belief which they knew they shared with little groups all over the empire. At a time when so many local barriers were being painfully and obscurely eroded, the Christians had already taken the step of calling themselves a "non-nation."

The Church was also professedly egalitarian. A group in which there was "neither slave nor free" might strike an aristocrat as utopian, or subversive. Yet in an age when the barriers separating the successful freedman from the *déclassé* senator were increasingly unreal, a religious group could take the final step of ignoring them. In Rome the Christian community of the early third century was a place where just such anomalies were gathered and tolerated: the Church included a powerful freedman chamberlain of the emperor; its bishop was the former slave of that freedman; it was protected by the emperor's mistress, and patronized by noble ladies.

For men whose confusions came partly from no longer feeling embedded in their home environment, the Christian Church offered a drastic experiment in social living, reinforced by the excitements and occasional perils of a break with one's past and one's neighbours.

This intense sense of the religious community was the legacy of Judaism. It saved the Christian Church. Because it thought of itself as "the true Israel," the Christian community was able to remain rooted in every town in which it was established, like a limpet on a rock when the tide recedes. In the late third century, the public religious ceremonies of the towns diminished; the dislocation of trade starved the oriental cults of immigrant devotees; but the Christian bishop remained, with a stable community and a long past behind him, to reap his harvest in the towns.

The wealth of the local notables was not so much impaired by the crisis of the late third century, as redirected: sums of money that had been spent on the townsfolk in the previous century were invested in more private living and on more frankly egotistical forms of competition for status. Naturally, the gods were affected by this change in the tempo of social life. Public competition in the second century had involved a large amount of religious activity—rites, processions, dedications of statues and temples. The Late Antique style of life, by contrast, was more blatantly personal, and so more secular: a magnate spent lavishly, but he gave shows and processions in order to emphasize his personal standing, his *potentia*; he did not care for reinforcing communal activities, such as religious festivals. Not surprisingly, therefore, the lavish inscriptions in honour of the traditional gods come to a halt after 250.

The Christian community suddenly came to appeal to men who felt deserted. At a time of inflation, the Christians invested large sums of liquid capital in people; at a time of increased brutality, the courage of Christian martyrs was impressive; during public emergencies, such as plague or rioting, the Christian clergy were shown to be the only united group in the town, able to look after the burial of the dead and to organize food-supplies. In Rome, the Church was supporting fifteen hundred poor and widows by 250. The churches of Rome and Carthage were able to send large sums of money to Africa and Cappadocia, to ransom Christian captives after barbarian raids in 254 and 256. Two generations previously, the Roman state, faced by similar problems after an invasion, had washed its hands of the poorer provincials: the lawyers declared that even Roman citizens would have to remain the slaves of the private individuals who bought them back from the barbarians. Plainly, to be a Christian in 250 brought more protection from one's fellows than to be a *civis romanus*.

But the true measure of the crisis of the towns is not to be found in the appeal of a few spectacular public gestures by the Christian Church. What marked the Christian Church off, and added to its appeal, was the ferociously inward-looking quality of its life. The Church did not scatter its alms indiscriminately: collected from the Christian community, they were presented by the bishop to God as the special "sacrifice" of the group. (The "sacrifice" of alms was quite as much part of the sacrificial offering of the Christians as was the Eucharist; this, in itself, was a most significant departure from pagan practice.) Thus blessed, the wealth of the community returned to the members of the community alone, as part of the "loving-kindness" of God to His special people.

Nor was Christian propaganda indiscriminate. The Christians did not adopt the market-place preaching of the Cynic philosophers. Instead, applicants for membership were supposed to be carefully scrutinized; they were slowly prepared for initiation; and, once initiated, a formidable penitential system made them constantly aware of the awesome chasm between belonging and not belonging to the religious group.

In the mid-third century, an educated Roman, Cyprian of Carthage, could simply disappear into this exotic and self-contained world. From 248 to 258 he spent the last part of his life performing feats of organization and diplomacy in order to maintain the Christian "faction" in Carthage. The appeal of Christianity still lay in its radical sense of community: it absorbed people because the individual could drop from a wide impersonal world into a miniature community, whose demands and relations were explicit.

The Christian Church enjoyed complete tolerance between 260 and 302. This, the "Little Peace of the Church," was of crucial importance, as we shall see . . . for the future development of Christianity in the Roman empire. As for the emperors, they were too preoccupied with the frontiers to care about the Christians. This is a sign of how far away the Rhine and the Danube were from the heart of the classical world; for a generation, the emperors and their advisers turned their backs on what was happening in the Mediterranean cities. When Diocletian finally established his palace in Nicomedia in 287, he was able to look out at a basilica of the Christians standing on the opposite hill. The Roman empire had survived; but in this Roman empire, Christianity had come to stay.

• • •

"If all men wanted to be Christians," the pagan Celsus wrote in 168, "the Christians would no longer want them." By 300 this situation had changed entirely. Christianity had put down firm roots in all the great cities of the Mediterranean: in Antioch and Alexandria the Church had become probably the biggest, certainly the best-organized single religious group in the town. The Christian gains had been made in just that part of the Roman world that had emerged comparatively unscathed from the troubles of the late third century. Silence descended on the stoutly pagan provinces of the West. By contrast, Syria and Asia Minor, with their vocal Christian elements, stood out more sharply than ever before as provinces of undimmed prosperity and intellectual ferment.

The most decisive change of that time, however, cannot be reduced to a matter of the size of the Christian communities. It was more significant for the immediate future of Christianity that the leaders of the Christian Church, especially in the Greek world, found that they could identify themselves with the culture, outlook and needs of the average well-to-do civilian. From being a sect ranged against or to one side of Roman civilization, Christianity had become a church prepared to absorb a whole society. This is probably the most important *aggiornamento* in the history of the Church: it was certainly the most decisive single event in the culture of the third century. For the conversion of a Roman emperor to Christianity, of Constantine in 312, might not have happened—or, if it had, it would have taken on a totally different meaning—if it had not been preceded, for two generations, by the conversion of Christianity to the culture and ideals of the Roman world.

Origen of Alexandria (*c.* 185–*c.* 254) was the towering genius whose works summed up the possibility of such a venture in assimilation. His work, continued by a succession of Greek bishops, culminated in the writings of a contemporary and adviser of the emperor Constantine, Eusebius, bishop of Caesarea, from about 315 to about 340. For Origen and his disciples, Christianity was the "natural," the "original" religion. The "seeds" of Christian doctrine had been sown by Christ in every man. Ever since the Creation they had been variously tended by Him. Christ, therefore, had "tended" the best in Greek culture—especially Greek philosophy and ethics—as deliberately as He had revealed the Law to the Jews; the foundation of the universal Christian Church by Christ had been expressly synchronized with the foundation of a universal Roman peace by Augustus. A Christian, therefore, could reject neither Greek culture nor the Roman empire without seeming to turn his back on part of the divinely ordained progress of the human race. Christ was the "schoolmaster" of the human race, and Christianity was the peak of His education, the "true" *paideia*, the "true" culture. Origen and his successors taught the pagan that to become a Christian was to step, at last, from a confused and undeveloped stage of moral and intellectual growth into the heart of civilization. On the sarcophagi and frescoes of the late third century, Christ appears as the Divine Schoolmaster, dressed in the simple robes of a professor of literature, lecturing—as Origen must have done—to a quiet circle of well-groomed disciples. The Christian bishop had become part of the intelligentsia of many a great Greek town: he, also, sat on a professor's "chair"—his *cathedra*; and he was thought of as "lecturing" his *didaskaleion*, his study-group, on simple and elevating ethical themes.

The early fourth century was the great age of the Christian Apologists—Lactantius (*c.* 240–*c.* 320), writing in Latin, and Eusebius of Caesarea, in Greek. Their appeals to the educated public coincided with the last, the "Great Persecution of the Church," from 302 to 310, and with the conversion and reign of Constantine as a Christian emperor from 312 to 337. The Christianity of the Apologists was not merely a religion that had found a *modus vivendi* with the civilization that surrounded it. They presented it as something far more than that. They claimed that Christianity was the sole guarantee of that civilization—that the best traditions of classical philosophy and the high standards of classical ethics could be steeled against barbarism only through being confirmed by the Christian revelation; and that the beleaguered Roman empire was saved from destruction only by the protection of the Christian God.

Such a message played on the "Great Fear" of the townsmen of the Mediterranean world of the late third century. One should always remember that classical civilization was the civilization of a fragile veneer: only one man in ten lived in the civilized towns. At no time did this urban crust feel its hold over a wide world to be more precarious than at the end of the third century. The townsmen had maintained their privileges. But they were dwarfed by a countryside whose face had become less recognizable to classical men. In many rural areas, from Britain to Syria, archaic cults, far removed from the classical Olympians, reared their heads more insistently than ever before. The primitive tribes from beyond the frontiers had made their presence felt in terrifying *razzias*. Furthermore, the traditional protectors of the towns, the emperors and their army, had never seemed so alien. The Roman army was stationed among, and recruited from, the populations of the frontiers. It had always been an outsider in the Mediterranean world: in the generation before the accession of Diocletian, in 284, it was in danger of becoming a foreign body. The Danubian provincials who saved the empire needed to be told by their commanders that they did so to preserve, not to terrorize, the civilians. When we compare the rough, uniformed figures of Diocletian and his colleagues with the exquisitely classical sarcophagi of contemporary upper-class Christians, we realize that, against the gulf which threatened to open between the new masters of the empire and the traditions of the ancient cities, the old division between pagan and Christian civilian might seem insignificant. By 300, the Christian bishop had at least become part of the landscape of most towns: in the civilized Greek world it was the Latin-speaking soldier who was the outsider.

With the return of peace after the accession of Diocletian, the wound began to close between the new, military governing class and the urban civilization of the Mediterranean. But there were now two groups who claimed to represent this civilization: the traditional pagan governing class, whose resilience and high standards had been shown in the revival and spread of Platonic philosophy in the late third century, were in danger of being outbid by the new, "middle-brow" culture of the Christian bishops, whose organizing power and adaptability had been proved conclusively in the previous generation.

At first, organization for survival was more important to the emperors than culture. Diocletian was a sincere, *borné* Roman traditionalist; yet he ruled for nineteen years without giving a thought to the Christians. The "Great Persecution," which began in 302 and continued spasmodically for a decade, came as a brutal shock to respectable Christians. They found themselves officially outcastes in the society with which they had so strenuously identified themselves. It was a terrifying and, on the whole, a deeply demoralizing experience. They were saved by an obscure event. In 312, a usurping emperor, Constantine, won a battle over his rival at the Milvian Bridge, outside Rome. He ascribed this victory to the protection of the Christian God, vouchsafed in a vision.

If God helps those who help themselves, then no group better deserved the miracle of the "conversion" of Constantine in 312 than did the Christians. For the Christian leaders seized their opportunity with astonishing pertinacity and intelligence. They besieged Constantine in his new mood: provincial bishops, notably Hosius of Cordova (*c.* 257–357), attached themselves to his court; other bishops, from Africa, swept him into their local affairs as a judge; Lactantius emerged as tutor to his son; and, when Constantine finally conquered the eastern provinces in 324, he was greeted by Eusebius of Caesarea, who placed his pen at the emperor's disposal with a skill and enthusiasm such as no traditional Greek rhetor had seemed able to summon up for Constantine's grim and old-fashioned predecessors—Diocletian and Galerius.

This prolonged exposure to Christian propaganda was the true "conversion" of Constantine. It began on a modest scale when he controlled only the under-Christianized western provinces; but it reached its peak after 324, when the densely Christianized territories of Asia Minor were united to his empire. Its results were decisive. Constantine could easily have been merely a "god-fearing" emperor, who, for reasons of his own, was prepared to tolerate the Christians: there had been many such in the third century (one of whom, Philip (244–249), was even regarded as a crypto-Christian). Given the religious climate of the age, there was no reason, either, why this decision to tolerate the Church might have been ascribed to intimations from the Christian God. Constantine rejected this easy and obvious solution. He came to be the emperor we know from his speeches and edicts: a crowned Christian Apologist. He viewed himself and his mission as a Christian emperor in the light of the interpretation of Christianity that had been presented to the average educated layman by the Christian Apologists of his age. In becoming a Christian, Constantine publicly claimed to be saving the Roman empire; even more—in mixing with bishops, this middle-aged Latin soldier sincerely believed that he had entered the charmed circle of "true" civilization, and had turned his back on the Philistinism of the raw men who had recently attacked the Church.

One suspects that Constantine was converted to many more aspects of Mediterranean life than to Christianity alone. The son of a soldier, he threw in his lot with a civilian way of life that had been largely ignored by the grey administrators of the age of Diocletian. From 311 onwards, Constantine put the landed aristocracy on its feet again: he is the "restorer of the Senate," to whom the aristocracy of the West owed so much. In 332, he gave these landowners extensive powers over their tenants. After 324, he grouped a new civilian governing class round himself in the Greek East. . . . He gave the provincial gentry of Asia Minor what they had long wanted: Constantinople, a "new" Rome, placed within convenient range of the imperial court as it moved along the routes connecting the Danube to Asia Minor. For the Greek senator and bureaucrat, roads that had long ceased to lead to Rome converged quite naturally at this new capital.

Constantine, very wisely, seldom said "no." The first Christian emperor accepted pagan honours from the citizens of Athens. He ransacked the Aegean for pagan classical statuary to adorn Constantinople. He treated a pagan philosopher as a colleague. He paid the travelling expenses of a pagan priest who visited the pagan monuments of Egypt. After a generation of "austerity" for everyone, and of "terror" for the Christians, Constantine, with calculated flamboyance, instituted the "Great Thaw" of the early fourth century: it was a whole restored civilian world, pagan as well as Christian, that was pressing in round the emperor.

In this restored world, the Christians had the advantage of being the most flexible and open group. The bishops could accept an uncultivated emperor. They were used to autodidacts, to men of genuine eccentric talent who—so they claimed—were taught by God alone. Constantine, one should remember, was the younger contemporary of the first Christian hermit, St Anthony. . . . Neither the Latin-speaking soldier nor the Coptic-speaking farmer's son would have been regarded as acceptable human material for a classical schoolmaster: yet Eusebius of Caesarea wrote the life of Constantine the soldier, and Athanasius of Alexandria—an equally sophisticated Greek—the life of Anthony the Egyptian. It was over the wide bridge of a "middlebrow" identification of Christianity with a lowest common denominator of classical culture, and not through the narrow gate of a pagan aristocracy of letters, that Constantine and his successors entered the civilian civilization of the Mediterranean.

THE MAKING OF EUROPE

In the fourth century, "Western Europe" did not exist as a political or cultural entity. Most of modern Germany lay outside the borders of the Roman state. Northern Gaul and Britain were mere outlying provinces of a Mediterranean empire which found its greatest centers of wealth and population in the East. By the time of Charlemagne's coronation (A.D. 800) a new, distinctively European society had emerged. It included numerous Germanic peoples; its main centers of power were in the north; it formed a political-religious unit clearly distinguished from the Byzantine civilization to the east and the Islamic civilization to the south.

Between A.D. 400 and A.D. 800, two basic processes of change—one religious, one economic—contributed to this outcome of events. Virtually all the people of Western Europe came to accept a common religion, Roman Christianity. And the trading activity that had linked the western provinces of the Roman empire to a Mediterranean system of commerce dwindled almost to nothing. Traditionally these changes have been seen as the slow working out of the consequences of the Germanic invasions. In 1925 the great economic historian Henri Pirenne proposed a radically different interpretation, upon which he elaborated in several subsequent works. The unity of the Mediterranean world survived the Germanic invasions, he maintained. The decisive changes that led to the emergence of Charlemagne's Europe were initiated by the Islamic conquests of the seventh and eighth centuries. For Pirenne the age of Charlemagne, usually seen as a time of reform and renewal, was an era of economic retrogression. As evidence for this he cited the change from a gold coinage to a silver one that was suitable for only small-scale transactions.

For more than half a century the "Pirenne thesis" was the focus of major debate among historians. In the course of that debate a great body of new evidence was unearthed (much of it literally unearthed by archaeological work). When the dust settled, it seemed that Pirenne was only partly right. The Muslim conquests certainly reshaped the political geography of the Mediterranean world; but it is not evident that they were a major cause of economic decline in eighth-century Gaul.

In the readings below, first the Pirenne argument is presented, then Daniel Dennett attacks a central argument of the Pirenne thesis and gives an explanation of the changes of coinage in the Merovingian era different from that of Pirenne. In the next reading Patrick Geary discusses the economy of Merovingian Gaul without finding it necessary to mention the Islamic invasions at all.

He associates the changing culture of the Carolingian era with religious rather than economic developments—a shift of religious centers from city-based bishoprics to rural monasteries, and increased contacts with the Roman church initiated by the missionary monk Boniface. Christopher Dawson especially emphasizes this last point. He sees the alliance between the Carolingian rulers and the papacy as a decisive step in the "making of Europe."

CHAPTER 4

Muhammad and Charlemagne

Henri Pirenne

The Mediterranean

The Roman Empire, at the end of the third century, had one outstanding general characteristic: it was an essentially Mediterranean commonwealth. Virtually all of its territory lay within the watershed of that great landlocked sea; the distant frontiers of the Rhine, the Danube, the Euphrates, and the Sahara, may be regarded merely as an advanced circle of outer defenses protecting the approaches.

The Mediterranean was, without question, the bulwark of both its political and economic unity. Its very existence depended on mastery of the sea. Without that great trade route, neither the government, nor the defense, nor the administration of the *orbis romanus* would have been possible.

As the Empire grew old this fundamentally maritime character was, interestingly enough, not only preserved but was still more sharply defined. When the former inland capital, Rome, was abandoned, its place was taken by a city which not only served as a capital but which was at the same time an admirable seaport—Constantinople.

The Empire's cultural development, to be sure, had clearly passed its peak. Population decreased, the spirit of enterprise waned, barbarian hordes commenced to threaten the frontiers, and the increasing expenses of the government, fighting for its very life, brought in their train a fiscal system which more and more enslaved men to the State. Nevertheless this general deterioration does not seem to have appreciably affected the maritime commerce of the Mediterranean. It continued to be active and well sustained, in marked contrast with the growing apathy that characterized the inland provinces. Trade continued to keep the East and West in close contact with each other. There was no interruption to the intimate commercial relations between those diverse climes bathed by one and the same sea. Both manufactured and natural products were still extensively dealt in: textiles from Constantinople, Edessa, Antioch, and Alexandria; wines, oils, and spices from Syria; papyrus from Egypt; wheat from Egypt, Africa, and Spain; and wines from Gaul and Italy.

From Henri Pirenne, *Medieval Cities: Their Origins and the Revival of Trade,* Frank Halsey, trans. (Princeton, N.J.: Princeton University Press), pp. 1–42. Copyright 1952, 1969 by Princeton University Press. Reprinted by permission of Princeton University Press.

There was even a reform of the monetary system based on the gold *solidus,* which served materially to encourage commercial operations by giving them the benefit of an excellent currency, universally adopted as an instrument of exchange and as a means of quoting prices.

· · ·

The appearance of the Germanic tribes on the shore of the Mediterranean was by no means a critical point marking the advent of a new era in the history of Europe. Great as were the consequences which it entailed, it did not sweep the boards clean nor even break the tradition. The aim of the invaders was not to destroy the Roman Empire but to occupy and enjoy it. By and large, what they preserved far exceeded what they destroyed or what they brought that was new. It is true that the kingdoms they established on the soil of the Empire made an end of the latter in so far as being a *State* in Western Europe. From a political point of view the *orbis romanus,* now strictly localized in the East, lost that ecumenical character which had made its frontiers coincide with the frontiers of Christianity. The Empire, however, was far from becoming a stranger to the lost provinces. Its civilization there outlived its authority. By the Church, by language, by the superiority of its institutions and law, it prevailed over the conquerors. In the midst of the troubles, the insecurity, the misery, and the anarchy which accompanied the invasions there was naturally a certain decline, but even in that decline there was preserved a physiognomy still distinctly Roman. The Germanic tribes were unable, and in fact did not want, to do without it. They barbarized it, but they did not consciously germanize it.

Nothing is better proof of this assertion than the persistence in the last days of the Empire—from the fifth to the eighth century—of that maritime character pointed out above . . . the economic organization of the world lived on after the political transformation.

In lack of other proofs, the monetary system of the Frankish kings would alone establish this truth convincingly. This system, as is too well known to make necessary any lengthy consideration here, was purely Roman or, strictly speaking, Romano-Byzantine. This is shown by the coins that were minted: the *solidus,* the *triens,* and the *denarius*—that is to say, the *sou,* the *third-sou,* and the *denier.* It is shown further by the metal which was employed: gold, used for the coinage of the *solidus* and the *triens.* It is also shown by the weight which was given to specie. It is shown, finally, by the effigies which were minted on the coins. In this connection it is worth noting that the mints continued for a long time, under the Merovingian kings, the custom of representing the bust of the Emperor on the coins and of showing on the reverse of the pieces the *Victoria Augusti* and that, carrying this imitation to the extreme, when the Byzantines substituted the cross for the symbol of that victory they did the same. Such extreme servility can be explained only by the continuing influence of the Empire. The obvious reason was the necessity of preserving, between the local currency and the imperial currency, a conformity which would be purposeless if the most intimate relations had not existed between Merovingian commerce and the general commerce of the Mediterranean. In other words, this commerce continued to be closely bound up with the commerce of the Byzantine Empire.

· · ·

Merovingian times knew, thanks to the continuance of Mediterranean shipping and the intermediary of Marseilles, what we may safely call a great commerce. It would certainly be an error to assume that the dealings of the Oriental merchants of Gaul were restricted solely to articles of luxury. Probably the sale of jewelry, enamels, and silk stuffs resulted in handsome profits, but this would not be enough to explain their number and their extraordinary diffusion throughout all the country. The traffic of Marseilles was, above all else, supported by goods for general consumption such as wine and oil, spices, and papyrus. These commodities, as has already been pointed out, were regularly exported to the north.

The Oriental merchants of the Frankish Empire were virtually engaged in wholesale trade. Their boats, after being discharged on the quays of Marseilles, certainly carried back, on leaving the shores of Provence, not only passengers but return freight. Our sources of information, to be sure, do not tell much about the nature of this freight. Among the possible conjectures, one of the most likely is that it probably consisted, at least in good part, in human chattels—that is to say, in slaves. Traffic in slaves did not cease to be carried on in the Frankish Empire until the end of the ninth century. The wars waged against the barbarians of Saxony, Thuringia, and the Slavic regions provided a source of supply which seems to have been abundant enough. Gregory of Tours speaks of Saxon slaves belonging to a merchant of Orleans, and it is a good guess that this Samo, who departed in the first half of the seventh century with a band of companions for the country of Wends, whose king he eventually became, was very probably nothing more than an adventurer trafficking in slaves. And it is of course obvious that the slave trade, to which the Jews still assiduously applied themselves in the ninth century, must have had its origin in an earlier era.

If the bulk of the commerce in Merovingian Gaul was to be found in the hands of Oriental merchants, their influence, however, should not be exaggerated. Side by side with them, and according to all indications in constant relations with them, are mentioned indigenous merchants. Gregory of Tours does not fail to supply information concerning them, which would undoubtedly have been more voluminous if his narrative had had more than a merely incidental interest in them. He shows the king consenting to a loan to the merchants of Verdun, whose business prospers so well that they soon find themselves in a position to reimburse him. He mentions the existence in Paris of a *domus negociantum*—that is to say, apparently, of a sort of market or bazaar. He speaks of a merchant profiteering during the great famine of 585 and getting rich. And in all those anecdotes he is dealing, without the least doubt, with professionals and not with merely casual buyers or sellers.

The picture which the commerce of Merovingian Gaul presents is repeated, naturally, in the other maritime Germanic kingdoms of the Mediterranean—among the Ostrogoths of Italy, among the Vandals of Africa, among the Visigoths of Spain. The Edict of Theodoric contained a quantity of stipulations relative to merchants. Carthage continued to be an important port in close relations with Spain, and her ships, apparently, went up the coast as far as Bordeaux. The laws of the Visigoths mentioned merchants from overseas.

In all of this is clearly manifest the vigorous continuity of the commercial development of the Roman Empire after the Germanic invasions. They did not put an end to the economic unity of antiquity. By means of the Mediterranean and the relations kept up thereby between the West and East, this unity, on the contrary, was preserved with a remarkable distinctiveness. The great inland sea of Europe no longer belonged, as before, to a single State. But nothing yet gave reason to predict that it would soon cease to have its time-honored importance. Despite the transformations which it had undergone, the new world had not lost the Mediterranean character of the old. On the shores of the sea was still concentrated the better part of its activities. No indication yet gave warning of the end of the commonwealth of civilization, created by the Roman Empire from the Pillars of Hercules to the Aegean Sea. At the beginning of the seventh century, anyone who sought to look into the future would have been unable to discern any reason for not believing in the continuance of the old tradition.

Yet what was then natural and reasonable to predict was not to be realized. The world-order which had survived the Germanic invasions was not able to survive the invasion of Islam.

It is thrown across the path of history with the elemental force of a cosmic cataclysm. Even in the lifetime of Mahomet (571–632) no one could have imagined the consequences or have prepared for them. Yet the movement took no more than fifty years to spread from the China Sea to the Atlantic Ocean. Nothing was able to withstand it. At the first blow, it overthrew the Persian Empire (637–644). It took from the Byzantine Empire, in quick succession, Syria (634–636), Egypt (640–642), Africa (698). It reached into Spain (711). The resistless advance was not to slow down until the start of the eighth century, when the walls of Constantinople on the one side (713) and the soldiers of Charles Martel on the other (732) broke that great enveloping offensive against the two flanks of Christianity.

But if its force of expansion was exhausted, it had none the less changed the face of the world. Its sudden thrust had destroyed ancient Europe. It had put an end to the Mediterranean commonwealth in which it had gathered its strength.

The familiar and almost "family" sea which once united all the parts of this commonwealth was to become a barrier between them. On all its shores, for centuries, social life, in its fundamental characteristics, had been the same; religion, the same; customs and ideas, the same or very nearly so. The invasion of the barbarians from the North had modified nothing essential in that situation.

But now, all of a sudden, the very lands where civilization had been born were torn away; the cult of the Prophet was substituted for the Christian Faith, Moslem law for Roman law, the Arab tongue for the Greek and the Latin tongue.

The Mediterranean had been a Roman lake; it now became, for the most part, a Moslem lake. From this time on it separated, instead of uniting, the East and the West of Europe. The tie which was still binding the Byzantine Empire to the Germanic kingdoms of the West was broken.

The Ninth Century

The tremendous effect the invasion of Islam had upon Western Europe has not, perhaps, been fully appreciated . . .

Of a regular and normal commercial activity, of steady trading carried on by a class of professional merchants, in short, of all that constitutes the very essence of an economy of exchange worthy of the name, no traces are to be found after the closing off of the Mediterranean by the Islamic invasion. The great number of markets (*mercatus*), which were to be found in the ninth century, in no way contradicts this assertion. They were, as a matter of fact, only small local marketplaces, instituted for the weekly provisioning of the populace by means of the retail sale of foodstuffs from the country. As a proof of the commercial activity of the Carolingian era, it would be equally beside the point to speak of the existence of the street occupied by merchants (*vicus mercatorum*) at Aix-la-Chapelle near the palace of Charlemagne, or of similar streets near certain great abbeys such as, for example, that of St. Riquier. The merchants with whom we have to do here were not, in fact, professional merchants but servitors charged with the duty of supplying the Court or the monks. They were, so to speak, employees of the seignorial household staff and were in no respect merchants.

There is, moreover, material proof of the economic decline which affected Western Europe from the day when she ceased to belong to the Mediterranean commonwealth. It is furnished by the reform of the monetary system, initiated by Pepin the Short and completed by Charlemagne. That reform abandoned gold coinage and substituted silver in its place. The *solidus* which had heretofore, conforming to the Roman tradition, constituted the basic monetary unit, was now only nominal money. The only real coins from this time on were the silver *deniers*, weighing about two grams, the metallic value of which, compared to that of the dollar, was approximately eight and one-half cents. The metallic value of the Merovingian gold *solidus* being nearly three dollars, the importance of the reform can be readily appreciated. Undoubtedly it is to be explained only by a prodigious falling off of both trading and wealth.

If it is admitted, and it must be admitted, that the reappearance of gold coinage, with the florins of Florence and the ducats of Venice in the thirteenth century, characterized the economic renaissance of Europe, the inverse is also true: the abandoning of gold coinage in the eighth century was the manifestation of a profound decline. It is not enough to say that Pepin and Charlemagne wished to remedy the monetary disorder of the last days of the Merovingian era. It would have been quite possible for them to find a remedy without giving up the gold standard. They gave up the standard, obviously, from necessity—that is to say, as a result of the disappearance of the yellow metal in Gaul. And this disappearance had no other cause than the interruption of the commerce of the Mediterranean. The proof of this is given by the fact that Southern Italy, remaining in contact with Constantinople, retained like the latter a gold standard, for which the Carolingian sovereigns were forced to substitute a silver standard. The very light weight of their *deniers*, moreover, testifies to the economic isolation of their Empire. It is inconceivable that they would have reduced the monetary unit to a thirtieth of its former value if there had been preserved the slightest bond between their States and the Mediterranean regions where the gold *solidus* continued to circulate.

• • •

We are so accustomed to consider the reign of Charlemagne as an era of revival that we are unconsciously led to imagine an identical progress in all fields. Unfortunately, what is true of literary culture, of the religious State, of customs, institutions, and statecraft is not true of communications and commerce. Every great thing that Charlemagne accomplished was accomplished either by his military strength or by his alliance with the Church. For that matter, neither the Church nor arms could overcome the circumstances in virtue of which the Frankish Empire found itself deprived of foreign markets. It was forced, in fact, to accommodate itself to a situation which was inevitably prescribed. History is obliged to recognize that, however brilliant it seems in other respects, the cycle of Charlemagne, considered from an economic viewpoint, is a cycle of regression.

The financial organization of the Frankish Empire makes this plain. It was, indeed, as rudimentary as could be. The poll tax, which the Merovingians had preserved in imitation of Rome, no longer existed. The resources of the sovereign consisted only in the revenue from his demesnes, in the tributes levied on conquered tribes, and in the booty got by war. The market-tolls no longer contributed to the replenishment of the treasury, thus attesting to the commercial decline of the period. They were nothing more than a simple extortion brutally levied in kind on the infrequent merchandise transported by the rivers or along the roads. The sorry proceeds, which should have served to keep up the bridges, the docks, and the highways, were swallowed up by the functionaries who collected them, the *missi dominici*, created to supervise their administration, were impotent in abolishing the abuses which they proved to exist because the State, unable to pay its agents, was likewise unable to impose its authority on them. It was obliged to call on the aristocracy which, thanks to their social status, alone could give free services. But in so doing it was constrained, for lack of money, to choose the instruments of power from among the midst of a group of men whose most evident interest was to diminish that power. The recruiting of the functionaries from among the aristocracy was the fundamental vice of the Frankish Empire and the essential cause of its dissolution, which became so rapid after the death of Charlemagne. Surely, nothing is more fragile than that State the sovereign of which, all-powerful in theory, is dependent in fact upon the fidelity of his independent agents.

The feudal system was in embryo in this contradictory situation. The Carolingian Empire would have been able to keep going only if it had possessed, like the Byzantine Empire or the Empire of the Caliphs, a tax system, a financial control, a fiscal centralization, and a treasury providing for the salary of functionaries, for public works, and for the maintenance of the army and the navy. The financial impotence which caused its downfall was a clear demonstration of the impossibility it encountered of maintaining a political structure on an economic base which was no longer able to support the load.

CHAPTER 5

Pirenne and Muhammad

Daniel C. Dennett

We must affirm that neither in the Koran, nor in the sayings of the Prophet, nor in the acts of the first caliphs, nor in the opinions of Muslim jurists is there any prohibition against trading with the Christians or unbelievers. Before Muhammad, the Arabs of the desert lived by their flocks and those of the town by their commerce. To these two sources of livelihood the conquest added the income of empire and the yield of agriculture, but the mercantile career remained the goal of many, as the caravan still crossed the desert and the trading vessel skirted the coast line of the Red Sea, the Persian Gulf, and the Indian Ocean. Pirenne has asserted that "it is a proven fact that the Musulman traders did not install themselves beyond the frontiers of Islam. If they did trade, they did so among themselves." This statement is a serious misrepresentation of fact. Arab merchants had established trading colonies which were centers not only for the exchange of goods but the propagation of the faith in India, Ceylon, the East Indies, and even China, by the close of the eighth century, and if one wishes to know why they did not establish similar centers in Gaul, let him ask the question—would Charlemagne have permitted a mosque in Marseilles?

In this respect the Muslims themselves were more tolerant and placed few obstacles in the path of Christian traders who came to their territory. Within the lands that had formerly submitted to the Emperor, the Christians were now subjects of the Muslim state, yet they were protected by law, and in return for the payment of their taxes and the discharge of obligations stipulated in the original terms of capitulation, they were specifically and formally guaranteed the freedom of Christian worship, the jurisdiction of Christian bishops in cases not involving Muslims, and the pursuit of trades and professions. The civil service and the language of administration remained Greek, and Arabic did not universally displace Greek in the government bureaus until the end of the first century following the conquest. In Egypt, at least, the change of rule brought an improvement in the social and economic life of the population, and the church of Alexandria enjoyed a liberty of faith which it had hitherto not experienced.

From Daniel C. Dennett, "Pirenne and Muhammad," *Speculum*, Vol. 23 (1948), pp. 167–170, 186–190. Reprinted by permission of the Medieval Academy of America.

In consideration of the fact that it has formerly been believed that internal causes produced a decline of industry and trade in Gaul, the burden of proof in Pirenne's thesis must show that the Arab raids were of a frequency and intensity *in themselves* to destroy the commerce of the western Mediterranean. It is not a just argument merely to assert that these raids were disastrous because commerce in Gaul declined. We have already noticed that in order to connect the decline of the Merovingian monarchy with the activity of the Arabs, Pirenne has been obliged to assign the date 650 as that point when Arab naval activity became formidable. What are the facts?

There may have been a raid on Sicily in 652. We are told that it was led by Muawia ibn Hudajj and resulted in taking much booty from unfortified places, but was called off when plague threatened the invaders. As Amari shows, there is a great deal of confusion among the Muslim authorities both as to the date (for an alternative, 664 A.D. is given), as to the leader (since it is highly probable that not Muawia but his lieutenant Abdallah ibn Quis commanded the actual expedition), and as to the port of embarkation (either Tripoli in Syria or Barka in North Africa). Becker does not accept the date 652 and argues that the first raid took place only in 664, but it is possible that there were two different expeditions, one in 652, the second in 664.

Three years after the presumed earliest assault on Sicily, the Emperor Constans II, in 655, received a serious blow to his prestige when the Byzantine fleet was beaten in the Aegean by the new Muslim navy in the first real test of sea power. The Arabs did not follow up their victory, but its consequence demonstrated to the Emperor the need for a vigorous naval policy, for, although Constantinople and the straits might be held against siege, the strategically vulnerable point of the Empire was not in the Aegean, but in the West, since (as events were to show two centuries later) once the enemy had a base in Sicily, South Italy would then be within easy grasp, and if South Italy were securely held, only immense naval exertions could protect Greece proper, and if Greece fell under Muslim control, a combined blockade by land and sea of the imperial city would be possible. Bury holds that this consideration, the guarding of the rear against attack from the West, was a strong motive in inducing Constans to concentrate naval power in the West and to go himself to Sicily in 662, where he reigned for six years until his assassination in 668.

The Arabs took advantage of the chaos following the assassination to raid the coasts of Sicily the next year, but when order was reestablished Sicily remained at peace again for thirty-five years.

Meanwhile the Greek fleet itself was far from inactive, raiding Egypt in 673 and, in a successful attack on Barka in 689, putting the Arabs to a rout in which the governor of North Africa, Zuheir ibn Qais, perished. Early attempts to take Carthage were frustrated because the Greeks had control of the seas, and the city fell in 698 only because the Arabs had constructed a fleet for the purpose and the Greek naval force was in the Aegean. Following Bury's argument, if the Emperor had established a permanent naval base at Carthage, the city would never have been taken.

Therefore, in view of the facts that the Arabs made only two (possibly three) raids on Sicily before 700, that these raids resulted in a vigorous naval policy of the Greeks in the West, that it was not until 698 that the Arabs had a fleet strong enough to operate at Carthage, and that they had not yet seized the straits of Gibraltar or occupied Spain, we are bound to acknowledge the absence of any evidence to indicate the closing of the Mediterranean thereby weakening the basis of royal power in Gaul before 700. Pirenne himself acknowledges this fact by admitting that spices and papyrus could be procured by the monks of Corbie in 716. Indeed, anyone who reads Pirenne closely will notice that he is careless with chronology and mentions results which were produced by the Arab conquest as beginning at various points within a period of 150 years.

• • •

. . . Pirenne turns to the problem of money and says, "In any case, the abundant circulation of gold compels us to conclude that there was a very considerable export trade." Now, in the absence of any banking system for settling by the shipment of bullion an accumulated disparity between exports and imports, one would certainly be prepared to believe it quite possible that the export of some products would bring foreign gold into the country, although the total supply might be diminishing due to larger imports, and this was undoubtedly the case, but Pirenne goes much farther and makes it very plain that he believes the exports from Gaul in early Merovingian days exceeded in value, or at least equalled, the imports of eastern products, since "if it [gold] had been gradually drained away by foreign trade we should find that it diminished as time went on. But we do not find anything of the sort." He argues that when the Muslim conquest closed the trade routes, gold became a rarity and was abandoned for silver as a medium of exchange. The employment of silver was the real beginning of the Middle Ages and is a witness of a reversion to natural economy. When gold reappeared, the Middle Ages were over, and "Gold resumed its place in the monetary system only when spices resumed theirs in the normal diet."

A natural question arises. If gold remained the medium of currency, unimpaired in quantity due to a favorable export balance until the Arabs cut the trade routes, what happened to it then? It could not have flowed East after the catastrophe on the assumption that exports suffered before imports, because Pirenne is insistent, and all the evidence he has collected is designed to show that it was the import of Eastern products which first disappeared. If gold *could not* flow East, why did it not remain in Gaul as a medium of local exchange?

There are at least three factors in the problem.

1. From the earliest times small quantities of gold were found in the beds of certain streams flowing from the Pyrenees, and even in the sands of the Rhine, but the supply was so negligible that one may assert that the West

produced no gold. On the other hand, there were substantial deposits of silver, and there were silver mines at Melle in Poitou and in the Harz mountains.

2. It should be unnecessary to point out that we have not the slightest idea of the total amount of gold in Gaul at any period. We occasionally hear of an amount confiscated by a king, of a loan given by a bishop, of a sum bequeathed the church by a landholder or merchant, of the size of booty or tribute, of a subsidy of 50,000 *solidi* sent by the Emperor, but that is all. In many cases, without doubt, a figure or instance is mentioned, not because it was usual, but because it was extraordinary. The number and importance of coin finds are not in any proportion to the probable facts and may not be relied on. Therefore when Pirenne speaks of "large" amounts of gold, he is merely guessing. Furthermore, as is well known, there was in general circulation a bronze and silver currency for use in smaller transactions.

3. Gregory the Great (590–604) testifies that Gallic gold coins were so bad that they did not circulate in Italy, and an examination of coins shows a progressive debasement before the Arab conquest. Since these coins did not come from the royal mint, but were struck by roving minters for people in more than a hundred known localities, one has evidence of the chaotic decentralization of the government and lack of interest in orderly financial administration, together with a possible indication of a growing scarcity of gold.

If gold disappeared in Gaul, this disappearance could be due to the following causes:

a. It might have been hoarded, buried, and lost.
b. It might have been exchanged or used for the purchase of silver.
c. It might have been drained off in purchase of commodities in a one sided trade, or paid in tribute.
d. Through the operation of Gresham's law, foreign merchants might have hoarded and removed the good gold coinage, leaving a debased coinage in local circulation.

There is no evidence to support the first two hypotheses, and considerable evidence for the last two—both of which amount to this same fact: gold *was* drained out of the country. This hypothesis is strongly supported by the best known authority and Bloch gives good reasons for accepting it. Gold, of course, did not completely disappear in the West, as the manufacture of jewelry and occasional references show, and it would be interesting to possess the full facts about the gold coin counterfeiting the Arab dinar—the *mancus*. However, it is difficult to accept the thesis advanced by Dopsch that there was enough gold to constitute with silver a truly bimetallic currency. But it is even more difficult to accept the proposition of Pirenne that the change from gold to silver meant a change from money to natural economy. The numerous instances which prove conclusively that money continued as a medium of exchange have been diligently collected by Dopsch (*Naturalwirtschaft und Geldwirtschaft*, pp. 110–145) and need not be repeated. It is not clear why silver coinage should equal natural economy. China and Mexico use silver today, and the coins of Arab mintage found in the Baltic regions are also silver, yet no one would pretend that in these instances we are dealing with a system of natural economy. Had a system of natural economy prevailed we might have expected an absence of all kinds of money, and the fact that the Carolingians introduced a pure, standard, centrally minted silver coinage would seem logically to prove just the contrary of Pirenne's thesis. . . .

To conclude: There is no evidence to prove that the Arabs either desired to close, or actually did close the Mediterranean to the commerce of the West either in the seventh or eighth centuries. Islam was hostile to Christianity as a rival, not as a completely alien faith, and the Muslims were invariably more tolerant than the Christians, but Islam as a culture, as the common faith of those who submitted and spoke Arabic, though not necessarily by any means of Arab blood, had far more in common with the Hellenized East and with Byzantium than did the Gaul of Pirenne's Romania. Much of what he says of Gaul was true of Islam. The Merovingians took over the administrative and particularly the taxation system of Rome intact. So did the Arabs. The Merovingians preserved Latin as the language of administration. The Arabs used Greek. Western art was influenced by Byzantine forms. So was Arab. But these are smaller matters. The crude Western barbarians were not able to develop—indeed, they were too ignorant to preserve the state and the culture they took by conquest, while the Arabs on the contrary not only preserved what they took but created from it a culture which the world had not known for centuries, and which was not to be equalled for centuries more. This culture was based on that of the Hellenized Eastern Mediterranean in one part and on that of Persia strongly permeated with both Hellenic and Indian elements, on the other. Arab theology, Arab philosophy, Arab science, Arab art—none was in opposition to late antique culture, as Pirenne seems to imagine, but was a new, fertile, virile, and logical development of long established forms. The decadence of the West—the so-called Middle Ages—was due to a complexity of causes, mostly internal, and largely connected with social and political institutions. Rostovtzeff, writing of economic conditions of the later Roman Empire, frequently warns against mistaking an aspect for a cause, and most of the economic factors of the Middle Ages are aspects and not causes. Thus, the man—whether he be a Pirenne or a Dopsch—who attempts to understand and to interpret either the Merovingian or Carolingian period in terms *purely* of an economic interpretation of history will be certain to fail, for the simple reason that economic factors play a subsidiary role and present merely aspects in the great causative process.

CHAPTER 6

Merovingian Society

Patrick Geary

The Economy of Countryside and City

The Roman society had continued to develop into the regionally fragmented and socially stratified world that we examined . . . [earlier]. This society was deeply rooted in the nature of its economic system, which was characterized by the monopoly of landowning in the hands of a small, extraordinarily wealthy elite, with the vast majority of the population, slave and free alike, destitute and often in desperate straits. The result was an agriculture woefully inadequate to the support of the population and a commercial and artisanal infrastructure catering almost exclusively to the elite.

This agricultural system, which characterized the early medieval economy for centuries, resulted in little surplus production in good years and frequent and often catastrophic famines in bad. Occasionally the fragility of this economic base has been blamed on the arrival of the barbarians, who in fact had little effect on either landholding or agricultural techniques. The continuity with late Roman field division, agricultural techniques, and manorial organization, when they had survived to the sixth century, was enormous. This was less the case in the Rhenish regions but was common elsewhere, both in the north of the Frankish kingdom and especially in the south. More disruptive than barbarians had been the general decline in population and flight from marginal or overtaxed lands beginning in the third century. The lack of sufficient agricultural labor continued to be a major problem, and the steps that had been taken since Diocletian had, if anything, probably exacerbated the situation. In 517 the council of Yenne forbade abbots to enfranchise slaves from the estates received from laymen because "It is unjust that slaves should enjoy liberty while monks work the land day and night." Well into the ninth century, kings, aristocrats, and churchmen were engaged in bringing abandoned and uninhabited lands into production.

The cultivation of the land relied on the techniques of provincial Rome, but they were, if anything, even more labor-intensive than previously. Machinery such as the mechanical harvester used in Gaul in the time of Pliny had disappeared; water mills, although in use along the Rhône and Ruiver, as well as in a few other areas, were rare; and the other tools, ploughs, scythes, hoes etc., were largely or even entirely of wood. Iron was a rare and precious commodity. So important was it that appeals were commonly made to local saints to find lost iron objects, and when they did so, the fortunate event was likely to be recorded among the saint's miracles. Carefully guarded, sparingly used, iron tools were employed primarily to make wooden ones.

Cereal production, which within the Roman world had consisted primarily of wheat, came to be dominated increasingly by darker grains such as barley, known to the Germanic peoples. This change reflected in part a change of taste from the traditional Mediterranean to a more northern one, but was also due to practical survival and efficiency. Dark grains were not only more hardy, but because they could be readily converted into a strong and nourishing beer, they could be conserved longer than the more delicate wheat.

One area of agriculture that actually expanded in the early Merovingian period was viniculture. Rome had introduced vines wherever it had come, but they were cultivated in the more northern areas of Europe only with the expansion of ecclesiastical institutions in these areas. Wine was not only essential for eucharistic liturgy, it was the drink of the elite. The increasing investment in wine cultivation at the expense of traditional subsistence-type agriculture probably indicates the growing dominance of agricultural decisions by the aristocracy.

The prehistoric concern of the Germanic peoples with cattle herding continued and expanded with the Frankish kingdom. Throughout the Salic Law and other early law codes, cattle figure prominently, and the detail with which cattle raising is treated reinforces the overall impression that these animals continued, as in the age of Stelus, to form the foundation of barbarian wealth and prestige.

Although the vast majority of the population still lived on the land, the cities of Francia played an important role in the kingdom, both as residences of bishops, counts, and kings and as centers of economic activity. The actual population of these cities is extremely difficult to determine. The only evidence comes from archaeology, and since it is largely based on the area included within the third-century city walls, there is abundant room for speculation about the size of the population residing in suburban quarters. Thus some historians have speculated that in the sixth century Paris might have had a population of 20,000 inhabitants and Bordeaux 15,000, while others have argued that these estimates should be reduced by almost 50 percent. What is certain is that the social, cultural, and political significance of these cities was far greater than what one might expect from their small populations.

Most of the Roman aristocracy had long before abandoned the cities for the security and autonomy of their vast country estates, but some had returned, and in the poetry of Sidonius Apollinarius and the lives of early saints we read of the presence of rich and powerful Romans living not only in the cities of Aquitaine and Gaul, but even in Trier, Metz, and Cologne. The most important Gallo-Roman residents were, however, the bishops. They and their clergy maintained much of the public life of the cities, undertaking the traditional civic obligations of poor relief and the maintenance of walls, aqueducts, and the like. So important were they that ancient cities which did not become the sees of bishops tended by and large to disappear in the early Middle Ages. The presence of an episcopal court made the difference between life and death for an urban center.

Although one hears much less about them than about the bishop and clergy in our sources, another important resident of the cities was the Frankish king or his representative, the count, and his military garrison. Frankish elites, like their Gothic and Burgundian counterparts, were attracted to Roman cities where they could both enjoy the good life they and their ancestors had long desired and find the safety in numbers that their political position and social rank demanded. Unlike the later Merovingians and certainly unlike the Carolingians, the early Merovingians and their representatives resided in cities, where they received and spent the revenues of estates they had acquired, thus contributing to a continuing mercantile and craft economy which flourished through the seventh century. While it is certainly true that the bishops and their clerics formed the central nucleus of urban continuity and that their building programs gradually came to dominate the physical space of the city with their cathedral groups, baptisteries, hospices, and, outside the walls, basilicas and cemeteries, one must not forget the effects on city life of a Theudebert, who had games held once more in the amphitheater of Arles, or of a Chilperic I, who built circuses in both Paris and Soissons.

The sixth-century city was more than the residence of the bishop and the Frankish count or king. It continued to play a vital commercial role as well. In spite of barbarian pillage and Gallo-Roman internal strife, in spite of depopulation and the archaization of Western society, the network of Roman roads and, more importantly, of commercial waterways continued to function. The nature of this circulation was, however, quite different from what had been the norm in previous centuries or was seen in the later Middle Ages when urban growth was accompanied by a resurgence of commercial activity. In order to understand the peculiar nature of commerce in the Merovingian world we must first understand the circulation of goods in general in sixth-century Francia.

Much ink has been spilled in the debate over the relative vitality of the Western economy in the sixth, seventh, and eighth centuries. On the one hand, numismatic evidence indicates the continued importance of gold coinage into the seventh century, and both archival and narrative sources mention merchants, import goods, and a functioning customs and tariff collection well into the eighth century. On the other hand, it often appears that precious metal was more important for display than for use as an exchange medium and that the primary means of circulation of goods and prestige objects was not commerce but military expeditions and local plundering, or else the exchange of gifts. Thus from one perspective the commercial world of late antiquity appears intact and perhaps even expanding in the north; Syrian, Greek, and Jewish merchants travel the length and breadth of Francia, sometimes in camel caravans, selling their wares, and local grain merchants buy and sell in flourishing markets. From the other, one sees an archaic society in which warfare and gift exchange characterize the modalities of circulation and in which gold is more prized for jewelry, for church ornamentation, or for horse trappings than for its exchange value. The confusion is the result of the complex nature of the Merovingian economy in which circulation mechanisms were intimately connected to social relationships. With different people, at different times, all of these mechanisms operated, and each played a vital role in the distribution of local, regional, and international goods and services.

The overwhelming majority of foodstuff were made available for local consumption either by the peasants who produced it or by their lords. The small surplus not consumed or lost to spoilage circulated by sale, gift, or theft, depending on the social and political relationships between the exchange partners. The second two were more significant than the first. Great aristocrats, whether Frankish or Roman, supported their followers and the members of their households by supplying them with food. clothing, arms, and other necessities of their livelihood and social rank. Bishops distributed alms to the poor inscribed in the municipal poor rolls as a continuation of the traditional obligation of imperial largesse and in order to maintain the support of the populace. Friendship was sealed by the exchange of gifts. This network of gifts and countergifts probably accounted for much of the equalization and distribution of agricultural surplus.

Between enemies, that is, any persons not bound by a mutual relationship of friendship, goods circulated by plunder and theft. This could mean warfare of simply periodic raids on enemies' goods and chattels as part of continuing feuds. Also, kings and their representatives received, in addition to taxes, gifts of livestock, wine, wax, and other products, which were essentially tribute.

Both of these sorts of transactions could and did take place within the city as well as the countryside. However, it was in the city that the less normal but still significant form of goods exchange between neutral parties took place—sale. One hears of the sale of foodstuffs primarily during times of crisis when those who had stockpiled them could realize enormous profits, although regular markets certainly existed. The more important types of commercial transactions were in commodities not everywhere available, relatively easy to carry, and in great demand. The most basic of these was salt, which was produced in low-lying coastal regions by evaporation and then transported inland. Also important were wine, oil, fish, and grain.

Products of artisanal workshops also circulated regionally and even over great distances, although the mechanisms of this circulation is uncertain. In the south, traditional Mediterranean pottery of late classical design continued to be produced into the eighth century; glass produced in the Ardennes and around Cologne found its way as far north as Frisia and even Sweden; Frankish weapons, which enjoyed a great reputation across Europe, have been found throughout Francia and in Frisia and Scandinavia. Textiles also circulated between regions: Provence was particularly known for its inexpensive cloth as far away as Rome, Monte Cassino, and Spain.

As reduced in size as the population of Frankish cities was, a diverse population of merchants continued to exist. Gregory of Tours mentions that the bishop of Verdun, Desideratus, obtained a loan from King Theudebert of 7,000 gold pieces guaranteed by the merchants of his city, who presumably specialized in foodstuffs. However, the story told by Gregory demonstrates the parallel existence of a gift-based circulation of wealth and commerce: Theudebert granted the loan as a favor to Desideratus to show his generosity. According to Gregory the load enriched "those practicing commerce," and the bishop was able to attempt to repay the loan with interest. The king refused repayment, saying that he had no need of it. That enough merchants existed in the city to repay such a loan indicates that commerce was not insignificant; that their repayment was later dismissed by the king out of generosity indicates that the system of commercial credit was alien to him—he preferred to have the city in his political debt. For a Merovingian king, gold was not primarily a form of money with which to make more money by clever investment; it was a means of manifesting his generosity and of cementing the bonds with his people.

In addition to urban merchants, the owners of great estates; both lay and ecclesiastic, had their own agents, sometimes Jews, in other instances members of their own households, either serf or freedmen, who were responsible for the sale of their surplus and the purchase of necessities not produced locally. Again, however, these agents operated not only in a commercial mode; the same individuals might be charged with the delivery of gifts to other magnates and with the reception of reciprocated gifts. One can suppose that much of the circulation in which they were involved was neither sale nor, strictly speaking, barter, but the delivery of goods that cemented relationships among the elite.

Finally, in every important city was a community of foreigners engaged in supplying luxury goods to the aristocracy. This long-distance commerce was largely in the hands of Greeks, Syrians, and Jews, who are found in Arles, Marseille, Narbonne, Lyon, Orléans, Bordeaux, Bourges, Paris, and elsewhere. They provided a supply of jewelry, precious cloths, ornaments, as well as papyrus, spices, and the like. These merchants could form considerable communities in Frankish cities with their own judicial officers or "consuls" and perhaps even took an active role in the wider community. Gregory of Tours mentions that a Syrian merchant, Eusebius, bribed his way into the position of bishop of Paris and, dismissing the household of his predecessor, replaced them with other Syrians. Clearly international merchants wielded considerable power.

They acquired this power because they could provide the aristocracy with the magnificent luxury goods they needed to make manifest their social positions. The merchants were also important because import duties and tariffs collected from them were a major source of liquid revenue for the Merovingians. Particularly in Provence, where the bulk of Mediterranean imports arrived, royal customs officers collected considerable sums which went to the royal coffers. The division of Provence among the subkingdoms of Francia probably involved as much a division of important customs dues as a division of land.

In return, the West had little to offer these international merchants but gold. This was nothing new. Gaul had never been a major exporter of anything but timber and, occasionally, of slaves. To this the Franks could add weapons. However the exportation of slaves was, in theory at least, forbidden—labor was scarce and the Franks themselves imported slaves from the Slavic regions—although it certainly did go on via the Rhône. Likewise, Frankish arms were a dangerous export item since they would be turned against them by other purchasers. Thus the East–West commerce was largely one-way. Gold that had been acquired as booty or subsidies from the Eastern Empire flowed back again in payment for luxury goods. As the amount of booty decreased in the later sixth, seventh, and early eighth centuries, commerce decreased with it. This gold drain, which temporarily ended only with renewed Frankish conquests under the Carolingians, ultimately reduced international trade to a trickle. And, as trade disappeared, so did the international communities of merchants which added color, sophistication, and excitement to the cities of Francia.

• • •

The Legacy of Merovingian Europe

The descendants of Clovis had lost the inheritance of his martial and ferocious spirit; and their misfortune or demerit has affixed the epithet of *lazy* to the last kings of the Merovingian race. They ascended the throne without power, and sunk into the grave without a name. A country palace, in the neighborhood of Compiègne, was allotted for their residence or prison: but each year, in the month of March or May, they were conducted in a wagon drawn by oxen to the assembly of the Franks, to give audience to foreign ambassadors and to ratify the acts of the mayor of the palace.

Thus Edward Gibbon described the last Merovingians in his great *History of the Decline and Fall of the Roman Empire.* He was being kind: traditionally most historians have suggested that the decline of the Merovingians was due largely to their personal depravity, congenital degeneracy, or both. The glorious brutality and faithless cruelty of Clovis and his successors was seen to have been followed by the impotence, passivity, and incompetence of his last heirs. The family has not gained much favorable appreciation in the past 1,200 years. Moreover, the whole period from the victory at Soissons to the anointing of Pippin has been an epoch with which heirs of the European tradition have been acutely uncomfortable.

While every country in the East seems eager to claim Charles the Great (Charlemagne, Karl der Grosse, Carlo magno) as their own, and pan-Europeanists term him the "Father of Europe," Clovis and even Dagobert are largely unclaimed. In Germany, generations of study of the tribal duchies and their origins have sought continuity between the migration period and the duchies which emerged with the dissolution of the Carolingian Empire. Scholars have tended to forget that these tribal duchies were artificial creations of the Merovingians and their agents.

In France, national memory jumps from the Gallo-Roman period of Syagrius (or perhaps even before, from the time of Asterix) to the glory of Charlemagne. A long tradition, nourished by three disastrous Franco-German wars, has encouraged the French to forget that before there was a "douce France" there was a Frankono lant," and that this Frankish land was centered in the lower Seine. "Les Francs sont-ils nos ancêtres?" reads the title of the lead article in a recent issue of the popular French journal *Histoire et Archeologie.* Through most of European history, the general desire on both sides of the Rhine has been to answer "no."

This disinclination to acknowledge the continuity between the Merovingian period and later European history is the result of a variety of factors. The first and most obvious is the tendency to accept in an uncritical manner the anti-Merovingian propaganda created and disseminated by the Carolingians and their supporters, which was intended to undermine the prestige of the Merovingian royal family. Too often this unflattering view of the Merovingians has been taken at face value and accepted as an accurate assessment of the dynasty and, in particular, its inglorious end.

This portrait of the Merovingian family explains why subsequent dynasties did not wish to be associated with it, but does not explain the negative view of the entire period. Perhaps a reason is offered by the peculiar nature of the society, culture, and institutions of the Merovingian period. The world we have been examining was at all times deeply rooted in late antiquity, a world little understood in comparison with earlier or subsequent periods. We must examine both of these factors in order to understand the negative image of the Merovingian period in European history.

• • •

The Uniqueness of Early Frankish Society

Merovingian civilization lived and died within the framework of late antiquity. Its characteristic political structure remained the kingdom of the imperial German military commander who, by absorbing the mechanism of provincial Roman administration, was able to establish his royal family as the legitimate rulers of the western provinces north of the Pyrenees and the Alps. His rule consisted primarily of rendering justice, that is, of enforcing Roman law and Romanized barbarian law where possible or appropriate within the tradition of his people, and of commanding the Frankish army. The economic basis for his power was on the one hand the vast Roman fisc and on the other the continuing mechanism of Roman taxation. The broader organization of society continued to be based on small communities, the late classical cities, with their local power structures virtually intact. Wherever possible, in the north of

Gaul around Soissons, in the Rhineland of Trier and Cologne, or in distant Regensburg and Salzburg, the Merovingians, and their agents integrated themselves into these existing Roman structures and derived their power and legitimacy from them. In a relatively short period of time, the warrior bands which had made up the mobile forces of the imperial Germanic commanders became territorially established and integrated into their corresponding indigenous populations. The distinguishing characteristic of this society as opposed to the Goths in Italy and Spain was its adherence to the orthodox Christianity of the indigenous population, making possible the rapid amalgamation of the various communities in Europe. By the eighth century this process was so complete that it not only had produced a new world but rendered the past virtually opaque to subsequent generations.

An essential characteristic of Francia was the fluidity of the political and cultural identities of its inhabitants. To many modern French, who identify with the Roman cultural tradition as opposed to Germanic conquest and occupation, and Gallo-Roman aristocracy of the Merovingian period were a disappointing lot. Gallo-Romans were ready to defend their Roman cultural tradition even while opposing any attempt by Roman imperial government to interfere with their local control. Thus they willingly and easily made common cause with any barbarian rulers who were prepared to accept them on their own terms. From Caesarius of Arles and Remigius of Reims through Eligius of Noyon and beyond, Romance identity was quite separate from political autonomy. In the political sphere, Aquitainian and Provençal elites acted exactly like their northern counterparts, stubbornly refusing to fit into modern categories of regional political structures based on cultural and ethnic identity and marrying into other elites without any hesitation. In short, in spite of sporadic attempts to portray the south as a region of heroic resistance to Germanic Frankish barbarity, the area's elites appear to the modern French like nothing so much as a society of collaborators.

The Franks of the north are even more perplexing, a curious blend of Germanic-speaking warriors governing through the institutions of a subclassical Roman administration whose primary characteristics, including even kingship, were the product of Roman military and civil tradition. Their pride in being Franks was only matched by their eagerness to serve the Roman state religion, orthodox Christianity, and to win recognition of their legitimacy in the eyes of the Roman emperor in Constantinople. The political fortunes of the Byzantine Empire fill almost as many pages of Merovingian chronicles as do those of Francia. The ease with which the Franks established themselves within a world of Roman cities, international commerce, literate government, written law, and Latin letters without abandoning their cherished feuds, kinship structures, and personal alliances is profoundly disturbing to those who expect the Franks to act like Germanic tribes of Tacitus. Small wonder, then, that when Germans of the nineteenth and early twentieth centuries looked back to find their ancient past, they largely bypassed these Roman Franks in favor of the myth of more authentic Germanic peoples east of the Rhine.

In reality, of course, both Romanized kingdoms of Gaul and western Germany and the "tribal" duchies east of the Rhine were the creations of the Merovingian world. In both areas, the intensely local interests at the end of the fifth century developed first into personal units around individual leaders or influential families, and then, in the course of the seventh century, these personal groupings, largely established for military purposes (for example, to counter the Basques in Aquitaine or the Slavs in Thuringia), evolved into territorial units that used the vocabulary of ethnic and cultural solidarity for political purposes. Thus the units of political organization which came to characterize Europe in the tenth and eleventh centuries—Aquitaine, Burgundy, Provence, "France," in the West; Bavaria, Alemannia, Thuringia, Saxony, in the East—first appeared in the Merovingian period. Although these areas took their names from preexisting geographical units or personal groups, they received their institutions, their geographical confines, and their leadership in the course of the seventh century. The Carolingian period would be but a hiatus in the development of regionalism of the late Merovingian world.

This profound localism was characteristic of the Merovingian period because its primary actors, "Frankish" and "Roman" alike, had been formed within the structures of Gallo-Roman antiquity and particularly within the provincial city. The shift of the center of cultural and political focus from city to countryside coincided with the disappearance of the Merovingian world. To a great extent, this also meant the shift in religious authority from the urban world of bishops to the rural monastery, a process already begun in the sixth century but carried to fruition by Irish and then Anglo-Saxon monks in the seventh and eighth. The ruralization of the Western Church was paralleled by the decay of the city as an economic and political center. With the decline in international commerce and the increasing importance of monasteries in the economic life of the West, towns lost their significance as commercial centers to monasteries, of which St. Denis, with its great fair, is the most important example. Also, the great monasteries such as Corbie, St. Bavon, and Fulda, the monastery of Boniface, because the principal centers for artisanal production and agents of distribution of both primary and manufactured goods. As the political importance of town decreased, kings and their agents took up principal residence in rural villas rather than in the cities favored by Clovis and his successors. The last Merovingians resided principally at Compiégne, while the Carolingians would spend most of their time at one or another favored rural estate until Charlemagne selected Aachen, an insignificant rural spa, as his primary residence.

The power centers of the Roman Empire had been progressively neglecting the West, a situation that largely suited its population. The language and ritual of international Roman culture was used to emphasize local concerns. This was particularly true in the essential elements of Merovingian power—saints, bishops, kings, and aristocrats. In late antiquity and in the Merovingian period, each of these derived its authority from local, indigenous roots. When these again became dependent on a wider order, the result was a new world.

In the sixth century, religious power was rooted in the local holy man, or even better in his relics. When a young girl from Toulouse possessed by demons was brought to St. Peter's in Rome for exorcism, the demon refused to leave her: it insisted that it could be exorcised only by Remigius of Reims. As Raymond Van Dam has pointed out, Gaul was presented as a direct rival to Rome in the force of its indigenous martyrs and special patrons. The West was prepared to look to its own devices in the religious as well as in the political sphere. By the eighth and early ninth century, Rome was again looking at the West. In the early ninth century a young girl from Aquitaine who was mute and deaf arrived at Seligenstadt, a monastery founded by Einhard in the Rhineland, where her father had brought her after unsuccessfully seeking a cure at many other sanctuaries. Upon entering the basilica, she was seized with violent convulsions, blood flowed from her mouth and ears, and she fell to the ground. When she was raised up she could speak and hear, and she announced that she had been cured by the saints venerated in the church, Marcellinus and Peter, Roman martyrs whose relics had been recently brought to Francia from Rome.

These two miracles indicate the shift in religious power from the Merovingian to Carolingian worlds. In both cases divine power is manifested through holy men, and in both the location of this action is north of the Alps. However by the end of the Merovingian period this power is mediated through Rome. Marcellinus and Peter had been transplanted to the north, and not to a city but to a rural monastery named paradoxically "the City of the Saints."

This transformation is paralleled, as discussed in the previous chapter, by the transfer of authority from Rome to the bishops of Francia appointed and supervised by Boniface and the Carolingians. The reestablishment of metropolitan sees, and the introduction of Roman usage and norms in the place of indigenous Gallo-Roman and Iro-Frankish ones tied the power of bishops to central rather than to local sources.

The Merovingians had been preeminently the embodiment of local authority. Never needing election or consecration, they were kings by their very nature, quite apart from any external religious or secular authority. The election and anointment of Pippin upon papal approval or even, according to some traditions, papal directive, fundamentally altered the nature of kingship, tying it to a particular religious and institutional tradition quite apart from the old Gallo-Roman and Frankish worlds.

Finally, along with the Carolingians, rose a new "imperial aristocracy" composed of nobles from many different backgrounds. Many were from old Austrasian families; others were from regional elites who had made the Carolingians secure in the various areas of Francia; still others had risen through service to the Carolingians or even to their predecessors but who had joined forces with the winning side at an early date. From this relatively small group of families the Carolingians drew their bishops and counts, whom they sent throughout the empire. Owing their positions to royal favor rather than primarily to local ties, these families, no less than Roman saints, Anglo-Saxon bishops, or Carolingian kings, depended on external sources of authority and power. Only after some time would these families intermarry, put down local roots in the areas into which they had been introduced, and produce the regional aristocracies of the High Middle Ages.

Although these transformations had been accomplished in the name of Roman tradition, by the end of the eighth century, when these new elements were firmly in place, little remained of the authentic late Roman West. The Rome that had sponsored Boniface was itself a new, artificial creation, as were the traditions of Latin letters and imperial destiny cultivated in Carolingian circles. And yet the transformed barbarian world so badly needed a Roman imperial tradition, even more than it had in the sixth century, that on Christmas Day in 800 Charles Martel's grandson received the title of emperor and Augustus. The barbarian world, that creature of Rome, had become its creator.

CHAPTER 7

Charlemagne and the Roman Church

Christopher Dawson

. . . There has never been an age in which England had a greater influence on continental culture. In art and religion, in scholarship and literature, the Anglo-Saxons of the eighth century were the leaders of their age. At the time when continental civilisation was at its lowest ebb, the conversion of the Anglo-Saxons marked the turn of the tide. The Saxon pilgrims flocked to Rome as the centre of the Christian world and the Papacy found its most devoted allies and servants in the Anglo-Saxon monks and missionaries. The foundations of the new age were laid by the greatest of them all, St. Boniface of Crediton, "the Apostle of Germany," a man who had a deeper influence on the history of Europe than any Englishman who has ever lived. Unlike his Celtic predecessors, he was not an individual missionary, but a statesman and organiser, who was, above all, a servant of the Roman order. To him is due the foundation of the mediaeval German Church and the final conversion of Hesse and Thuringia, the heart of the German land. With the help of his Anglo-Saxon monks and nuns he destroyed the last strongholds of Germanic heathenism and planted abbeys and bishoprics on the site of the old Folkburgs and heathen sanctuaries, such as Buraburg, Amoneburg and Fulda. On his return from Rome in 739 he used his authority as Papal Vicar in Germany to reorganise the Bavarian Church and to establish the new dioceses which had so great an importance in German history. For Germany beyond the Rhine was still a land without cities, and the foundation of the new bishoprics meant the creation of new centres of cultural life. It was through the work of St. Boniface that Germany first became a living member of the European society.

This Anglo-Saxon influence is responsible for the first beginnings of vernacular culture in Germany. It is not merely that the Anglo-Saxon missionaries brought with them their custom of providing Latin texts with vernacular glosses, nor even that the earliest monuments of German literature—the old Saxon *Genesis* and the religious epic *Heliand*—seem to derive from the

From Christopher Dawson, *The Making of Europe* (London: Sheed and Ward, 1946), pp. 166–171. Reprinted by permission of Christina Scott as the literary representative of the Estate of Christopher Dawson.

Anglo-Saxon literary tradition. It is that the very idea of a vernacular culture was alien to the traditions of the continental Church and was the characteristic product of the new Christian cultures of Ireland and England, whence it was transmitted to the continent by the missionary movement of the eighth century.

But in addition to this, Boniface was the reformer of the whole Frankish Church. The decadent Merovingian dynasty had already given up the substance of its power to the mayors of the palace, but in spite of their military prowess, which saved France from conquest by the Arabs in 735, they had done nothing for culture and had only furthered the degradation of the Frankish Church. Charles Martel had used the abbeys and bishoprics to reward his lay partisans, and had carried out a wholesale secularisation of Church property. As Boniface wrote to the Pope, "Religion is trodden under foot. Benefices are given to greedy laymen or unchaste and publican clerics. All their crimes do not prevent their attaining the priesthood; at last rising in rank as they increase in sin they become bishops, and those of them who can boast that they are not adulterers or fornicators, are drunkards, given up to the chase, and soldiers, who do not shrink from shedding Christian blood," Nevertheless, the successors of Charles Martel, Pepin and Carloman, were favourable to Boniface's reforms. Armed with his special powers as Legate of the Holy See and personal representative of the Pope, he undertook the desecularisation of the Frankish Church.

In a series of great councils held between 742 and 747, he restored the discipline of the Frankish Church and brought it into close relations with the Roman see. It is true that Boniface failed to realise his full programme for the establishment of a regular system of appeals from the local authorities to Rome and for the recognition of the rights of the Papacy in the investiture of the bishops. But, though Pepin was unwilling to surrender his control over the Frankish Church, he assisted St. Boniface in the reform of the Church and accepted his ideal of co-operation and harmony between the Frankish state and the Papacy. Henceforward the Carolingian dynasty was to be the patron of the movement of ecclesiastical reform, and found in the Church and the monastic culture the force that it needed for its work of political reorganisation. For it was the Anglo-Saxon monks and, above all, St. Boniface who first realised that union of Teutonic initiative and Latin order which is the source of the whole mediaeval development of culture.

$$\bullet \ \bullet \ \bullet$$

The historical importance of the Carolingian age far transcends its material achievement. The unwieldy Empire of Charles the Great did not long survive the death of its founder, and it never really attained the economic and social organisation of a civilised state. But, for all that, it marks the first emergence of the European culture from the twilight of pre-natal existence into the consciousness of active life. Hitherto the barbarians had lived passively on the capital which they had inherited from the civilisation which they had plundered; now they began to co-operate with it in a creative social activity. The centre of mediaeval civilisation was not to be on the shores of the Mediterranean, but in the northern lands between the Loire and the Weser which were the heart of the Frankish dominions. This was the formative center of the new culture, and it was there that the new conditions which were to govern the history of mediaeval culture find their origin. The ideal of the mediaeval Empire, the political position of the Papacy, the German hegemony in Italy and the expansion of Germany towards the East, the fundamental institutions of mediaeval society both in Church and State, and the incorporation of the classical tradition in mediaeval culture—all have their basis in the history of the Carolingian period.

The essential feature of the new culture was its religious character. While the Merovingian state had been predominantly secular, the Carolingian Empire was a theocratic power—the political expression of a religious unity. This change in the character of the monarchy is shown by the actual circumstances of the installation of the new dynasty; for Pepin obtained Papal authority for the setting aside of the old royal house and was anointed king in the year 752 by St. Boniface according to the religious coronation rite which had grown up under ecclesiastical influence in Anglo-Saxon England and Visigothic Spain, but which had hitherto been unknown among the Franks. Thus the legitimation of the rule of the Carolingian house sealed the alliance between the Frankish monarchy and the Papacy which St. Boniface had done so much to bring about, and henceforward the Frankish monarchy was the recognised champion and protector of the Holy See. The Papacy had already been alienated from the Byzantine Empire by the Iconoclastic policy of the Isaurian emperors, and the extinction of the last survival of the Byzantine power at Ravenna by the Lombards in 751 forced the Pope to look for support elsewhere. In 754 Stephen II visited Pepin in his own dominions, and obtained from him a treaty which secured to the Papacy the Exarchate of Ravenna and the former Byzantine possessions in Italy, together with the duchies of Spoleto and Benevento. In return the Pope reconsecrated Pepin as King of the Franks, and also conferred on him the dignity of Patrician of the Romans. This was an epoch-making event, for it marked not only the foundation of the Papal State which was to endure until 1870, but also the protectorate of the Carolingians in Italy, and the beginning of their imperial mission as the leaders and organisers of Western Christendom.

The Carolingians were naturally fitted to undertake this mission since they were themselves the representatives of both sides of the European tradition. They traced their descent from Gallo-Roman bishops and saints as well as from Frankish warriors, and they combined the warlike prowess of a Charles Martel with a vein of religious idealism, which shows itself in Carloman's renunciation of his kingdom in order to enter the cloister, and Pepin's sincere devotion to the cause of the Church. But it is in Pepin's successor, Charles the Great, that both these elements find simultaneous expression. He was above all a soldier with a talent for war and military enterprise which made him the greatest conqueror of his time. But in spite of his ruthlessness and unscrupulous ambition he was no mere barbaric warrior; his policy was inspired by ideals and universal aims. His conquests were not only the fulfillment of the traditional Frankish policy of military expansion; they were also crusades for the protection and unity of Christendom. By his destruction of the Lombard Kingdom he freed the Papacy from the menace which had threatened its independence for two hundred years and brought Italy into the Frankish Empire. The long drawn out struggle with the Saxons was due to his determination to put an end to the last remains of Germanic heathenism as well as of Saxon independence. His conquest of the Avars in 793–794 destroyed the Asiatic robber state which had terrorised the whole of Eastern Europe, and at the same time restored Christianity in the Danube provinces, while his war with the Saracens and his establishment of the Spanish March were the beginning of the Christian reaction to the victorious expansion of Islam. In the course of thirty years of incessant warfare he had extended the frontiers of the Frankish monarchy as far as the Elbe, the Mediterranean and the Lower Danube, and had united Western Christendom in a great imperial state.

The coronation of Charles as Roman Emperor and the restoration of the Western Empire in the year 800 marked the final stage in the reorganisation of Western Christendom and completed the union between the Frankish monarchy and the Roman Church which had been begun by the work of Boniface and Pepin.

FEUDAL SOCIETY: PROBLEMS AND APPROACHES

Charlemagne's empire disintegrated in the ninth century. Out of the near-anarchy that ensued there emerged a new ordering of society that modern historians describe by the word *feudal*. Some historians, notably Karl Marx, have seen feudalism as a necessary stage in the evolution of all civilizations. Others have regarded it as a specifically European phenomenon. This is largely a question of definition. If, like Marx, we mean by the term *feudal society* essentially a society that is based on the exploitation of a subject peasantry, then evidently many feudal regimes have existed in many different times and places. But modern Western historians more commonly use the word *feudal* to describe the relationships existing among the medieval nobility, among the knights and greater lords. Here we find an aristocracy of mounted warriors, holding fiefs from overlords to whom they are bound by oaths of personal loyalty, and exercising substantial rights of government over the lands they control. This is a much more rare—perhaps unique—form of social structure.

The problem of definition continues to interest medieval historians. In the following readings, Marc Bloch presents a classic account of the shift in emphasis from ties of kinship to ties of vassalage in the ninth and tenth centuries. Joseph Strayer's discussion is concerned with the political aspects of feudalism. Strayer argues that the "informal and flexible" arrangements of feudal society made possible the emergence of new kinds of governmental institutions in the Western world. But he also observes in a footnote that the great legal historian, Maitland, long ago complained about the vagueness and inadequacy of the term *feudalism*. Taking up this theme, Elizabeth A. R. Brown launches a frontal attack on the use of this abstract noun, *feudalism,* as a "simple label" to designate a very complex medieval reality. She urges that we abandon the term altogether. Brown's argument evoked a vigorous discussion among historians that is still continuing. In considering it, one should note that her argument about "feudalism" could apply to many other abstract nouns ending in *-ism:* e.g., *capitalism, socialism, liberalism, Catholicism, Protestantism.* So a reader has to decide whether the use of such terms is useful and necessary in our discourse or, as Brown maintains, merely confusing.

Feudal Society

Problems and Approaches

CHAPTER 8

Kinship and Lordship

Marc Bloch

The Structure of the Family

Vast *gentes* or clans, firmly defined and held together by a belief—whether true or false—in a common ancestry, were unknown to western Europe in the feudal period, save on its outer fringes, beyond the genuinely feudalized regions. On the shores of the North Sea there were the *Geschlechter* of Frisia or of Dithmarschen; in the west, Celtic tribes or clans. It seems certain that groups of this nature had still existed among the Germans in the period of the invasions. There were, for example, the Lombard and Frankish *farae* of which more than one Italian or French village continues today to bear the name; and there were also the *genealogiae* of the Alemans and Bavarians which certain texts show in possession of the soil. But these excessively large units gradually disintegrated.

The Roman *gens* had owed the exceptional firmness of its pattern to the absolute primacy of descent in the male line. Nothing like this was known in the feudal epoch. Already in ancient Germany each individual had two kinds of relative, those "of the spear side," and those "of the distaff side," and he was bound, though in different degrees, to the second as well as to the first. It was as though among the Germans the victory of the agnatic principle had never been sufficiently complete to extinguish all trace of a more ancient system of uterine filiation. Unfortunately we know almost nothing of the native family traditions of the countries conquered by Rome. But, whatever one is to think of these problems of origins, it is at all events certain that in the medieval West kinship had acquired or retained a distinctly dual character. The sentimental importance with which the epic invested the relations of the maternal uncle and his nephew is but one of the expressions of a system in which the ties of relationship through women were nearly as important as those of paternal consanguinity. One proof of this is the clear evidence from the practices of name-giving.

The majority of Germanic personal names were formed by linking two elements, each of which had a meaning of its own. So long as people continued to be aware of the distinction between the two stems, it was the common custom, if not the rule, to mark the filiation by borrowing one of the components. This was true even in Romance-speaking regions where the prestige of the

From Marc Bloch, *Feudal Society*, L. A. Manyon, trans. (Chicago: University of Chicago Press, 1961), pp. 137–140, 160–162. English translation copyright 1961 by Routledge & Kegan Paul Ltd. Reprinted by permission of The University of Chicago Press.

conquerors had led to the widespread imitation of their name system by the native peoples. Children took their names either from the father or the mother; there seems to have been no fixed rule. In the village of Palaiseau, for example, at the beginning of the ninth century, the peasant *Teud-ricus* and his wife *Ermen-berta* baptized one of their sons *Teut-hardus*, another *Erment-arius*, and the third, by way of a double memorial, *Teut-bertus*. Then the practice developed of handing down the whole name from generation to generation. This was done again by taking the name from each side alternately. Thus of the two sons of Lisois, lord of Amboise, who died in 1065, one was named after his father but the other, who was the elder, was named Sulpice like his maternal grandfather and uncle. Still later, when people began to add patronymics to Christian names, they vacillated for a long time between the two modes of transmission. "I am called sometimes Jeanne d'Arc and sometimes Jeanne Romée," said the daughter of Jacques d'Arc and Isabelle Romée to her judges. History knows her only by the first of these names; but she pointed out that in her part of the country it was customary to give daughters the surname of their mother.

This double link had important consequences. Since each generation thus had its circle of relatives which was not the same as that of the previous generation, the area of the kindred's responsibilities continually changed its contours. The duties were rigorous; but the group was too unstable to serve as the basis of the whole social structure. Worse still, when two families clashed it might very well be that the same individual belonged to both—to one of them through his father and to the other through his mother. How was he to choose between them? Wisely, Beaumanoir's choice is to side with the nearest relative, and if the degrees are equal, to stand aloof. Doubtless in practice the decision was often dictated by personal preference. When we come to deal with feudal relations in the strict sense, we shall encounter aspects of this legal dilemma in the case of the vassal of two lords. The dilemma arose from a particular attitude of mind and in the long run it had the effect of loosening the tie. There was great internal weakness in a family system which compelled people to recognize, as they did in Beauvaisis in the thirteenth century, the legitimacy of a war between two brothers, sons of the same father (though by different marriages), who found themselves caught up in a vendetta between their maternal relatives.

How far along the lines of descent did the obligations towards "friends by blood" extend? We do not find their limits defined with any precision save in the groups that maintained the regular scale of compensation, and even here the customs were set down in writing only at a relatively late date. All the more significant is the fact that the zones of active and passive solidarity which they fixed were surprisingly large, and that they were, moreover, graduated zones, in which the amount of the indemnity varied according to the closeness of the relationship. At Sepulveda in Castile in the thirteenth century it was sufficient, in order that the vengeance wreaked on the murderer of a relative should not be treated as a crime, for the avenger to have the same great-great-grandfather as the original victim. The same degree of relationship entitled one to receive a part of the blood money according to the law of Oudenarde and, at Lille, made it obligatory to contribute to its payment. At Saint-Omer they went so far as to derive the obligation to contribute from a common founder of the line as remote as a grandfather of a great-grandfather. Elsewhere, the outline was vaguer. But, as has already been pointed out, it was considered only prudent in the case of alienations to ask the consent of as many collaterals as possible. As for the "silent" communities of the country districts, they long continued to gather together many individuals under one roof—we hear of as many as fifty in eleventh-century Bavaria and sixty-six in fifteenth-century Normandy.

On close examination, however, it looks as if from the thirteenth century onwards a sort of contraction was in process. The vast kindreds of not so long before were slowly being replaced by groups much more like our small families of today. Towards the end of the century, Beaumanoir felt that the circle of people bound by the obligation of vengeance had been constantly dwindling—to the point where, in his day, in contrast with the previous age, only second cousins, or perhaps only first cousins (among whom the obligation continued to be very strongly felt), were included. From the latter years of the twelfth century we note in the French charters a tendency to restrict to the next of kin the request for family approval. Then came the system under which the relatives enjoyed the right of redemption. With the distinction which it established between acquired possessions and family possessions and, among the latter, between possessions subject, according to their origin, to the claims of either the paternal or the maternal line, it conformed much less than the earlier practice to the conception of an almost unlimited kinship. The rhythms of this evolution naturally varied greatly from place to place. It will suffice here to indicate very briefly the most general and most likely causes of a change which was pregnant with important consequences.

Undoubtedly the governmental authorities, through their activities as guardians of the peace, contributed to the weakening of the kinship bond. This they did in many ways and notably, like William the Conqueror, by limiting the sphere of lawful blood-feud; above all, perhaps, by encouraging refusal to take any part in the vendetta. Voluntary withdrawal from the kindred group was an ancient and general right; but whilst it enabled the individual to avoid many risks, it deprived him for the future of a form of protection long regarded as indispensable. Once the protection of the State had become more effective, these "forswearings" became less dangerous. The government sometimes did not hesitate to impose them. Thus, in 1181, the count of Hainault, after a murder had been perpetrated, forestalled the blood-feud by burning down the houses of all the relatives of the guilty man and extorting from them a promise not to give him succour. Nevertheless the disintegration and attenuation of the kindred group, both as an economic unit and as an instrument of the feud, seems to have been in the main the result of deeper social changes. The development of trade conduced to the limitation of family impediments to the sale of property; the progress of inter-communication led to the break-up of excessively large groups which, in the absence of any legal status, could scarcely preserve their sense of unity except by staying together in one place. The invasions had already dealt an almost mortal blow at the much more solidly constituted *Geschlechter* of ancient Germany. The rude shocks to which England was subjected—Scandinavian inroads and settlement, Norman conquest—were doubtless an important factor in the premature decay in that country of the old framework of the kindred. In practically the whole of Europe, at the time of the great movement of land reclamation, the attraction of the new urban centres and of the villages founded on the newly cleared lands undoubtedly broke up many peasant communities. It was no accident if, in France at least, these brotherhoods held together much longer in the poorest provinces.

• • •

The Formation of the Classical Type of Vassalage

The collapse of the Carolingian state represented the swift and tragic defeat of a little group of men who, despite many archaisms and miscalculations but with the best of intentions, had tried to preserve some of the values of an ordered and civilized life. After them came a long and troubled period which was at the same time a period of gestation, in which the characteristics of vassalage were to take definitive shape.

In the state of perpetual war—invasions as well as internal strife—in which Europe henceforth lived, men more than ever looked for chiefs, and chiefs for vassals. But the extension of these protective relationships no longer redounded to the benefit of the kings. Private ties now increased in number, especially in the neighbourhood of the castles. With the beginning of the Scandinavian and Hungarian invasions, more and more of these fortresses sprang up in the country districts, and the lords who commanded them—either in their own name or in that of some more powerful personage—endeavored to assemble bodies of vassals for their defence. "The king has now nothing save his title and his crown . . . he is not capable of defending either his bishops or the rest of his subjects against the dangers that threaten them. Therefore we see them all betaking themselves with joined hands to serve the great. In this way they secure peace." Such is the picture which, about 1016, a German prelate drew of the anarchy in the kingdom of Burgundy. In Artois, in the following century, a monk pertinently explains how among the "nobility" only very few have been able to avoid the ties of seignorial domination and "remain subject to the public authority alone." Even here it is obviously necessary to understand by this term not so much the authority of the crown, which was much too remote, as that of the count, the repository, in place of the sovereign, of all that remained of a power by its very nature superior to personal ties.

It goes without saying that these ties of dependence spread through all ranks of society and not only among those "nobles" to whom our monk refers. But the lines of demarcation which the Carolingian age had begun to trace between the different kinds of relationships, characterized by different social atmospheres, were now more firmly drawn.

Certainly language and even manners for a long time preserved vestiges of the old confusion. Some groups of very modest manorial subjects, dedicated to the despised labours of the soil and tied to responsibilities which from now on were considered servile, continued till the twelfth century to bear that name of "commended men" which the author of the *Chanson de Roland* applied to the greatest vassals. Because the serfs were the "men" of their lord, it was often said of them that they lived in his "homage." Even the formal act by which an individual acknowledged himself the serf of another was sometimes described by this name and indeed at times, in its ritual, recalled the characteristic gestures of the homage "of hands."

This servile homage, however, where it was practised, was in sharp contrast with vassal homage; it did not have to be renewed from generation to generation. Two forms of attachment now began to be distinguished more and more clearly. One was hereditary. It was marked by all manner of obligations considered to be of a rather low order. Above all, it allowed of no choice on the part of the dependant, and so was regarded as the opposite of what was then called "freedom." It was in fact serfdom, into which most of those of inferior status who commended themselves descended imperceptibly, in spite of the "free" character which had marked their original submission in a period when social classifications were based on different principles. The other relationship, which was called vassalage, terminated in law, if not in fact, on the day when one or other of the two lives thus bound together came to an end. By this very characteristic, which relieved it from the stigma of an hereditary restriction on the individual's liberty of action, it was well suited to the honourable service of the sword. And the form of aid which it involved was essentially warlike. By a characteristic synonymity the Latin charters from the end of the eleventh century speak almost indifferently of a man as being the vassal, or the *miles*, of his lord. Literally, the second term should be translated by "soldier." But the French texts, from the moment of their appearance, rendered it by "knight" and it was certainly this vernacular expression which the notaries of an earlier day had had in mind. The soldier was typically a man who served on horseback in heavy armour, and the function of the vassal consisted above all in fighting in this manner for his lord. So that, by another avatar of the old word which not long before had been so humble, "vassalage" in popular speech came into common use as a name for the finest of the virtues known to a society perpetually at war—to wit, bravery. The relation of dependence thus defined was formally sealed by homage with joined hands, which was henceforth almost entirely restricted to this use. But, from the tenth century, this rite of profound dedication seems generally to have been completed by the addition of the kiss which, by placing the two individuals on the same plane of friendship, lent dignity to the type of subordination known as vassalage. In fact, this relationship was now confined to persons of high—sometimes even of very high—social status. Military vassalage had emerged by a slow process of differentiation from the ancient and disparate practice of commendation, and had come in the end to represent its highest form.

CHAPTER 9

Feudalism in Western Europe

Joseph R. Strayer

Feudalism, in Western European history, is a word which has been given many meanings,[1] but most of them can be brought into two general categories. One group of scholars uses the word to describe the technical arrangement by which vassals became dependents of lords, and landed property (with attached economic benefits) became organized as dependent tenures or fiefs. The other group of scholars uses feudalism as a general word which sums up the dominant forms of political and social organization during certain centuries of the Middle Ages.

There are difficulties with both usages. In the first category there is no agreement on the relationships which are to be considered typically feudal. Is it the act of becoming a vassal, or the act of granting a fief, or a combination of the two which makes feudalism? Retainers, clients, armed dependents of a great man—all these we have in both Germanic and Roman society from the fourth century on, but does that entitle us to speak of the late Roman or primitive German feudalism? Under Charlemagne there are vassals, and these vassals receive dependent tenures. Yet the king still keeps close control over all men and all lands, and the relationships of dependency are not necessarily hereditary. If this is feudalism, then we need another word to describe conditions in the eleventh century. In the seventeenth century, in both France and England all the technical forms of feudalism survive—most nobles are vassals and much of their land is held as fiefs. Yet it is only the form which has survived; the ideas which control the relationship of king and noble no longer conform to the feudal pattern. In short, the difficulty in concentrating on the technical aspects of feudalism is that it sets no chronological limits and provides no standards by which feudalism can be clearly distinguished from preceding and succeeding types of organization.

In the second category this difficulty is overcome by assuming at the onset that there is a "feudal age," a "feudal period" with definite chronological limits. The limits may vary, but there is general agreement on the core of the period—all authorities would admit that feudalism reached its height in the

From Joseph R. Strayer, "Feudalism in Western Europe," in *Feudalism in History*, Rushon Coulborn, ed. (Princeton, N.J.: Princeton University Press, 1956), pp. 15–25. Copyright 1956, renewed 1984 by Princeton University Press. Reprinted by permission of Princeton University Press.

eleventh and twelfth centuries. But while this approach clears up the chronological confusion, it introduces a functional confusion by applying the feudal label to all social phenomena between the tenth and the thirteenth centuries. For example, the class structure of the late Middle Ages was very different from that of the early Middle Ages—are they both feudal? Lords used a different technique in exploiting their lands in 1200 from that in vogue in 1000—which technique should be accepted as typical of feudalism? We meet the sort of difficulties here that a modern historian would find if he assumed that the factory system were an integral part of democracy.

To obtain a usable concept of feudalism we must eliminate extraneous factors and aspects which are common to many types of society. Feudalism is not synonymous with aristocracy—there have been many aristocracies which were not feudal and there was no very clear concept of aristocracy in the early days of feudalism. Feudalism is not a necessary concomitant of the great estate worked by dependent or servile labor—such estates have existed in many other societies. Feudalism is not merely the relationship between lord and man, nor the system of dependent land tenures, for either can exist in a nonfeudal society. The combination of personal and tenurial dependence brings us close to feudalism, but something is still lacking. It is only when rights of government (not mere political influence) are attached to lordship and fiefs that we can speak of fully developed feudalism in Western Europe. It is the possession of rights of government by feudal lords and the performance of most functions of government through feudal lords which clearly distinguishes feudalism from other types of organization.

This means that Western European feudalism is essentially political—it is a form of government. It is a form of government in which political authority is monopolized by a small group of military leaders, but is rather evenly distributed among members of the group. As a result, no leader rules a very wide territory, nor does he have complete authority even within a limited territory—he must share power with his equals and grant power to his subordinates. A fiction of unity—a theory of subordination or cooperation among feudal lords—exists, but government is actually effective only at the local level of the country or the lordship. It is the lords who maintain order, if they can, who hold courts and determine what is the law. The king, at best, can merely keep peace among the lords and usually is unable even to do this.

The men who possess political power also possess important sources of wealth—land and buildings, markets and mills, forests and rivers—and this wealth is naturally useful in maintaining or increasing their political authority. Yet wealth alone does not give political power—loyal vassals and courageous retainers are more important. Any sensible feudal lord will surrender much of his land in order to increase the number of his vassals, and the most powerful lords, such as the Duke of Normandy, actually possess relatively few estates. It is also true that political and economic rights do not always correspond. A lord may have rights of government where he has no land and may hold land where some other lord has superior political authority. No one finds this inconsistent, because the distinction which we have been making between political and economic rights has almost no meaning for the early Middle Ages. Public authority has become a private possession. Everyone expects the possessor of a court to make a profit out of it, and everyone knows that the eldest son of the court-holder will inherit this profitable right, whatever his qualifications for the work. On the other hand, any important accumulation of private property almost inevitably becomes burdened with public duties. The possessor of a great estate must defend it, police it, maintain roads and bridges and hold a court for his tenants. Thus lordship has both economic and political aspects; it is less than sovereignty, but more than private property.

Effective feudal government is local, and at the local level public authority has become a private possession. Yet in feudalism the concepts of central government and of public authority are never entirely lost. Kingship survives, with real prestige though attenuated power, and the Church never forgets the Roman traditions of strong monarchy and public law. The revival of Roman law in the twelfth century strengthens these traditions and by the thirteenth century most lawyers insist that all governmental authority is delegated by the king and that the king has a right to review all acts of feudal lords.

Feudal lordship occupies an intermediate place between tribal leadership and aristocratic government. It differs from tribal leadership in being more formalized and less spontaneous. The feudal lord is not necessarily one of the group whom he rules; he may be a complete stranger who has acquired the lordship by inheritance or grant. It differs from aristocracy in being more individualistic and less centralized. The feudal lord is not merely one of a group of men who influence the government; he *is* the government in his own area. When feudalism is at its height, the barons never combine to rule jointly a wide territory but instead seek a maximum degree of independence from each other. One of the signs of the decay of feudalism in the West is the emergence of the idea of government by a *group* of aristocrats.

As the last paragraphs suggest, we must distinguish between an earlier and a later stage of Western feudalism. In the early stage feudalism was the dominant fact in politics, but there was almost no theoretical explanation or justification of the fact. In the later stage feudalism was competing with and slowly losing ground to other types of political organization, and many able writers tried to explain how and why it functioned. The great law-books of the thirteenth century—the Norman *Summa de Legibus,* Bracton, Beaumanoir—fit the facts of feudalism into a logical and well-organized system of law and government. Naturally most writers of secondary works have relied on these treatises and as a result the modern concept of feudalism is largely that of feudalism in the late twelfth and thirteenth centuries—a feudalism which was much better organized, much more precise, and much less important than that of the earlier period.

The first period of feudalism is best exemplified by the institutions of northern France about 1100. In northern France the one basic institution was the small feudal state dominated by the local lord. He might bear any title (the ruler of Normandy was called at various times duke, count, or marquis) and he was usually, though not always, the vassal of a king. But whatever his title, whatever his nominal dependence on a superior, he was in fact the final authority in his region. No one could appeal from his decisions to a higher authority; no one could remain completely indifferent to his commands. His position was based on his military strength. He had a group of trained fighting men in his service; he held fortified strategic positions throughout his lands; he possessed sufficient economic resources to pay for both the army and the fortifications. There might be lesser lords within his sphere of influence who had accepted his leadership in order to gain protection or because his military power left them no choice but submission. Some of his retainers—not necessarily all—would have fiefs for which they rendered service, in which they had limited rights of government. Relations between the lord and these subordinates were still undefined. The exact amount of service to be rendered by the vassal, the rights of government which he could exercise, the degree to which these rights could be inherited by his descendants depended far more on the power and prestige of the lord than on any theory of law. It was up to the lord to defend his territory and his rights; if he failed he would either lose his lands to a stronger neighboring lord or to his more powerful subordinates. There could be great fluctuations in power and in amount of territory controlled, not merely from one generation to another, but even from one decade to another. The only thing which was relatively stable was the method of government. The customs of a region remained the same, even if the lordship changed hands, and every lord had to govern through and with his vassals. They formed his army; they made up the court in which all important acts of government were performed; they performed most of the functions of local government in their fiefs.

The second stage of feudalism—the stage described by the great lawyers of the thirteenth century—bears a closer resemblance to the neat, pyramidal structure of the textbooks. The bonds of vassalage have been tightened at the upper and relaxed at the lower level; the ruler of a province now owes more obedience to his superior and receives less service from his inferiors. Early feudalism might be described as a series of overlapping spheres of influence, each centered around the castles of some strong local lord. Later feudalism is more like a series of holding corporations; the local lord still performs important functions but he can be directed and controlled by high authority. Appeals from the local lord to his superior are encouraged; petty vassals are protected against excessive demands for service or attempts to seize their fiefs; the central government in some cases deals directly with rear-vassals instead of passing orders down a long chain of command. Royal law-courts play a great role in this reorganization. The institution of the assizes at the end of the twelfth century in England protected the rear-vassal and brought him into direct contact with the king. The development of appeals to the king's court at Paris gave the same results in thirteenth-century France. In this much more highly organized feudalism rights and duties are spelled out in great detail. The amount of service owed is carefully stated, rules of inheritance are determined, the rights of government which can be exercised by each lord are defined and regulated. Force is still important, but only the king and the greatest lords possess sufficient force to gain by its use; the ordinary lord has to accept judicial solutions to his controversies.

There is obviously a great difference between these two stages of feudalism, and yet the transition from one to the other was made so smoothly, in many places, that it was almost imperceptible. It is true that in the later stage rulers were aided by concepts which were not derived from early feudalism, such as the revived Roman law and the Church's ideas of Christian monarchy. Yet, giving due weight to these outside influences, there must still have been some principle of order and growth in early feudalism which made possible the rapid development of relatively advanced systems of political organization in the twelfth and thirteenth centuries. Early feudal society, turbulent as it was, was never pure anarchy. There was always some government, even if rudimentary and local; there were always some centers of refuge and defense. Early feudal government, primitive as it was, was still more sophisticated and complicated than tribal government. There was a higher degree of specialization—the fighting men and the men with rights of government were clearly marked off from the rest of the group. There was a little more artificiality in political organization. Feudal government was not (necessarily) part of the immemorial structure of the community; it could be imposed from the outside; it could be consciously altered by the lord and his vassals. Early feudalism was rough and crude, but it was neither stagnant nor sterile. Flexible and adaptable, it produced new institutions rapidly, perhaps more rapidly than more sophisticated systems of government.

To understand the real vitality of feudalism we shall have to consider briefly the circumstances in which it first appeared in Europe. The Roman Empire had collapsed in the West, largely because none of its subjects cared enough for it to make any great effort to defend it. The Germanic rulers who succeeded the Emperors were not hostile to Roman civilization. They preserved as much of it as they were able; they kept together as large political units as they could. They were not entirely successful in these efforts, but they did preserve real power for the central government and they did thwart the growth of independent local lordship. The greatest of the Germanic rulers, Charlemagne, even united a large part of Western Europe in a new Empire. This was a *tour de force* which has impressed men for over a thousand years; he made his bricks not only without straw but very nearly without clay. The Latin and Germanic peoples he united had no common political tradition, no common cultural tradition and very few economic ties. Their interests were predominantly local, as they had been for centuries; only the clergy remembered with longing the peace and good order of Rome. With the moral support of the Church and the physical support of the army of his own people, the Franks, Charlemagne held his Empire together, but it was always a shaky structure. The Church profited by its existence to extend the parish system and to improve the education of the higher clergy. These developments helped to soften some of the cultural differences among Western European peoples, and to lay the foundations for a common European civilization, but the forces of localism were still stronger than those which worked for unity. Local government was in the hands of counts, men of wealth and high social position who held their authority from the king but who were not always fully obedient to him. The counts, in turn, were not always able to dominate the great landowners of their districts. Vassalage was becoming common and something very like fiefs held of the king or of lords appeared about the middle of the eighth century. Charlemagne tried to reinforce the doubtful loyalty of his subjects by making the great men his vassals, but this expedient had only temporary success. The ties between the magnates and their retainers were far closer than those between Charlemagne and the magnates, for the retainers lived with their lords while the lords visited the imperial court only occasionally. As a result the magnates had great power in their own provinces, subject only to the intermittent intervention of the king. This was not yet feudalism: there was still public authority, and the great men held political power by delegation from the king and not in their own right. But it was very close to feudalism; a strong push was all that was needed to cross the line.

The push came in the fifty years which followed Charlemagne's death. His heirs were less competent than he and quarreled among themselves. The magnates took advantage of these quarrels to gain independence; they began to consider their offices private possessions, to be inherited by their sons. Meanwhile invasions from outside threatened the security of all inhabitants of the Empire. The Saracens raided the south coast of France, the west coast of Italy, and even established a permanent fort at Garde-Frainet which interfered seriously with overland travel between France and Italy. The Magyars occupied Hungary, and from this base sent great cavalry expeditions through southern Germany, eastern France and northern Italy. Worst of all were the Northmen. For over a century their shallow-draft ships pushed up all the rivers of northern Europe and sent out raiding parties which plundered the countryside. The central government was almost helpless; it could not station troops everywhere on the vast periphery of the Empire and it could seldom assemble and move an army quickly enough to catch the fast-moving raiders. Defense had to become a local responsibility; only the local lord and his castle could provide any security for most subjects of the Empire.

It was in these conditions that feudal governments began to appear in northern France—a region which had suffered heavily from both civil war and Viking raids. We could hardly expect these early feudal governments to be well organized and efficient—they were improvised to meet a desperate situation and they bore all the signs of hasty construction. But they did have two great advantages which made them capable of further development. In the first place, feudalism forced men who had privileges to assume responsibility. In the late Roman Empire, the Frankish kingdom, and the Carolingian monarchy wealthy landlords had assisted the central government as little as possible while using their position and influence to gain special advantages for themselves. Now they had to carry the whole load; if they shirked they lost everything. In the second place, feudalism simplified the structure of government to a point where it corresponded to existing social and economic conditions. For centuries rulers had been striving to preserve something of the Roman political system, at the very least to maintain their authority over relatively large areas through a hierarchy of appointed officials. These efforts had met little response from the great majority of people; large-scale government had given them few benefits and had forced them to carry heavy burdens. Always there had been a dangerous discrepancy between the wide interests of the rulers and the narrow, local interests of the ruled. Feudalism relieved this strain; it worked at a level which was comprehensible to the ordinary man and it made only minimum demands on him. It is probably true that early feudal governments did less than they should, but this was better than doing more than was wanted. When the abler feudal lords began to improve their governments they had the support of their people who realized that new institutions were needed. The active demand for more and better government in the twelfth century offers a sharp contrast to the apathy with which the people of Western Europe watched the disintegration of the Roman and Carolingian Empires.

Feudalism, in short, made a fairly clean sweep of obsolete institutions and replaced them with a rudimentary government which could be used as a basis for a fresh start. Early feudal government was informal and flexible. Contrary to common opinion, it was at first little bound by tradition. It is true that it followed local custom, but there were few written records, and oral tradition was neither very accurate nor very stable. Custom changed rapidly when circumstances changed; innovations were quickly accepted if they seemed to promise greater security. Important decisions were made by the lord and his vassals, meeting in informal councils which followed no strict rules of procedure. It was easy for an energetic lord to make experiments in government; for example, there was constant tinkering with the procedure of feudal courts in the eleventh and twelfth centuries in order to find better methods of proof. Temporary committees could be set up to do specific jobs; if they did their work well they might become permanent and form the nucleus of a department of government. It is true that many useful ideas came from the clergy, rather than from lay vassals, but if feudal governments had not been adaptable they could not have profited from the learning and skill of the clergy.

Feudalism produced its best results only in regions where it became the dominant form of government. France, for example, developed her first adequate governments in the feudal principalities of the north, Flanders, Normandy, Anjou and the king's own lordship of the Ile de France. The first great increase in the power of the French king came from enforcing his rights as feudal superior against his vassals. Many institutions of the French monarchy of the thirteenth century had already been tested in the feudal states of the late twelfth century; others grew out of the king's feudal court. By allowing newly annexed provinces to keep the laws and institutions developed in the feudal period, the king of France was able to unite the country with a minimum of ill-will. France later paid a high price for this provincial particularism, but the existence of local governments which could operate with little supervision immensely simplified the first stages of unification.

England in many ways was more like a single French province than the congeries of provinces which made up the kingdom of France. In fact, the first kings after the Conquest sometimes spoke of the kingdom as their "honor" or fief, just as a feudal lord might speak of his holding. As this example shows,

England was thoroughly feudalized after the Conquest. While Anglo-Saxon law remained officially in force it became archaic and inapplicable; the law which grew into the common law of England was the law applied in the king's feudal court. The chief departments of the English government likewise grew out of this court. And when the combination of able kings and efficient institutions made the monarchy too strong, it was checked by the barons in the name of the feudal principles expressed in Magna Carta. Thus feudalism helped England to strike a happy balance between government which was too weak and government which was too strong.

The story was quite different in countries in which older political institutions prevented feudalism from reaching full development. Feudalism grew only slowly in Germany; it never included all fighting men or all lands. The German kings did not use feudalism as the chief support of their government; instead they relied on institutions inherited from the Carolingian period. This meant that the ruler acted as if local lords were still his officials and as if local courts were still under his control. In case of opposition, he turned to bishops and abbots for financial and military aid, instead of calling on his vassals. There was just enough vitality in this system to enable the king to interfere sporadically in political decisions all over Germany, and to prevent the growth of strong, feudal principalities. But while the German kings of the eleventh and twelfth centuries showed remarkable skill in using the old precedents, they failed to develop new institutions and ideas. Royal government became weaker, and Germany more disunited in every succeeding century. The most important provincial rulers, the dukes, were also unable to create effective governments. The kings were jealous of their power, and succeeded in destroying or weakening all the great duchies. The kings, however, were unable to profit from their success, because of their own lack of adequate institutions. Power eventually passed to rulers of the smaller principalities, not always by feudal arrangements, and only after the monarchy had been further weakened by a long conflict with the papacy. Thus the German kings of the later Middle Ages were unable to imitate the king of France, who had united his country through the use of his position as feudal superior. Germany remained disunited, and, on the whole, badly governed, throughout the rest of the Middle Ages and the early modern period.

Italy also suffered from competition among different types of government. The German emperor was traditionally king of (north) Italy. He could not govern this region effectively but he did intervene often enough to prevent the growth of large, native principalities. The Italian towns had never become depopulated, like those of the North, and the great economic revival of the late eleventh century made them wealthy and powerful. They were too strong to be fully controlled by any outside ruler, whether king or feudal lord, and too weak (at least in the early Middle Ages) to annex the rural districts outside their walls. The situation was further complicated by the existence of the papacy at Rome. The popes were usually on bad terms with the German emperors and wanted to rule directly a large part of central Italy. In defending themselves and their policies they encouraged the towns' claims to independence and opposed all efforts to unite the peninsula. Thus, while there was feudalism in Italy, it never had a clear field and was unable to develop as it did in France or England. Italy became more and more disunited; by the end of the Middle Ages the city-state, ruled by a "tyrant," was the dominant form of government in the peninsula. There was no justification for this type of government in medieval political theory, and this may be one reason why the Italians turned with such eagerness to the writings of the classical period. In any case, the Italian political system was a failure, and Italy was controlled by foreign states from the middle of the sixteenth to the middle of the nineteenth century.

There are certainly other factors, besides feudalism, which enabled France and England to set the pattern for political organization in Europe, and other weaknesses, besides the absence of fully developed feudalism, which condemned Germany and Italy to political sterility. At the same time, the basic institutions of France and England in the thirteenth century, which grew out of feudal customs, proved adaptable to changed conditions, while the basic institutions of Italy and Germany, which were largely non-feudal, had less vitality. Western feudalism was far from being an efficient form of government, but its very imperfections encouraged the experiments which kept it from being a stagnant form of government. It was far from being a just form of government, but the emphasis on personal relationships made it a source of persistent loyalties. And it was the flexibility of their institutions and the loyalty of their subjects which enabled the kings of the West to create the first modern states.

Note

1. Pollock and Maitland, *History of English Law*, 2nd ed. (Cambridge, 1923), I, 66–67: ". . . *feudalism* is an unfortunate word. In the first place it draws our attention to but one element in a complex state of society and that element is not the most distinctive: it draws our attention only to the prevalence of dependent and derivative land tenure. This however may well exist in an age which can not be called feudal in any tolerable sense. What is characteristic of 'the feudal period' is not the relationship between letter and hirer, or lender and borrower of land, but the relationship between lord and vassal, or rather it is the union of these two relationships. Were we free to invent new terms, we might find *feudo-vassalism* more serviceable than *feudalism*. But the difficulty is not one which could be solved by any merely verbal devices. The impossible task that has been set before the word *feudalism* is that of making a single idea represent a very large piece of the world's history, represent the France, Italy, Germany, England, of every century from the eighth or ninth to the fourteenth or fifteenth. Shall we say that French feudalism reached its zenith under Louis d'Outre-Mer or under Saint Louis, that William of Normandy introduced feudalism into England or saved England from feudalism, that Bracton is the greatest of English feudists or that he never misses an opportunity of showing a strong antifeudal bias? It would be possible to maintain all or any of these opinions, so vague is our use of the term in question."

CHAPTER 10

The Tyranny of a Construct

Elizabeth A. R. Brown

At a recent conference Thomas N. Bisson introduced his paper "Institutional Structures of the Medieval Peace" by cautioning his audience that in his discussion of peace movements, peace associations, and peace institutions in southern France and Spain he would not attempt to relate his findings to "feudalism."[1] His approach was descriptive—and thoroughly enlightening—and no further reference to any ism occurred until the question period. Then, bestowing the double-edged praise that is his hallmark, Professor John F. Benton asked how historians could have managed to overlook for so long such abundant evidence that would necessitate the revision of numerous lectures on medieval society. Responding to this remark, Professor Bisson again alluded to the eventual necessity of evaluating his conclusions with reference to the general topic of feudalism, but time prevented him from elaborating. It occurred to me as this interchange was taking place that the failure of historians to take account of the data used by Bisson may well have resulted from their concentration on feudalism—as model or Ideal Type—and their consequent tendency to disregard to dismiss documents not easily assimilable into that frame of reference.

Whatever their relevance to the subject of Professor Bisson's paper, feelings of uneasiness concerning the term "feudalism" are not uniquely mine. Historians have for years harbored doubts about the term "feudalism" and the phrase "feudal system," which has often been used as a synonym for it. One of the first, and certainly one of the wittiest and most eloquent, to comment on the problem was Frederic William Maitland. In lectures on English constitutional history prepared in 1887 and 1888 he wrote:

> Now were an examiner to ask who introduced the feudal system into England? one very good answer, if properly explained, would be Henry Spelman, and if there followed the question, what was the feudal system? a good answer to that would be, an early essay in comparative jurisprudence. . . . If my examiner went on with his questions and asked me, when did the feudal system attain its most perfect development? I should answer, about the middle of the last century.[2]

From Elizabeth A. R. Brown, "The Tyranny of a Construct: Feudalism and Historians of Medieval Europe," *The American Historical Review,* Vol. 79 (1974), pp. 1063–1088. Reprinted by permission of the author.

Thanks to J. G. A. Pocock, it is now known that Henry Spelman, a learned English antiquarian of the seventeenth century, used neither the term "feudal system" nor the word "feudalism," but this does not detract from the validity or the importance of Maitland's observations. Following in the steps of the Scottish legal scholar Sir Thomas Craig, Spelman held that the social and political relationships of medieval England had been uniform and systematic enough to be described adequately as regulated by a " 'feudal law' [which] was an hierarchical system imposed from above as a matter of state policy." The work of Craig and Spelman had its virtues, for they were the first British historians to attempt to relate British institutions to continental developments. Both, however, relied for their knowledge of continental institutions on Cujas's and Hotman's sixteenth-century editions of the twelfth-century Lombard *Libri Feudorum,* which gave, to paraphrase Pocock, a precise and detailed "definition of the *feudum* whereby it could be recognized in any part of Europe," or, as he says, "a systematic exposition of the principles of tenure, forfeiture and inheritance." These criteria Craig and Spelman employed to classify the evidence from Scottish and English sources, and their simplification and regimentation of phenomena notably offset the advantages to historical thought of their demonstration that the development of England and Scotland could be understood only in the context of the European experience.[3]

Given these beginnings, it is no wonder that eighteenth-century British writers began to accept the concept of a uniform feudal government and to concentrate on the system, the construct, instead of investigating the various social and political relationships found in medieval Europe. "They were," Pocock observes, "making an 'ism' of [feudalism]; they were reflecting on its essence and nature and endeavoring to fit it into a pattern of general ideas."[4] In so doing they resembled Boulainvilliers and Montesquieu, who wrote of *féodalité* and *lois féodales* as distinguishing a state of society, thus, incidentally, expanding the concept to include a far wider range of phenomena than it had for legal scholars.[5] The writers of the eighteenth century, like those of later times, assigned different meanings to the term *féodalité,* or, in English, "feodality." Some used it to designate a system of government, some to refer to conditions that developed as public power disappeared. By 1800 the construct had been launched and the expression "feudal system" devised; by the mid-nineteenth century the word "feudalism" was in use. The way was prepared for future scholars to study feudalism—whatever it was conceived to be—scientifically and for others to employ the ism to refer, abusively, to those selected elements of the past that were to be overthrown, abolished, or inexorably superseded.[6]

Since the middle of the nineteenth century the concepts of feudalism and the feudal system have dominated the study of the medieval past. The appeal of these words, which provide a short, easy means of referring to the European social and political situation over an enormous stretch of time, has proved virtually impossible to resist, for they pander to the human desire to grasp—or to think one is grasping—a subject known or suspected to be complex by applying to it a simple label simplistically defined. The great authority of these terms has radically influenced the way in which the history of the Middle Ages has been conceptualized and investigated, encouraging concentration on oversimplified models that are applied as standards and stimulating investigation of similarities and differences, norms and deviations. As a result scholars have disregarded or paid insufficient attention to recalcitrant data that their models do not prepare them to expect.

But let us return to Maitland. Implicit in his assessment of Spelman and the feudal system is a clear objection to applying the label "feudal system" to medieval England, presumably because of a belief that England never underwent a systematization of social and political life—or, as Maitland puts it, never experienced "the development of what can properly be called a feudal system." Less evident, perhaps, is a hesitancy about the propriety of using the phrase "feudal system" at all. That Maitland questioned the wisdom of applying it to conditions of medieval society is hard to dispute, however, for in his lectures he remarks,

> The phrase [feudal system] has thus become for us so large and vague that it is quite possible to maintain that of all countries England was the most, or for the matter of that the least, feudalized; that William the Conqueror introduced, or for the matter of that suppressed, the feudal system.[7]

Still, having bemoaned the terminological situation, Maitland proceeds to use the term "feudalism," equated by him with "feudal system."[8] He announces that "the feudalism of the thirteenth is very different from that of the eleventh century." He then goes on to give his own definition of feudalism, emphasizing ties of vassalage, fiefs, service in arms owed the lord, and private administration of justice. Using this definition, he discusses the question of the progress toward such an organization that England had been making before the Norman Conquest, and he concludes, "Speaking generally then, that ideal feudalism of which we have spoken, an ideal which was pretty completely realized in France during the tenth, eleventh and twelfth centuries, was never realized in England." Here, he says, "the force of feudalism [was] limited and checked by other ideas."[9]

As these statements show, Maitland's tolerance for unresolved contradictions was high, and other historians have demonstrated a similarly striking capacity for living with inconsistency. Although they attack the term "feudalism," they are still unwilling and perhaps unable—whether from habit, inertia, or simple inattention—to jettison the word. Consider H. G. Richardson and G. O. Sayles. In a book published in 1963 they denounce "feudal" and "feudalism" as "the most regrettable coinages ever put into circulation to debase the language of historians." "We would, if we could," they declare, "avoid using them, for they have been given so many and such imprecise meanings." They confess, however—without apology or explanation—that they cannot "rid [themselves] of the words and must live with them" and therefore proclaim their determination to "endeavor, when [they use] them, to do so without ambiguity." They evidently have some sense of attachment, however grudging, to the terms, and their feelings are reflected in their insistence that "if the concept and the term are to be in the least useful"—thus implying that they can be—"there must be precise definition." Such definition they do not, unfortunately, offer. Nonetheless they doggedly persist in using the words, and they spend a large portion of their book dealing with their "thesis of the relative unimportance of any element of 'feudalism' in post-Conquest England" and of "the essential continuity of English institutions."[10]

Such an approach logically requires isolating those elements that can properly be called feudal from those that cannot. Since Richardson and Sayles never explicitly objectify the enemy, however, their readers are left to deduce from their arguments just what phenomena they consider essential components of feudalism. Homage, " 'feudal' incidents," honors and honorial courts, knightly service connected with fiefs, and the use of military tenures for military purposes are all linked in one way or another with feudalism, although Richardson and Sayles clearly suggest that, unless found in their Franco-Norman forms, these elements should not be considered truly feudal. Thus the authors attempt to validate their hypothesis by showing either that these or similar institutions existed in England before 1066—and hence are to be classified as Old English and therefore not Norman feudal—or that they had to real importance after that date.[11] In the end, coming to grips with the problem of definition, they abruptly abandon their previous criteria. So that they can pronounce England safely nonfeudal and therefore, non-French, they fall back on what they call "the classical theory of feudalism," described as the idea of lordship diminished by fragmentation or of "sovereignty . . . divided between the king and his feudataries," neither of which was ever found in England. They warn that feudalism should not be defined simply in terms of tenure, since if it is it will be found everywhere.[12]

As their lengthy discussion and conclusion make clear, Richardson and Sayles were never fully convinced, despite their initial volleys, that feudalism was in fact no "more than an arbitrary pattern imposed by modern writers upon men long dead and events long past." Although they end their analysis by remarking of the word "feudal" that "an adjective so ambiguous and so misleading is best avoided," their repeated use of the term belies their alleged distaste.[13]

If numerous arguments in defense of feudalism have been advanced, "utility" and "indispensability" are the chief rallying cries of the term's defender. Let us turn first to the criterion of utility.

In the introduction to his classic study *Feudalism*, F. L. Ganshof states that he intends his book to facilitate the work of students of medieval society. In analyzing and describing feudal institutions he says he has "endeavored to bring out as clearly as possible their essential features, since, once these are grasped, it is easy for the student to disentangle the elements that can properly be described as feudal in the institutions of the period or country with which he is primarily concerned."[14] Helping the scholar as well as the student to evaluate, analyze, and categorize the past is also important to Michael Postan, and in his foreword to the English edition of Marc Bloch's *Feudal Soci-*

ety he argues that the usefulness of "generalized concepts" such as feudalism lies in their ability to "help us to distinguish one historical situation from another and to align similar situations in different countries and even in different periods." For Postan greater complexity apparently means greater utility, and he prefers Bloch's definition of feudalism, which embraces "most of the significant features of medieval society," to "constitutional and legal concepts of feudalism" centering on "military service" and "contractual principles." These latter concepts, he feels, may have some virtue as pedagogical devices, to promote "intellectual discipline," and to serve as "an antidote to the journalistic levities of modern historiography." Still, they cannot validly be considered "an intellectual tool, to be used in the study of society."[15]

If Postan draws a rather unsettling distinction between pedagogy on the one hand and research and sound intellectual endeavor on the other, it is clear that he is not alone in considering appropriate for the student what is decried for the scholar. This "track" approach to feudalism is widespread, even though those who espouse it may differ concerning what should be taught at different levels. Postan envisions progression from a partial to a more complex model, always retaining the term "feudalism" to denote the model. Others, expressing fundamental objections to the misleading impression of simplicity and system they believe inevitably associated with isms, still argue that authors of basic textbooks—as opposed to advanced studies—would be lost without the concept of feudalism. This rather inconsistent attitude apparently springs from two convictions: first, that beginning students are incapable of dealing with complex and diverse development and must for their own good be presented with an artificially regular schema; and second, that the term "feudalism" somehow helps these students by serving as a handy, familiar tag to which to attach consciously oversimplified generalizations. Later, as graduate students, they are presumably to be introduced to qualifications and complications, and finally, as scholars and initiates into the mysteries of the trade, they are to be encouraged to discard the offending ism for purposes of research, if not for purposes of teaching their own beginning students. Charles T. Wood, although not explicitly endorsing the use of the term "feudalism," writes that "the feudal pyramid . . . makes for clear diagrams, and schoolboys have to begin somewhere." Still, he admits, "where they do begin is rather far removed from reality."[16]

Postan, and presumably Ganshof, feels that employing the construct has the virtue of enabling scholars to distinguish likenesses among different times and areas. Similarly John Le Patourel advocates formulating a definition of feudalism that could be used "as a measuring-rod,"[17] and such a standard could presumably be relied on not only, as he wants, to clarify "the old argument" over the introduction of feudalism into England but also, as Postan argues, to advance the work of those concerned with comparing developments in different countries.

If feudalism is praised as a teaching device and as a means of understanding societies, it is also said to be "indispensable," and that for a number of reasons. Marc Bloch maintains that scientists cannot function without abstractions and that since historians are scientists, they also require abstractions. The specific abstractions "feudal" and "feudalism" are defended on the grounds that, however awkward and inappropriate in terms of their original connotations these words and others like them may be, the historian is in this respect no worse off than the scientist, who must also make do with inconvenient and unsuitable terminology.[18] Michael Postan goes beyond Bloch to declare that "without generalized terms representing entire groups of phenomena not only history but all intelligent discourse would be impossible," and he maintains that no difference exists between such a word as "feudalism" and other general terms like "war" and "agriculture."[19] Equally positively, if less aggressively, Fredric Cheyette has insisted that the term "feudalism" cannot "simply be discarded—the verbal detours one would have to make to replace it would be strained as well as disingenuous."[20] Otto Hintze argues that the concept is indispensable not only for reasons of practicality and convenience but also because of the deficiencies of the processes of human thought, assumed to be incapable of comprehending the complexities of the real world. Hintze asserts that since "it is impossible to grasp the complicated circumstances of historical life, so laden with unique occurrences, in a few universal and unambiguous concepts—as is done in the natural sciences," historians must use "intuitive abstractions" and create "Ideal Types, and such types indeed underlie our scholarly terminology."[21]

Even its most eloquent advocates readily acknowledge the difficulties associated with the use of the term "feudalism." Marc Bloch, for one, states that "nearly every historian understands the word as he pleases," and "even if we do define, it is usually every man for himself." He admits that the word is charged with emotional overtones[22] and is in fact "very ill-chosen,"[23] and he acknowledges that, in general, abstractions which are "ill-chosen or too mechanically applied" should be avoided.[24] He goes so far as to declare that the word "capitalism" has lost its usefulness because it has become burdened with ambiguities and because it is "carelessly applied to the most diverse civilizations," so that, as a result, "it almost inevitably results in concealing their original features."[25] Even Postan, whose loyalty to Bloch exceeds Bloch's sense of commitment to his own ideas, grants that comprehensive terms like "feudalism" "over-simplify the reality they purport to epitomize," and he confesses that

> in some contexts the practice of giving general names to whole epochs can even be dangerous, [luring] its practitioners into the worst pitfalls of the nominalist fallacy, and [encouraging] them to endow their terms with real existence, to derive features of an epoch from the etymology of the word used to describe it or to construct edifices of historical argument out of mere semantic conceits.[26]

The variety of existing definitions of the term and the general unwillingness of any historian to accept any other historian's characterization of feudalism constitute a prime source of confusion. The best definition would doubtless be, as Cheyette suggests, one that helped "to make the body of evidence on medieval institutions coherent," but he himself has not found or formulated any definition to accomplish this purpose.[27] In the absence of consensus, the play with meanings has flourished and still continues.

The sweeping perspective adopted by Marc Bloch produced a definition of European feudalism—equated by Bloch with feudal society and, in the translation of his book, with feudal system[28]—that in effect summarizes the topics treated in the central section of his *La Société féodale*. It encompasses a wide range of aspects of medieval life.

> A subject peasantry; widespread use of the service tenement (i.e. the fief) instead of a salary, which was out of the question; the supremacy of a class of specialized warriors; ties of obedience and protection which bind man to man and, within the warrior class, assume the distinctive form called vassalage; fragmentation of authority—leading inevitably to disorder; and, in the midst of all this, the survival of other forms of association, family and State, of which the latter, during the second feudal age, was to acquire renewed strength.[29]

Some historians have accepted this inclusive list as a definition of feudalism, but others would prefer to link it only with feudal society, which they feel can and should be distinguished from a more narrowly conceived feudalism, in which the fief is accorded greater prominence than Bloch gives it.[30] Ganshof, for one, believes that in the Middle Ages "the fief, if not the cornerstone, was at least the most important element in the graded system of rights over land which this type of society involved." The definition of feudalism he prefers— "the narrow, technical, legal sense of the word"—concentrates on service and maintenance and emphasized the fief, while it excludes entirely the private exercise of public justice and jurisdiction. For Ganshof feudalism is envisaged as

> a body of institutions creating and regulating the obligations of obedience and service—mainly military service—on the part of a free man (the vassal) towards another free man (the lord), and the obligations of protection and maintenance on the part of the lord with regard to his vassal. The obligation of maintenance had usually as one of its effects the grant by the lord to his vassal of a unit of real property known as a fief.

Although Ganshof admits that "powers of jurisdiction [in particular what one normally calls feudal jurisdiction] were . . . very closely bound up with feudal relationships," he states firmly that "there was nothing in the relationships of feudalism . . . which required that a vassal receiving investiture of a fief should necessarily have the profits of jurisdiction within it, nor even that he should exercise such jurisdiction."[31]

Ganshof may have his followers, particularly among historians of the Normans and the English.[32] On the other hand, many scholars insist that the private exercise of public governmental authority—an element rejected by Ganshof—is the single essential component in any definition of feudalism. Several years ago Joseph R. Strayer adopted this position when he advocated a definition focusing on jurisdiction and omitting most of the other factors contained in the definitions just examined. "To obtain a usable concept of feudalism,"

Strayer argued, "we must eliminate extraneous factors and aspects which are common to many types of society." Having lopped off aristocracy, "the great estate worked by dependent or servile labor," "the relationship between lord and man," and "the system of dependent land tenures," he concluded that it is "only when rights of government (not mere political influence) are attached to lordship and fiefs that we can speak of fully developed feudalism in Western Europe."[33] Subsequently Strayer decided that this definition was defective,[34] and in 1965 he advanced one that included a military as well as a political element. Then he presented as "the basic characteristics of feudalism in Western Europe . . . a fragmentation of political authority, public power in private hands, and a military system in which an essential part of the armed forces is secured through private contracts." Thus feudalism was seen not only as a "method of government" but also as "a way of securing the forces necessary to preserve that method of government." It seems clear, however, that Strayer still considered the jurisdictional element fundamental, for in concluding his discussion he wrote that "a drive for political power by the aristocracy led to the rise of feudalism."[35]

Other approaches to the problem of defining feudalism have been taken. In 1953 Georges Duby states a bit hesitantly that "what one refers to as feudalism" (*ce qu'on appelle la féodalité*) should be understood to have two aspects, the political—involving the dissolution of sovereignty—and the economic—the constitution of a coherent network of dependencies embracing all lands and through them their holders.[36] Thus he created a bridge of sorts, reconciling the definitions of Strayer and Ganshof. Later, however, Duby turned from government and land to mentalities, and in 1958 he suggested that feudalism might best be considered

> a psychological complex formed in the small world of warriors who little by little became nobles. A consciousness of the superiority of a status characterized by military specialization, one that presupposes respect for certain moral precepts, the practice of certain virtues; the associated idea that social relations are organized as a function of companionship in combat; notions of homage, of personal dependence, now in the foreground, replacing all previous forms of political association.[37]

Definitions of feudalism abound, and student and scholar have available to them broad ones that lump together numerous facets of medieval society and narrow ones that center on carefully chosen aspects of that society—tenurial, political, military, and psychical. The possibilities for bewilderment and dispute are dizzying, particularly since a single author's interpretation of the term can undergo marked shifts.

Another difficulty posed by feudalism and its system is the fact that those employing the terms, in whatever sense they use them, are constantly found qualifying and limiting the extent to which they believe them applicable to any particular time and locality in medieval Europe. Marc Bloch writes,

> In the area of Western civilization the map of feudalism reveals some large blank spaces—the Scandinavian peninsula, Frisia, Ireland. Perhaps it is more

important still to note that feudal Europe was not all feudalized in the same degree or according to the same rhythm and, above all, that it was nowhere feudalized completely.

Nostalgically, and with regret only a confirmed Platonist could harbor, he concludes, "No doubt it is the fate of every system of human institutions never to be more than imperfectly realized."[38]

While Robert S. Hoyt could write of the growth and development of feudalism and could state that by the mid-eleventh century "an essentially feudal society had emerged throughout western continental Europe," he felt obliged, first, to deny that there was a " 'feudal system' common to all Europe," and second, to assert that "there were endless diversity and variety."[39] In the introduction to *Feudalism* Ganshof notes that he proposes

> to study feudalism mainly as it existed in France, in the kingdom of Burgundy-Arles and in Germany, since in these countries its characteristics were essentially the same, and to concentrate on the regions lying between the Loire and the Rhine, which were the heart of the Carolingian state and the original home of feudalism. Further afield, in the south of France and in Germany beyond the Rhine, the institutions that grew up are often far from typical of feudalism as a whole.[40]

In his foreword to the book, F. M. Stenton praises Ganshof's self-imposed limitations and suggests that they result from a realization "that social arrangements, arising from the instinctive search for a tolerable life, vary indefinitely with varieties of time and circumstance." While it is easy to agree with Stenton that students should be disabused of the idea that "an ideal type of social order" dominated Western Europe, it comes as something of a shock to find him readily accepting the doctrine that in the huge area on which Ganshof focuses a single "classical feudalism" was to be found.[41] The expectation of infinite variety in social arrangements seemingly ends for Stenton at the Loire and the Rhine, a good safe distance from the Thames.

The variety of definitions of feudalism and the limitations imposed on their relevance are confusing. Equally disconcerting is the pervasive tendency on the part of those who use the word to personify, reify, and to coin two words, occasionally "bacterialize," and even "lunarize" the abstraction. How often does one read that feudalism, like a virus, spread from one area to another, or that, later on, it slowly waned. In a single study feudalism is assigned a dazzling array of roles. It is found giving birth, being extremely virile, having vitality, being strong, knowing a long tradition, being successfully transplanted, surviving, being replaced, teetering, being routed, declining and falling, and finally dead and in its grave. Another author sees it destroying the Frankish Empire and making a clean sweep of outmoded institutions. For another it makes onslaughts on the power of the kings of France and England; "les forces féodaux" end the confusion of spiritual and temporal authorities. Still another work reassuringly attributes a home to feudalism, which is said to have exercised, rather adventurously, "paralyzing action" over "many forms of royal activity," and, more decorously, to have been "introduced into

England in its French form" by the duke of Normandy.[42] In concluding *Seigneurie et féodalité* Boutruche in fact triumphantly proclaims it madness to consider feudalism an abstraction. "In actuality, it is a person. . . . Feudalism is medieval. . . . It is the daughter of the West."[43]

Another problem is the inclination to employ the idea of fully developed, classical, or perfectly formed feudalism as a standard by which to rank and measure areas or societies. Territories are regularly divided into categories: some highly or thoroughly feudalized; others never, gradually, or only partly feudalized.[44] Non-European countries are evaluated in this manner, and the standard has often been applied to Japanese modes of social and political organization.[45] Such assessments can also be made of institutions. The Church in Norman Italy, for instance, has been judged "never feudalized to the same extent as . . . the Church in Norman England."[46]

These examples all involve inanimate phenomena, geographical or institutional, but it is also possible to attribute to an individual or a group the aim of achieving complete feudalization or of introducing an articulated feudal system and then judge the person or group a success or failure in achieving this hypothesized objective. The precise nature of the goal would naturally depend on how the historian making the attribution defined feudalism or feudal system, but such assessments immediately imply that the person or group in question consciously planned and then attempted to implement a system based primarily on the granting of fiefs but also involving the establishment of a graded hierarchy of status and command and the delegation of sovereign power. D. C. Douglas transposes feudalism from the realm of the abstract into a concretely human framework when he says that in England William the Conqueror "was concerned to establish a completed feudal organization by means of administrative acts" and when he indicates that the conquest of England enabled William to realize the "feudal organization in Normandy." Before 1066, Douglas says, the Normans were "as yet unorganized in any rigid feudal scheme," the feudal structure "had not yet been fully formed," "the structure of Norman society had [not] as yet been made to conform to an ordered feudal plan."[47] A similar transformation of abstract model into consciously held goal occurs as Christopher Brooke asserts that "only in the Norman and the crusading states, colonized in great measure from the homeland of French feudalism, did one find any attempt to live up to a conception of feudalism as coherent as that of northern France."[48]

Appraising in terms of an ideal standard need not involve making value judgments, but such assessments are ordinarily expressed in value-loaded terms. To say that a person or a group is attempting to live up to or realize a standard certainly suggests virtuous dedication on the part of the people in question. To declare that a country which is not feudalized is lagging behind is to indicate that the area is in some sense backward. Even more evidently evaluative are such expressions as decayed, decadent, and bastard feudalism, all of them implying a society's failure or inability to maintain pure principles that were once upheld.[49] One is occasionally struck by a rather sentimental regret that the societies, individuals, and groups which might have been encouraged by high marks to persevere or shamed by low ones into exerting an additional push are unable to benefit from them. Even if formulated in value-free terms, analyses of societies on the basis of their conformity to or deviation from a norm offer little insight into the societies themselves, however much the process of comparison may stimulate and challenge the ingenuity of historians. To produce helpful insights, comparative history must involve the examination of the widest possible range of elements, not those idiosyncratically dubbed essential by the historians devising the standard to be applied.

Asserting that individual rulers actively and consciously aimed at establishing feudalism and judging them in terms of this aim is, at another level, equally misconceived and misleading. That William the Conqueror, the Normans, and the Crusaders wanted to establish control within the areas they conquered as effectively as circumstances permitted is, I think, unquestionable; that they used and molded the institutional forms and arrangements with which they were familiar and which were available to them is equally undeniable. To suggest, however, that they operated on the basis of a definite, preconceived scheme focused primarily on the fief, and to measure their accomplishments by such a standard, is to give a distorted, simplistic picture of their actions and policies, projecting into the minds of people who dealt creatively and flexibly with numerous options and who manipulated a variety of institutional devices to achieve their purposes a degree of calculation, narrowness of vision, and rigidity that the surviving evidence does not suggest characterized them and in which even a contemporary management specialist might have difficulty believing.

What of the other virtues attributed to feudalism as a means of comprehending medieval social and political life? As far as pedagogy is concerned, students should certainly be spared an approach that inevitably gives an unwarranted impression of unity and systematization and unduly emphasizes, owing to the etymology of the word, the significance of the fief. Even if historians agreed to define feudalism as feudal society and included within its scope all facets of social and political development, the practical problem would remain. There are other, more basic, disadvantages. To advocate teaching what is acknowledged to be deceptive and what must later be untaught reflects an unsettling attitude of condescension toward younger students. Furthermore, not only does such a procedure waste the time of teacher and student, but its supporters apparently disregard the difficulty of, as a student of mine puts it, " 'erasing' an erroneous concept or fact from the mind of a child who has been taught it, mistakenly or intentionally, at a lower school level." This student, Marie Heinbach, who teaches social studies in a New York junior high school, goes on to point out that "the difficulty becomes almost insurmountable when the amazing retentive powers of a young and impressionable child are considered. In addition, as the amount of time between the learning and unlearning of a concept increases, it becomes nearly impossible totally to correct the misconceptions that a student may have."[50] Experts who knowingly mislead their students appear to be unsure of their own ability to present a simplified account of the conclusions concerning medieval society that historians have now reached. Those of their students who do not progress beyond the introductory stage are denied the knowledge that most medieval historians study the actions and interrelationships of human beings rather than concentrating on the formulation and refinement of definitions of abstractions. Such students are never exposed to the problems of social and family structure and their corresponding etiquettes or to the problems of territorial loyalties and group attachments that historians are now examining. Presented with an abstract model and sternly cautioned against assuming its general relevance and applicability, only the staunchest will be motivated to pursue the individuals and groups lurking behind and beyond the ism.

For scholars the approach has equally little use. Applying an artificially fabricated standard in which certain components are divorced from the context in which they existed is essentially sterile. And those who investigate the workings of medieval society run the risk of having their vision narrowed, their perspective anachronistically skewed, and their receptivity to divergent data consequently blunted unless they firmly divorce themselves from the preconceptions and sets associated with the oversimplified models and abstractions with which they have been indoctrinated and which they themselves pass on to their students.

What of the indispensability of feudalism? Here a distinction must be made. While the creation of intuitive abstractions and simple Ideal Types can indeed be explained by invoking the infinite and confusing variety of human experience, it is quite another matter to suggest that the procedure is obligatory, necessary, or laudable. Alternative modes of classifying and describing exist and can be used. Again, attempting to justify the formulation and use of such models and abstractions by maintaining that scholarly and scientific terminology and common usage assume their existence is patently circular, avoiding as this argument does the obvious fact that scholarly terminology can be revised and common usage clarified. Far more appropriate to express regret and to apologize for measures attributable to the weaknesses and defects of human modes of expression and perception. Historians and social scientists can, like natural scientists, devise multifactor, heuristic models that encompass and account for the available evidence, are reformulated to include newly discovered data, and are not misleadingly labeled so as to suggest either system and conscious organization where none existed or the predominant importance of one element in a situation in which many elements are known to have been significant.[51] Such multifactor models and descriptive, narrative accounts, which emphasize complexity and the unique, can convincingly be said to encourage fuller, less distorted, and hence more acceptable understanding of the past than any "one-sided accentuation of one or more points of view."[52]

The contention that such general terms as "feudalism" are essential for intelligent discourse is also debatable, and those who advance this defense reveal their own discomfiture when they invoke other commonly used abstractions, such as "war" and "agriculture," to serve as buttressing middle elements. Intelligent discourse devoid of general abstract terms is, the argument runs, inconceivable. All abstractions—feudalism, war, agriculture—are similar in nature. Therefore the isms are indispensable if intelligent discourse is to occur. This chain of reasoning is, however, flawed in its second step, for there is an evident difference between, on the one hand, those collective descriptive abstractions arrived at by isolating common features of different phenomena similar enough to permit the use and assure the acceptance of single words to denote them, and, on the other hand, those abstract analytic constructs formulated and defined as a shorthand means of designating the characteristics that the observers consider essential to various time periods, modes of organization, movements, and doctrines. To a degree to which the first type is not, the second sort of general term is inevitably and often intentionally affected by the theories and assumptions of the formulators and users. Disagreements over the exact meaning of "war" or "agriculture" do occur, but they can ordinarily be resolved by introducing greater precision and clarity into the definitions of the terms, whose core signification is not generally contested. In distinction, infinite disagreement about the meanings of the isms is possible and perhaps inevitable, since the terms were not devised to designate the basic elements of fundamentally similar classes of phenomena but rather to refer to selected elements of complex phenomena, the choice of which inevitably involves the idiosyncratic value judgments of the terms' inventors and employers. Thus, however easy it is to say what the words "fief," "capital," and "merchant" mean, it is another thing entirely to see consensus on the definitions of "feudalism," "capitalism," and "mercantilism," precisely because of the subjective nature of the definitions of these words. To raise the level of discourse and make it truly intelligent, there should be general agreement to consider the isms no more than the artificialities they are.

Direct expressions of discontent with the term "feudalism" have increased in number and strength over the past two decades. From time to time there has seemed reason to hope that, with a resounding whoop, historians would join together, following the example of the National Assembly, to annihilate the feudal regime and, with the good members of the Legion of Honor, agree "to combat . . . any enterprise tending to reestablish it."[53] At least partly responsible for the mounting volume of protest is the reorientation of perspective that took place in 1953 with the publication of two remarkable books, one French and one English, both dealing with the political and social life of Western Europe in the tenth through the twelfth centuries, both concerned with individuals rather than abstractions, and both avoiding the medieval isms.

Of these books the purest—in that it does not, as far as I can tell, contain the word "feudalism"—is Richard W. Southern's study, *The Making of the Middle Ages.* In a section devoted to "The Bonds of Society" Southern presents an illuminating introduction to the political life of the eleventh and twelfth centuries by concentrating on a single, "unusually instructive" example of "what happened where the control exercised by the past was least effective, and where the disturbing elements of trade, large towns and active commercial oligarchies were not conspicuous." Discussing the emergence of the county of Anjou, Southern uses such abstract terms as "the disintegration of authority" and "the shaping of new political order." He writes, generally, of "an age of serious, expansive wars waged by well-organized and strongly fortified territorial lords." The term "feudal" is sometimes used in a general sense, in context in which it clearly implies more than connection or involvement with the fief. When the term is given this broader meaning, however, it seems to be so used out of force of habit rather than from any conscious conviction that it is the most appropriate and meaningful word to be found. "The art of feudal government" and "the early feudal age," neither phrase explicitly defined by Southern, are reminiscent of Bloch's *La Société féodale,* a book Southern recommends, and they strike a jarring note of vagueness and imprecision in a discussion otherwise notable for its concreteness. On the few other occasions when Southern employs the term "feudal" in this general way, alternative expressions that he devises to describe the phenomena in question are strikingly more informative. "Knightly" is one of these alternative terms, and, on a more extended scale, "the straightforward feudal-contract view of society" is far less subtle and suggestive than his evocative description of an "imagination . . . circumscribed by the ties of lordship and vassalage, by the recollection of fiefs and honours and well-known shrines, by the sacred bond of comradeship."[54]

Only a small portion of Southern's book is devoted to social and political ties and the exercise of governmental power, but Georges Duby, in his study of the Mâconnais in the eleventh and twelfth centuries, dedicates an entire volume to these subjects. Hence it is all the more noteworthy that in his index, as in Southern's, there is no reference to *féodalité,* although the index does list the indisputably acceptable terms *feudataire, fidéle, fidélité,* and *fief,* which are derived from and accurately reflect the terminology and usage of the eleventh and twelfth centuries.[55] Duby's avoidance of the term *féodalité* is consistent with his avowed purpose in writing his book. In his preface he announces that he is studying a small province in order to approach human beings directly, without isolating them from their milieu.[56] This he does, describing first the state of society in the Mâconnais at the end of the tenth century, then the period of independent castellanies from 980 to 1160, and finally the movement between 1160 and 1240 from castellany to principality. His conclusions are significant, first because of the wealth of data on which they are founded but even more because the Mâconnais lies within—if at the southern extreme of— the area between the Loire and the Rhine where countless scholars have seen "classical feudalism" emerging, and also because its history does not exemplify the characteristics associated with this development.

Stressing the survival of comital power and superiority until the end of the tenth century, Duby shows that among the higher ranks of society the ties of fidelity linking those agreeing to some sort of mutual support were vague and imprecise, like family ties, and can best be described as confirming a relationship of *amicitia.* As the count's power declined and as that of the castellans increased, bonds of dependence among the higher classes became more important, and grants of land were used to solidify the ties until by 1075 land outweighed loyalty as their determinant. Obligations were still indefinite, however, and military service was not a significant component. Between men of unequal status, dependent relationships were closer, but the strength and meaning of these ties were limited by the small value of the fiefs that the lords gave their followers, who generally possessed large allodial holdings, and by the multiplicity of the ties. According to Duby, "feudal institutions"—by which he apparently means not only fiefs but also homage and vassalage—had only superficial importance. They constituted a sort of superstructure that formalized without affecting pre-existing relationships.

> Feudal institutions were adapted to the previous structure of the higher class without significantly modifying it. Between great lords or knights, homage is a simple guarantee, an agreement not to harm; between a small noble and a powerful one, it is a true dedication, an agreement to serve. Vassalage and the fief, customary practices born in private usage, organized the relations that unequal division of wealth and power had already determined; they created no additional ones. In eleventh-century Mâconnais, there was no pyramid of vassals, there was no feudal system.[57]

Duby concludes that for the higher classes "feudalism was a step toward anarchy," but by this he evidently means not that any ill-conceived and abortive attempt had been made to create harmony by introducing homage, vassalage, and the fief, but that the links ordered by these institutions were not strong or meaningful enough to serve as effective restraints. These were instead provided by the teachings and intervention of the Church, by family bonds, and by a variety of oaths. Thus, "although violent and disturbed, the world of lords was not anarchic."[58] In this period the nobility exercised for their own benefit governmental powers over the lower classes, but their actual control over land did not increase.[59]

In the late twelfth and early thirteenth century the economy of the Mâconnais was transformed, and the king of France, long absent from the area, reappeared there. Economic pressures and royal policy produced a proliferation of ties of dependence and a marked decrease in allodial holdings; concomitantly, services may have become more definite and heavier. As far as justice was concerned, "the peace of the prince replaced the peace of God," and judicial procedures developed in the eleventh century were regularized and made more effective.[60]

Duby occasionally uses the word *féodalité*, but the term has no central significance in his book, thanks to his determination to focus on individuals and their actions. In his general conclusion he relates his findings to his own definition of feudalism, which, as has been seen, involves the disintegration of central authority and the development of an inclusive web of dependencies. In the Mâconnais, he reminds his readers, these two characteristics appeared successively rather than simultaneously, since in the eleventh and twelfth centuries, when most lands were freely held, jurisdictional powers were in the hands of private lords, and in the thirteenth century, when most lands were involved with dependent relationships, sovereignty reappeared in the persons of kings and princes.[61] Duby refuses to comment on the districts outside the Mâconnais, and he calls for additional local studies. Nonetheless he notes that "the society of the Mâconnais did not evolve in isolation." Pointing out that the Mâconnais was "a province of feudalism with marked individual characteristics,"[62] he implicitly suggests that other areas lying within the fabled heartland of feudalism were equally distinctive.

Duby does not openly attack the use of the concept of feudalism, nor does he denounce the idea that institutions in the Loire-Rhine region were similar enough to be described as a single phenomenon. Still, his conclusions demonstrate the futility of generalizations that are not based on the study of successive generations of human beings inhabiting a restricted area. They also suggest the inappropriateness of descriptive terms that fail to convey a sense of the variety of experience and development to be found throughout Western Europe between the tenth and the late twelfth centuries. When I once asked Monsieur Duby what difference there was between his book on the Mâconnais and Ganshof's study of feudalism, he replied with a modest shrug of the shoulders, "Toute la différence du monde, Madame." His own book is a testimony to his conviction that understanding the workings of medieval society necessarily involves exploring the intricate complexities of life rather than elaborating definitions and formulas designed to minimize, simplify, and, in the last analysis, obscure these complexities.[63]

Southern and Duby had their predecessors—historians who probed beyond or disregarded the construct feudalism and who concentrated on analyzing and describing the many different ties and modes of dependency binding human beings to one another. Unquestionably, the work of Duby and Southern has acted as an additional, powerful stimulus, prompting more scholars to study the actual functioning of society in different areas. In general, however, and certainly in words directed at a popular rather than a scholarly audience, the situation remains much the same as it has been, and there is virtually universal resistance and opposition to abandoning the term "feudalism" and to confining the word "feudal" to its narrow sense—"relating to fiefs." The reservations regarding the use of the generalized constructs implicit in the books of Southern and Duby have not yet had the widespread effect that might have been hoped.

Exceptions do, of course, exist. In the books he has published since 1953 Southern has consistently employed his brilliant descriptive techniques and has assiduously avoided the term "feudalism."[64] R. H. C. Davis is now following a similar path, having apparently undergone something of a conversion. In the history of medieval Europe that he wrote in 1957 the word "feudalism" occasionally appears. England after William's conquest is called "the best and simplest example of a feudal monarchy." The index refers readers wishing to learn about "fully-developed feudalism" to pages Davis evidently considers relevant to this subject. How refreshing, then, to turn to an article on the Norman Conquest written ten years later and to find there a convincing analysis of William's accomplishments that contains no reference to the ism or its associated forms.[65]

Southern and Davis are unfortunately in a minority. Far more numerous are the scholars who, while attacking the concept feudalism, still use the term and even encourage its propagation by suggesting new and better definitions. The contradictions in the work of Richardson and Sayles have already been discussed. Fully as puzzling is the case of Duby himself. Having implicitly questioned the aptness of the term in his study of the Mâconnais, he proceeded in 1958 not only to employ it but also, as has been seen, to advance an alternative definition, unusual and idiosyncratic, which he appears subsequently to have rejected. In a still later work, directed at a less scholarly audience, Duby employs the term *féodal* which, while undefined, clearly refers to something more general than the fief. It is found modifying such nouns as *éparpillement, forces, cours, princes,* and *seigneur;* a section of the book is entitled "Les féodaux," and the construct feudalism is several times personified.[66] A popular work published in 1973 shows that Duby's dedication to and reliance on the term have, in recent years, simply increased. He repeatedly refers to *féodalité* and uses the adjective *féodal* in a vague, indefinite way, and he goes so far as to designate the period from the mid-eleventh to the late twelfth century "les temps féodaux."[67] Saying that feudalism was characterized by the disintegration of monarchical authority and associating it with the institutions of the *seigneurie,* Duby presents feudalism as being implanted and established; he refers to feudalization, a feudal epoch, feudal society, feudal Europe, feudal peace, feudal structures, and a feudal economy and economic system.[68]

Striking inconsistencies appear in Christopher Brooke's five-page discussion of barons and knights in a book he published in 1963. Having begun by declaring that "few historical labels are more ambiguous than 'feudal' " and by proclaiming that he would therefore "use it as little as possible," having then warned that "it is doubtful whether [strict feudalism] ever existed outside the imaginations of historians," he proceeds, without defining the term "feudal," to use it, imprecisely and ambiguously, in writing of "the feudal bond," "feudal conceptions," "the feudal contract," "the feudal oath," and "feudal and quasi-feudal institutions." He also refers to "highly developed" feudalism, "classical feudalism," "French feudalism," and "strict feudalism." Finally he both reifies feudalism and uses the phrase "coherent feudalism" to designate a consciously formulated and adopted set of goals and principles.[69]

The hesitancies, contradictions, and inconsistencies that have been reviewed—and that are wholly typical of statements found in the books on medieval society published in the past twenty years—clearly demonstrate how necessary it is to reassess the value of the words "feudal" and "feudalism." It must be admitted that there is little possibility of ridding the historical vocabulary of them, adopted as they have been by the scholarly community in general and by the economists in particular. The terms exist. They have been and probably will be used for many years. As words students know if they know nothing else about the Middle Ages, they cannot be avoided. But confrontation need not mean capitulation, for it is perfectly possible to instruct students at all levels to use "feudal" only with specific reference to fiefs and to teach them what feudalism is, always has been, and always will be—a construct devised in the seventeenth century and then and subsequently used by lawyers, scholars, teachers, and polemicists to refer to phenomena, generally associated more or less closely with the Middle Ages, but always and inevitably phenomena selected by the person employing the term and reflecting that particular viewer's biases, values, and orientations. Illustrations of the many meanings attached to "feudal" and "feudalism" can be given, and students with a flair for historiography can be encouraged to explore the eccentricities of usage associated with the terms.

Other students will be directed to the study of medieval society and politics, and they and their instructors will be faced with the necessity and challenge of finding an adequate means of describing the elements historians have investigated and should explore and the positive conclusions that have been reached.[70] Throughout, the terminology and word usage of those who lived in the Middle Ages must be emphasized, and attention must be paid to the shifting meanings of key words, as well as to the gulf between actual practice and the formal, stylized records that have survived. Some elements will be pointed to as constants of general importance: the slowness and difficulty of communication, the general insecurity, the sluggish rate of technological change, and the reverence for tradition. The varying effects and significance of terrain, warfare, and violence must be emphasized. Stress must also be given to the resultant regional and diachronic variations in forms of government, modes of military organization, social and family structure, social mobility, the relationship between social class and function, styles of agricultural exploitation and commercial activity, and urban growth. Attention must be called to the different social and political relationships in which human beings were involved, to the ceremonies through which these relationships were fixed and manifested, and to the varying sorts of ties that superficially similar ceremonies could be used to create: bonds of obligation, fidelity, and support between sovereigns and their subjects, created and confirmed by oaths, pledges, and services; ties of loyalty, solidarity, and mutual assistance among people of similar and different social classes, formalized in communes, confraternities, gilds, leagues, and alliances, constituted through mutual undertakings that were sometimes left vague and sometimes clearly defined, solidified through privileges granted to and demanded by these groups; religious ties binding members of local congregations, regional churches, and similar faiths; ties of dependence forged between individuals or inherited from the past, sometimes involving friendship, sometimes service, sometimes protection, reinforced by gestures and oaths, resulting in benefits—material, monetary, territorial, social—to one or both parties; family bonds, revealed and consolidated in testamentary provisions, marriages, special festivities, and feuds and vendettas. The written and unwritten rules governing these ties and relationships must be considered, as must the ways in which and the different degrees to which these principles were systematized and enforced.

But to be properly understood, these elements must be observed as they developed, interacted, and changed, and thus the importance of presenting searching and detailed descriptions of areas characterized by different forms of governmental and social structure and organization and by different modes of development. Regions where strong monarchies developed and survived must be given as extensive consideration as areas where they disappeared, so that any given region—the Empire, England, Italy, Normandy, the Ile-de-France, the Mâconnais—will be considered neither abnormal nor typical but will be viewed as an instance of the varying ways human beings responded to similar and dissimilar circumstances, whose impact was conditioned by the total pasts of the people they affected. Those who are introduced to the study of medieval social and political life in this way will be far less likely than those presented with definitions and monistically oriented models to be misled about the conditions of existence in the Middle Ages. They will find it difficult to contrive and parrot simplistic and inaccurate generalizations about medieval Europe, and they may be challenged to inquire into subjects and areas as yet uninvestigated and to seek solutions to problems as yet unanswered.

The unhappiness of historians with the terms "feudal" and "feudalism" is, thus, understandable. Far less comprehensible is their willingness to tolerate for so long a situation often deplored. Countless different, and sometimes contradictory, definitions of the terms exist, and any and all of these definitions are hedged around with qualifications. Using the terms seems to lead almost inevitably to treating the ism or its system as a sentient, autonomous agent, to assuming that the medieval people—or at least the most perspicacious of them—knew what feudalism was and struggled to achieve it, and to evaluating and ranking societies, areas, and institutions in terms of their approximation to or deviation from an oversimplified Ideal Type.

Despite the examples set by Southern and Duby some twenty years ago and followed in the interim by some scholars, historians have been generally loath to restrict the term "feudal" and discard the term "feudalism," particularly in dealing with general rather than specialized audiences. Feudalism's reign has continued virtually unchallenged, with ambivalence characterizing the attitudes of most historians toward the subject. The situation, however, can and should change. The arguments advanced to defend using the terms as they have been used in the past are weak, based as they are on vaguely articulated assumptions concerning the concept's utility as a verbal and intellectual tool, as a teaching device, or as a mode of evaluation—none of which is convincingly established. Similarly unsatisfactory are justifications founded on hypothesized requirements: the historian's need, as scientist, for abstractions like feudalism; the basic demands of discourse; or necessities created by the fundamental and seemingly insurmountable limitations of the human mind. Preferable alternative perspectives and terms exist, and there seems no reason to delay channeling all available energies to the study of human beings who lived in the past, thus putting an end to the elaboration of arid definitions and the construction of simplistic models. The tyrant feudalism must be declared once and for all deposed and its influence over students of the Middle Ages finally ended. Perhaps in its downfall it will carry with it those other obdurate isms—manorial, scholastic, and human—that have dominated for far too long the investigation of medieval life and thought.

Notes

An earlier version of this article was presented to a meeting of the Columbia University Seminar on Medieval Studies, May 8, 1973. I am grateful to the members of the seminar for their questions and suggestions. For their advice and counsel I would also like to express my thanks to Professor Fredric Cheyette of Amherst College, Professor John Bell Henneman of the University of Iowa, Professor Joshua Prawer of the Israel Academy of Sciences and Humanities, Professor Thomas N. Bisson of the University of California at Berkeley, Professor John F. Benton of the California Institute of Technology, Professors Edwin Burrows, Philip Dawson, Charlton Lewis, and Hyman Sardy of Brooklyn College of the City University of New York, Barbara W. Tuchman, and finally the members of the History Club and my students at Brooklyn College.

1. Thomas N. Bisson, "Institutional Structures of the Medieval Peace," a paper presented to a colloquium held at Princeton University on March 31, 1973.
2. Frederic William Maitland, *The Constitutional History of England*, ed. H. A. L. Fisher (Cambridge, 1908), 142. See also Fisher's introduction to this edition, p. v.
3. J. G. A. Pocock, *The Ancient Constitution and the Feudal Law: English Historical Thought in the Seventeenth Century* (Cambridge, 1957), 70 n.2, 93–94, 249, 79–80, 97–99, 70–79, 72, 84, 99, 103, 102. Pocock perhaps exaggerates these advantages (p. 102) because of the strength of his admiration for the boldness and imagination with which Craig and Spelman challenged the distortedly insular approach taken by Coke and the common lawyers. It seems clear, furthermore, that Pocock himself does not question the validity or the usefulness of the term "feudalism."
4. Ibid., 249; see also Robert Boutruche, *Seigneurie et féodalité: Le premier âge des liens d'homme à homme* (Paris, 1959), 15 nn, 16–17, 16 n.20.
5. Boutruche, *Seigneurie et féodalité*, 13–14; Marc Bloch, *La Société féodale* (Paris, 1949), I: 1–3. The English edition, with a foreword by M. M. Postan, was translated by L. A. Manyon and is entitled *Feudal Society* (Chicago, 1961); the corresponding pages are xvi–xviii.
6. Boutruche, *Seigneurie et féodalité*, 16, 18–23. See also the *Oxford English Dictionary*, s.v. "feudal," "feudalism," and "feudality."
7. Maitland, *Constitutional History*, 161, 143. See also Sir Frederick Pollock and Frederic William Maitland, *The History of English Law before the Time of Edward I* (2d ed., introd. S. F. C. Milsom; Cambridge, 1968), I: 66–67; and Frederic William Maitland, *Collected Papers*, ed. H. A. L. Fisher (Cambridge, 1911), I: 489.

8. Maitland does not subject the word "feudalism" to the same critical scrutiny he applies to the phrase "feudal system," and he is far less wary of using the former than the latter. At one point in his lectures he seems to be distinguishing between the two—"we do not hear of a feudal system until long after feudalism has ceased to exist"—but he also uses them as equivalents. In his conclusion he indicates that he considers "the development of . . . a feudal system" the same as the realization of "ideal feudalism." *Constitutional History*, 141–143, 161–163.

9. Ibid., 143–164.

10. H. G. Richardson and G. O. Sayles, *The Governance of Mediaeval England from the Conquest to Magna Carta* (Edinburgh, 1963), 30, 92, 117–118, 30–31, 105, 116.

11. Ibid., 36–38, 77, 99, 105–112, 115; see also 85–91, 147, and the comments on p. 116: "The Normans were already familiar with much that they found in England, but we are not thereby warranted in terming those familiar things 'feudal' or in asserting that England was already 'feudal.' "

12. Ibid., 117–118.

13. Ibid., 92, 118.

14. F. L. Ganshof, *Feudalism*, foreword F. M. Stenton, tr. Philip Grierson (London, 1952), xviii; see also 151.

15. Postan, foreword to Bloch, *Feudal Society*, xiv, xiii.

16. Wood's own description of medieval society deals with human beings rather than schemas, but he occasionally uses the terms "feudal" and "feudalism," which are not defined. *The Quest for Eternity: Medieval Manners and Morals* (New York, 1971), 28, 55–56, 177. Wood's index (p. 227) shows that he has not discarded the term "feudalism," which he seems to see as closely linked with vassalage.

17. John Le Patourel, review of Richardson and Sayles, *Governance of Mediaeval England*, in *English Historical Review*, 80 (1965): 117 n.1; and see also Max Weber, *The Theory of Social and Economic Organization*, ed. Talcott Parsons, tr. A. M. Henderson and Talcott Parsons (New York, 1947), 329.

18. Marc Bloch, *Apologie pour l'histoire ou Métier d'historien* (Paris, 1949), 86–87. The corresponding pages in the English edition—*The Historian's Craft*, ed. Lucien Febvre, tr. Peter Putnam (New York, 1953)—are 169–171.

19. Postan, foreword to Bloch, *Feudal Society*, xiv.

20. Fredric L. Cheyette, "Some Notations on Mr. Hollister's 'Irony,' " *Journal of British Studies*, 5 (1965): 4; see also Cheyette, ed., *Lordship and Community in Medieval Europe: Selected Readings* (New York, 1968), 2–3.

21. Otto Hintze, "Wesen und Verbreitung des Feudalismus" (1929), in Hintze, *Gesammelte Abhandlungen*, ed. Gerhard Oestreich, 1 (2d ed.; Göttingen, 1962): 85; for an English translation of the article, entitled "The Nature of Feudalism," see Cheyette, *Lordship and Community*, 22–31. See, too, the comments of Michael Lane and particularly the enlightening passage quoted from Max Weber, in which Weber describes how ideal types are formulated. *Introduction to Structuralism* (New York, 1970), 25–26.

22. Bloch, *Apologie,* 89, 87 (*Historian's Craft,* 176, 171).
23. "Un mot fort mal choisi." Bloch, *Société féodale,* 1: 3 (*Feudal Society,* xviii).
24. Bloch, *Apologie,* 88 (*Historian's Craft,* 173). Bloch comments that the feudalisms which scholars have located in different parts of the world "bear scarcely any resemblance to each other." *Apologie,* 89 (*Historian's Craft,* 175–176).
25. Ibid., 88 (*Historian's Craft,* 174). For a fuller, if less extreme, analysis of the similar problems posed by using the terms capitalism and feudalism, see the review of J. Q. C. Mackrell, *The Attack on 'Feudalism' in 18th Century France* (London, 1973), in the *Times Literary Supplement,* Feb. 15, 1974, p. 160.
26. Postan, foreword to Bloch, *Feudal Society,* xiv.
27. Cheyette, "Some Notations on Mr. Hollister's 'Irony,' " 4, 12; see also 5–6, where he states that the usefulness of the term (he may in fact mean of the definition) "is determined by how it helps to order the evidence."
28. Bloch, *Société féodale,* 2: 244–249(*Feudal Society,* 443–445). In the translation (p. 443) "the feudal system" replaces Bloch's "le régime féodal" (2: 245). Similarly, Bloch's "les féodalités d'importation" (1: 289–292) become in translation "the imported feudal systems" (pp. 187–189). Both Ganshof and David Herlihy have indicated—misleadingly it seems to me—that Bloch perceived a fundamental difference between feudalism and feudal society. Ganshof, *Feudalism,* xvi; David Herlihy, ed., *The History of Feudalism* (New York, 1970), xix.
29. Bloch, *Société féodale,* 249–250 (*Feudal Society,* 446).
30. Herlihy, *History of Feudalism,* xix; Ganshof, *Feudalism,* xv. Ganshof's description of feudalism as a form of society on the same page diverges at many points from Bloch's: "a development pushed to extremes of the element of personal dependence in society, with a specialized military class occupying the higher levels in the social scale; an extreme subdivision of the rights of real property; a graded system of rights over land created by this subdivision and corresponding in broad outline to the grades of personal dependence just referred to; and a dispersal of political authority amongst a hierarchy of persons who exercise in their own interest powers normally attributed to the State and which are often, in fact, derived from its break-up." Here there is no mention of peasantry or family; here the state is mentioned only by virtue of its dissolution (although see also pp. 141–151 for a lengthy discussion of feudalism and the state); here there is a stress on landed rights and property missing in Bloch's definition.
31. Ganshof, *Feudalism,* xvi–xvii, 143, 141.
32. Similar to but narrower than Ganshof's is the definition of feudalism offered by D. C. Douglas. Since Douglas's works deal primarily with Normandy and the Norman conquests it is understandable that, like Ganshof, he should not consider the disintegration of central control a basic element. For Douglas two ideas are important: "the principle that the amount of service owed should be clearly determined before the grant of

the fief" and "the notion of liege-homage." *The Norman Achievement, 1050–1100* (Berkeley, 1969), 177; see also 179. Douglas also emphasizes the idea of contractual military service, isolating this as the core of the "Norman feudal custom," which, he says, William the Conqueror interpreted "in a sense advantageous to himself" when he "[suddenly introduced] military feudalism into England." *William the Conqueror: The Norman Impact upon England* (Berkeley, 1964), 100, 101, 103, 283. See also Cheyette, who counsels historians to "consider feudalism a *technique*, rather than an *institution*, . . . a technique involving above all a relation of personal dependence and service normally sealed by the grant of a dependent tenure or some other form of material support, and confined to that group of professional warriors who in time become the nobility, the *miles* [sic], the *domini*—a technique used to achieve certain purposes in certain places at certain time." "Some Notations on Mr. Hollister's 'Irony,'" 12.

33. Joseph R. Strayer, "Feudalism in Western Europe," in Rushton Coulborn, ed., *Feudalism in History* (Princeton, 1956), 16, reprinted in Cheyette, *Lordship and Community*, 13. A similar definition appears in a lecture presented by Strayer in 1963 and published four years later as "The Two Levels of Feudalism," in Robert S. Hoyt, ed., *Life and Thought in the Early Middle Ages* (Minneapolis, 1967), 52–53, reprinted in Joseph R. Strayer, *Medieval Statecraft and the Perspectives of History: Essays by Joseph R. Strayer*, ed. John F. Benton and Thomas N. Bisson (Princeton, 1971), 63–65. In this essay Strayer maintains that a broader definition, referring to economic and social conditions, "in fact defined nothing," and he asserts that "the narrow, military definition of feudalism" ("a way of raising an army of heavy-armed calvarymen by uniting the two institutions of vassalage and the fief"), while laudably precise, is "too limited" to be useful, since, if defined in this way, feudalism "would have little historical significance." In Hoyt, *Life and Thought*, 52–53 (in Strayer, *Medieval Statecraft*, 64–65). See also Strayer's comments in *Feudalism* (Princeton, 1965), 13–14. This point of view was again expressed, in modified form, in an essay Strayer published in 1968: "The Tokugawa Period and Japanese Feudalism," in John W. Hall and Marius B. Jansen, eds., *Studies in the Institutional History of Modern Japan* (Princeton, 1968), 3, reprinted in Strayer, *Medieval Statecraft*, 90. In this essay Strayer states that "in political terms, feudalism is marked by a fragmentation of political authority, private possession of public rights, and a ruling class composed (at least originally) of military leaders and their followers." Note that this definition, explicitly couched "in political terms," does not exclude the possibility of formulating other definitions phrased in different terms.

34. This modification resulted from a reorientation of approach that occurred in 1962 and 1963, when Strayer established his concept of two levels of feudalism. In reviewing Marie Fauroux's *Recueil des actes des ducs de Normandie, 911–1066* (Caen, 1961), Strayer commented that "many scholars have failed to see that there were really two feudalisms—the feudalism of the armed retainer or knight, and the feudalism of the counts and other

great lords who were practically independent rulers of their districts. The two feudalisms began at different times and under different circumstances, and it was a long time before they were fully meshed together." In *Speculum,* 37 (1962): 608. Although Strayer did not explicitly define feudalism, his discussion revealed that "Norman feudalism of the classic type" required the holding of "land in return for a definite quota of military service." "Knights and other vassals" were important not only "for military purposes" but also as "part of the governing group," whose aid and counsel the duke needed to rule effectively, and who possessed local administrative authority (pp. 608–609). It is hard to reconcile this analysis with a definition of feudalism that emphasizes the disintegration of central authority and the consequent distribution of political power among numerous members of a ruling group, and in 1963 Strayer acknowledged that in Normandy political fragmentation—an essential element of the political definition of feudalism he described in the same essay as the original and "best" definition—was tardy and incomplete. "Two Levels of Feudalism," in Hoyt, *Life and Thought,* 51–52, see also 63–65 (in Strayer, *Medieval Statecraft,* 63, see also 74–75). In addition see Strayer, *Feudalism,* 39. Even outside Normandy it was not until the eleventh century—and then not consistently and regularly—that the lower as well as the higher social and military orders distinguished by Strayer can be said to have exercised independent political power. With the inadequacy of the political definition of feudalism exposed, it must have become evident that some additional element or elements would have to be added to produce a satisfactory definition of the term.

35. Strayer, *Feudalism,* 13, 74. Note, too, that in "The Tokugawa Period," published in 1968, Strayer still laid heavy emphasis on the political aspect of feudalism.

36. Georges Duby, *La société aux XIᵉ et XIIᵉ siècles dans la région mâconnaise* (Paris, 1953), 643, the corresponding page in the reprint (Paris, 1971) is 481. Duby's evasive approach to the word *féodalité* reappears in his book *Guerriers et paysans, VIIᵉ–XIIᵉ siècle: Premier essor de l'économie européenne* (Paris, 1973). Here he uses terms reminiscent of those he employed in 1953 as he refers to "ce que les historiens ont coutume d'appeler la féodalité" (p. 179). Calling it "un mouvement de très grande amplitude," he does not define it precisely and explicitly, although he says that it was characterized by "la décomposition de l'autorité monarchique" and coincided with the development of a new sort of warfare and the establishment of a new conception of peace; he discusses "un système économique que l'on peut, en simplifiant, appeler féodal"; he concludes that "au plan de l'économie, la féodalité n'est pas seulement la hiérarchie des conditions sociales qu'entend représenter le schéma des trois ordres [elsewhere described as le clergé, les spécialistes de la guerre, et les travailleurs"], c'est aussi—et d'abord sans doute—l'institution seigneuriale" (pp. 179, 184, 185, 187, 191). Thus, on the economic plane, Duby substitutes the develop-

ment of the lordship for the coherent network of dependencies that he stressed in 1953.

37. Georges Duby, "La Féodalité? Une mentalité médiévale," *Annales: Économies, Sociétés, Civilisations,* 13 (1958): 766. See also the comments of J. M. Wallace-Hadrill in a review of Bloch's *Feudal Society,* in *English Historical Review,* 78 (1963): 117.

38. Bloch, *Société féodale,* 2: 248, 249 (*Feudal Society,* 445).

39. Robert S. Hoyt, *Europe in the Middle Ages* (2d ed.; New York, 1966), 185, 190–196.

40. Ganshof, *Feudalism,* xvii.

41. Stenton, foreword to ibid., vii–viii.

42. See Bryce D. Lyon, *From Fief to Indenture: The Transition from Feudal to Non-Feudal Contract in Western Europe* (Cambridge, Mass., 1957), 272–273; Georges Duby, *Adolescence de la Chrétienté occidentale, 980–1140* (Geneva, 1967), 61, 83. The corresponding pages in the English edition—translated by Stuart Gilbert and entitled *The Making of the Christian West, 980–1140* (Geneva, 1967)—are 61, 83. See also Bloch, *Feudal Society,* 59, 142, 443, where the statements found in *Société féodale,* 1: 95, 221 and 2: 245, are sometimes given a rather free interpretation. Finally, see Ganshof, *Feudalism,* xvii, 54, 59, 61.

43. "La féodalité est présentée parfois comme une abstraction. Folie! En vérité, c'est une personne. . . . La féodalité est médiévale. . . . Elle est fille de l'Occident." Boutruche, *Seigneurie et féodalité,* 297.

44. Lyon, *From Fief to Indenture,* 23–24; Joseph R. Strayer, "The Development of Feudal Institutions," in Marshall Clagett, Gaines Post, and Robert Reynolds, eds., *Twelfth-Century Europe and the Foundations of Modern Society* (Madison, 1961), 79, reprinted in Strayer, *Medieval Statecraft,* 78–79.

45. Bloch, *Société féodale,* 2: 250–252 (*Feudal Society,* 446–447); Strayer, "The Tokugawa Period." For hesitations expressed by Ganshof and by Bloch himself concerning the validity of this approach, see Ganshof, *Feudalism,* xv–xvi; Bloch, *Société féodale,* 2: 242 (*Feudal Society,* 441), and *Apologie,* 89 (*Historian's Craft,* 175–76).

46. Douglas, *Norman Achievement,* 176.

47. Douglas, *William the Conqueror,* 281, 98, 283, 96, 104; see also note 32 above. See the more convincing analysis presented by Strayer in his review of Fauroux's *Recueil des actes,* 609–610. Like Douglas, however, Strayer concludes that although "Norman feudalism of the classic type was not fully developed until the second half of the eleventh century . . . it was William the Conqueror, more than any other ruler, who gave it definitive form." Note the warnings given by Richardson and Sayles against assuming that William had any "grand designs or well devised plans." *Governance of Mediaeval England,* 71. For a clearly integrated account of William's accomplishments—which only once mentions the adjective "feudal"—see D. C. Douglas, "William the Conqueror: Duke and King," in Dorothy Whitelock, D. C. Douglas, C. H. Lemmon, and Frank Barlow, *The Norman Conquest: Its Setting and Impact* (London, 1966), 45–76; see p. 65 for "feudal."

48. Christopher Brooke, *Europe in the Central Middle Ages, 962–1154* (New York [1963]), 100.

49. See the comments of K. B. McFarlane, " 'Bastard Feudalism,' " *Bulletin of the Institute of Historical Research,* 20 (1943–1945): 161–162.

50. This statement was made in an examination submitted on March 27, 1974.

51. See, for the natural sciences, N. R. Hanson, *Observation and Explanation: A Guide to Philosophy of Science* (New York, 1971), 77–84; T. S. Kuhn, *The Structure of Scientific Revolutions,* vol. 2, no. 2 of the International Encyclopedia of Unified Science (2d ed.; Chicago, 1970), 100–102; George Gamow, *Thirty Years That Shook Physics: The Story of Quantum Theory* (Garden City, 1966), 155; and James D. Watson, *The Double Helix* (New York, 1969), 18, 38, 47, 49, 61, 83, 123.

52. Max Weber, *The Methodology of the Social Sciences* (Glencoe, 1949), 90, quoted and discussed in Lane, *Introduction to Structuralism,* 25.

53. Bloch, *Société féodale,* 1: 2–3 (*Feudal Society,* xvii); see also Boutruche, *Seigneurie et féodalité,* 20–21.

54. Richard W. Southern, *The Making of the Middle Ages* (New Haven, 1953), 90–91, 80–81, 87, 86, 262, 55, 241. When Southern mentions "the straightforward feudal-contract view of society," he associates the term "feudatory" with the "holding [of] land in return for military service" (p. 55); see also p. 56 for a reference to "the formula of feudal government" and p. 242 for "feudal custom" and "feudal etiquette"; for "knightly ideal" see p. 241; see also pp. 55, 243.

55. Duby, *Société aux XIe et XIIe siècles,* 666 (reprint, 501).

56. "J'ai volontairement conduit mes recherches dans le cadre étroit d'une petite province. La méthode des monographies régionales permet en effet d'approcher directement les hommes sans les isoler de leur milieu." Ibid., ix (reprint, 7). In his conclusion, Duby again describes his approach: "Pour approcher de plus prés les hommes, nous avons concentré notre attention sur une toute petite région" (p. 644 [reprint, 482]).

57. Ibid., 94–116, 140–141, 172, 177–185, 194–195, see also 185–193, 291 (reprint, 93–108, 124–125, 149, 153–158, 164–165, see also 158–164, 235–236).

58. Ibid., 204 (reprint, 170). For a full discussion of these restraints see pp. 196–204 (reprint, 165–170).

59. Ibid., 329–330 (reprint, 261–262). For the close connection Duby now posits between the development of the ideology of the peace of God and "les premiers phases de la féodalisation," see note 36 above and Duby, *Guerriers et paysans,* 185).

60. Duby, *Société aux XIe et XIIe siècles,* 473–569, 571 (reprint, 361–427, 429).

61. Using Bloch's periodization, Duby concludes that only in this sense could there be said to have been "two feudal ages." The second age—a time of fiefs, censives, and feudal principalities—contrasted with the earlier age of independent castellanies, and Duby believes that it began no earlier than 1160 and that it ended in 1240. Ibid., 642–643 (reprint, 481–482).

62. Ibid., 644 (reprint, 482).

63. See, however, his more restrained comments in "La Féodalité?" 765–766. Duby recommended Ganshof's study of feudalism as a guide and reference work but suggested that the very clarity, simplicity, and Cartesian rigor which are among its chief virtues may give the reader a false impression of order and regularity.

64. See his book *Western Society and the Church in the Middle Ages* (Harmondsworth, 1970). Under the circumstances it is not difficult to forgive him for translating the word *homo*, which literally means no more than "man," as "vassal" in his edition of the *Vita Anselmi: The Life of St. Anselm, Archbishop of Canterbury, by Eadmer* (Edinburgh, 1962), 111. Southern recently told me that he thinks "deplorable" not only the term "feudalism" but also the words "humanism" and "scholasticism." He said that he had never knowingly used the word "feudalism" to refer to actual conditions in the Middle Ages. He offered, however, a tentative and qualified defense of the word in *Medieval Humanism and Other Studies* (Oxford, 1970), 29. Southern's work suggests that he thinks the words "humanism" and "scholasticism" may have some practical value, however defective he may judge them on a theoretical plane. Medieval humanism is the central subject of his collected essays, and in a lecture, "The Origins of Universities in the Middle Ages," given at Philadelphia on April 8, 1974, Southern emphasized the importance of "scholasticism" and "scholastic" thought, calling the universities "the power house of scholasticism." In his conclusion, however, he warned that "European scholastic development" should be envisioned not as a single whole but as marked by diversity and variety.

65. R. H. C. Davis, *A History of Medieval Europe from Constantine to Saint Louis* (London, 1957), s.v. "feudalism" in the index, and see also p. 127, where he enclosed the term "feudalism" in quotation marks; and see pp. 295, 414. Davis, "The Norman Conquest," *History*, 51 (1966): 279–286, reprinted in C. W. Hollister, ed., *The Impact of the Norman Conquest* (New York, 1969), 123–133.

66. Duby, *Adolescence de la Chrétiente occidentale*, 60–61, 84. The translation of this book exaggerates these tendencies: see the corresponding pages, *Making of the Christian West*, 61–62, 83–84, and note that the section Duby entitled "Les féodaux" is called "Feudalism" in the translation. In *L'économie rurale et la vie des campagnes dans l'Occident médiéval* (Paris, 1962), Duby may refer to "la seigneurie des temps féodaux" (p. 379), but he generally avoids the term, and *féodalité is not listed in the index. Note, however, that in the translation of the book published in 1968, "temps féodaux" becomes "the feudal period," and "rente seigneuriale" is transformed into "feudal rent." Rural Economy and Country Life in the Medieval West*, tr. Cynthia Postan (London, 1968), 171, 232–259.

67. Duby, *Guerriers et paysans*, 179–204, and see note 36 above.

68. See also ibid., 194 ("l'implantation de la féodalité"), 262 ("l'établissement de la féodalité), 184 ("l'établissement des structures féodales"), 185 ("la féodalisation"), 278 ("l'époque féodale"), 192 ("la société féodale"), 201

("l'Europe féodale"), 300 ("la paix féodale"), 184 ("les structures féo-dales"), 189 ("l'économie féodale"), 187 ("un système économique que l'on peut, en simplifiant, appeler féodal"). It is heartening to note that the review of Duby's *Guerriers et paysans* in the *Times Literary Supplement* does not contain the words "feudal" or "feudalism." Aug. 17, 1973, pp. 941–942.

69. Brooke, *Europe in the Central Middle Ages*, 95–96, 99–100. Brooke writes that "in its origin feudalism provided for the recruitment of vitally needed cavalry troops" (p. 100). See also pp. 1076–1077 above. Note, too, that having just questioned the validity of the idea of "strict feudalism," Brooke scrupulously encloses "feudal" in quotation marks when he refers to " 'feudal' means" of raising troops (p. 100).

70. See Joseph R. Strayer, "The Future of Medieval History," *Medievalia et Humanistica*, n.s. 2 (1971): 182. Only since the appearance in 1968 of Fredric Cheyette's invaluable collection of translated essays, *Lordship and Community*, has it been practically possible to direct beginning students to the recent literature in which this perspective on medieval society is reflected.

ECONOMIC LIFE AND SOCIAL CHANGE

In the tenth and eleventh centuries a great economic recovery took place in Western Europe; eventually it provided the material foundations for a new civilization.

Population increased. New patterns of trade became established. Once a profitable market for surplus agricultural products existed, lords and peasants found a new incentive to expand agricultural production, and great tracts of wasteland were brought under cultivation for the first time. Total output rose very substantially, mainly because of this extension of arable land but also because of the use of improved farming methods. Subsequently the development of the economy and the growth in the number of workers led on to a geographical expansion of European civilization in the twelfth and thirteenth centuries.

The readings in this section illustrate different aspects of these widespread changes. The excerpt from Georges Duby describes the social and economic structure of an early medieval manor. Léopold Génicot discusses the demographic expansion that made possible all the other achievements of the age. A. B. Hibbert considers the emergence of the new merchant class. Finally, Robert Bartlett discusses the distinctive characteristics of the medieval "expansion of Europe."

CHAPTER 11

Manorial Economies

Georges Duby

The Great Landed Estates

Some tenants of the manor were rich and some were poor, but all tilled the land of a master who was far wealthier than they. It was for the benefit of this landed aristocracy that the documents which illuminate the rural scene for us were put together; and they are solely concerned with their possessions.

The picture they reflect is that of a highly stratified society, in which power was vested in a small group of people who controlled from above the activities of the vast mass of country folk. It is true that there existed between tenants and lords a class of modest farmers who succeeded in preserving at least some of their economic independence. [There was] a peasant family numbering twenty souls whose existence is known to us by accident because their forebear had recently presented his land to a great monastery. Before this act of charity the family's possessions had been free from any overlordship. From other sources, and particularly from those which recorded service in the royal army, we catch glimpses of the existence and vitality of this class of peasants who farmed their own *manses*.* It was more than likely that what enriched the great abbeys of south Germania in the ninth century were donations from such small farmers, each gift a modest one but commensurate with the donor's means. But however they were assembled it cannot be denied that very large accretions of *manses* and waste were concentrated in the hands of the ruling princes, the great ecclesiastical establishments and a few wealthy families. Enormous landed estates thus came into existence. The part of the temporal property of St. Bertin which was devoted to the support of the monks in the ninth century consisted of 25,000 acres, and the area of the lay estate of Leeuw St. Pierre in Brabant was reckoned to be more than 45,000 acres in extent.

Of all the forms which rural activity took at that time, these great estates were the first—and indeed very nearly the only—ones to be clearly revealed

From Georges Duby, *Rural Economy and Country Life in the Medieval West*, Cynthia Postan, trans. (Columbia, S.C.: University of South Carolina Press, 1968), pp. 33–42, 48–52. Reprinted by permission of the University of South Carolina Press and Edward Arnold (Publisher) Limited.
*The term *villa* refers to a great landed estate. The *manse* was a peasant's small-holding on the estate, i.e., his dwelling and a surrounding plot of land. The more well-to-do peasants also held strips of land in the open fields. These are referred to as *appendicia*.—Ed.

by written evidence. These carefully ordered institutions, run for the profit of their owners, were called in the scholarly parlance of the time *villae*, the same word which had been used in classical Latin texts. Those situated in the region of Carolingian civilization between Loire and Rhine, or in Lombardy, which can be more satisfactorily observed, belonged to the great monasteries. Inventories and descriptions have enabled historians to trace the characteristics of this economic organization which it is convenient to call "the manorial system." As it has been the subject of many studies, often very detailed, we shall not need to linger long over it.

The aspects of the system revealed by the most famous of the documents, the first to be described by scholars and represented by them as the "classical" type, are the two, complementary, halves of the *villa*. One of these was farmed by direct management. French historians have been accustomed to call this part *la réserve*, but when medieval lords and peasants spoke of it, they used the word *le domaine*—the demesne—and I, too, shall use the same word. The second half of the *villa* was composed of tenancies; small holdings let out on lease.

A demesne bore the same appearance as a *manse*, for it was after all the *manse* of the master, *manse indominicatus*. But it was an outsize *manse*, because it corresponded to a specially numerous, productive and demanding "household" or *familia*. Even so, its structure was no different from that of other *manses*. At the centre was an enclosure, the courtyard, the space surrounded by a solid palisade, enclosing as well as the orchard and kitchen garden a collection of buildings which amounted to a hamlet. Here is a description of Annapes, which belonged to the king. Around a well-built stone palace containing three halls on the ground floor and eleven rooms upstairs stood a cluster of wooden buildings, a cowhouse, three stables, kitchen, bakehouse and 17 huts to shelter the servants and store the food. As for the *appendicia*, attached to the central plot, there were extensive stretches of arable and meadow, as many vineyards as possible, and finally huge tracts of waste. The farm of Somain, near Annapes, had attached to it fields measuring 625 acres, meadow measuring 110 acres and 1,970 acres of woods and pasture. Other "farms" were not always so well provided for; the one belonging to the abbey of St. Pierre-du-Mont-Blandin at Ghent possessed less than 250 acres.

However, generally speaking, the *mansus indominicatus* was equal in size to several dozen peasant *manses* held as tenancies. And the picture most frequently given by the evidence is of a number of tenanted *manses* supporting the one farmed by the master. The area of arable possessed by the tenanted *manses* varied very greatly in size, as we have seen, but was always less than the quantity of land which theoretically corresponded to the physical capacity of a peasant family. Those holdings called "free" were on the average endowed with attached fields larger in extent than the "servile" holdings—but the status of the *manse* was not always the same as the personal status of its tenant.

The primary function of the great demesnes was to allow a few men to live in idleness, abundance and the exercise of power. They maintained a narrow circle of the magnates in a magnificent way of life. In a society still primitive, and at a time when food supplies were limited, the "man of power" showed himself first of all as the man who could always eat as much as he wished. He was also open handed, the man who provided others with food, and the yardstick of his prestige was the number of men whom he fed, and the size of his "household." Around the great lay and religious leaders congregated vast retinues of relatives, friends, people receiving patronage (the latter were known officially at the court of Charlemagne as *les nourris*), guests welcomed with liberality who would spread tales of the greatness of a house, and a host of servants, amongst whom would be found those artists in metal, woodcarving and weaving who could fashion weapons, jewellery and ornaments, and thereby enhance the luxurious setting appropriate to the exalted rank of the ruler. This way of life assumed housekeeping on a gigantic scale; barns and cellars filled to overflowing; well tended and fruitful gardens, trellises and vineyards; the cultivation of fields of almost limitless extent to provide sufficient grain in spite of low yields; and lastly the existence of enormous forests and wastes to harbour game and give pasture to the riding and warhorses which were the mark of the aristocrat. The springs of wealth had to be inexhaustible. It was the privilege of the noble at all times to avoid any appearance of shortage. He had to be prodigal in the midst of famine, but, as harvests fluctuated from year to year, his steward, anxious never to find himself in short supply, naturally tried to increase output, especially of corn.

• • •

Farming the Demesne

Scholars have in recent years constructed economic "models" of what they choose to call the classic demesne system (*le régime domanial classique*), based on the evidence of the few authoritative documents, and in this ideal system the *villa* is shown as a centre for the direct exploitation of the land: a widely spread centre, it is true, because agricultural yields were so low. At the beginning of the tenth century the monastery of San Giulia of Brescia consumed 6,600 *muids* of grain per annum. To assure themselves of this quantity the monks had to sow 9,000 *muids*. So rudimentary was agricultural technique that a single aristocratic family needed for its support a vast arable area, usually the extensive *appendicia* of several *villae*. Consequently the chief problem which faced estate managers was that of manpower.

The solution of this problem was much simplified by the existence of slavery. At that period the whole of western Europe practised slavery, and probably nowhere more actively than on the less advanced fringes closer to pagan lands, such as England and Germania. In any case there were very large numbers of men and women described in Latin texts by the classical names of *servus, ancilla,* or the collective noun of neuter gender, *mancipium*. Their legal condition, only slightly ameliorated by a Christian environment, was the same as that of Roman or heathen slaves. Their marriages were recognized, they could save small sums of money and acquire land. But their bodies were entirely at the lord's disposal and could be bought and sold: they, together with their offspring and their possessions, formed part of the equipment of the household. Their duty to obey was unlimited and their labour was without reward. Many were set up by their masters on *manses* where they could raise families and make a living, and these enjoyed a degree of freedom. But many more lived and worked in the lord's house where their position was the same as that of the farm animals. They were fed and looked after and became objects of capital value, and they worked at the lord's will. It may be that household slaves were more numerous than other slaves, and there is some evidence to show that some peasants employed them in their homes. The man of modest means who managed the demesne of the monks of St. Bertin at Poperinghe had four slaves in his service; his neighbour who managed a *manse* of 62 acres of arable at Moringhem kept a dozen slaves for his own personal use. In the houses of the nobles and the headquarters of the *villae*, there were of course hordes of them.

Our documents seldom mention the farm personnel as such. Slaves working with their hands (*servi manuales*), from whom these workers were drawn, and the *mancipia non casata*—the slaves who had no habitation in which to lead a separate family life but who were lodged in outhouses in the courtyard, and were also known as "prebendaries," since their master gave them food—all these were lumped together in a capitulary of 806 with household movables which were not always listed in inventories. Personnel of this character existed everywhere and agricultural production everywhere depended primarily on them. On a demesne *manse* of about 60 acres which had just been presented to St. Germain-des-Pres when the *polyptyque* of Irminon was drawn up the work was done by three *mancipia*. And 22 household slaves worked on the 200 acres of demesne arable on the *villa* of Ingolstadt presented by Louis the Pious to the abbey of Niederalteich. On the Lombardy possessions of the abbey of San Giulia of Brescia there were in the years 905–906 between eight and forty-nine slaves in each household.

The support of these servants was not an insurmountable problem. On estates where there were mills, the profits of multure were often sufficient to maintain the servile *familia*. Nor must it be thought that recruitment of domestics was difficult. It is true that the spread of Christianity somewhat hindered the slave traffic, but the market remained well supplied. Furthermore, some of the servants were married (as was the case with two of the *homines manuales* who worked in the household of one of the abbey of Farfa's *villae*) and many had legitimate or illegitimate children. It was probably not thought profitable to bring these children up in the master's household, since it would have meant feeding them until they were old enough to work. On the other hand it is more than likely that the lord's personal servants, both male and female, were the offspring of the slaves who had been settled on the servile *manses*. The latter could have been nurseries for rearing young domestic servants, and perhaps this was one of their chief economic functions.

There was one overwhelming reason, nevertheless, why masters did not leave all the fieldwork in the hands of their household staff. This was because the work itself was unequally spread over the agricultural calendar. Unlike animal husbandry or viticulture, cereal-growing alternates long seasons of inactivity with feverish periods when fieldworkers are needed in extraordinary numbers. Ploughing, harvesting and making hay to feed the draught animals in winter had to be accomplished with great speed in uncertain weather, and were times of frantic activity. To have enough personal servants to fulfill all the needs of the moment would have meant maintaining them in virtual idleness throughout the rest of the year. The food they ate would have been wasted and would have reduced the already restricted yield of agriculture. As a consequence the delicately poised economy of the demesne would have been disturbed. A far better solution was to supplement the small domestic labour force required to perform the daily tasks with the seasonal appointment of some hired labourers.

Economic conditions of the time did not absolutely preclude the possibility of wage labour. At Corbie the official in charge of cultivating the garden employed helpers for digging the borders, for planting and for weeding. Every year he was given towards the upkeep of these dayworkers 100 loaves, one *muid* of peas and beans and one of barley beer (which proves that these workers by the day were paid with meals), but 60 *deniers* were set aside as well "to take on men." But even so the monetary medium lacked flexibility, and money wages remained exceptional. It was much more convenient to reward the temporary farmworkers of the demesne with a plot of land, and to settle them upon a *manse*. The productive effort of these men and their families was thus divided. One part was left to provide themselves and their families with a living from their own plot of land. But the other had to remain at the disposal of the landlord. Here then was another economic function of the satellite holdings of the demesne.

In return for their endowment the peasant "households" owed to the "household" of their master various dues the nature of which was usually the same for each category of *manses* on the *villa* and also on other *villae* belonging to the same landowner. There were to begin with the various dues which had to be taken to the lord's hall on certain days of the year. The amounts were fixed, a few pieces of money, some chickens, eggs, one or two small animals such as sheep or pigs. These payments can be taken either as payments for the use of the woods and wastes of the lord, or as taxes of public origin. Some of them were the relics of the charges formerly imposed on peasants for supplies to the royal armies. It was the duty of the landlord to collect these, and in time he appropriated them for himself. These different dues were never heavy and the profit of the recipient was minimal. Their impact on the economy of the *villa* cannot have affected the real struggle for existence, the toil connected with garnering the main food supply, but was more a marginal matter of backyard poultry and small surplus items of diet. They formed only a superficial charge on the tenants' own farm production; and to the lord, as well, these odd amounts of food and small sums of money were trifling matters which contributed little if anything to his standard of living.

On the other hand the labour services imposed on the holdings were the essential economic link between them and the demesne and formed the very nexus of the demesne system. The manpower available on each satellite farm unit was, as we have seen, greater than that required to cultivate its fields. And this surplus manpower had to go to the demesne. It might take the form of periodic deliveries of objects upon which labour had been expended: thus, each *manse* might have to prepare a load of firewood, or a certain number of stakes, beams or planks, or perhaps some of those simple tools which could be constructed by any unskilled person. On servile holdings the women would weave cloth for the demesne. But the main tasks were agricultural, and they took three distinct but often interconnected forms.

1. The *manse* could in the first place be charged with a definite task. It could be responsible, for instance, for erecting in springtime a certain length of temporary fencing to protect the crops and the hay. More usually it was given the responsibility for an entire season's cultivation of a given plot of land, the *ansange*, taken from the demesne arable; activities which began with preliminary ploughing and continued right until storing of the grain in the lord's barn. In this way, every year some parcels of the demesne arable which needed cultivating were temporarily detached from the rest and were joined to the *appendicia* of the peasant *manses*. They rounded off the latter and absorbed the underemployed productive effort of the tenant population.

2. Other obligations were more exacting, since they left the workers less freedom. To perform them they were periodically taken away from the family group and put to join a team of workers on the lands attached to the demesne. The demands—the *corvées* in the real sense of the term, since the word means "demand" or "requisition"—only affected one labour unit in each *manse*, a worker either by hand or with a draught animal, i.e. a man or a plough team. If a *manse* was occupied by several families, or if the tenants themselves owned servants, as was fairly frequent, the service would be much lightened. Sometimes the *manse* owed a fixed number of days either at certain seasons, or else each week, and sometimes the man subject to the *corvée* assisted in a definite task until it was completed. In certain cases it was really manual labour (*manoperae*), for the man in question would come in the morning to the lord's hall to join the farm servants and await his orders whilst his implements and plough team were left behind at the *manse*. Another kind of forced labour was specially assigned to certain tasks. The work of the women from the servile *manses* in the demesne workshops was of such a kind, and so were the errands and cartage requiring the use of cart and draught animals, which were usually the responsibility of the better-equipped, so-called "free" *manses*.

3. Tasks referred to in the inventories as "nights" were the third kind of work which might be required. These placed the tenant at the service of the lord for several days at a stretch without the certainty of returning home each evening. This enabled him to be employed at a distance or to be sent away on a mission, and it is clear that these obligations of an indeterminate nature pro-

vided the demesne with a reserve of immediately available and reliable labour in cases of unforeseen need.

These different tasks were often combined. But for the free *manse* they were usually lighter, more limited, and of less degrading nature. The free *manses* were generally occupied by peasants of free status, whose ancestors had often been independent, but who, because they were poor or weak, had allowed their lands to become part of the economic system of the *villa* in exchange for help and protection. But even where rural migration, mixed marriages and the alienation of land had obliterated the connection between the "freedom" of the tenancy and the free status of the tenants, the holdings were of sufficient size to support the larger domestic animals. To be able to provide oxen or a horse, and thus to take part in ploughing, cartage and contacts with the outside world, was probably their most valuable contribution to the demesne activities; they could supply ploughmen, drivers and horsemen, rather than unskilled labourers. On the other hand, it is easy to believe that when landlords created servile *manses* to house some of their domestic serfs in order to be rid of responsibility for their maintenance and to let them bring up their own children, they did not for one moment relax their right to command obedience or to use them at their will. They had to do manual labour because they did not usually possess draught animals. It was they who guarded the headquarters of the demesne at night, did the laundry, dipped and sheared sheep, while their wives and daughters worked in the demesne workshops. Servile *manses* were also burdened with the weekly labour services of undefined nature. In Germania they had usually to put a man at the disposal of the lord for three days a week; or in other words each *manse* had to provide one half-time servant throughout the year. This explains their smaller allocation of arable land than that of the free *manses*. Their holders were forced to work away from home for longer and could thus devote less time to their own farms, but on the other hand, when performing forced labour in the demesne they ate in the refectory, and their consumption of food at home was accordingly reduced.

Since the profit to be derived from a tenancy did not correspond to the services which it owned, the tenancy was not exactly a wage. The letting out of the *manses* ought primarily to be thought of as a way of relieving the demesne management of the necessity to provide the servants with board and lodging. The demesne could in this way have an abundant source of labour at its disposal. It has been calculated that the 800 dependent families of the abbey of San Giulia of Brescia at the beginning of the tenth century owed service to their masters amounting to 60,000 working days. The lord, here as elsewhere, wanted to dip into a bottomless well, to be permanently able to command instant service in the event of unforeseen need. But in normal times it is unlikely that all the labour services owing were actually called upon.

This then was the manorial system. The surplus productive effort of the peasant families was appropriated by the lord, to whose rule they were subject, for the purpose of farming his lands. But since human labour could by itself produce so little, this surplus was also limited. And because of this, the demesne needed a large number of satellite *manses*.

CHAPTER 12

On the Evidence of Growth of Population in the West

Léopold Génicot

Economic expansion, religious ferment, renaissance of letters and development of science, creation of an original art, territorial gains at the expense of the infidel world, all these phenomena of which the life of Christian Europe was woven between the 11th century and the 13th are in some way related to a net growth of the population. Consequently, almost all historians hold that, during what Marc Bloch called the second feudal age, the West went through a strong demographic surge.

This virtual unanimity is, however, a little deceptive: no one ordinarily doubts the fact or its importance yet we really know little about it. Actually, no one has had the courage to study it very closely. The documentation is so poor as at first sight to seem unable to sustain more than vague general conclusions. It has not been interrogated methodically, for fear that the effort would be futile. Perhaps this pessimism is justified, but how can we tell? We cannot be certain until at least one scholar has carried out systematic and exhaustive research in some definite region, and has then tried to draw together all the forms of evidence that reveal the shape of demographic trends from the post-Carolingian period up to the end of the Middle Ages.

This article tries to show what types of research would be feasible. It offers, not a finished history of the population of the different regions of the West between the years 1000 and 1300—indeed, the present state of knowledge would barely permit of an outline—but a list of the various indices of population growth that the monographs we need ought to collect and analyze. We shall illustrate the uses and the significance of each of these indices. Perhaps this will stimulate more careful research into "demographic prehistory." In any case I hope it will show that, although some historians may have exaggerated in speaking of the "demographic revolution of the 11th, 12th, and 13th

From Léopold Génicot, "On the Evidence of Growth of Population in the West from the Eleventh to the Thirteenth Century," Sylvia L. Thrupp, trans., in *Change in Medieval Society* (New York: Appleton-Century-Crofts, 1964), pp. 14–23. Article from the *Journal of World History*, Vol. 1:2. Copyright 1953 by Unesco. Reproduced by permission of Unesco.

centuries" and although our knowledge is still far from precise, the impression that population was growing is well founded.

To speak of demography means that we must seek quantitative measures, even though the figures may only partially reflect the reality and be no more than a basis for interpretation. Accordingly, we shall classify the numerous and varied indices of population growth in order of decreasing precision, that is to say, according as they may be expressed in more or less rigorous mathematical form, or better still—for history is concerned with evolution—in statistical series. They might be ranged as follows: the evidence given in military or fiscal documents; information gained from inventories of seigneurial property and rights; birth rates to be deduced from genealogical study and from the descriptions of families to be found in many charters; long-term price trends, in particular of agricultural prices; the multiplication and expansion of towns; land clearance, technological advances, and the fragmentation of traditional land holdings; changes in ecclesiastical geography and construction or alteration of public buildings, especially of churches and chapels; and colonization of the vast regions seized from the Infidel.

Medievalists do not hope to find a complete census of any population. They are happy enough to find incomplete or indirect data, such as lists of men liable to military service, or accounts of hearth taxes or poll taxes. The former are rather rare and late; only in Italy do we have any that antedate the 14th century. Again, they concern only the towns and we cannot be certain that urban population fluctuated in the same way as rural population. And their use depends on the calculation of a multiplier, usually on uncertain grounds, that will represent the ratio between the number of men capable of bearing arms and the total population. The second type of data, as presented by the celebrated "Etat des paroisses et des feux" of 1328 and the poll tax returns of 1377, is more valuable because it ordinarily covers a wide region, not just a single town. But it raises even more difficult problems. What was a hearth and what is the average number of individuals it indicates? Or what was the ratio between the number of adults who paid a poll tax and the number of children? What percentage of the population did exempt groups form— clergy, often nobles and their households, and vagrants? Were the enumerators and collectors conscientious? Was it hard to evade payment? How are we to fill the frequent gaps in the records? To what extent and under what conditions is it legitimate to argue from the part to the whole? All these questions are extremely delicate. On the other hand, again with exceptions in Italy (the *generales subventiones* of Frederick II and Charles of Anjou), the fiscal records, like the military lists, are all later than 1300. Yet for our purpose they are still relevant and useful, even for the earlier period. They furnish figures which, when compared with earlier data from other sources, show very convincingly that the population of the West had grown before the 14th century, and they help us to form a rough idea of the amplitude and the rhythm of this growth. Without the poll tax referred to above, J. C. Russell would not have been able to establish so firmly the fact that the population of England more than tripled in some 250 years, between 1086 and 1346.

Among the oldest of the other auxiliary sources are the surveys known as the polyptyques. Sometimes these give a fully detailed inventory of all the lands and dues belonging to a lay or ecclesiastical lord. In the 13th century many great and middling lords whose classical manorial regime had weathered a crisis drew up surveys of this kind in order, so to speak, to take their bearings. Sometimes the survey is merely a concise description of a single manor, compiled on the occasion of a pious donation or of a dispute or of what was later called a *dénombrement* of a fief. But whatever their form or scope, the polyptyques all contain similar statistical data: the number of settlements on the estate, for at least from the 11th century this often comprised more than one; the number of holdings of each type; the total area, in the ancient and the current measures, of fields and meadows; the number of tenants and the average extent of their holdings; and finally, in so far as one can tell from figures based on dues levied on individuals or on hearths, the total population and its density. If one has, then, for all or part of an estate, several polyptyques or related documents, such as accounts, it is possible to establish these facts at a series of dates and hence to deduce, more or less exactly, the demographic trend of the period and region in question. New settlements may appear, or the older ones may come to be more densely populated. For example, the 81 people living on the lands of Weedon Beck in 1248 had by 1300 grown to 110. Such a record is a valid measure of population growth if all other things remain equal at the two dates, namely, the area of land in question and the hearth or household unit. We must also be certain that an increase in one item is not offset by a decrease in another, for example, that an increase in the number of tenants does not simply reflect a decrease in the number of subtenants or of landless people.

Another way of measuring population change is through calculations of the average number of children per household. With luck, if our documentation is good enough, there will be two ways of doing this. One is through compiling genealogies. If genealogies compiled in the Middle Ages are used they of course have to be checked, and may sometimes be amplified, by new research. In this way it was discovered that the eldest branches of two of the greatest families of the region of Namur in each generation between the dates 1000 and 1250 had respectively a minimum of 5.75 and 4.30 children who came of age. The method is however applicable only in the case of great families. And the average number of children surviving may have varied considerably between one social level and another. There is however another procedure, one that to my knowledge has never been tried, namely, the gathering of the descriptions of complete families to be found in charters. These quite often, when referring to pious donations of land, or in the case of *liberi* who donated themselves or of serfs who were donated to a religious foundation, name parents and their children. This information should be classified by date, by social class, by regions, etc. It would then show how the average number of children altered between one period and another. It might also resolve other problems, especially the question whether, as many historians have maintained, the serfs died out through having a particularly low birth rate. Having obtained the average by one or the other of these methods, one then has to estimate the number of children per couple, in the period and region in question, that would have been requisite simply to maintain the population level. Ideally one would deduce this from local documents of the period. In practice the best plan is to take a coefficient calculated by modern specialists, say 2.7, modifying it in the light of differences in the relevant variables. We are unable to take account of infant mortality, because the documents mention only children who have lived for some years, indeed usually only those who have grown up. But we have to take account of the nuptiality rate. This was undoubtedly lower in the Middle Ages than today because of a more pronounced disequilibrium between the sexes and because of more frequent entry into religious orders. Again, we have to bear in mind that the average duration of life was also lower in that age of all too frequent famine and epidemic.

Price trends, especially in agricultural prices, also demand attention. They are or may be, to an extent which has to be determined for every case, a function of demographic change. A fall in the rent of fields and meadows, accompanied by a rise in wages, especially of farm hands, such as we see in 14th-century England, is an unequivocal sign of a fall in population. Inversely, a rise in the value of arable land, above all if it is accompanied by a fall in wages, is a clue to population increase. Although we may never be able to trace the course of wages with any exactness before 1300, it is possible to form a general idea of their movement in the regions that are better documented. As to land values, at least in the 13th century, it is quite easy to show that they were rising: one may do so either by comparing average figures in successive years or, more surely, by charting the course of the rents on specific pieces of land.

Other indices lend themselves less easily to measurement, chief among these being the growth of towns. In some regions, such as the Low Countries, these probably originated in the 9th century; in others, such as Lombardy, they were revivified in the 10th century; everywhere they were in full expansion between the 11th century and the 13th. Proof of this lies in the continual enlargement of their bounds that is revealed by the successive construction of new outworks and by the reordering of their ancient parish divisions. The extension of their areas was not, however, exactly proportionate to increase in the number of inhabitants, for the density of urban population was not a constant. It varied from one town to another and within the same town, not only from one period to another but from one quarter to another, as, for example, between the market quarter and what modern architects would call the residential quarters, or from the ancient *civitas* to newly built suburbs. Besides, the walled area was seldom if ever completely built up; especially towards the close of the Middle Ages, it might include fields and meadows and other vacant sites. Yet in default of any more exact measure, the extension of the area enclosed is of some significance. To cite only two instances, the area enclosed by the fortifications of Ghent, one of the greatest towns of the age, had by the 14th century grown from 80 hectares to 644; the fortified area of Aix, a lesser town, grew from 50 hectares to 175.

Parallel with this urban movement ran another which some historians overlook: the transformation of villages into little towns. Places that had hitherto been simply agricultural acquire market rights and a market place, and sometimes a fair. They become petty commercial centers.

One should beware of exaggerating the demographic significance of these urban phenomena. Urban growth is not a precise index of total population growth. Even if the area of Ghent grew almost tenfold in 250 years or the population of some town in central Italy grew in the same period from 5,000 to 30,000, it does not follow that the population of Flanders or of Tuscany or of Umbria had grown tenfold or sixfold. Towns have always tended to absorb the people of their immediate environs; in some regions, as in Italy, they have attracted the artisans of whole regions, and even the peasants. They have continually drained the open country. All the same, and this is the point to be emphasized here, they did not empty the countryside. They drained off only its surplus human output.

They did not even take the whole of that surplus. Between the 11th and the 13th century, the rural population grew appreciably. The considerable extension of arable land during this period is sufficient evidence of this. For this was the age of the great work of dyking and drainage in fenlands. In Flanders, nature and man combined in the 11th century to push back the sea. In Lombardy, bishops, monasteries, and finally communes, endeavoured to tame the Po and make its valley fertile. By 1250 the work was finished: Milan by then, for instance, had its great irrigation canal, the Muzza, while downstream, between the tributaries of the Oglio and the Molinella, the river was well under control.

This is also, notably in such regions of France as the Parisian basin, the great age of the "villes neuves." The "villes neuves" were new settlements founded on open waste and in forest clearings by enlightened lords and their colonists (*hôtes*). We have the foundation charters of some of these places. For others the place name attests their origin by referring to new foundation (the French *Villeneuve*) or to the proprietor (Créon, Libourne), or by indicating their privileged status (the Italian *Villafranca*), or by copying the name of some great city far off (Bruges or Ghent in Béarn), or above all, by preserving the memory of the ancient forests and of the clearing process which eroded it, as in the German place names ending in *rade, raut, rode, roth, reut, riet, holz, wald, forst, hausen, hain, hagen, bruch, brand, scheid, schlag*, etc. Often the ground plan is our evidence, a grid pattern or the angling of intersections proving that the whole place was laid out in one operation.

Even where there was no dyking, no drainage, and no planting of new settlements, there was still new activity, although it may be more difficult for us to trace it. Yet careful examination of the old landscapes and attentive reading of the documents relating to them will often reveal that arable and pasture areas were being enlarged. Sometimes the structure of villages is significant, as in the intercalary type of settlement. Here there is a nucleus around which lie hamlets, scattered houses, or, less frequently, isolated manors. Records and source data prove these to be relatively new. They may, for example, be mentioned as inhabited places only rather late; they may be served by a little chapel dependent on the church in the central settlement, or they may be located in the middle of a huge tract of land owned by a single tenant, while the surrounding lands lie in open fields cultivated in strips, etc. Sometimes holdings are classified in such a way as to indicate that new clearing has taken place. A 13th century polyptyque, for instance, distinguishes the older tenements—manses, *més*, quarters, and *masale* land—from the assarts (newly broken land). Or study of the names of fields and holdings reveals the presence of *courts, vents, artigues, arsis*, and *mesnils*, dating from Roman or early Frankish times. Again, the documents may speak of the tithes known as *novales*, those levied on newly cultivated land, which may go back to a 9th century origin but more often only to the 11th century. Finally, a charter or a saint's life may mention the new development of forest or wasteland: for example, a property may be deeded to an individual or to a religious foundation to be cleared (*ad extirpandum*), or someone struck by paralysis has to lease out land that he had brought under cultivation.

All of these indices of the advance of cultivation have been known to us for a long time. The need now is to examine them in a more methodical and rigorous way. Research should focus on clearly defined areas and should exploit every existing source of information. Local study should deal simultaneously with water problems, with the appearance, the number and the importance of *villes neuves*, and with clearing operations within older lands in order to identify and date each assart. By doing so, it would be possible to measure the advance of cultivation in the region in question as accurately as possible.

The increase of the cultivated area would be a main clue to the degree of population growth. Yet although the two phenomena certainly move together, there is nothing to show that they must vary equally. Conceivably the breaking in of more land might be due less to an increase in population than to a fall in the number of the landless, or to a general rise in standards of living. The problem in each case would be to decide how far the movement was the result of population pressure. To know the motivation of the people or the communities concerned would be helpful. The founding of a *ville neuve* by a king or a territorial prince whose aims were political, strategic, or fiscal rather than truly economic and whose call for immigrants drew a response mainly from more or less remote countries, or the creation of a grange (outlying farm) by some Cistercian abbey would be less significant for the region we were studying than clearing planned by the cadets of seigneurial families or by peasants. Work of this kind was often more important than has been generally recognized.

To attack forest and wasteland is one means of dealing with population pressure. Another way is to improve technique. Agricultural methods progressed through fallowing every third year instead of every second and, on some plots, by sowing legumes in the fallow, through plowing more frequently and more deeply and fertilizing the soil more, and by specialization, for example, in vine culture or market gardening. All this was going on in the valley of the Rhine in the 12th and 13th centuries. What was achieved there may have been achieved elsewhere. In studying the demographic history of a region, it is important to look into all this.

But not everyone with too many children made an effort to get more land or to farm better. When population began to grow families at first continued to live on their patrimony. After a time, if juridical and other customs permitted, they would simply divide it. Fragmentation of manorial units, both of a whole vill and of the peasant *mansus*, was thus to some extent a consequence of population growth. It is one of our indices. It is true that the movement began well before 1100; in some places, for example in Lorraine, it was by then general. Of greater interest for us is the further fragmentation of the units, especially the quarter, into which the ancient manse had been split, but its occurrence is not easy to date.

Population growth bore not only on the secular "cell" of the social organism, the vill, but also on its religious "cell", the parish. Sometimes the parish disintegrated, though less often than has been supposed. The proprietors and the incumbents of the old churches, both rural and urban, defended their privileges fiercely and often victoriously. Thus the spiritual problems consequent on the growth of the flock had to be met by other means than subdivision of parishes. The old churches, and the bodies of clergy serving them, had to be enlarged or else new *loci religiosi* had to be set up, that is, chapels served more or less regularly by a priest, so that the faithful could at least hear Sunday Mass. Construction or alteration of churches and chapels is thus evidence of population growth; here the historian should consult the archeologist.

Finally, along with chance references to the development of this or that rural industry, we have clear proof of a rise in the population curve—in the expansion of the West. *Reconquista*, the feudal operations of the Hautevilles and their rivals in Southern Italy and Sicily, Crusades, and the *Drang nach Osten*—these movements are too familiar and too far-reaching to be discussed here. Between the 11th century and the 13th, and even into the 14th century, they were drawing colonists from all parts of the Christian West. In research in the population history of a region one must never forget to find out whether any of its people emigrated—either in large groups, like the Flemish peasants who went off to the Baltic fenlands, or singly, like the barons of Perche or of Béarn who straggled off to Spain. One should also try to find out why they went. Land hunger need not have been the only motive.

These then are the kinds of evidence which tend to show that from 1000 or 1050 to 1300 or 1350 the Christian West was becoming more thickly settled. Taken by itself, each piece of evidence is debatable. For example, the clearing of new land is not in itself "decisive evidence of an unusual growth of population, of a demographic revolution." It is the consistency of the evidence that brings conviction. Increase in the number of households or of individuals within a given area, birth rates higher than would have been necessary to mere maintenance of the population, a rise in land values coinciding with a probable fall in wages, growth in the size and number of towns, the promotion of more and more villages to the status of a little town and the rise of God knows how many new villages and hamlets, the pushing back of seas, marshes, wasteland, and forest by the advance of fields and pastures, improvements in the yield of land, fragmentation of old manorial units, subdivision of parishes or enlargement of churches and building of chapels, the expansion of the West to the South and to the East—how are we to explain all this going on at the same time, except by a net increase of population?

But though the nature of the process is clear enough, its working is in many respects still hazy. The evidence has not been systematically interrogated. We are still much in the dark about the starting points, the duration, the intensity and the phasing of the movement. When did it begin? We say, in the mid-11th century. But is this true of Italy? Or of Germany? Or of the Low Countries, Flanders or Normandy? When did it die down? Most historians would say, in the 14th century; many towns were then stagnating or declining, while marginal lands and even whole villages were being deserted. But there is still controversy as to whether these developments came in the early or middle years of the century. Those who believe that they came around 1300 point to the impossibility of bringing any more land under wheat, and to evidence of soil exhaustion on many of the assarts. They argue that in these circumstances population must already have ceased to grow and may already have begun to fall. But the majority still holds to the contrary thesis that the Black Death was responsible for reversing the trend. Again, some researchers take an entirely different view of the phasing of the movement. One writer claims that the Bavarian plain was already fully exploited by the end of the 13th. Another claims, after comparing two fiscal records, that between 1312 and 1427 the population of the Tirol grew by 50%.

The extent to which population grew is also a matter of debate. To speak of a revolution is perhaps to exaggerate. Even by the rather generous estimates of Levasseur or of Lamprecht, the average annual increase comes out far below that of England or Germany between 1800 and 1850—a percentage of 3.8 or 4.8 instead of 14 or 11. As to the possible phases of the movement, we are still unable to distinguish and describe them.

Almost everything that we know or postulate on this subject therefore requires to be verified and restated in quantitative terms. This can be done only through meticulously careful regional study. We cannot even be certain of reaching precise quantitative results. But the attempt has to be made, for although it has been long neglected, the problem is nonetheless important. Indeed, in all medieval history there are few questions so fundamental as this one.

P.S. On reading the manuscript of this article my esteemed colleague and friend Professor Philippe Wolff of the University of Toulouse suggested to me that the improvement in the status of peasants, especially the relaxation of the bonds attaching them to the soil, may equally be a consequence of population growth. This is certainly true, yet the interpretation of this index is a particularly delicate matter, one that does not lend itself well to statistical study.

CHAPTER 13

The Origins of the Medieval Town Patriciate

A. B. Hibbert

This article is concerned with the theory advanced by Henri Pirenne to explain the origins and early history of medieval towns. This theory may be summarized as follows.[1] During the 9th and much of the 10th centuries long-distance trade in Europe was at its lowest ebb, and during this period the only settlements which were not purely agricultural were the ecclesiastical, military and administrative centres which served the major needs of the feudal ruling classes: fortresses, monasteries, episcopal seats, royal residences and the like.[2] These had none of the characteristics of true towns and knew neither commercial nor industrial activity, but when long-distance trade revived in the 10th and 11th centuries the merchants and artisans produced by changing economic conditions settled round them. The influx of such people made it possible for true town life to develop.

From the very beginning the incoming traders differed from the older inhabitants. They were set apart by their origins, for they were "new men" and indeed outsiders to the feudal order itself, living on the margins of that society; they were set apart in a purely physical sense, for they lived outside the walls of the old feudal settlement or "pre-urban nucleus" in a separate trading and manufacturing colony, the suburb.

The feudal "core" of such double settlements remained static, inert, but the colony formed by the newcomers grew in numbers and in strength. Finally a time came when the traders and craftsmen felt themselves strong enough to challenge the control which the feudal element had hitherto exercised over them. They or their leaders struggled for independence, and by money or force of arms established a new regime which contrasted in all essentials with the old order. A distinctive social, economic and legal unit was brought into being, the medieval town, and this was the work of the merchants and artisans alone.

From A. B. Hibbert, "The Origins of the Medieval Town Patriciate," *Past and Present*, No. 3 (February 1953), pp. 15–27. World copyright The Past and Present Society, 175 Bauxbury Road, Oxford England. This article is reprinted with the permission of the Society and the author from *Past and Present, A Journal of Historical Studies*.

A group of the more important merchants commonly took the lead in the struggle to achieve these various changes, and after the town had thrown off or modified feudal control, this group developed into the characteristic medieval "patriciate." This patriciate was an increasingly narrow class which enjoyed social, political and economic control in the town and whose power and influence rested on the control of the wholesale and long-distance trades of the town. The changing relations between this dominant element and the rest of the townsmen were to determine a great deal of later town history.

This theory is certainly both powerful and fertile, and yet it may be questioned at many points. What follows is not an original or exhaustive examination of the hypothesis. I intend merely to probe some of its weak points in a preliminary way. I shall only deal with one theme in detail, that of the origin of the patriciate, and shall choose my facts and arguments from among those likely to be familiar to students of the subject.

We can most profitably criticise Pirenne's views in two ways: on theoretical grounds and by reference to fact. In the first instance we may ask whether he was right in his view of the role of the revival of long-distance trade in the 10th and 11th centuries, and in his views on the relationship between trade and feudal society in general. In the second, we may ask whether a sharply contrasted feudal "nucleus" and a trading suburb really occurred in the early stages of all towns and whether the patriciate really developed along the lines he suggested.

I shall make the only the briefest reference to the effects and nature of the expansion of long-distance trade from the late 10th century onwards. Has long-distance trade as opposed to local trade any special virtue as a stimulant of town growth? Was long-distance trade before 1000 A.D. as unimportant as Pirenne's theory assumes? We may leave these questions aside, though Pirenne's answers to them may be, and have been challenged. There are other grounds for disquiet. Pirenne treats a trade revival as though it were something which happens of itself, independent of surrounding circumstance.[3] Such treatment of historical fact is often justifiable, it is a useful piece of shorthand to prevent an infinite regress from cause to cause but it loses its justification if instead of condensing argument to a convenient size, it involves the elimination of arguments vital to the discussion.

Just such a difficulty arises here. Pirenne's theory leans heavily on the idea that there is a natural incompatibility between arrangements of society suited to feudal lords and those suited to merchants and artisans, or between a "feudal" settlement and one allowing the development of trade and industry. One cannot deny that such an antagonism between "feudal" and "burgess" interests did develop later in the Middle Ages. It may even be granted that it was potential or latent from the beginning. If, however, we consider how trade *must* originally have developed in the context of a feudal society, and how the earlier concentrations of merchants and artisans must equally have been the outcome of feudal circumstance, we may properly question any theory which assumes that the two were originally and inherently incompatible.

Both fact and theory suggest that in earlier medieval times trade was by no means a solvent of feudal society, but that it was a natural product of that society and that feudal rulers up to a point favoured its growth. There is the simple fact that whatever area and whatever century we may choose to take as being most typically "feudal" there is still trade and there are still merchants. Feudalism could never dispense with merchants. The very structure, technical level and economic habits of society always made some local and long-distance trade necessary. It is possible to press this point further. It can be argued that the development of feudal lordships and of related changes in agricultural organization both increased total productivity and concentrated the wealth so produced. Ever greater and wealthier feudal establishments appeared and these acted as ever greater and more demanding consumers— thus directly stimulating trade and concentrating those who supplied the goods for them. Again, a substantial class of merchants and craftsmen had to be fed by the agricultural labours of the other groups; these therefore had to provide extra food. It may thus be suggested that growth of such a class depended essentially on changes in rural society which made either for increased productivity or lower consumption per head among the tillers, thus providing more food. Such changes must have been wrought *within* the "feudal" structure and were a basic prerequisite of any town development.

The mass of evidence about what attitude feudal lords took in practice towards towns and trade adds weight to these arguments. They founded towns, encouraged merchant and artisan settlement, sketched out a staple policy in their attempts to direct trade through centres under their own control and, especially in Southern Europe, took an active and direct part in town life. There were two obvious reasons why they should do this. They had to provision large private and public establishments, and they wished to gain profit from trade and industry, either by becoming traders themselves or by tapping the wealth produced by trade and industry through levies and charges upon goods or upon those who produced and distributed them.

Portions of Pirenne's theory can be tested by a more direct appeal to facts. Two questions seem particularly prominent: the nature and role of the "pre-urban" or "feudal" nucleus and the origins of the patriciate. For the sake of brevity I shall discuss only the second of these here. Pirenne's description of the social history of the burgess class and the rise among them of an urban patriciate is of prime importance in his theory. For him the patricians were the main creators and moulders of urban life and institutions; they were the mainspring of town development. It is therefore of some consequence to establish who and what they were.

Pirenne answers this question in a fairly simple way. The more prosperous burgesses were the descendants of those newcomers who in the 11th century and onwards had settled round fortresses, monasteries and similar centres for the sake of security. Each had originally been "a little pedlar, a sailor, a boatman, a docker" or something of the sort.[4] Those who had prospered had become great merchants and from among the most notable of these was recruited, during the 12th and 13th centuries, the ruling clique of the towns, a patriciate whose class dominance was based on their position as great wholesale traders.[5]

Any attempt to find out whether the patriciate really did originate among merchants and "new men" encounters very great difficulties, above all the sheer lack of documentary material. The obvious way to answer the question would be to sample the family histories of members of the early patriciate, but in practice this is almost impossible. Of course this difficulty cuts both ways and Pirenne himself has to rely more on inference than on direct evidence for his own theory. The career of St. Godric of Finchale, which he uses as a picturesque illustration, is a rather shaky foundation on which to build a great theoretical edifice.[6]

The basic facts about many Italian towns are perhaps too well known to need much comment. There the petty nobility and the greater among the free landowners played a part which Pirenne himself admits to be different from that generally allotted to them in this theory.[7] They were favourably disposed towards the development of trade, they took a direct part in commercial activities and they were sometimes the most prominent subscribers of capital and the final controllers of commercial life.

At *Genoa* for example where the first trading partnerships are found in the documents of the early 11th century, the typical sleeping partner is a landowner who has some surplus capital to invest, presumably derived from land rents, loot from expeditions against the Moslems, or from feudal office. Later, during the course of the 11th and 12th centuries, it becomes even clearer that the greatest leaders of trade expansion were the men who already possessed influence and money because of their high position in a feudal society, men who received larger revenues from rents or customs or market dues. In the very front rank, commercially as well as socially and politically, were great 12th century vice-comital families like the Burone, della Volta, Mallone and di Castro. They and people of the same general standing, such as the Embriaco family, dominated all aspects of Genoese life during this period. Then, in the later 12th and 13th centuries, their position was challenged by new men who had risen from the lower ranks of society by the ladder of successful trade. Such newcomers were the Doria, Cigala and Lercari families who were to be so important in the period of Genoese maturity.[8]

This class of lesser nobles and landowners were equally important in the constitutional development of Italian towns. They took a prominent part, and characteristically the lead, in the struggle against episcopal control. We find them to be the essential element of many of the earliest urban ruling groups; they provided the membership of the earliest Italian patriciates. From the earliest date *Milan* chose its consuls from the "capitanei," "valvassores" and "cives."[9] Elsewhere the "grandi" were typically recruited from the lesser nobility and great landlords, from the group which had usurped seignorial control. This group was so little composed of great merchants alone that these latter had subsequently to lead revolutions to secure a share of control with the earlier patriciate. Long after the towns had achieved a marked degree of independence, in the 13th century, great merchants combined against the old patriciate of semi-feudal nature in revolutionary movements at *Florence* and elsewhere. Few things could be more significant, for if the patriciate had already been simply composed of great merchants such struggles would have been superfluous. Hence A. Sapori, summing up the present state of investigations into Italian town history, sees town development as due to the formation of a group stronger and richer than the rest, which usurped the public and financial functions of the overlord and gave its personal and class unity a territorial basis. It was essentially formed, he holds, of petty vassals, great emphyteutic tenants and large-scale "farmers," all of whom had developed a direct interest in trading matters.[10]

It therefore seems no exaggeration to say that in Italy the first stages of urban history in the Middle Ages were associated with the formation of a ruling group of largely aristocratic and feudal origin, which controlled town life and trading conditions. The later history of this patriciate would vary. Sometimes the original patriciate adapted itself to the changing volume and nature of trade by taking an interest in its development or by recruiting members from among the merchants themselves. In such cases an upper group, part feudal-aristocratic, part mercantile would arise, a group of mixed nature like the "magnates" of *Bologna* formed of nobles made *bourgeois* by business and *bourgeois* ennobled by city decree, both fused together in law.[11] In other towns the old patriciate would prove too unadaptable and powerful new groups would build up outside its ranks. Then the day would come when the controllers of the great trades either overthrew the rule of the "grandi" or else forced them to share their powers. In the first case the history of the patriciate clearly consists, in various proportions, of the transformation of the old ruling group of feudal origin and the recruitment of new men into it. Even when events had the most revolutionary appearance, however, we have still to face two facts. An aristocratic patriciate held sway in the earlier and most formative period, and the supplanting group usually made little change in town organization and quickly formed itself into a body barely distinguishable from that which it had replaced.

Leaving aside the evidence of other southern regions, which is often so similar to the Italian, let us turn to northern Europe, for Pirenne in fact based his theory on the evidence of northern towns.

J. W. F. Hill has collected the information available about the families which dominated *Lincoln* immediately after it achieved some degree of self-government.[12] Take the three most prominent families of all, those which provided the first three mayors to be known by name. Adam, mayor between 1210 and 1216, had as grandfather a landowner and church benefactor, as uncles the holder of a fee and a bailiff of the lord; his father was a property owner, a man who leased houses to tradesmen, and supervisor of repairs of the castle gaol. His brothers-in-law were lords' bailiffs and considerable landowners within the city and in surrounding villages, his cousin another landowner. He himself possessed numerous lands, houses and rents, including land in the Bail, the area which remained under the feudal jurisdiction of the constable of the castle. His nephew, John Fleming de Holm, held a lordship at Langton as well as being an alderman of Lincoln, and John's son and grandson followed in his footsteps. The latter, Peter de Holm, held property within the Bail by homage and fealty to the Bishop of Durham, and his case is the first in which we *may* have evidence that the family engaged in trade: in 1268 he was granted life exemption from all tallages assessed in the city provided that he did not trade in town. This seems very dubious and negative evidence on which to base a claim that the family was one of merchants. We must not make too much of an argument from silence, but it remains true that between 1150 and 1250 the family was one of important landowners, rentiers and feudal officials, on the fringe of the nobility.

The second known mayor, William "nephew of Warner," had relatives of the same generation who held the rectory of St. Paul in the Bail, held half a Knight's fee from the bishop, were owners of houses and market stalls, bailiffs and great landowners. William himself was bailiff to the lord on several occasions and a rich rentier into the bargain. There were trading interests in the family however; a certain Osbert, probably William's uncle, and owner of considerable landed property, was once fined for selling wine contrary to the assize. Even so it is very arguable whether trade or land and office-holding ranked as the original and basic activity, and Osbert's sons and grandsons figured as prominently as bailiffs, landed proprietors and rent holders as they did as men with commercial interests. The third family, that of the mayor Peter de Ponte, conformed more closely to the pattern of the first. This family "had its roots in the Bail," contained two bailiffs in Peter's father's generation, and was characteristically made up of large landowners and rentiers in the 12th and early 13th centuries.

Naturally such evidence is not conclusive as to the origins of the 13th century patriciate of Lincoln. Somewhere in an unrecorded past these men *may* have first climbed to fortune by the profits of the Scandinavian trade. What the facts do tell us is that at its very first documented appearance the patriciate has the character of a land-owning and rentier group, holding feudal office and then town office without a break, merging with the smaller kind of feudal noble and landlord. If we can discriminate at all on such slender evidence we are shown that trading was at least as likely to be something taken up as time went on, as something to be dropped as part of a shameful family past.

Evidence of varied nature comes from other places. In *Poland* Rutkowski derives the trading patriciate of those towns whose population remained on the whole Polish, from the feudal nobles who settled in the towns while retaining their interests as great landholders.[13] In *Norway* the chief merchants in the 12th and 13th centuries were great ecclesiastics and great landowners, while the ruling class of *Bergen* and its dominant trading clique before the days of Hanseatic hegemony, was made up of important officials and the principal owners of "gaards" (curtes) within the town, to whom were joined as more recent and less substantial elements, some professional merchants and shipowners.[14] Pirenne himself goes so far as to agree that in the 11th century there was at least some fusion between the knightly class and the upper rank of traders to form the patriciate in the northern towns, and he has also to admit that in some towns of his area, and especially in the episcopal cities of the *Rhineland* and the *Liége* region, the "ministeriales" of the lord entered into the patriciate.[15]

It is interesting that the evidence for his own theory is so very dubious in the one town on which Pirenne has published a detailed study—*Dinant*.[16] Here, under the presidency of the "villicus" of the bishop of Liége, the chief officials were the "monetarii" who acted as judges in the town court and were the instruments of episcopal control. Pirenne describes this feudal group as "gradually giving way before the slow but irresistible invasion of the bourgeoisie,"[17] the echevinage replacing the "monetarii" in the 12th and 13th centuries. Pirenne's case would be firmer if the "monetarii-judices" survived by the side of the "échevins" as a contrasted group. As it is, their disappearance allows us to guess that both groups might in fact have been recruited from the same class of men and that one was transformed into the other. In fact, the evidence suggests just this. In 1227 when the four "monetarii" are mentioned for the last time, two of them *were* "échevins," and another almost certainly belonged to a family which provided more than one "échevin" later in the century. In other words, three out of the four episcopal officials furnished direct proof of continuity and fusion with the echevinage. It should be noted that "échevins" were probably still elected by the bishop, that the law they administered was seigneurial, that they clung above all other things to competence in cases involving real estate. If the echevinage was the original form of the *bourgeois* patriciate as Pirenne says, then it must be conceded that it derived in great part, if not entirely from the same class as the original feudal officials. "Their possession in the city and its surrounds of vineyards, curtileges, houses and land rents" was a primary basis of their economic power and their large-scale trading interests were probably derivative.

J. Lestocquoy's researches into the great patrician families of *Arras*[18] provide most important direct evidence. He examines in detail five of the families who were in the top rank from the 12th century onwards and in no case does he find their origins among landless newcomers or among a population of professional merchants some of whom gradually improved their position. Instead they seem to spring from a group who were feudal officials and moderately important landowners in the 11th century. The Crespin family, which produced some of the greatest financiers of the Middle Ages and lent several times their annual income to most of the cities of Flanders, first appeared as modest landed proprietors and possessors of a mill in the mid-12th century. They took up money-lending on a moderate scale about the 1220s. The Huquedieu family started in the service of St. Vaast monastery, as officials of the Count of Flanders and as cathedral canons about the same time. They may have had a military origin, and seem to have been high feudal officials; one of them was an échevin in 1111 when these officers receive their first mention.

Similar cases can be multiplied. At *Cambridge* we find that the alderman of the Gild Merchant and perhaps the first mayor of the town, Hervey Dunning, held land in half-a-dozen villages, claimed the rank of knight and twice demanded wagers of battle in suits concerning landed property. His father, uncle and grandfather were all land owners.[19] At *Brussels* the patriciate dominated the Gild Merchant at the beginning of the 14th century and contained the most prominent merchant-employers in the drapery industry; yet no 13th century document shows the patrician "lignages" engaged in trade. Of course this is in part due to the chances of documentary survival, yet the further back patrician family histories are pushed, the more clearly the patricians appear as landholders and lesser feudatories. Families like the Clutines and Eggluys were farmers of tithes, tenants of castellanies, holders of ducal fiefs—they owed their wealth to lands, rents and the farming of feudal revenues.[20]

Perhaps there is much more similar evidence to be found. Who were the 11th and early 12th century aldermen of *London*? Who were the "possessores" who lived near *Ghent* in the 11th century and took their wool to the town to be woven? Who were the leading citizens of early *Douai,* two of whom can be found in the 12th century selling their share in the town tolls to the Abbey of Andin?[21] The whole problem of patrician origins requires much more detailed investigation, but the evidence does seem to call for an interim revision of Pirenne's theory.

This revision must take account of two main facts: the evidence which shows that old-established families could adapt themselves to new economic conditions, and use their old power to achieve power in a new context; and the truth in Pirenne's contention that the more successful merchants among the newcomers to a town could make their way into the ruling class. Two processes are involved in the formation of the patriciate, the internal transformation of an old dominant class and the recruitment of new families from the more successful merchants and artisans, who were often immigrants or the descendants of immigrants. Let us take each process in turn.

In the earlier stages of town development there was often a class between the actual lords on the one hand, and agricultural workers, craftsmen, petty traders, porters, innkeepers and the like, on the other. This group comprised large freeholders and emphyteutic tenants, sometimes the lower grades of the nobility (especially in Italy), prominent officials in the service of a lay or ecclesiastical lord, like the more important among the "ministeriales" in Germany, and, possibly, such elements as burhthegns, cnihts, lawmen, or members of a witan, dimly discernible in early English towns. The economic position of the group was intimately associated with the possession of land and feudal office. At the same time its members were willing to take advantage of any opportunity to improve their position—by leasing their land or renting the buildings they had constructed on it, by letting out stalls in the market place, by farming mints, tolls or mills from the lord, by raising loans wherever required, and by engaging their capital in commercial and industrial enterprises beyond the scope of lesser men.

Two things would happen to such a group, made up of quite wealthy men, used to freedom and possessing initiative, men accustomed also to running the affairs of the town on the lord's behalf, or at least to being consulted by him. What more natural than that they should be in the lead of movements for freedom from seigneurial control? The new municipal powers created economic and political opportunities of which they were in the best position to take advantage. Psychologically, socially and politically they were in the most suitable position to conduct a successful attack.

Secondly, these men would probably have had an interest in trade from the earliest times. As seigneurial officials many of them were well placed for controlling supplies to one of the best of the early markets, the feudal households, and the group as a whole possessed land and land rents, one of the greatest potential sources of liquid capital during the Middle Ages. They would therefore include the capitalization of trade among their varied activities, and where trade developed quickly they might be merchant capitalists among other things at a very early date. As M. Postan comments: "It can well be doubted whether the conventional picture of a vagrant trader, travelling with his goods . . . ever represented the upper strata of the medieval merchant class."[22] At first, however, trading, if present at all, would not normally be the greatest or most typical of their economic activities; but as economic change proceeded in Europe, trade and finance would come to rival, perhaps to overshadow, other means of gaining wealth. The leading families, or the more adaptable among them, invested proportionately more in the new activities, because men of their group characteristically seized all opportunities of advancement of any kind. They would retain, and even intensify their old land-owning and office-holding interests by means of the new wealth, as methods of social and financial investment. By and large, however, the influence and power of the class increasingly depended on commerce and finance.

Thus the formation of the 12th and 13th century patriciate involved *internal transformation* of a dominant class which already existed, and which was opportunist enough to shift the emphasis of its activities as conditions changed. Some of the leading townsfolk were, however, too conservative and rigid in outlook to adapt themselves. They were left as survivals of an older stage, like the "grandi" in Italy, opposing the great trades rather than merging with them; or like the échevins in some towns of the *Liége* group who refused to join their more progressive fellows in leadership of the new council of jurés; or like the Avvocato and Gavi families of 12th century *Genoa* who failed to join the rush of many of their social equals into trade. Sometimes the class as a whole failed in adaptability, especially when it was faced with fundamental economic changes like those of the late 13th and 14th centuries. Then there were challenges of varying seriousness, and the ensuing battles filled much of town history in the later Middle Ages.

These problems cannot be treated here. Instead we must complete the explanation of patrician origins by looking at the recruitment of new men. Outsiders, and especially those merchants and artisans who had made more than a modest competence through their ability and good fortune, could and did enter the patriciate. Such recruitment could take two principal forms. There was the normal continuous inflow of rich parvenus into the ruling group, which was all the more easily assimilated when the patriciate itself had developed large trading interests. The rate of recruitment however would vary greatly and depended particularly on the attitude of the patricians themselves. This suggests the second form. If the ruling group proved unadaptable and exclusive, a class of nouveaux riches was likely to build up in opposition to them, particularly when economic conditions had opened up new ways of obtaining wealth. Recruitment was, so to speak, dammed back, and would therefore produce tensions and greater or lesser crises in which the new men would try to seize power or at least to share it with the old.

A satisfactory explanation of the origin of the medieval patriciate seems possible along these lines. Moreover, the explanation can be adjusted to suit the divergent circumstances of different towns and regions by allowing for variations in the relative importance of the two main processes, the internal transformation of a "feudal" upper class and the recruitment of the new man.

Sometimes for instance the social constitution of an early town did not favour any large number of men of the "feudal" type. This type seems to have been especially common in Southern Europe, and particularly where there was substantial continuity of town life from late Roman times. It was fairly common in most of the episcopal centres and other large and old-established settlements in the North. But the old "feudal" group might be weaker, and the association of the "new" merchants coming up from below the stronger, for many social reasons. Then "recruitment" would be a major factor and merchants rising from among the commons more important than an element of officials and landowners who had taken to trade. In the South such conditions may have obtained exceptionally, as in *Venice,* but in the non-episcopal towns of the North they were much more common, especially in England and "new" Germany, where they were often associated with the peculiar importance of the merchant gild. It is on such evidence that Pirenne founds his theory, on part of the evidence for part of Europe. We may freely admit that in certain cases his explanation seems close to the truth, but what matters is that the explanation, appropriate to cases at one end of the spectrum, is applied to the whole range. In fact even those examples best suited to Pirenne's theory usually show some small effects due to another type of development. Even in the North of Europe there are many important towns in which "transformation" was at least as important as "recruitment," and most towns in the South require a different approach altogether. Further, if there is a Pirennian extreme at one end of the scale, there seems to be an equally "feudal" extreme at the other. This is constituted by such towns as those in northern Italy and especially in *Piedmont* where communes sprang from seigneurial families whose multiplying offspring formed themselves into an association, each the nucleus of a town commune.

We may in conclusion note a few auxiliary advantages of the foregoing explanation. Trade revival and economic change generally are retained as integral parts of the scheme of development, and merchant capitalists keep an important role though a different one from that postulated by Pirenne. The explanation tallies well with what we know of the forms of economic and political power actually exercised by established patriciates. It allows for a source of mercantile capital additional to or alternative to the windfalls of petty pedlars and porters. Finally it will allow for the idea that novel techniques or fresh markets might first be exploited by new men who in order to expand relied on association with wealthy men of older standing so that capital was gradually shifted from an older to a new use.

Notes

1. H. Pirenne's theory was first advanced in articles on "L'Origine des Constitutions Urbaines au Moyen Age" in the *Revue Historique* 1895, and expanded in various later works. All these can be most conveniently consulted in the collection of his writings on urban history published as *"Les Villes et les Institutions Urbaines"* (2 vols.), henceforward quoted as V.I.U.

2. The word "feudal" will be used in this article to refer to a kind of society in which economic and political power derive from large-scale land-holding, and where there is direct and indirect exploitation of this land by means of dependent cultivators.

3. "Que l'origine des villes du Moyen Age se rattache directement, comme un effet à la cause, à la renaissance commerciale . . . c'est ce dont il est impossible de douter," V.I.U., I, p. 376. "L'idée fondamentale . . . qui voit dans le commerce la cause essentielle de la formation des villes, est incontestablement vraie," Ibid., II, p. 259.

4. H. Pirenne, *Economic and Social History of Medieval Europe,* p. 48.

5. Ibid., p. 201.

6. Ibid., p. 47.

7. Ibid., p. 48.

8. Y. Renouard, *Les Hommes d'Affaires Italiens,* pp. 24, 47–54.

9. V.I.U., p. 400.

10. A. Sapori, article in *International Historical Congress* 1950, Vol. I, Rapports.

11. Ibid.

12. J. W. F. Hill, *Medieval Lincoln,* Appendix V.

13. J. Rutkowski, *Histoire Economique de la Pologne avant les Partages,* p. 39.

14. J. A. Gade, *The Hanseatic Control of Norwegian Commerce,* pp. 27–28.

15. V.I.U., I, pp. 54, 103–104, 216.

16. *Histoire de la Constitution de la Ville de Dinant au Moyen Age;* V.I.U., II, pp. 1–94.

17. J. Lestocquoy, *Les Dynasties Bourgeoises d'Arras du XIe au XVe Siècle.* Since writing this article, I have been able to see Lestocquoy's *Les Villes de Flandre et d'Italie sous le gouvernement des patriciens Xie—XVe siècles,* which attacks the Pirenne thesis in greater detail along lines similar to those here indicated.

18. H. Cam, *Liberties and Communities of Medieval England,* pp. 23–24.

19. Favresse, *Le Régime Démocratique à Bruxelles,* pp. 32–33.

20. V.I.U., I, p. 137 n. 1.

21. G. Espinas, *Douai,* I, p. 306.

22. Power and Postan, *English Trade in the Fifteenth Century,* p. 146.

CHAPTER 14

The Expansion of Europe

Robert Bartlett

Medieval and Modern Colonialism

The 'expansion of Europe' in the High Middle Ages clearly shared many characteristics with the overseas expansion of post-medieval times. It showed, also, however, certain distinctive structural features. One characteristic in particular distinguishes it sharply from, say, European imperialism of the nineteenth and twentieth centuries, at least as that phenomenon is classically described. Modern imperialism, it is usually held, intensified the large-scale regional differentiation of the globe: industrialized areas, greedy for raw materials and markets, became enmeshed in a pattern of systematic interdependence with regions which supplied the raw materials and helped to purchase the products of the industrial zones. There is, doubtless, an element of caricature in this picture, but even a rudimentary acquaintance with the history of rubber or copper in modern times shows that there is some truth in this image.

The colonialism of the Middle Ages was quite different. When Anglo-Normans settled in Ireland or Germans in Pomerania or Castilians in Andalusia, they were not engaged in the creation of a pattern of regional subordination. What they were doing was reproducing units similar to those in their homelands. The towns, churches and estates they established simply replicated the social framework they knew from back home. The net result of this colonialism was not the creation of 'colonies,' in the sense of dependencies, but the spread, by a kind of cellular multiplication, of the cultural and social forms found in the Latin Christian core. The new lands were closely integrated with the old. Travellers in the later Middle Ages going from Magdeburg to Berlin and on to Wroclaw, or from Burgos to Toledo and on to Seville, would not be aware of crossing any decisive social or cultural frontier.

This is indeed one reason why the formulation 'core–periphery' is not entirely fortunate (though hard to avoid) as a tool to describe the expansionism of the High Middle Ages. On the one hand, of course, there is a sense in which the centre-outwards perspective is perfectly justifiable: by 1300 the descendants of men from France ruled in Ireland and Greece, those of men from Germany in

Prussia and Brandenburg, those of men from England in Ireland and Wales, those of men from Italy in Crete, those of men from Castile in Andalusia. There is clearly an outward movement of people and power not balanced by movement in the other direction. But 'core–periphery' is still perhaps misleading, for the concept is often taken to imply a permanent or long-term functional subordination of the periphery to the core. This is exactly what high medieval colonialism was not—it was a process of replication, not differentiation.

This expansion through replication had, as its characteristic agents, not the powerful monarchies—we might be tempted to say, not the state—but consortia, entrepreneurial associations of Frankish knights, Latin priests, merchants, townsmen and, as non-voting members, peasants. The freelance nature of such expansionary enterprises as the Anglo-Norman penetration of the Celtic world or the spread of Germans into eastern Europe has often been remarked. One consequence was the creation of many independent or virtually independent lordships on the fringes of Europe—the Villehardouin principality of the Morea, the early Norman lordships in southern Italy, autonomous Valencia under the Cid, Strongbow's Leinster and de Courcy's Ulster, Brandenburg under its margraves. Only in a few cases did the expansion take the form of a growth of kingdoms, with the Iberian peninsula providing the main example. Even here, although monarchical direction was crucially important in the Spanish Reconquest, there was a significant place for autonomous urban communities, with their own *fueros*, militias and regime of local border warfare.

The situation along the eastern frontiers of the kingdom of Germany shows clearly how a lack of central direction need be no hindrance to successful expansionary movement. In the twelfth and thirteenth centuries conquest and colonization virtually doubled the sphere of German settlement and political control. The involvement of the German kings in this process was minimal. In the tenth century, by contrast, full-blooded German royal involvement under the Ottonian dynasty had been a prerequisite for territorial expansion on the eastern frontier. In that earlier period the concentration of resources under monarchical leadership had been the only thing that made even a precarious conquest possible; in the High Middle Ages there was a spontaneous many-headed movement that took German lords and settlers deep into eastern Europe.

Indeed, it may be that the strengthening of some of the major kingdoms of western Europe that is noticeable around the year 1300 actually provided some kind of brake on the expansion of Latin Europe. The amorphous petty warfare of the eleventh and twelfth centuries had left plenty of energy, i.e. manpower, resources and political will, for enterprises external to the Frankish world; but by the thirteenth century the larger princely states were seeking to monopolize aggression, and though more powerful than the smaller powers of the earlier period, would often concentrate their resources upon each other to the neglect of expansionary enterprises further afield. Charles of Anjou, whose far-flung claims to overlordship embraced such classic products of the expansionary period as Sicily, the Morea and the kingdom of Jerusalem, was actually far too busily engaged in fighting his western rivals to be a prop to the Latin states of the eastern Mediterranean. As Outremer finally fell to the Muslims in 1291, the two great powers of France and Aragon were at each other's throats. Philip the Fair of France was the most powerful ruler in Christendom, but none of his efforts were directed towards the expansion of Christendom. The example of his contemporary, Edward I of England, whose incorporation of Wales may be seen as the final consummation of Anglo-Norman expansion in that part of the Celtic world, shows that when the great unitary polities of the thirteenth and fourteenth centuries did concentrate upon expansion, they could be devastatingly effective; but more characteristic of this period was the endless struggle between the western European powers dubbed the Hundred Years War.

It was thus the knightly-clerical-mercantile consortium, not the apparatus of kingly power, that orchestrated the most characteristic expansionary movements of the eleventh and twelfth centuries. The classic case of an enterprise launched by such a consortium was the eastern Mediterranean crusade. The political map of the Levant was transformed in the twelfth and thirteenth centuries not by royal or imperial statecraft but by a curious assemblage of western magnates and knights, ecclesiastics of both a papalist and an independent bent and Italian merchants, impelled by motives as diverse as their status and origins. Contemporaries remarked how the armies of the First Crusade were 'without lord, without prince' or how they 'fought without king, without emperor'; but the establishment of Outremer was only the most striking example of the way the warrior-aristocrats, clerical élite and urban merchants of the Latin West could combine forces, often in the complete absence of monarchical orchestration, to produce new polities and new settlements. The colonization of the eastern Baltic shows how an entirely new social and political form, the *Ordensstaat,* the 'Order State,' could emerge from the activities of German merchants and missionaries, land-hungry nobles and peasants, all under the general direction and authority of one of the international military orders.

The interests of the knights, merchants, peasants and clerics who were members of these consortia did not, of course, always harmonize. In pagan eastern Europe the missionary priest raised his voice against the avarice and brutality of the secular conquerors, whose greed and violence provided the native population no incentive to peaceful conversion. The Teutonic Knights might blithely tell the German merchants that 'we have been fighting to expand the faith and your trade,' but in virtually every theater of crusade commercial interests were intertwined with the crusading movement in a way that was as often mutually destructive as it was symbiotic. The repeated and futile papal prohibitions on Italian merchants trading war materials with Muslim powers are an unambiguous example. The merchants' position is comprehensible. Alexandria, to take an instance, was not only a great Islamic centre, but also one of the biggest commercial cities of the Mediterranean. It was not at all clear that the Venetian, Genoese or Pisan trader would prefer to sack it in alliance with Frankish nobles rather than buy and sell there under the protection of a Muslim ruler. The Frankish aristocrats of the eastern Mediterranean often had no autonomy or authority in regard to the Italian traders who controlled their maritime lifelines. In 1298 the king of Cyprus told a Venetian merchant who complained of being robbed by some Genoese that 'the king did not interfere between Genoese and Venetians.' It was prudent for this Frankish crusader king to keep out of Italian mercantile disputes altogether.

The absence of political masterminding in the colonial ventures of the Middle Ages is illustrated not only by the prominent role of these eclectic consortia, that is, by the agents of expansion, but also by the distinctive nature of the form of expansion. With the exception of Ireland—which can perhaps be termed a colony in the modern sense—the eventual result of the outward movements of the Middle Ages was never the permanent political subordination of one area to another. The kingdom of Valencia, the kingdom of Jerusalem and the dominions of the Teutonic Knights in Prussia and Livonia were autonomous replicas, not dependencies, of western and central European polities. And the east with which these 'new colonies of Holy Christendom' could become replicas without political subordination is best explained by the existence, in the Latin West, of international legal forms or blueprints, which could generate new structures quite independently of an encompassing political matrix.

The expansionary power and deepening cultural uniformity of the Latin West between the tenth and thirteenth centuries is partly explained by the development in western Europe of these legal and institutional blueprints or models which were easily exportable and adaptable but also resistant. In new circumstances these forms could be modified and survive, but they also transformed their surroundings. Codifiable blueprints such as the chartered town, the university and the international religious order crystallized in the West between 1050 and 1200. As the image of crystallization suggests, many of the elements that composed them were already in existence but not yet in the exact arrangement or relationship that they were to assume. From a fusion of the monastic rule and the knightly ethos came the military orders; from the immunity and the market, the chartered town; from the priesthood and the guild, the university. What was characteristic of these forms was their uniformity and reproducibility. They were vectors of expansion because they could be set down anywhere and still thrive. They all show how a legal blueprint, codifiable and transmissible, was able to diffuse new forms of social organization throughout Europe quite independently of centralized political direction. Such forms were perfect instruments for the lay-ecclesiastical consortia we have just described.

These forms were distinguished by two vital features: they were legal and they were international. The two features were linked. Because social forms were defined legally, they were codifiable and transmissible. They gained a certain independence from local circumstances and were able to be transplanted into alien environments and survive. The town, as envisaged in innumerable borough charters, *Stadtrechte* and *fueros*, was a picture, a set of norms that could be adapted to, rather than swamped by, local situations. Hence, . . . German urban law formed the model for towns far into eastern Europe, Norman customs could be transplanted to Wales, and the *fueros* of Christian Spain could be introduced into the towns of the Reconquest. Like the towns, the new monastic orders of the twelfth century had a normative and self-defining quality. Compared with their Cluniac predecessors, the Cistercians, achieved new levels of legal articulation and international organization. Cistercian affiliation tied together hundreds of religious communities from Ireland to Palestine. As in the case of the chartered town, new members of such orders could be created with the confidence that they would change their environment as much as adapt to it. Here was a formula for successful expansion.

• • •

The process of cultural diffusion and assimilation so far described was not effortlessly smooth. It encountered opposition and generated tensions. For, as Frankish knights and Latin ecclesiastics carried their cultural and social dreams and habits into diverse parts of the world, native responses were not lacking. There was cultural resistance as well as cultural assimilation. For many, the conquests and expansionary movements of the High Middle Ages were a loss, a pain and a tragedy. 'What? Have they not, marked it with ignominy?' grieved the Muslim poet Ibn Hamdïs of Sicily. 'Have they not, Christian hands, changed its mosques into churches . . . ? I see my homeland abused by the Latins, which was so glorious and proud under my people.' The Welsh cleric Rhigyfarch, witness to the Norman conquest of south Wales in the late eleventh century, sounded a similar note:

> The people and the priest are despised
> By the word, heart and deeds of the Frenchmen.
> They burden us with tribute and consume our possessions.
> One of them, however lowly, shakes a hundred natives
> With his command and terrifies them with his look.
> Alas, our fall, alas the deep grief.

Native peoples subject to the violence of the military aristocracy of the Latin world did not only grieve. Sometimes reaction on the part of native societies was strong enough to produce enduring states, hammered out in the very process of resistance. The Lithuanian state was born in response to the German threat and went on to outlast the *Ordensstaat* and, by the late Middle Ages, to dominate eastern Europe. Faced with the challenge of German crusaders in the Baltic, the pagan Lithuanians reacted not only by engaging in stubborn military resistance but also by creating a more centralized state structure with unitary dynastic leadership. The birth of this dynamic and expansionary political structure was linked to a vigorous reavowal of their traditional religion. It is sometimes overlooked that by the mid-fourteenth century this state, ruled by pagans, was the largest in Europe. There was nothing atavistic about it: its deployment of artillery was as sophisticated as anyone's. Its gods were old, but its guns were new.

Native reactions elsewhere, if less dramatic, were equally dogged. In areas such as Ireland, where the invaders were unable to establish undisputed authority, one can find complex situations in which a partial conquest produced a strong reaction from native rulers, who were, nevertheless, unable to oust the conquerors completely. The native rulers of the north and west of the island preserved their autonomy during the high tide of Anglo-Norman colonialism, then, from the late thirteenth century, began to roll back English control. In the fourteenth and fifteenth centuries it was the local English population that began to Gaelicize, much to the dismay of the colonial authorities. The 'half-conquered' state of Ireland involved a mutual borrowing in the military as well as the cultural field. By the fifteenth century the Irish were building stone castles, but many of the Anglo-Normans, strangely enough, had abandoned the stirrup.

In Spain the conquered Muslims, the Mudejars, usually submitted only on condition that they were granted free exercise of their religion and judicial autonomy. There were some mass expulsions from certain cities, and the chief mosques were rededicated as cathedrals; but down to the time of Columbus there were large Muslim minorities—Muslim even if, as was increasingly the case, they spoke Spanish and bore Christian names—practising the Islamic religion in the Christian kingdoms of the West. They were largely debarred from political power and suffered some social and legal disabilities, but they showed no signs of disappearing.

Lithuania, Ireland, the Mudejars: the extremities of Europe experienced the process of homogenization as a process of polarization. The very same forces that drew the English, the Pomeranians or the Danes into a more uniform cultural world could, in these outlying areas, actually erect starker cultural boundaries. By the fourteenth century a large part of Europe, including England, France, Germany, Scandinavia and northern Italy and Spain, had come to possess a relatively high degree of cultural homogeneity. The whole fringe around this area, however, was characterized by a mixture of, and often conflict between, languages, cultures and, sometimes, religions. Everywhere in this fringe zone race relations mattered in a way they scarcely did in the more homogeneous central zone—and these relations were not between equals: they involved domination and subordination, control and resistance.

This book then tells both how a more uniform cultural pattern was created and extended on the continent of Europe and also how that same process produced a surrounding ring of linguistically and ethnically divided societies. This tale of increasing cultural homogeneity coupled with stark cultural divisions should have a familiar ring for those who study later periods of history, including our own. There is a connecting thread. It has been shown, reasonably conclusively, how the mental habits and institutions of European racism and colonialism were born in the medieval world: the conquerors of Mexico knew the problem of the Mudejars; the planters of Virginia had already been planters of Ireland.

Humanism and "Renaissance" in The Twelfth Century

The idea of a medieval "Renaissance" was popularized by Charles Homer Haskins in a book called *The Renaissance of the Twelfth Century.* Haskins presented his thesis thus: "There was an Italian Renaissance, whatever we choose to call it. . . . But—this much we must grant—the great Renaissance was not so unique or decisive as has been supposed. The contrast of culture was not nearly so sharp as it seemed to the humanists and their modern followers, while within the Middle Ages there were intellectual revivals whose influence was not lost to succeeding times, and which partook of the same character as the better known movement of the fifteenth century."

This argument attracted a good deal of comment and criticism. Erwin Panofsky dissented from it in a study titled *Renaissance and Renascenses in Western Art.* Panofsky preferred to use words such as "renascence" or "proto-Renaissance" for the medieval revivals of culture in Carolingian times and in the twelfth century in order to distinguish them from the Italian Renaissance—which he regarded as the only real Renaissance—that came later. He maintained that "the two medieval Renascences were limited and transitory; the Renaissance was total and permanent." Panofsky added, "Since the Renaissance the Antique has been constantly with us whether we like it or not. It lives in our mathematics and natural sciences. It has built our theatres and cinemas as opposed to the mediaeval mystery stage. It haunts the speech of our cab driver—not to mention the motor mechanic or radio expert—as opposed to that of the medieval peasant."

At first this dispute seems to be a rather sterile squabble, mere quibbling about how historians ought to use the word "Renaissance." But it really involves the whole problem of how we look at the course of Western history. Is the emergence of modern civilization really due to the revival of classical culture in the Italian Renaissance? Did the Middle Ages produce any distinctive ideas or institutions that have survived to help shape the modern world? The role of humanism in present-day culture (usually in the guise of "secular humanism") is often debated nowadays. What types of humanism existed in earlier periods, and how are we to evaluate them? These are some of the serious questions raised by the initial dispute about a "twelfth-century Renaissance."

In the following readings, David Knowles finds evidence of a real humanism in the twelfth century, but holds that this humanism was short-lived. It was soon overwhelmed by the rise of scholasticism. Richard Southern argues that the scholastic culture of the thirteenth century was itself humanistic. Eva M. Sanford discusses the views of Haskins and Panofsky and other contributors to the debate.

CHAPTER 15

The Humanism of the Twelfth Century

David Knowles

The two centuries that follow the millennium, which have been so closely studied by the historians of politics, economics and art, have perhaps not yet yielded up all their secrets in the realm of cultural life. It is only too easy to regard the medieval period as a prelude and preparation for the modern world, and to consider the history of Western civilization as that of an ordered progress towards the material and intellectual perfection of man; within the medieval centuries themselves it is equally inviting to discover a steady and straightforward evolution from barbarism to enlightenment. Yet even in constitutional, legal and economic history where such a view is least misleading, the conception of an ordered and unhalting progress, familiar to Victorian writers, must receive modification in more than one respect; in the history of intellectual development and the changes of religious sentiment any idea of an unfaltering advance is wholly false.

This, perhaps, is particularly true in respect of the first great flowering of culture in Western Europe which began shortly after the year 1000. This age, save for its artistic life, had until recently been unduly neglected by historians of thought. The great moral and intellectual leaders—Anselm, Abelard and Bernard, and their lesser contemporaries such as Peter the Venerable or John of Salisbury—were indeed familiar figures, but they had been treated only in isolation; and even during the last twenty years, when the various schools of medieval philosophy and theology have at last attracted something of the attention they deserve, there has been a tendency to regard the eleventh and twelfth centuries as but a dawning, a prelude, to the thirteenth, the "greatest of centuries," which opened with Innocent III and St. Francis, which saw the earliest and purest masterpieces of Gothic architecture spring into being at Chartres, at Paris, at Salisbury and at Westminster, which embraced all the glories of scholastic theology, and which closed upon the year in which Dante,

From David Knowles, "The Humanism of the Twelfth Century," *Studies*, Vol. 30 (1941), pp. 43–58; reprinted in Knowles, *The Historian and Character and Other Essays* (Cambridge, 1963), pp. 16–30. Reprinted by permission of Professor C. N. L. Brooke, the author's literary executor, and the publisher.

waking in the hillside forest, passed in imagination through the realms beyond the grave. In consequence, even those who, like the late Professor Haskins, have done most to extend our knowledge of the twelfth century or who,
like Denifle and Ehrle and Mandonnet and Grabmann, have studied the
growth of the universities, the origins of scholasticism and the pre-history of
the friars—even these, when treating of earlier years, have given their attention to the seeds that were still to bear fruit rather than to the ripe ears of the
summer's harvest. Yet to a careful observer the latter half of the twelfth century appears as a decline as well as a dawn, and as he looks back over the brilliant creative achievement of the hundred years between 1050 and 1150 and
notes its deep and sympathetic humanism, which anticipated to an extraordinary degree much that is considered typical of the age of the Medici and of
Erasmus, he becomes sensible of a very real change and declension between
1150 and 1200 which helped to make the culture of the thirteenth century, for
all its intense speculative force and abiding power, less universal, less appeal-
ing and, in a word, less humane than what had gone before.

It is the purpose of these pages to direct attention to the earlier years, to
the brilliant and original creative energies of the late eleventh century, and to
the wide and sympathetic humanism which between 1050 and 1150 made its
appearance for the first time in Western Europe. This first great re-birth—the
proto-Renaissance as it has sometimes been called by historians of art and architecture—took place earlier than is generally supposed; the movement
reached maturity between 1070 and 1130; it changed and declined in the fifty
years between the death of St. Bernard and the pontificate of Innocent III, and
the intellectual atmosphere of the thirteenth century which followed, though it
was in some ways more rare, more bracing and more subtle, lacked much of
the kindly warmth and fragrant geniality of the past. The culture of the
schools was, in fact—to drop the language of metaphor—without many of the
elements that make a society fully humane, and that the preceding age had
possessed for a time and subsequently lost.

The first stages of all great creative movements are hard to trace. The pre-
Socratic philosophy, the sculpture which preceded the age of Ictinus and Phei-
dias, the constitutional legislation of Solon and Cleisthenes, though in many
ways more original and admirable than the later developments in the golden
age of Pericles, have but partially and recently been rescued from oblivion and
reconstructed from the fragmentary monuments that survive. Similarly, few
decades in European history are darker than those between 970 and 1030 in
which the first generations of the new age were growing to maturity, and only
those familiar with the writings and artistic achievements of the previous centuries can appreciate the change that then began. Consequently, there has been
a general tendency to set the dawn too late—when, in fact, it is no longer
dawn but a sunlight visible to all, at the end of the century, and in northern
France. Yet it is clear that the real moving of the waters was in the decades immediately before the millennium, and in northern Italy.

That the schools of Italy, and in particular those of Lombardy, were the
first by some thirty or forty years to develop new life, is clear not only from

the calibre of their alumni but from the express testimony of contemporaries. How solid the literary training was may be seen from Peter Damian, who had himself been a master in the schools during early manhood. Damian after his conversion inveighed ceaselessly against secular learning and the poets, but in doing so he used, even in spite of himself, the very instruments against which his attack was turned; for all his writings are those of one who has not only been well trained in all the arts of expression and persuasion, but who is, besides, gifted with a real sense of the beauty of language in both prose and verse, and who is possessed of oratorical and poetic powers of a high order.

While the revival of intellectual life was a reality in Italy already between 1000 and 1020, the tide did not reach Touraine, Maine and the Ile de France till about the middle of the century; but, when it came, the spring there was even more brilliant than in Italy. Historians have often noted that while the Italian revival speedily developed into an intensive cultivation of civil and canon law, the French schools turned almost at once to dialectic. Neither of these developments was, properly speaking, humanistic in character; but whereas in Italy the purely literary education was soon abbreviated into a preparation for the study of law, in France, for almost a century, some of the monasteries and a group of schools, of which Chartres is the most important, kept to a purely literary culture, looking to philosophy, such as they knew it, for a general illumination of life and conduct rather than for a lifelong intellectual pursuit and the key to the understanding of the deepest mysteries of the faith.

The three notes of the new humanism, which set the great men of the eleventh and twelfth centuries apart from those who had gone before and those who came after, may be put out as: first, a wide literary culture; next, a great and what in the realm of religious sentiment would be called a personal devotion to certain figures of the ancient world; and, finally, a high value set upon the individual, personal emotions, and upon the sharing of experiences and opinions within a small circle of friends.

Since the ideas and emotions thus shared were often of a religious or, at least, of a philosophical character, and since the writers were in every case men who wrote little or nothing that could be called pure poetry or secular literature, the fundamental humanism of their outlook has been overlooked or, at best, has been recognized only in those who, like John of Salisbury or Hildebert of Lavardin, were classical scholars of an eminence that would attract notice in any age. In one celebrated case, indeed, it has been obscured by the persistent attempts that have been made to romanticize the past in a totally unhistorical fashion. Nevertheless, the men of the early twelfth century, if they are regarded with attention and sympathy, show themselves as possessed of a rare delicacy of perception and warmth of feeling. It is to the sixteenth century, not to the thirteenth, that one looks for the spiritual kin of Anselm, of John of Salisbury, and of Héloïse.

The hall-mark of the revival, and the accomplishment that was most widely possessed by all whom it affected, was a capability of self-expression based on a sound training in grammar and a long and often loving study of the foremost Latin writers. The great ecclesiastics, one and all, who flourished between 1030 and 1180, could express themselves not only in fluent, correct and often elaborate language, but also in phrases and sentences of true dignity and eloquence. Peter Damian, John of Fécamp, Anselm, Abelard, Bernard, William of Malmesbury, Peter the Venerable, John of Salisbury—all these, and a hundred others, were masters of a flexible style and a wide vocabulary; they can be read with ease and pleasure; they are capable of giving adequate expression to their ideas and emotions, and do not fail to do so. Indeed, a student of the period comes to take this for granted—just as, in the use of contemporary manuscripts, he takes for granted the uniform, clear and beautiful script. Yet all this is in contrast alike to the age which had gone and to that which was to follow. Even the most learned men of the previous century, such as Abbo of Fleury, are narrow in the range of their ideas and awkward in their utterance; in England, among those who write Latin, the ideas are still less mature and the expression often laboured to the point of incomprehensibility. As for the century that came after, it may seem paradoxical to suggest that the great churchmen and thinkers of the age were inarticulate; yet those who have read in their entirety the correspondence of Adam Marsh, Robert Grosseteste and John Pecham, or who have endeavored to pierce through to the personal experience and intimate characteristics of Albert the Great, Thomas Aquinas or Robert Kilwardby—to say nothing of the enigmatic Roger Bacon or Duns Scotus—will readily admit that in all the arts of language, in all manifestations of aesthetic feelings or personal emotions, in fine, in all the qualities of self-revealing intimacy, the great men of the thirteenth century are immeasurably poorer than their predecessors a hundred years before. And though the luminous and adequate expression of ideas and emotions does not of itself alone constitute a character which we call humanist—for neither Anselm nor Bernard, past masters of the craft of letters, are precisely humanists—yet the power of self-expression grounded upon, or at least reinforced by, a wide literary culture is a condition *sine qua non* of a humanist's growth.

The second trait of the humanism of the twelfth century was, it is suggested, a personal devotion to one or more of the great figures of the distant past. To look to the past as to an age wider and more accomplished than the present, to imitate its masterpieces and hand on its doctrine, had been a common tendency in every country since the end of the Empire wherever any sort of enlightenment found scope. To rediscover and repeat the past had been the watchword of Charlemagne, as it was to be the watchword, differently understood, of Hildebrand, of the early fathers of Cîteaux and of the early promulgators of the newly revived civil and canon law. What was peculiar to many of the humanists, and at the same time a striking anticipation of the sentiment of leading circles in the later Italian Renaissance, was a reverence for the precepts and a conscious endeavour to imitate the lives of celebrated writers or characters of antiquity considered as human beings or sages, rather than precisely as saints or legislators. If we wish to see the more intimate aspects of this trait, we cannot perhaps do better than consider the ways of thinking and acting of three individuals, all endowed with eminent intellectual gifts and exquisite emotional sensibilities and all eager to give expression to a part, at least, of their experience.

Abelard, Héloïse and Ailred of Rievaulx are among the comparatively few personalities of the early twelfth century whose lives and words will continue to attract and move the minds of men throughout the ages. All three are, though in very different ways, essentially of their own period and remote from ours in the circumstances of their lives and in the cast of their thought. The problems, the catastrophe and the fate of Abelard and Héloïse are, quite as much as the austere monastic life of Ailred, typical of the twelfth century and remote from the experience of the twentieth. All three, on the other hand, by reason of their intense sensibility to emotions shared in some degree by all civilized mankind, and by reason also of a vivid power of self-expression, are not only of an age but for all time. With neither of the characteristics just mentioned are we concerned here, however, but with a third: the peculiar cast, that is, given to their thoughts and emotions by the humanistic training which they had undergone.

This appears, as has been said, most clearly in the reverence and devotion with which they regarded certain great figures of antiquity. With Abelard and Héloïse it is Cicero, Seneca, Lucan and St. Jerome who are principally revered; with Ailred it is Cicero (at least in youth) and St. Augustine. That in the case of all three the influence has a strong religious colour and that its primary object is a saint (for St. Jerome is the exemplar to whom both Abelard and Héloïse turn most readily) does not affect its peculiar character. There is a world of difference between Abelard's attitude to Jerome or Ailred's to Augustine and the liturgical, quasi-feudal devotion of so many of their contemporaries to an apostle or an eponymous saint; equally, the reverence paid to the word of Seneca or Cicero is something personal, something coloured by emotion, and quite distinct from the immense but purely scientific authority given to Aristotle by St. Thomas or to Cicero by the grammarians. It is Jerome the man, inveighing against marriage or counselling Paula and Eustochium; it is Cicero the friend and the philosopher as pictured (however unhistorically) by the imagination of the twelfth century; it is "my own Augustine" of Ailred, the Augustine who loved and was loved by others, the Augustine of the *Confessions*, not the Doctor of Grace. Yet we may see a difference between Ailred and the other two. He is a humanist to the extent that he chooses out and turns for counsel to those minds of the past who had felt and suffered and striven as he had. Abelard and Héloïse "date" more clearly than Ailred because they, like their scholar-successors of the later Renaissance, take for masters and guides and models a few great men of the past chosen with a scholar's rather than with a Christian's mind, and set them on a pedestal, not indeed opposed to that on which Christ and His saints stand, but without direct reference to revealed, supernatural religion. Both, when coming to closest grips with their own tragic and most real and keenly felt problems, find their securest counsel and stay in the Stoics of the Empire—Seneca, Persius and Lucan—and in the letters of Jerome. Héloïse, indeed, who was at once the more absolute and final in her self-surrender and the one less susceptible of any spiritual influence, frankly turned for a model to Lucan and his Cornelia at the moment when she devoted herself irrevocably to the life for which she had no spiritual vocation. The passage in which Abelard described this crisis is so vivid as to deserve quotation in full:

> And she, as I remember well, when many full of sympathy for her youth were vainly endeavoring to deter her from submission to the monastic Rule as though it were an unbearable punishment—she, I say, breaking out as best she could amid her tears into Cornelia's famous lament, cried aloud: "O most renowned of husbands! O thou deemed unworthy of my bed! Had fortune, then, power thus far over such a one as thee? Why did I marry so rashly above my star, only to make him unhappy? Accept from me the penalty which I pay of my free choice." And with these words she hastened to the altar, and took from it the veil blessed by the bishop, and before all bound herself with the monastic vows.

It is hard to conceive a scene less characteristic than this of the monastic life of the twelfth century as commonly pictured: the despairing self-immolation of Héloïse, with the Stoic's cold phrases ringing in her ears, would be more in character in a heroine of Corneille or in some tragic story of a noble Roman house of the fifteenth century.

The third trait common to Abelard, Héloïse and Ailred, though again issuing in very different courses of action, is the importance which all attached to their personal emotions. With Abelard the crisis came comparatively late in life, when he was near his fortieth year. Previously, we may suppose, the vivid interests and brilliant successes of his intellectual life had kept all else suppressed; for the deterioration of character, due to wealth and fame, to which he attributed his fall, may supply a moral explanation, but does not of itself reveal the psychological background of the drama. In any case, his passion ran a not unusual course, though the genius of the man and the tragical *dénouement* of the affair have to some extent sublimated it in the eyes of posterity. From frank sensuality he rose to a deeper, if still wholly selfish, emotion; self-centered as he was, he must give his every mood expression (for in this, as in much else, he resembled a Newman or a Cicero), and the most acute dialectician of the schools, the successful rival of William of Champeaux and Anselm of Laon, became a singer of love lyrics which by their words and melody carried the name of Héloïse beyond the barriers of land and sea. All have perished, but when we read the hymns which Abelard wrote in a still later phase, we are not disposed to accuse of partiality the judgement passed upon his earlier verses by the one who was the theme of their praise.

Abelard's love for Héloïse long remained selfish; the sacrifices which it entailed were, as he himself pointed out somewhat coldly, the unwilled consequences and punishments of his fault, not a willing gift of self-surrender. Only when he had become a monk and a priest and was, partially at least, "converted" to the religious life, did his affection for Héloïse show itself in actions inspired by a genuine and selfless devotion. Indeed, it is by reason of the care shown by this strange ex-abbot for his wife who still more strangely found herself abbess, rather than by the earlier phases of his emotional drama, that Abelard stands among the humanists, in contrast to the more conventional religious sentiments of his day.

Héloïse, on the other hand, at once greater and not so great as her lover, gave all in a very real sense from the beginning. With her, motives of the intellectual order meant nothing, and those of the spiritual order little more. Héloïse in truth, so far as her own deepest utterances go, has nothing of the Christian in her. What renders her unique and gives her nobility and even sublimity is the combination of exceptional mental power and unshakable resolve with the most complete and voluntary self-sacrifice—not, indeed, the surrender of her own will and life to God or to any ethical demand, but the surrender of herself in totality to another. Clinging to this sacrifice with an intensity worthy of a heroine of Scandinavian legend—and indeed the blood of the pagan North may well have flowed in her veins—she found her model not in any saint of the Christian or even of the Hebrew centuries, but in the haughty and despairing women of ancient Rome, as they were depicted by the Stoic poet.

The life story of St. Ailred, when compared with those of Abelard and Héloïse, may have appeared tranquil enough to those who saw the distinguished abbot of the Yorkshire Rievaulx only on his travels up and down England or at his appearances at court. Yet in his life's journey, too, as in that of "his" Augustine, the heart had shared the traces with the head and if, here also like Augustine, he had found a final peace where both head and heart might rest secure, he underwent no violent change of character and retained to the end his fresh, warm, spontaneous readiness to give and to receive love—a love transmuted into a wholly benevolent and unselfish goodwill, embracing all who would accept it, yet having for each the delicate individuality of a mother's love, to which indeed his biographer, writing half a century before St. Francis had made the expression familiar, did not hesitate to compare it.

St. Augustine the thinker, the preacher and the theologian, had dominated and saturated the intellectual life of the West to a degree which even now is not, perhaps, sufficiently realized; Augustine "the man," the Augustine of Monica and the *Confessions*, appears but rarely. It is the peculiar characteristic of Ailred that he was, until Petrarch's day, almost the only one to approach his Augustine through the *Confessions*, to recognize in him a fellowship of deep feeling, and to look to him as a predecessor and a guide in his own pilgrimage. To him, as to his illustrious exemplar, the April days of his boyhood, days of shine and shower in a Northumbrian school where he had for fellow and friend the Prince Henry, son of King David of Scotland, were an abiding memory, rich in moulding influence.

> When I was still a boy at school [wrote Ailred later at Rievaulx], and took great delight in the charm of the companionship of those around me, it seemed good to me to give myself up unreservedly to my heart's leading and to dedicate myself to friendship. Nothing to me seemed more delightful, more sweet, or more profitable than to love and to be loved.

As Augustine had been stung to thought by Cicero, so Ailred, reading the Roman orator's *De Amicitia*, was humiliated at the contrast between his own impulsive, dominating emotions and the calm dignity, as it seemed to him, of Cicero's judgements, and though he had none of Augustine's intellectual crises, he found at the court of King David of Scotland, where he held for a time official rank, ties of ambition and affection not dissimilar to those which had held the great African shackled. When he describes his struggle to us, he falls naturally into the very rhythm of the *Confessions*, though the sincerity of personal experience is all his own.

When once he had found his spiritual home at Rievaulx, Ailred's great and in some ways unique gifts of mind and soul found full scope. To the visitor of today, who surveys the white ruins across the lawns and foliage of their exquisite setting, the past inevitably takes shape in a vision of the hard, sparing life of Cîteaux, shut out for ever from the world. The Rievaulx of St. William, St. Waldef and St. Ailred had indeed an observant, austere and deeply spiritual life, but perhaps no greater surprise in all the varied life of the twelfth century awaits the student familiar only with feudalism, Domesday and the crusades than his first glimpse of the fermenting life at Rievaulx in its secluded dale—an overflowing household of more than a hundred monks and five hundred lay brothers, with its centre of acute intellectual debate and its interplay of eager and ardent personalities. Here indeed, far from the familiar centres of European life, is the quintessence of the humanism of the twelfth century; Ailred, the novice-master and teacher, surrounded by a small group of finely educated young minds absorbed in living debates—Ailred, the friend and guide, learning recollection and true charity from his contact with others—Ailred the abbot, in middle age and in premature old age brought on by long and sharp illness, the centre of an ever shifting gathering of his sons to whom he, with his old charm intensified by suffering and sanctity, was all things to all, now discussing the nature of the soul in a dialogue left unfinished at his death, now counselling an illiterate lay-brother with equal care, while around him the fixed life of choir and farm-work, of changeless routine and sparing diet, went on unchanged.

> We his monks were around him [writes Walter Daniel of his last days on earth], now twelve in number, now twenty, now forty, now even a hundred, for he who loved us all was thus loved exceedingly by us in return . . . and he considered it his greatest happiness that he should be thus loved. No one ever said to us "Depart, be off, do not touch your abbot's bed," but stepping upon his pallet or sitting upon it we spoke with him as a child speaks with its mother.

And so he died, surrounded by his monks, lying on the sackcloth and ashes of the monastic custumal, with his eyes upon the crucifix on the wall.

The familiarity of all educated men of the age with the masterpieces of Latin literature has often been remarked upon. The mention of Héloïse touches upon another aspect of this renaissance: the share, that is, of women in the higher culture of the day. Héloïse, indeed, was something of a prodigy, but nowhere is there any suggestion that her uncle, Fulbert, was acting in an eccentric or even in an unconventional manner when he decided to give his niece a perfect education in letters. Nor did she stand wholly alone. It may not be easy to point to individual *bas bleus* in Paris or even in the convents of France in general, but in England there was no lack of them. The daughter of Margaret of Scotland, the future Queen Maud, was given a thorough literary education at Romsey; Shaftesbury, a little later, sheltered Marie de France, and Muriel of Wilton was not the only other poetess in England, as is shown by the numerous copies of Latin verses attached by the convents of women to the bead-rolls of exalted personages. These cloistered elegists, however, scarcely differ in kind from their sisters who, four hundred years before, had corresponded with St. Boniface; Héloïse, alike in her single-minded enthusiasm, in her real literary powers, and in her devoted, even pedantic reverence for her classical models, is a true predecessor of Camilla Rucellai, Margaret Roper and Lady Jane Grey; to her, as to these, Dorothea in George Eliot's novel would have looked with admiration.

Héloïse may well have outdistanced all rivals of her own sex. In deploring the lack of letters among men, however, Peter the Venerable, in his celebrated letter to the widowed abbess, is using the language of exaggeration, for no one acquainted with the literature of the age can be unaware of the wide familiarity shown by so many with Latin literature. Ailred of Rievaulx can assume a familiarity with Cicero's *De Amicitia* as a matter of course in a young Cistercian of his abbey; quotations from the poets are common in almost all the more elaborate chronicles and letters of the period; the greatest humanists, such as Hildebert of Lavardin, Abelard and John of Salisbury, quote aptly and copiously from a very wide range of Latin poetry. Rarely, perhaps, are the poets quoted solely on account of the intrinsic beauty of their words; Abelard, however, and John of Salisbury often give evidence of their appreciation of the purely poetic. For most the favourite authors are the rhetoricians and satirists of the Silver Age and the learned, artificial poets of the later Gallo-Roman culture. Though Virgil has pride of place, it may be suggested that even he may appear rhetorical to a superficial and unintuitive mind; Horace, significantly enough, is often quoted from the *Satires* and *Epistles,* rarely from the *Odes*—their beauty, it may be, was too sophisticated and too exquisite to be appreciated, their urbanity too unfamiliar, and their pagan morality and religion too obvious. For similar reasons Tibullus and Propertius rarely occur, and scarcity of manuscripts is sufficient of itself to account for unfamiliarity with Lucretius and Catullus. Juvenal, on the other hand, Lucan and the difficult Persius were, relatively speaking, more familiar to the contemporaries of Abelard than to classical scholars of today.

Nothing, perhaps, shows both the reality and the extent of the training on classical models than the facility with which numbers were able to compose sets of perfectly correct Latin verses, and that not only in hexameters and elegiacs, but in the lyric metres used by Horace and Catullus. That the inhabitants of nunneries in Wessex should have been able to write passable elegiacs, and that it should have seemed natural to a monk when composing a saint's life to break without warning or apparent reason into alcaics, hendecasyllabics and the still more elaborate iambic and trochaic metres, are phenomena of the late eleventh century to which it would be hard to find a parallel save in the late fifteenth or early sixteenth. That only a few—a Peter Damian, an Abelard, a Hildebert—should have attained real poetry in their compositions should be no occasion for wonder; the rest fail where the most felicitous versus of a Jebb, of a Calverley, and even of a Milton fail; the remarkable fact is that so many had achieved a mastery of the language and the metre without any aid from a Gradus or dictionary. Occasionally, indeed, the level of true poetry is attained, together with perfect felicity of vocabulary; Peter Damian's Sapphic hymns to St. Benedict, like the earlier hymn to the Baptist, *Ut queant laxis,* are supreme in their kind, and it would be difficult for a scholar, familiar only with ancient Latin literature, to assign their composition to the eleventh rather than to the sixth or the sixteenth century. More often, however, the nearest approach to true poetry is made in the simpler accentual metres and the lyrics that verge upon the vernacular.

The decline of this humanism, like its rise, was comparatively rapid. The phase of sentiment we are considering touched its apogee between the rise of Hildebert of Lavardin and the central years of the literary life of John of Salisbury. With Peter of Blois the decline is beginning, and though in England there was something of a time-lag, the end was reached with Walter Map, Gerald of Wales and their circle; Gerald, indeed, lived on into another world and lamented the change. By the death of King John the transformation was complete. The great figures of the early thirteenth century, whether thinkers or administrators, are all but inarticulate when not in their schools or chanceries. It is from the class of the unlettered, from a Francis of Assisi or a Joinville, that the clearest utterances come, "the earliest pipe of half-awakened birds," heralding another dawn in Europe. Literary, philosophical, scholarly humanism was dead, and it is significant that the supreme and balanced art, the Pheidian assurance and repose of the sculptures of Chartres, of Wells, of Amiens and of Rheims, was the expression of life as seen, not by a Leonardo or a Michelangelo, but by unlettered handicraftsmen living wholly in the present and wholly ignorant of the literature and culture of the past.

This is not to say that the new age owed no debt, paid no homage, to the past. In one sense the debt of no century had been heavier; for, as recent scholarship has shown, a larger and larger portion of the corpus of Aristotelian writings and numerous dialogues of Plato and Greek philosophers of the Empire were becoming familiar to the West, together with works of science, Greek and Arabian. St. Thomas rests upon Aristotle, "the Philosopher," more completely and unreservedly than does Abelard upon Augustine or Jerome or Seneca; and, as regards language, all metal is tested upon the touchstone of Cicero. Plato, Aristotle and Augustine, in their various ways, are not merely the foundations of the fabric of scholasticism; they are its *materia prima,* the very medium in which Aquinas works. Yet scholars of today who, when rightly demonstrating the traditional and wholly European character of medieval culture, emphasize the debt of the schoolmen to the ancients, may perhaps mislead those familiar only with modern history when they speak of the humanism, or of the classical tradition, of the great scholastics. The attitude of

St. Thomas towards the masters of the past differs by a whole heaven from that of Abelard and Ailred, as it does from that of Erasmus and More. The humanists, though living in times so very different from those of Greece and Rome, scrutinize the lives and emotions of the ancients, imitate their modes of expression and seek to reach the heart of their thought by long and sympathetic examination; the schoolmen revere the past no less deeply, but it is the external, visible fabric of thought, the purely intellectual, impersonal element that they absorb, and so far from submitting themselves to its moulding influence, they adapt it without hesitation to serve a wholly new system of philosophy, an utterly different *Weltanschauung*. To the schoolmen the personalities, the emotions, the external vicissitudes of the lives of Aristotle and Augustine meant nothing; the skeleton of their thought was all in all. To Ailred and to Héloïse, as to the contemporaries of Cosimo de' Medici, the joy and anguish of an Augustine or a Cornelia were a consolation and a light; they turned to them, and to the poets of the past, for guidance and sympathy. "Then 'twas the Roman, now 'tis I." So the humanists, but never the schoolmen, found strength in a community of feeling with those who, centuries before, had trodden the same path, and it is this consciousness of the unchanging mind of man that divides the culture of the first Renaissance from the more familiar culture of the later Middle Ages.

CHAPTER 16

Medieval Humanism

R. W. Southern

As a general rule medieval historians do well to avoid words which end in "ism." They are words which belong to a recent period of history, and their use injects into the past the ideas of a later age. But some of these words like feudalism, romanticism, and humanism have become so closely bound up with our conception of various periods of history that it is almost impossible to write of these periods without some reference to the words which have been so often used to describe their main characteristics. They distort, but they also summarise a large assortment of facts and impressions; and we are obliged sometimes to ask what they mean and whether they correctly describe the main traits of the ages to which they have been applied.

One of the main difficulties with the word "humanism" is that it has two distinct, though related, meanings, and historians have used the word sometimes in one sense and sometimes in the other, and sometimes in a mixture of the two. This has caused a good deal of confusion. The most general meaning of the word according to the Oxford English Dictionary is "any system of thought or action which is concerned with merely human interests or with those of the human race in general." It is in this sense that this word is now in popular use, especially among those who call themselves humanists. This meaning of the word associates humanism with the extension of the area of human knowledge and activity, and consequently with the activity of limiting (or abolishing) the supernatural in human affairs. Its main instrument is scientific knowledge leading ultimately to a single coherent rational view of the whole of nature, including the nature of men. I shall call this the "scientific" view of humanism. I suppose that most people who support this type of humanism look on the medieval period—with its emphasis on the supernatural end of man, with its insistence on the primacy of theology among the sciences, with its predominantly clerical culture and hierarchical organization under a universal papal authority—as the embodiment of all that they most bitterly oppose.

From R. W. Southern, *Medieval Humanism* (Cambridge: Basil Blackwell, Ltd., 1970), pp. 29–41, 48–50, 58–60. Reprinted by permission of Basil Blackwell Publisher. A revised and much enlarged version of this essay will appear in Vol. I of R. W. Southern's *Scholastic Humanism and the Unification of Europe*.

Alongside this popular view of humanism, there is also an academic view which goes back to the Renaissance. In this view, the essential feature of humanism is the study of ancient Latin and Greek literature: hence the use of phrases like "Professor of Humanity" and "literae humaniores" in our academic jargon. These studies were regarded as pre-eminently *humane* in contrast to the formal and systematic studies of the Middle Ages in scholastic theology, canon law and logic, which were thought to have excluded humanity, destroyed style, and to have dissociated scholarship from the affairs of the world and men. I shall call this the "literary" view of humanism. On this view of the matter the Middle Ages, in the eyes of the early literary humanists, represented the enemy, not only in their comparative neglect of the literary qualities of the ancient masterpieces, but also in their supposed neglect of the human qualities which the study of these masterpieces inculcated.

The protagonists of both these types of humanism, therefore, have generally looked on the Middle Ages as hostile country. Historians indeed have protested, and on many grounds. They have pointed out that the Middle Ages cannot be lumped together in a single undifferentiated period of a thousand years, and they have singled out the Carolingian age and the twelfth century as periods of "Renaissance" and "humanism" in one sense or another; they have brought to light medieval lovers of classical literature and writers of elegant Latin prose and poetry; they have spoken of medieval science, and medieval Platonism, and medieval influences on Renaissance scholarship and so on. But there is a confusion of voices. Those who have spoken most forcibly about the humanism of the twelfth century have been inclined to admit that it was short-lived, and that there was a falling-away long before the beginning of the thirteenth century. Those who have extolled the medieval stylists and lovers of the classics have found them disconcertingly indifferent to the authors whose words they quoted so lavishly. As we watch so notable a humanist as John of Salisbury striding through the classics, heaping up each page with quotations from half a dozen authors, with sovereign indifference to the source, we are forced to ask what kind of sensitivity to ancient literature this great man possessed. Certainly it was not the sensitivity of a Petrarch.

The confusions of the subject could be discussed without end—confusions in the use of words, confusions in the views of historians, confusions in the subject itself. Instead of pursuing these shadows let me attempt to state quite simply why, and in what sense, I believe the period from about 1100 to about 1320 to have been one of the great ages of humanism in the history of Europe: perhaps the greatest of all. As a corollary of this I shall argue that, far from the humanism of the twelfth century running into the sand after about 1150 to re-emerge two centuries later, it had its fulfillment in the thirteenth and early fourteenth centuries—in the period which the humanists of the Renaissance most despised. Lastly I shall ask why the humanism of this period appeared so repellent to the humanists of a later age.

In order to discuss these questions, we must first be clear [about] what we are looking for. What are the symptoms which will establish the existence of a deep-seated humanism in the period we are to study? I take them to be these:

In the first place there can be no humanism without a strong sense of the dignity of human nature. That man is a fallen creature, that he has lost his immediate knowledge of God, that his instincts and reason are often in conflict, and that he is radically disorganized and disorientated—all this is common ground to all Christian thinkers. We must not expect a denial of these facts in the Middle Ages, or even for that matter in the Renaissance; but we may expect a humanist to assert not only that man is the noblest of God's creatures, but also that his nobility continues even in his fallen state, that it is capable of development in this world, that the instruments exist by which it can be developed, and that it should be the chief aim of human endeavour to perfect these instruments.

Along with this large view of man's natural dignity there must go a recognition of the dignity of nature itself. This second feature of humanism is a consequence of the first, for if man is by nature noble, the natural order itself, of which he forms part, must be noble. The two are linked together by indissoluble ties, and the power to recognize the grandeur and splendour of the universe is itself one of the greatest expressions of the grandeur and splendour of man. Thus man takes his place in nature; and human society is seen as part of the grand complex of the natural order bound together by laws similar to those which tie all things into one.

Finally the whole universe appears intelligible and accessible to human reason: nature is seen as an orderly system, and man—in understanding the laws of nature—understands himself as the main part, the key-stone, of nature. Without this understanding it is hard to see how men can experience that confidence in human powers which humanism implies.

When those elements of dignity, order, reason and intelligibility are prominent in human experience, we may reasonably describe as humanistic the outlook which ensues. This humanism will be much nearer to the type I have described as "scientific" than to "literary" humanism, but I believe that this must be our starting point in any study of the central period of the Middle Ages.

The starting point is important because the subject has been confused by the tendency to start with the humanism of the Renaissance. This has given the love of ancient literature and the ability to imitate the style of ancient authors an exaggerated importance in judging medieval humanism. If we start with the concepts of natural nobility and of reason and intelligible order in the universe, the whole subject takes on a different appearance.

We may at once say that there is little evidence that these concepts played an important part in medieval experience before about 1050. In the main tradition of the early Middle Ages nearly all the order and dignity in the world was closely associated with supernatural power. There was order in symbolism and ritual, and order in worship and sacrament, and both of them were very elaborate and impressive. Man's links with the supernatural gave his life a framework of order and dignity; but in the natural order the chaos was almost complete. Almost nothing was known about secondary causes in natural events. Rational procedures in law, in government, in medicine, in argument, were scarcely understood or practised even in the most elementary way. Man chiefly knew himself as a vehicle for divine activity. There was a profound sense of the littleness and sinfulness of man. Both physically and mentally human life had narrow limits: only in prayer and penance, in clinging to the saints, was there any enlargement. Man was an abject being, except when he was clad in symbolic garments, performing symbolic and sacramental acts, and holding in his hands the earthly remains of those who already belonged to the spiritual world.

That at least is how I interpret the main evidence for the period before the late eleventh century. Perhaps this awe-struck, sacramental view of man's place and powerlessness in the world gives a more satisfactory account of man's situation in the universe than the optimism of the succeeding centuries; and optimism never overcame the final impotence of man and his need for supernatural aid. But there is a sharp change of emphasis after about 1050. It is this change of emphasis that we are to examine.

We shall look first into the monasteries, for they were the great centres of supernatural influence in the early Middle Ages, and it is in them that we see the first signs of a change that had a profound effect on the religious life of Europe. Briefly, the change took the form of a greater concentration on man and on human experience as a means of knowing God. This was a significant step towards the restoration of the dignity of man, for it made the study of man an integral part of religious life. The search for God within the soul became one of the chief preoccupations of the monastic leaders of the late eleventh and twelfth centuries and this search expanded into a general demand for self-knowledge. The search took many forms and can be found in many places. For my part I find one of its most significant moments in Normandy in 1079. In this year Anselm at Bec entered into the chamber of his mind, excluded everything but the word "God," and found that suddenly the word articulated itself into a demonstration of God's existence, which he believed to be both new and true. It was new, and whether or not it was true, it was a triumph of an analytical introspective method. It seemed to show that men could find new truths of the greatest general importance simply by looking within themselves. The idea of finding something new was itself new to a generation which had believed itself to be at the end of the road; and to find the new things so close at hand, and so entirely central, was a revelation of the powers that lay within man's mind.

It was St. Bernard, a generation later, who popularized the method of introspection and made it the property of a school of monastic writers. He gave the whole exercise a new direction. He was not interested, like Anselm, in logic or analysis, but only in spiritual growth. According to Bernard, man's love of God begins with man's love of himself for himself alone. This love can be refined by reason and virtue until it gives birth to the love of one's neighbour, and this in turn to the love of God. So here too we find a programme of spiritual growth starting with man, and with a most unpromising aspect of man, his self-love. The programme is rooted in nature, and it uses the instruments of natural virtue to reach a supernatural end. From nature itself arises the necessity for turning to God.

To begin with man and nature and to find in them the road to God is very characteristic of the new age. As St. Bernard's younger contemporary, Richard of St. Victor, said:

> A man raises his eyes in vain to see God who has not yet succeeded in seeing himself. Let a man first learn to understand the invisible things of himself before he presumes to stretch out to the invisible things of God . . . for unless you can understand yourself, how can you try to understand those things which are above yourself?

This search for man was at first a monastic programme, and it was in the monasteries also that another aspect of human experience began to be appreciated—the experience of friendship. Without the cultivation of friendship there can be no true humanism. If self-knowledge is the first step in the rehabilitation of man, friendship—which is the sharing of this knowledge with someone else—is an important auxiliary. This was understood by the humanists of the Renaissance; but the discovery was made in the monasteries of the late eleventh century.

Here again, it was St. Anselm who first in his generation groped for words to express the intensity of his feelings for his friends. But very soon in many places friendship came to appear an essential part of a full religious life. By 1160 Aelred of Rievaulx was able to sum up the results of the monastic experience of the past century in the words "Friendship is widsom," "*amicitia nihil aliud est quam sapientia*," or even "God is friendship," "*Deus est amicitia*." He was careful to say that these phrases had to be accepted with some reserve, but they expressed the close relationship between human friendship and the nature of God. The experience of friendship lay along the road to God. Nature, said Aelred, makes man desire friendship, experience fortifies it, reason regulates it, and the religious life perfects it. So here again we start with nature and end with God. The treatise that Aelred wrote on friendship is the most beautiful example of the casting of an ancient humanistic theme into a Christian mould, and the sequence which it elaborates—nature prompting, reason regulating, experience strengthening, religion prefecting—is the basis of all religious humanism.

Of all the forms of friendship rediscovered in the twelfth century, there was none more eagerly sought than the friendship between God and man. This may seem a commonplace theme, and one which had been debased by countless sentimentalities and trivialities. But it was once fresh, and it lifted a great weight from men's lives. In the early Middle Ages God had not appeared as a friend. By great labour and exertion, by crippling penances and gifts to the Church, by turning from the world to the monastic life, men might avert God's anger: but of God as a friend they knew little or nothing. It was terribly difficult to approach Him. Then quite suddenly the terror faded and the sun shone.

There were many forces working in this direction. One of them was just a new way of thinking about God. Prayers, poems, devotions of all kinds, poured forth from the twelfth century onwards, which had one predominant theme—the humanity of God. I do not forget that one of these poems—the greatest of them, of about 1250—begins with the tremendous words:

Dies irae, dies illa,
solvet saeclum in favilla . . .
[That day of wrath, that dreadful day,
Shall the whole world in ashes lay]

But it is wrong to think that this superb poem simply describes a scene of terror. Its second half mitigates the terror by an appeal to the sufferings and humanity of Christ:

Recordare, Jesu pie
quod sum causa tuae viae,
ne me perdas illa die.
Quaerens me sedisti lassus;
redemisti, crucem passus:
tantus labor non sit cassus.
[Forget not what my ransom cost,
Nor let my dear-bought soul be lost
In storms of guilty terror tost
Thou who for me didst feel such pain
Whose precious blood the cross did stain
Let not these agonies be in vain—*

This is just one of the many signs that since the days of St. Anselm the God of human sufferings and emotions had become an object of tender contemplation. The whole creation had become filled with humanity. The theme is capable of an infinite amount of illustration, but I shall quote only a few sentences from an anonymous thirteenth century treatise on the use of adversity. It shows how even this theme so redolent of sin, misery and impotence has been sweetened by the common humanity of God and man:

Tribulations illuminate the heart of man with self-knowledge, and this is the perfection of the human condition.

Just as lovers send letters to each other to refresh their memories one of another, so Christ sends tribulations to refresh our memories of him and his sufferings.

By denying us earthly satisfactions God forces us to seek those which are heavenly, just as an earthly lord who wants to sell his own wine orders the public houses to close until he has sold it.

We may object that these gentle similes cover the harsh realities of the world with sentimentality, and this may be an inevitable result of humanism

*Trans. Wentworth Dillon.

in religion. But it is a form of humanism that has survived all the religious divisions of Europe, and it has made a lasting contribution to the way in which ordinary people have looked at the universe. Popular piety has never lost this sentimental familiarity.

Some may think that these religious themes, however expressed, are far from the themes of humanism. But if we are looking for a growing sense of human dignity, and for an enlargement of man's powers and place in the universe, the hymns and meditations of the twelfth and thirteenth centuries supply us with abundant evidence. Indeed these religious developments are perhaps the greatest triumph that humanism has ever achieved, for they conquered the universe for humanity, and made God so much man's friend that his actions became almost indistinguishable from our own.

The greatest triumph of medieval humanism was to make God seem human. The Ruler of the Universe, who had seemed so terrifying and remote, took on the appearance of a familiar friend. The next triumph was to make the universe itself friendly, familiar, and intelligible. This is an essential part of the heritage of western Europe which we owe to the scholars of the twelfth and thirteenth centuries. The experience of earlier centuries had suggested that so far as man could see, the universe was a scene of chaos and mystery, and that renunciation, submission to the supernatural, and a grateful acceptance of miraculous aid were the best that men could aim at. But in the late eleventh century, secular schools began to multiply which were dedicated to the task of extending the area of intelligibility and order in the world in a systematic way.

The importance of these schools for the intellectual development of Europe is very great. They provided permanent centres of learning which faced the world instead of facing away from it. The studies of the monasteries were necessarily dominated by the needs of the monastic life, but the secular schools belonged to the world. They were normally found in centres of urban life. They drew their scholars from a class of men who expected to live in the world and to make their careers in the government of church and state. The greatest of these schools became the prototypes of all modern universities. Oxford, Paris and Bologna have had a continuous history since the twelfth century: likewise our academic faculties and disciplines have had an unbroken development since that time. These schools and universities and disciplines have many achievements to their credit, but their first achievement was the foundation of all others: they brought the idea of an indefinitely expanding order and rationality into every area of human experience.

The emancipating role of the medieval schools has been obscured partly by the prejudices and misconceptions of a later age, and partly by the hardening of the arteries that afflicts all institutions in the course of time. Later scholars, who saw that the medieval secular schools existed to train tonsured clerks in sciences necessary for running ecclesiastical courts and institutions, could not understand that they had once been the great liberating force in European thought. They could not see how small was the gap that separated the clerks of these schools from the secular world. The masters and scholars wore the ecclesiastical tonsure and were subject to ecclesiastical courts, but many of them looked forward to employment in secular business. They were willing to use their skills as much to oppose ecclesiastical claims as to promote them. They had no sense of separation from secular affairs. Contemporaries criticised them for wasting the resources of the Church on studies irrelevant or hostile to the purposes of the Church, and though this was a narrow-minded criticism it was nearer the truth than the later charge of subservience to ecclesiastical interests. Certainly it would be difficult to imagine a less clerical body, in any modern sense of the word, than the unruly and undisciplined communities of the medieval universities. This was an aspect of the medieval schools hidden from the view of later critics who could only see them engaged in a long struggle to preserve a clerical monopoly in academic effort.

As for the curriculum and methods of study of the schools, they came to seem very arid to almost all thinking men. In the early days of the revival of medieval studies, no more than a century ago, the best that a deeply learned and serious observer could find to say about medieval scholastic writers was that:

> those men handed down to us much precious knowledge, with much verbiage and false logic. . . . They ticketed every portion of man's moral anatomy, found a rule for every possible case of choice, a reason and a reward for every virtue, and a punishment for every conceivable crime; they turned generalizations into law, and deduced from them as laws the very facts from which they had generalized. They benefited mankind by exercising and training subtle wits, and they reduced dialectics, almost, we might say, logic itself, to absurdity. . . . In reading Thomas Aquinas one is constantly provoked to say, What could not such a mind have done if it had not been fettered by such a method?

These are in their way very judicious remarks: this is what it all came to in the end. But in the beginning, the medieval scholastic curriculum met an urgent need for order in the intellectual outlook of a Europe first rising to independent thought. At that time the only available instrument of intellectual order was a thorough command of the sciences and techniques of the Greco-Roman world so far as they had been preserved in the West. This command was achieved, and it brought intellectual order into human life in a wonderfully short space of time. No doubt it is possible to imagine better starting-points. But none other was available, and we must judge the achievement in the light of the problems and the tools that lay to hand.

I have said that there can be no humanism without a strong sense of the dignity and intelligibility of man and nature; and if God exists, the same qualities must characterize the relations of God with his creation. These phrases could almost be taken as a description of the programme of the medieval secular schools. One of the first things they did was to renew a sense of the dignity and nobility of man. These terms are rare in the eleventh century, but very common in the twelfth. They meant that man's powers of reason and will, cultivated as they can be by study, give him a splendour which survives all the effects of sin and degeneration. As a twelfth century schoolmaster, Bernard Silvestris, wrote:

The animals express their brute creation
By head hung low and downward looking eyes;
But man holds high his head in contemplation
To show his natural kinship with skies.
He sees the stars obey God's legislation:
They teach the laws by which mankind can rise.

These images were largely borrowed from Ovid, but whereas in Ovid they were a poetic fiction, for the twelfth century scholar they were a scientific fact. They provided a basis for intellectual ambition and optimism. For scholars of an earlier generation the dignity of man and nature had been lost through sin, and could only be restored by supernatural means. But the leading scholars of the secular schools, from the beginning of the twelfth century onwards, stressed the natural remedies to the ravages of sin, and saw the seven liberal arts as instruments for the mitigation of human frailties.

This view of the nature of man and his hopes for the future was based on man's apparently unlimited capacity for knowledge. It may seem strange that scholars who had so recently emerged from an extremely pessimistic view of human capacities, and who believed that man's faculties had been grievously impaired by sin, should rush to the other extreme and proclaim that everything, or almost everything, could be known. But in intellectual affairs almost all revolutions are violent, and this was no exception. Scholars discovered that there existed a scientific basis for optimism. They learnt from their sources that man's affinity with every part of nature gives him the power to understand everything in nature; that his elements and humours, and the influences playing upon his birth and development, are the raw materials for the whole universe. Hence man, being the epitome of the universe, is built to understand the universe. Despite the ravages of sin, he can still intellectually trace the primitive perfection of the creation, and collaborate with God in its restoration.

The instrument of this collaboration with God in the regeneration of nature is reason. With comprehensive enthusiasm, the secular masters of the early twelfth century began to let fall such *dicta* as these: "The dignity of our mind is its capacity to know all things"; "We who have been endowed by nature with genius must seek through philosophy the stature of our primeval nature"; "In the solitude of this life the chief solace of our minds is the study of wisdom"; "We have joined together science and letters, that from this marriage there may come forth a free nation of philosophers." These were ancient thoughts, but for the first time for many centuries we find men confident that all those things could be done and that nature could be known. Hence the future seemed bright. Men knew little as yet, but they could know everything, and already, as it seemed to those optimistic masters, they knew more than had ever been known before. At last, in a famous phrase of Bernard of Chartres, they "stood on the shoulders of the giants, and could see further than their great predecessors." They had mastered the past:

His eagle eye could clearly see
through each perplexed obscurity

of all the seven liberal arts.
He knew them well in all their parts,
and made quite clear to everyone
truths that for Plato dimly shone.

This was the epitaph of Thierry, one of the great masters who died about
1150. The idea that he could see further than Plato, not through revelation but
through superior science, was surely very bold. Thierry was only one of a
large number of masters responsible for the intellectual revival I have been describing. A surprisingly high proportion of them died or retired in the decade
before 1150; Abelard, Hugh of St. Victor, William of Conches, Thierry, Bernard
Silvestris. It has seemed to many scholars that humanism died with them. Certainly some freshness and charm died with them. But if we look at the principles of enquiry for which they stood, the main current of their work suffered
no setback. These men represented the intellectual adolescence of Europe, and
it is natural to mourn the passing of youth. But we must not exaggerate their
youthful achievement. What they made was partly a ground-plan and partly a
castle in the air. It still remained to build on the foundation and to give reality
to the vision.

• • •

No reality is ever as beautiful as the vision. When people see the elaborate
structures of thirteenth century thought and compare them with the visions of
the age of William of Conches they find them less interesting in detail, less liberating in their effects, and less beautiful in their expression. Consequently
they are apt to think that the intention of the later thinkers was quite different
and much less humane. But the main difference is that the later writers knew
vastly more than their predecessors and they had to work harder to integrate
their material. The lack of new material, which had threatened to bring the humanism of the early twelfth century to a halt, was abundantly made good by
the flow of new translations in the century after 1150. By 1250 virtually the
whole corpus of Greek science was accessible to the western world, and scholars groaned under its weight as they strove to master it all. The days had gone
when two large volumes could hold all that was essential for the study of the
liberal arts. There was no time for artistic presentation and literary eloquence.
This was a grave loss, but the achievement was there all the same. The main
ideas of the earlier masters—the dignity of man, the intelligibility of the universe, the nobility of nature—not only remained intact, but were fundamental
concepts in the intellectual structures of the thirteenth century.

These concepts were so much taken for granted that they no longer seemed
to call for poetic expression. They were introduced as a matter of course into
the most technical discussions on the most unlikely subjects. I have in front of
me a highly abstract argument about the Incarnation, written by the first great
Oxford master, Robert Grosseteste, about 1230. If we compare it with Anselm's
great treatise on the same subject, completed just a hundred and thirty years

earlier, we see the great difference that the scientific humanism of the intervening period had made. Anselm is far superior in literary grace, but Grosseteste is inspired by a much more profound humanism. Anselm had argued that the Incarnation was necessary because man had sinned beyond the possibility of redemption by any other means, and that God necessarily became man, not because of any quality in man, but because of his otherwise total ruin. For Grosseteste the picture was quite different. He too saw God's Incarnation as necessary for man's salvation. But it was not man's sin that made it necessary: it was necessary for the completion of man's nature, and it would have happened if man had never sinned. It was therefore not a last desperate throwing of God's final reserves into a battle that was almost lost. It was a final act in the unfolding drama of creation: it made Man and Nature complete, and it bound the whole created universe together in union with God.

Whether this is good theology or good science I do not know. But it is certainly profoundly humanistic in a way that Anselm's argument is not. It is filled with a conception of a human dignity so exalted that God could not stop short of Incarnation, and of a natural order so sublime that it required to be completed by a God-perfected man. This is the final step in scientific humanism. It was not a step that was generally taken by Grosseteste's contemporaries, but a large body of the theological work of the thirteenth century displays a similar faith in man and nature. Indeed the chief objection that can be brought against scholastic theology is not its lack of humanism, but its persistent tendency to make man appear more rational, human nature more noble, the divine ordering of the universe more open to human inspection, and the whole complex of man, nature and God more fully intelligible, than we can now believe to be plausible. But—regarded simply as an effort to comprehend the structure of the universe and, in the striking image of William of Conches, to demonstrate the dignity of the human mind by showing that it can know all things—this body of thought is one of the most ambitious displays of scientific humanism ever attempted.

From this point of view, the two *Summae* of Thomas Aquinas mark the highest point of medieval humanism. . . . The reader is tempted to say as he reads: "Of course there are things man cannot yet understand—but not many; of course man is a sinner—but how wonderfully the ravages of sin have been restored by reason, and how easy, how natural, how rational the steps to salvation." The natural faculties are no longer in ruins. Reason and nature have inherited the world. The work of Thomas Aquinas is full of illustrations of the supremacy of reason and nature. His judgements nearly always give the natural man rather more than his due. He reversed the ancient opinion that the body is the ruined habitation of the soul, and held with Aristotle that it is the basis of the soul's being. Everywhere he points to the natural perfection of man, his natural rights, and the power of his natural reason. The dignity of human nature is not simply a poetic vision; it has become a central truth of philosophy.

Thomas Aquinas died in 1274, and it is probably true that man has never appeared so important a being in so well-ordered and intelligible a universe as in his works. Man was important because he was the link between the created universe and the divine intelligence. He alone in the world of nature could understand nature. He alone in nature could understand the nature of God. He alone could use and perfect nature in accordance with the will of God, and thus achieve his full nobility.

• • •

Many reasons may be given for rejecting the kind of humanism we have been considering. We may disagree with its theological basis, or its belief in the intelligibility of the universe, or the central position accorded to man, or the optimism about man's rational powers. But it is at first sight puzzling that men who had no quarrel with God or with reason, and who sought to glorify man, should have denied that the ways of thinking I have described had any claim to be called humanistic. Anyone who knew anything about the world of the eleventh century would have had to agree that the dignity of man, the intelligibility of the world and of God, and the application of reason to practical affairs had made such progress in the twelfth and thirteenth centuries that they had become the central features of all thought and experience. Why then did these two centuries come to seem in retrospect so hostile to humanistic values?

I think the main explanation to this puzzle lies in the early fourteenth century. Europe then entered a period when the optimism which had buoyed up the efforts of the previous two centuries was abruptly destroyed: the flow of new intellectual materials came to an end; the forward movement in settlement and expansion came to a halt; the area of disorder in the world was everywhere increasing; everything began to seem insecure. Until this time it had seemed that, however horrible the present might be, the future was likely to be better. It was reasonable to believe that all the new information about the universe could be fitted into one grand universal plan, and it was not unreasonable to think that the papal, or perhaps the imperial, system of universal authority would in time bring universal peace. There was very little ground for thinking that the universe and God might after all be beyond the reach of reason, and humanly speaking chaotic.

But quite quickly this whole situation changed. It does not need a dramatic disaster to change the intellectual outlook of a generation. It only needs a slight change of direction, the end of expansion, the drying up of sources of information, a series of small setbacks, a persistent sense that nothing is going well. Petrarch, who above all stood for a new kind of humanism in the mid-fourteenth century, had reason to be disillusioned with the achievements of the last two centuries. The kind of intellectual and practical order at which men had aimed suddenly seemed quite unattainable:

> Turn where you will, there is no place without its tyrant; and where there is no tyrant, the people themselves supply the deficiency. When you escape the One, you fall into the hands of the Many. If you can show me a place ruled by a just and mild king, I will take myself there with all my baggage. . . . I will

go to India or Persia or the furthest limits of the Garamantes to find such a place and such a king. But it is useless to search for what cannot be found. Thanks to our age, which has levelled all things, the labour is unnecessary.

The hopes of the past had to be buried. But such hopes are never buried with simple quiet resignation: they have to be buried with scorn and derision and a sense of betrayal. Hence the clerical schools with their formalised procedures and legalistic distinctions came to be seen, not simply as the agents of a great failure, but as the promoters of a great enslavement.

All systems of thought have some pervasive weakness built into their structure, and the weakness is all the more ineradicable when it forms in some sense the strength of the system. The characteristic weakness of medieval scientific thought was its dependence on *auctoritates* and *sententiae*. These were the bricks from which the system was formed; they provided the material for argument and the foundations for the most daring conclusions. But they also defined limits beyond which the system could not develop. So the moment of stasis was bound to come sooner or later. This is not a phenomenon peculiar to medieval thought or to scholastic processes of argument; it is a universal phenomenon in the development of every system; but the moment arrived in the Middle Ages with a peculiarly paralysing effect because it arrived without warning.

As soon as men lost confidence in the system and its aims, the details all appeared intensely repellent. No books have ever been written that give less invitation to study by their physical appearance than the manuscripts of the medieval schools; their illegible script, crabbed abbreviations, and margins filled with comments even less legible than the text, invite derision. As soon as men lost confidence in the end toward which this whole apparatus of learning moved, the adjuncts were bound to seem barbarous and inhumane. They had no beauty of style or vivacity of wit to support them.

Hence, as the residuary legatee of the scientific and systematic humanism of the twelfth and thirteenth centuries, a new kind of humanism came into existence. It was the product of disillusion with the great projects of the recent past. When the hope of universal order faded, the cultivation of sensibility and personal virtue, and the nostalgic vision of an ancient utopia revealed in classical literature, remained as the chief supports of humane values. Instead of the confident and progressive humanism of the central Middle Ages, the new humanism retreated into the individual and the past; it saw the aristocracy rather than the clergy as the guardians of culture; its sought inspiration in literature rather than theology and science; its ideal was a group of friends rather than a universal system; and the nobility of man was expressed in his struggle with an unintelligible world rather than in his capacity to know all things. When this happened the humanism of the central Middle Ages came to be mistaken for formalism and hostility to human experience.

CHAPTER 17

Renaissance or Proto-Renaissance?

Eva Matthews Sanford

There are two phases of our problem: what do we mean by a renaissance, and does the twelfth century conform to this definition sufficiently to justify giving it the name? Since the term was first applied to the humanism of the Italian *Quattrocento* and to the appropriation of the antique in combination with direct observation of man and nature in its art, its original connotations were in the fields of classical scholarship and of literature and art. The humanists' reaction against their own concept of mediaevalism, as a period of dull stagnation dominated by blind acceptance of authority, and limited by indifference to the material world, gave rise to the idea of "rebirth" or *renaissance,* and to Michelet's classic phrase, "the rediscovery of the world and of man." Few scholars would now insist on the literal meaning of the word "Renaissance," with its suggestion of a preceding state of coma, if not of actual death, though it is difficult to wean undergraduates from this prejudiced view of the Middle Ages. If we substitute the criterion of intensified interest and vitality for re-birth and rediscovery, we still have to reckon with the Renaissance factors of individualism, secularism, skeptical criticism of traditional authority, and the creation of new standards and techniques in scholarship, literature and the arts, based in part on the interworking of classical and contemporary factors. We have also to consider the conspicuous influence on humanistic scholars and artists, and on Renaissance thought in general, of the "notion of belonging to a new time" and of the historical definition of the Renaissance as the transition from the mediaeval to the modern world.

In a recent paper Professor Wallace Ferguson has discussed our need of a new synthesis of the Renaissance as "an age of moral, religious, intellectual and aesthetic crisis, closely interrelated with acute economic, political and social crisis." He considers the revival of antiquity as a great, but secondary, causative force in this age. He notes decisive changes in all countries of western Europe from the beginning of the fourteenth century, and therefore proposes that the Renaissance, as the transition from mediaeval to modern culture, should be

From Eva Matthews Sanford, "The Twelfth Century—Renaissance or Proto-Renaissance?" *Speculum,* Vol. 26 (1951), pp. 635–641. Reprinted by permission of the Mediaeval Academy of America.

dated from about 1300 to 1600. This proposal embodies a most comprehensive view of the Renaissance. It accents the principle of crisis as a determinant, an extension of the "new age" emphasis, and it reminds us of a chronological problem. If we consider the twelfth century, according to Professor Haskins' chronology, as extending to about 1250, when "the signature of the thirteenth century" became clearly recognizable in literature, art, and thought, the period between a Renaissance of the twelfth century and the inauguration of the major Renaissance would be only fifty years long. This may lead us to a fruitful application of the obvious differences between the organic phenomena of the two periods, the one representing the height of mediaeval culture, and the other a decidedly transitional phase, but both contributing directly in their different ways to the emergence of the modern world.

As far as literature and art are concerned, Erwin Panofsky, in his brilliant essay on "Renaissance and Renascences," proposed the terms "proto-humanism" and "proto-Renaissance" for the twelfth century, on the ground that (1) the appropriation of the antique in this period, however notable in its immediate results, was subjective and fragmentary, as contrasted with the focussed perspective and comprehensive interests of the true Renaissance, and (2) it was limited both by the strong sense of continuity with antiquity and by Christian antagonism to pagan culture. He held that the elements taken over from antiquity were so fully assimilated into the mediaeval patterns that they did not inspire further progress, whereas the Italian Renaissance, though academic, was permanent, because of the changes it created in the minds of men. I find the specific illustrations by which he supports this thesis more convincing in art than in literature. But he brings out an essential difference between the two periods in their attitude toward the classical models that both used so much in their various ways. Writers and artists of the twelfth century did not recognize a cultural break between antiquity and their own time, whereas those of the fifteenth century not only recognized but emphasized it. The distinction between the twelfth century and the later Renaissance in regard to direct stimulus provided for further development, however, does not hold good in all the fields that interest historians.

Professor McIlwain has demonstrated the fallacy of contrasting the political theories and institutions of the twelfth century with those of the Renaissance in this respect. In "Mediaeval Institutions in the Modern World" he wrote: "In the field of political institutions and ideas, I venture to think that what Professor Haskins has termed 'the Renaissance of the Twelfth Century' marks a more fundamental change than the later developments to which we usually attach the word 'Renaissance'; that the constitutionalism of the modern world owes as much, if not even more, to the twelfth and thirteenth centuries than to any later period of comparable length until the seventeenth." He cited especially the mediaeval limitations of governmental authority by private rights, the development of parliamentary institutions, and the gradual assimilation of Roman constitutionalism. The slow process of assimilation of Roman law was speeded up in twelfth-century Italy by the rivalries of empire, papacy, and north Italian communes, which in this period developed the autonomous institutions that contributed so much to their leadership in fifteenth century culture. The University of Bologna and the work of the great glossators show that in the field of Roman law the twelfth and thirteenth centuries left no opportunity for fundamental "discovery" but only for continued study and application of foundations already well and truly laid.

In the field of the natural sciences, we are increasingly aware that the basis for the phenomenal progress of the sixteenth and seventeenth centuries was established before the Renaissance, and that the translations of Greek and Arabic scientific works in the twelfth and thirteenth centuries provided the initial stimulus for such significant research in scientific theory and techniques as that carried on at Padua from about 1300. It is now generally recognized that Roger Bacon, as his own words testify, was not the first mediaeval scholar to set a high value on experimental science, and to formulate sound criteria for it. The net results of mediaeval science, in comparison with the achievements of the sixteenth century, are small indeed, yet the period of incubation began here rather than in the fifteenth century. In the latter period, although many humanists tended to scorn the natural sciences in favor of classical learning (as some have been known to do even in later times), the careful re-examination of mediaeval scientific works together with those of the Greeks and Romans, and the increasing interchange of ideas and techniques between scholars, artists, and craftsmen, prepared the way more fully for the dynamic scientific achievements of the sixteenth century. It would seem that in the scientific as well as in the political field the twelfth century exerted a sufficiently direct influence on later developments to make its definition as a "proto-Renaissance" untenable.

Unqualified insistence on a twelfth-century Renaissance, however, involves the risk of emphasizing the Renaissance characteristics of the period at the expense of its essentially mediaeval qualities. In many respects, like all periods of dynamic activity, it was an age of transition, but the factors of change, significant though they were, still operated to extend and enrich the traditional pattern of a unified Christian culture, with its closely knit communities and personal ties, rather than to destroy them. There were many crises in the twelfth century, but there was not, it seems to me, the over-all motivation in terms of crisis that Professor Ferguson attributes to the later Renaissance. For all the new phases of economic, political, social, aesthetic and intellectual life in the twelfth century, I have not found in it that prevalent consciousness of a new age, or the determination of ideas by the sense of newness, that is so conspicuous in the fifteenth century.

The conviction of continuity with the ancient world is one controlling factor here. We see it in the "Christian synthesis" of Hebrew, Greek, Hellenistic, and Roman with Christian history, and in the historical pattern of the four empires, ending with the Roman, which was expected to endure till the end of the created world. Mediaeval historians, even those who fully recognized that the imperial power in the west had been transferred from Roman to Frankish and German rulers, often echoed the old statement, "The last age is the Roman, in which we now live." They did not look back to the ideas and achievements of antiquity for fresh inspiration from a distant source, but as a direct inheritance and a native possession. This conviction of the unity of history made them unconscious of anachronism and blocked of many approaches to historical criticism, but it also saved the ancient world from the aspect of unreality that it has had for many students in later ages. With the great increase in historical writing in the twelfth century, the theme of *renovatio* appears, as it does also in the political theories of the imperial partisans. Peter of Blois' famous defence of the study of ancient history may serve to illustrate this "Renaissance" attitude, which appears frequently in the works of the chief twelfth-century writers, but, as in this case, within the framework of the mediaeval pattern of world history: "However dogs may bark at me, and pigs grunt, I shall always imitate the writings of the ancients: these shall be my study, nor, while my strength lasts, shall the sun find me idle. We are like dwarfs on the shoulders of giants, by whose grace we see farther than they. Our study of the works of the ancients enables us to give fresh life to their finer ideas, and rescue them from time's oblivion and man's neglect." Here is no blind reverence for ancient authority, but a dignified, though not unmodest assumption that a twelfth-century scholar could and should see farther than the giants of the past. Here, also, is one of many possible answers to the common charge that mediaeval scholars in general feared and distrusted the influence of pagan ideas. The strictures of Bernard of Clairvaux and other ascetic Christians represent a significant but by no means a universal mediaeval attitude. They were often occasioned by the genuine devotion to classical literature displayed by contemporary humanists. Not only the intimate knowledge that twelfth-century writers exhibit of the works of Virgil, Ovid, Horace, and other Latin authors, but the frequent occurrence, even in theological works, of pagan *exempla virtutis* and the wide range of mediaeval quotations from classical authors, show that the classics were commonly read and used for their own value, and not merely to assail pagan corruption or to despoil the Egyptians. The extensive use of classical citations, chiefly for ethical purposes, in Petrus Cantor's *Abbreviated Word*, is one striking example of this. Another significant clue to mediaeval attitudes toward the classics is afforded by marked passages in manuscripts of the authors most read, which indicate the sentiments that the scribe, or some mediaeval reader, found particularly valuable. In the case of Juvenal, for example, one of the pagan writers classified as an *auctor ethicus*, the passages marked in many manuscripts that I have examined show clearly that he was read as a source of ethical precepts, and not merely, as some modern critics state, for evidence of pagan vice.

To those Renaissance historians who broke away from the mediaeval scheme of history, antiquity was an age long past, separated by a thousand years from their own time, and hence studied more objectively, for its possible contributions to their new and rapidly changing world. In the twelfth century, the sense of continuity with the past is conspicuous in the leading cultural centers of northern France, England, the Rhineland and the upper Danube, where the Latin language and literature were not native to the same degree that they were in southern France and Italy. Though Latin was no longer a mother tongue, even in the latter areas, it was in many respects a living language, flexibly handled by educated men, without the artificial restrictions on style and vocabulary that extreme Ciceronians later imposed on it. The hymns and lyric and narrative poems of the twelfth and thirteenth centuries testify that poets found in Latin a natural medium for the expression of their ideas and emotions. The occurrence of both Latin and vernacular versions of the same themes, and the evidences of cross-fertilization between Latin and vernacular literature, deserve serious consideration in this connection. Greek literature, however, remained unknown, aside from the arid and prosaic Latin epitomes of Homer, and such works as had been earlier incorporated in the Latin tradition by the great translators of the Roman period, or by the popular versions of Aesop's fables and the romance of Apollonius of Tyre, for example. The names of Greek authors were known from histories of literature; the scholars who diligently sought out and translated Aristotle's books on logic and natural science might presumably have recovered literary texts also, if they had wished, but they left this important phase of the appropriation of the antique for a later time.

Secularism, individualism, and criticism of established authority are much stressed as distinguishing characteristics of the Renaissance. How far should our appraisal of the twelfth century be influenced by the ecclesiastical character of its culture as contrasted with later secularism? Professor Boyce has wisely pointed out that the terms "secular" and "ecclesiastical" are not mutually exclusive in the Middle Ages. When education was provided chiefly by monastic and cathedral schools, and private tutors were usually monks or priests, when there were few non-clerical careers for intellectual men, and students, however worldly, could claim benefit of clergy, when all society, except for the small minority of Jews and avowed heretics, was united in one Christian fellowship, there could be no clear line of demarcation between the religious and the secular except that drawn by extremists. Not all priests and bishops, monks and friars were insulated from the world by an ecclesiastical ivory tower. Those whose undue worldliness aroused the righteous indignation of contemporary reformers were sometimes, though not always, among the intellectual leaders of their day, and some very secular works were dedicated to ecclesiastical patrons. The learning and literature of the courts of Henry II, Eleanor of Aquitaine, and the Norman rulers of Sicily remind us that patronage was not entirely clerical, though there were fewer wealthy lay patrons—as indeed, there were fewer wealthy men—than in the fifteenth century. Professor Thompson and others have taught us that not all the laity were illiterate; the twelfth century saw a marked increase in the reading public, and the desire of the new readers for edification and entertainment from books met with a notable response on the part of both Latin and vernacular writers. Honorius Augustodunensis, a priest and monk who chose the extremely unworldly life of an "inclusus," shows in his varied works a lively appreciation of the variety and beauties of the natural world, and a keen understanding of the material problems of the congregations for whom he composed his sermons. His writings deal not only with theological and ethical questions, but with secular history, geography, political theory, and the liberal arts. He considered this life a pilgrimage, but he made every effort to help the pilgrim live a well-rounded life during the journey of his soul to God, though he himself had narrowly restricted his own physical activities. He defined man as "a rational soul, clothed with a body," and he provided appropriate nourishment for all three elements.

The most notable buildings that afforded opportunity for the development of architecture and the decorative arts were churches, but in their decoration secular motifs were blithely introduced with apparent unconsciousness of incongruity. Though the traditional symbolism of many of these motifs is well established, the naturalism and freshness with which they are often presented make them no less convincing evidence that details of the physical world were recognized as belonging in the religious context. As the church was the unifying factor in society, its interests embraced many secular elements which later ages associate with the body politic and social rather than with the communion of saints. Obviously, however, the ecclesiastical side of the scales was more heavily weighted than the secular, whereas the next few generations were to change the balance. Here there is a fundamental difference between twelfth-century and Renaissance culture, though the contrast is relative rather than absolute.

The question of individualism is also a relative one. We no longer identify outstanding individuals in the Middle Ages as forerunners of the Renaissance, but recognize Abelard, for example, as a natural product of his time, albeit an exceptional one. In what age would Abelard not have been exceptional? The personal tone of much lyric and satirical poetry is pertinent here. Anonymity was not always due to the Christian subordination of individual claims to creative talent in favor of the Creator. Sometimes, as in Honorius' case, it was expressly attributed to fear of malicious opponents, and sometimes, as in the case of the most popular treatise on education, the Pseudo-Boethius, *De disciplina scholarium*, to the desire to gain a wider public by fathering one's book on a noted ancient authority. Again there is a marked difference in proportion between the two periods; individualism is by no means exceptional in the twelfth century, but it runs rampant in the fifteenth.

Outspoken criticism of traditional authority was not unknown in the twelfth century, when the range of ecclesiastical questions open to dispute was somewhat wider than it was on the eve of the Reformation. The risk of a trial for heresy was not always a deterrent to scholars convinced of their own sound judgment. Skepticism and the spirit of objective inquiry did not always provoke condemnation, and Abelard's critical method survived numerous attacks before his works were incorporated in the curriculum of the University of Paris. His rational thesis, "By doubting we are led to inquire, and by inquiry we perceive the truth," represents the constructive theological approach of the period better than the attacks it provoked from the more intellectually inert of his contemporaries. Bishop Otto of Freising stated the case of the imperial party against the Donations of Constantine in a brief and matter of fact fashion without the elaborate display of learning that was to make Lorenzo Valla's treatise on the same subject a landmark of the critical spirit of the Renaissance. While he left the case open, as a problem not within the province of his *Chronicle* to decide, his presentation leaves no doubt as to his own point of view. Honorius openly attacked the performance for unworthy motives of such "good works" as pilgrimages and crusades, without any inhibitions about criticizing activities sponsored by the church.

For the Age of Faith assumed the exercise of reason, within the bounds of its clearly defined and finite world, which still provided ample range for speculative and critical thought. In his memorable Harvard Tercentenary lecture on Mediaeval Universalism, Etienne Gilson pointed out the intellectual obligations imposed by the mediaeval conviction of universal truth as valid for all men at all times and places. In the twelfth century a unified society with a common meaning for all its members still transcended local differences; its culture was still non-national and non-racial, though there was an increasing consciousness of local and national distinctions. Changes were being wrought by the expansion of commerce and industry with their new contacts, implements and techniques, and their new types of communities and opportunities. Many political and social adjustments were required by these changes and by the concomitant increase in population and production. In their later stages these changes were to create a new world and in so doing, break down the unity of the old, but they had not as yet destroyed the equilibrium.

As we look back at the twelfth century, it is difficult to remember that feudal and agrarian institutions were still actively developing, with more conscious definition of their functions and principles than before, and were still being furthered rather than weakened by the expanding horizons of the age.

To sum up: the designation of the twelfth century as a proto-Renaissance seems both misleading and inadequate. But if we describe it, without considerable qualifications, as a Renaissance period, do we not risk underestimating and even distorting its real character? Can we use this term without implying more identity than the twelfth century really had with the later Renaissance, with its atmosphere of crisis and its consciousness of a new age, in which the secular motivation of political, social, economic and intellectual life replaced the universalism that still directed and inspired the thought and action of the twelfth century? I must confess that I have found the idea of a twelfth-century Renaissance very useful in teaching undergraduates mediaeval history, and I have not really questioned its validity before I wrote this paper. Now I am not so sure. If the men of the Renaissance had not put mediaevalists on the defensive by insistence on their rescue of the world and man from mediaeval ignorance and oblivion, should we feel the need of defining the earlier period as a renaissance? Should we not rather be satisfied to let the twelfth century stand on its own merits as a dynamic period of mediaeval culture, which made fruitful contributions to the development of modern man and the modern world without forfeiting its own essentially mediaeval character?

Women and Family

In recent decades there has been a huge increase in our knowledge of women's lives in the Middle Ages and of medieval attitudes to women. In the following readings C. S. Lewis reminds us of the striking originality and enduring influence of the courtly love tradition. Turning from romance to realism, the next selection, from Barbara Hanawalt, describes the daily life of medieval peasant women. Christiane Klapisch-Zuber discusses the child-bearing role of women in the merchant class of medieval Florence. Caroline Bynum's essay shows how some distinctive spiritual experiences of medieval women reacted on the whole religious culture of the Middle Ages.

CHAPTER 18

Courtly Love

C. S. Lewis

Every one has heard of courtly love, and every one knows that it appears quite suddenly at the end of the eleventh century in Languedoc. The characteristics of the Troubadour poetry have been repeatedly described. With the form, which is lyrical, and the style, which is sophisticated and often 'aureate' or deliberately enigmatic, we need not concern ourselves. The sentiment, of course, is love, but love of a highly specialized sort, whose characteristics may be enumerated as Humility, Courtesy, Adultery, and the Religion of Love. The lover is always abject. Obedience to his lady's lightest wish, however whimsical, and silent acquiescence in her rebukes, however unjust, are the only virtues he dares to claim. There is a service of love closely modelled on the service which a feudal vassal owes to his lord. The lover is the lady's "man." He addresses her as *midons*, which etymologically represents not "my lady" but "my lord." The whole attitude has been rightly described as "a feudalisation of love." This solemn amatory ritual is felt to be part and parcel of the courtly life. It is possible only to those who are, in the old sense of the word, polite. It thus becomes, from one point of view the flower, from another the seed, of all those noble usages which distinguish the gentle from the vilein: only the courteous can love, but it is love that makes them courteous. Yet this love, though neither playful nor licentious in its expression, is always what the nineteenth century called "dishonourable" love. The poet normally addresses another man's wife, and the situation is so carelessly accepted that he seldom concerns himself much with her husband: his real enemy is the rival. But if he is ethically careless, he is no light-hearted gallant: his love is represented as a despairing and tragical emotion—or almost despairing, for he is saved from complete wan-hope by his faith in the God of Love who never betrays his faithful worshippers and who can subjugate the cruellest beauties.

The characteristics of this sentiment, and its systematic coherence throughout the love poetry of the Troubadours as a whole, are so striking that they easily lead to a fatal misunderstanding. We are tempted to treat "courtly love" as a mere episode in literary history—an episode that we have finished with as we have finished with the peculiarities of Skaldic verse or Euphuistic

From C. S. Lewis, *The Allegory of Love* (Oxford: Oxford University Press, 1936), pp. 2–12. Reprinted by permission of Oxford University Press.

prose. In fact, however, an unmistakable continuity connects the Provencal love song with the love poetry of the later Middle Ages, and thence, through Petrarch and many others, with that of the present day. If the thing at first escapes our notice, this is because we are so familiar with the erotic tradition of modern Europe that we mistake it for something natural and universal and therefore do not inquire into its origins. It seems to us natural that love should be the commonest theme of serious imaginative literature: but a glance at classical antiquity or at the Dark Ages at once shows us that what we took for "nature" is really a special state of affairs, which will probably have an end, and which certainly had a beginning in eleventh-century Provence. It seems—or it seemed to us till lately—a natural thing that love (under certain conditions) should be regarded as a noble and ennobling passion: it is only if we imagine ourselves trying to explain this doctrine to Aristotle, Virgil, St. Paul, or the author of *Beowulf*, that we become aware how far from natural it is. Even our code of etiquette, with its rule that women always have precedence, is a legacy from courtly love, and is felt to be far from natural in modern Japan or India. Many of the features of this sentiment, as it was known to the Troubadours, have indeed disappeared; but this must not blind us to the fact that the most momentous and the most revolutionary elements in it have made the background of European literature for eight hundred years. French poets, in the eleventh century, discovered or invented, or were the first to express, that romantic species of passion which English poets were still writing about in the nineteenth. They effected a change which has left no corner of our ethics, our imagination, or our daily life untouched, and they erected impassable barriers between us and the classical past or the Oriental present. Compared with this revolution the Renaissance is a mere ripple on the surface of literature.

There can be no mistake about the novelty of romantic love: our only difficulty is to imagine in all its bareness the mental world that existed before its coming—to wipe out of our minds, for a moment, nearly all that makes the food both of modern sentimentality and modern cynicism. We must conceive a world emptied of that ideal of "happiness"—a happiness grounded on successful romantic love—which still supplied the motive of our popular fiction. In ancient literature love seldom rises above the levels of merry sensuality or domestic comfort, except to be treated as a tragic madness, [a folly] which plunges otherwise sane people (usually women) into crime and disgrace. Such is the love of Medea, of Phaedra, of Dido; and such the love from which maidens pray that the gods may protect them. At the other end of the scale we find the comfort and utility of a good wife acknowledged: Odysseus loved Penelope as he loves the rest of his home and possessions, and Aristotle rather grudgingly admits that the conjugal relation may now and then rise to the same level as the virtuous friendship between good men. But this has plainly very little to do with "love" in the modern or medieval sense; and if we turn to ancient love-poetry proper, we shall be even more disappointed. We shall find the poets loud in their praises of love, no doubt. . . . "What is life without love, tra-la-la?" as the later song has it. But this is no more to be taken seriously than the countless panegyrics both ancient and modern on the all-consoling virtues of the bottle. If Catullus and Propertius vary the strain with cries of rage and misery, this is not so much because they are romantics as because they are exhibitionists. In their anger or their suffering they care not who knows the pass to which love has brought them. They are in the grip of the [folly]. They do not expect their obsession to be regarded as a noble sorrow—they have no "silks and fine array."

Plato will not be reckoned an exception by those who have read him with care. In the *Symposium*, no doubt, we find the conception of a ladder whereby the soul may ascend from human love to divine. But this is a ladder in the strictest sense; you reach the higher rungs by leaving the lower ones behind. The original object of human love—who, incidentally, is not a woman—has simply fallen out of sight before the soul arrives at the spiritual object. The very first step upwards would have made a courtly lover blush, since it consists in passing on from the worship of the beloved's beauty to that of the same beauty in others. Those who call themselves Platonists at the Renaissance may imagine a love which reaches the divine without abandoning the human and becomes spiritual while remaining also carnal; but they do not find this in Plato. If they read it into him, this is because they are living, like ourselves, in the tradition which began in the eleventh century.

Perhaps the most characteristic of the ancient writers on love, and certainly the most influential in the Middle Ages, is Ovid. In the piping times of the early empire—when Julia was still unbanished and the dark figure of Tiberius had not yet crossed the stage—Ovid sat down to compose for the amusement of a society which well understood him an ironically didactic poem on the art of seduction. The very design of his *Art of Love* presupposes an audience to whom love is one of the minor peccadilloes of life, and the joke consists in treating it seriously—in writing a treatise, with rules and examples *en règle* for the nice conduct of illicit loves. It is funny, as the ritual solemnity of old gentlemen over their wine is funny. Food, drink, and sex are the oldest jokes in the world; and one familiar form of the joke is to be very serious about them. . . .

The fall of the old civilization and the coming of Christianity did not result in any deepening or idealizing of the conception of love. The fact is important, because it refutes two theories which trace the great change in our sentiments respectively to the Germanic temperament and to the Christian religion—especially to the cult of the Blessed Virgin. The latter view touches on a real and very complex relationship; but as its true nature will become apparent in what follows, I will here content myself with a brief and dogmatic statement. That Christianity in a very general sense, by its insistence on compassion and on the sanctity of the human body, had a tendency to soften or abash the more extreme brutalities and flippancies of the ancient world in all departments of human life, and therefore also in sexual matters, may be taken as obvious. But there is no evidence that the quasi-religious tone of medieval love poetry has been transferred from the worship of the Blessed Virgin: it is just as likely—it is even more likely—that the colouring of certain hymns to the Virgin has been borrowed from the love poetry. Nor is it true in any unequivocal sense that the medieval church encouraged reverence for women at all: while it is a ludicrous error (as we shall presently see) to suppose that she regarded sexual passion, under any conditions or after any possible process of refinement, as a noble emotion. The other theory turns on a supposedly innate characteristic in the Germanic races, noted by Tacitus. But what Tacitus describes is a primitive awe of women as uncanny and probably prophetic beings, which is as remote from our comprehension as the primitive reverence for lunacy or the primitive horror of twins; and because it is thus remote, we cannot judge how probably it might have developed into the medieval *Frauendienst*, the service of ladies. What is certain is that where a Germanic race reached its maturity untouched by the Latin spirit, as in Iceland, we find nothing at all like courtly love. The position of women in the Sagas is, indeed, higher than that which they enjoy in classical literature; but it is based on a purely commonsensible and unemphasized respect for the courage or prudence which some women, like some men, happen to possess. The Norsemen, in fact, treat their women not primarily as women but as people. It is an attitude which may lead in the fullness of time to an equal franchise or a Married Women's Property Act, but is has very little to do with romantic love. The final answer to both theories, however, lies in the fact that the Christian and Germanic period had existed for several centuries before the new feeling appeared. "Love," in our sense of the word, is as absent from the literature of the Dark Ages as from that of classical antiquity. Their favourite stories were not, like ours, stories of how a man married, or failed to marry, a woman. They preferred to hear how a holy man went to heaven or how a brave man went to battle. We are mistaken if we think that the poet in the Song of Roland shows restraint in disposing so briefly of Alde, Roland's betrothed. Rather by bringing her in at all, he is doing the opposite: he is expatiating, filling up chinks, dragging in for our delectation the most marginal interests after those of primary importance have had their due. Roland does not think about Alde on the battle-field: he thinks of his praise in pleasant France. The figure of the betrothed is shadowy compared with that of the friend, Oliver. The deepest of worldly emotions in this period is the love of man for man, the mutual love of warriors who die together fighting against odds, and the affection between vassal and lord. . . . Germanic and Celtic legend, no doubt, had bequeathed to the barbarians some stories of tragic love between man and woman—love "star-crossed" and closely analogous to that of Dido or Phaedra. But the theme claims no preeminence, and when it is treated the interest turns at least as much on the resulting male tragedy, the disturbance of vassalage or sworn brotherhood, as on the female influence which produced it. Ovid, too, was known to the learned; and there was a plentiful literature on sexual irregularities for the use of confessors. Of romance, of reverence for women, of the idealizing imagination exercised about sex, there is hardly a hint. The centre of gravity is elsewhere—in the hopes and fears of religion, or in the clean and happy fidelities of the feudal hall. But, as we have seen, these male affections—though wholly free from the taint that hangs about "friendship" in the ancient world—were themselves lover-like; in their intensity, their wilful exclusion of other values, and their uncertainty, they provided an exercise of the spirit not wholly unlike that which later ages have found in "love." The fact is, of course, significant. Like the formula "Ovid misunderstood," it is inadequate to explain the appearance of the new sentiment; but it goes far to explain why that sentiment, having appeared, should make haste to become a "feudalization" of love. What is new usually wins its way by disguising itself as the old.

The new thing itself, I do not pretend to explain. Real changes in human sentiment are very rare—there are perhaps three or four on record—but I believe that they occur, and that this is one of them. I am not sure that they have "causes," if by a cause we mean something which would wholly account for the new state of affairs, and so explain away what seemed its novelty. It is, at any rate, certain that the efforts of scholars have so far failed to find an origin for the content of Provencal love poetry. Celtic, Byzantine, and even Arabic influence have been suspected; but it has not been made clear that these, if granted, could account for the results we see. A more promising theory attempts to trace the whole thing to Ovid; but this view—apart from the inadequacy which I suggested above—finds itself with the fatal difficulty that the evidence points to a much stronger Ovidian influence in the north of France than in the south. Something can be extracted from a study of the social conditions in which the new poetry arose, but not so much as we might hope. We know that the crusading armies thought the Provencals milk-sops, but this will seem relevant only to a very hardened enemy of *Frauendienst*. We know that this period in the south of France had witnessed what seemed to contemporaries a signal degeneracy from the simplicity of ancient manners and an alarming increase of luxury. But what age, what land, by the same testimony, has not? Much more important is the fact that landless knighthood—knighthood without a place in the territorial hierarchy of feudalism—seems to have been possible in Provence. The unattached knight, as we meet him in the romances, respectable only by his own valour, amiable only by his own courtesy, predestined lover of other men's wives, was therefore a reality; but this does not explain why he loved in such a new way. If courtly love necessitates adultery, adultery hardly necessitates courtly love. We come much nearer to the secret if we can accept the picture of a typical Provencal court drawn many years ago by an English writer, and since approved by the greatest living authority on the subject. We must picture a castle which is a little island of comparative leisure and luxury, and therefore at least of possible refinement, in a barbarous country-side. There are many men in it, and very few women—the lady, and her damsels. Around these throng the whole male *meiny*, the inferior nobles, the landless knights, the squires, and the pages—haughty creatures enough in relation to the peasantry beyond the wall, but feudally inferior to the lady as to her lord—her "men" as feudal language had it. Whatever "courtesy" is in the place flows from her: all female charm from her and her damsels. There is no questions of marriage for most of the court. All these circumstances together come very near to being a "cause"; but they do not explain why very similar conditions elsewhere had to wait for Provencal example before they produced like results. Some part of the mystery remains inviolate.

CHAPTER 19

Peasant Life

Barbara Hanawalt

A women's work is never done, we say, and yet we do not know what work rural women did in the late Middle Ages. The hours must have been very long and the work hard, for the only literary piece that speaks of the peasant woman's day with envy is that old saw of the tyrannical husband who taunts his wife into changing places for a day because he thinks her work is easier. He, of course, learns his lesson. Since the basic unit of economic production and consumption was the peasant household, a woman's contribution was made within the context of her family. Because medieval English peasant families were not normally extended with many female kin to lend a hand, a household relied heavily on the wife's contribution to the home economy. But what was the nature of her contribution? The tyrannical husband of the ballad argues: "And sene the good that we have is halfe dele thyn,/Thow shalt laber for thy part as I doo for myne." Two areas are traditionally assigned to the wife: the daily running of the household and raising and training the next generation. But women performed a variety of other tasks, including the classical occupation of spinning, that supplemented the routine management of house and family by bringing in extra earnings.

The problem for historians has been to find evidence on how married couples divided the economic responsibilities of the household. Men's contributions emerge more quickly because they frequently appeared in the manorial court rolls in cases related to their work and landholding or in the account rolls where their wages were recorded. Women's work was more often directed toward the private household economy than the public one of the manor. One might take the excellent studies that have been done of early modern and modern peasant women and project their picture back into earlier centuries, but the early modern economy was different in many ways from the medieval one. Women in early modern Europe had many more opportunities to work in cottage industry or to sell their labor in the rapidly expanding cities. The economy of the thirteenth through late fifteenth centuries in England was still largely centered around the exploitation of individual holdings on manors. Manorial records do contribute something to our knowledge of women's work, and information can be gleaned from wills, poll tax returns, and coroners' inquests.

Most rural women would eventually marry, because they could find few positions outside the household economy. Peasant women would not become nuns and the position of servant was usually a temporary one within the teenage years of the life cycle. The other options for unmarried peasant girls were not entirely attractive. They could stay at their brother's home and work for his family; they could hope to find work in an urban center or on a manor as a servant; or they could become prostitutes. J. C. Russell's work on the 1377 poll tax showed that, in villages with populations up to eight hundred, 75 percent of the women were married. This percentage tended to decrease in boroughs. The figure represents all women over fourteen years of age (the taxable age) but does not indicate widows or those who would eventually marry. As we have seen, determining the number of men and women who remained single is difficult but has been estimated to be 7 percent of the population in the mid-sixteenth century. Thus the number of permanently celibate women was very low.

A woman's first contribution to the household economy, therefore, was the money, goods, animals, or land that she brought to the marriage in her dowry, dower from a former husband, or inheritance in her own right. These possessions came from a variety of sources, but wills give the most detailed information. One must remember, however, that they are a biased source since they tend to overrepresent the wealthier elements in the community. Since men left the vast majority of wills, women appear as beneficiaries of husbands, fathers, grandfathers, godfathers, and masters.

A father dying without a son to inherit could will his property to his daughters. In the customary law of the manor and in common law, as we noted in the section on inheritance, the property would be divided equally among the surviving daughters. A will gave a man of property an opportunity to divide the inheritance himself, so that he could favor one daughter, usually the eldest, and keep the family lands intact. Of the 319 married men leaving wills in Bedfordshire in the late fifteenth and early sixteenth centuries, 44 of them, or 14 percent, had only daughters as heirs. Sometimes the daughter was already married and the will makes clear that the son-in-law would have control over the land, but the right to the land remained to the issue of the marriage. Since heiresses were much sought after in marriage, the father would have carefully selected the son-in-law. After all, the father might retire and live with them. Other fathers died young and left the lands in care of their widows until the daughters were of marriageable age.

Even if the daughter was not the chief heir, she could claim some part of the family wealth, usually payable in animals, grain, household goods or money. These inheritances might have been in addition to an earlier dowry or they might be a provision for it. Only 9 percent of the wills specifically mention that the bequest to a woman was for her marriage. Henry Davy, a prosperous man, died with two daughters still unmarried. He left them both considerable grants of land that they were to receive on their marriage. Monetary bequests for dowries ranged from 13s. 4d. to £40. John Derlynge, who left his daughter 20s., was fairly typical of the humbler will makers. Other relatives might also contribute toward a girl's marriage. An uncle on the father's side was the usual source, but one grandfather generously gave each of his grand-daughters £10 toward her marriage. In the poem "How the Good Wife Taught Her Daughter," the mother meets her obligations to her daughter's dowry by collecting household goods for her as soon as she is born.

Dying men also raised the issue of their wives' remarriage and made provision for them accordingly. Of the 319 married men leaving wills, 74 percent were survived by a widow. Common law allowed a widow a third of the husband's property for life and would permit her to take this land into a new marriage. Wills, however, gave husbands greater flexibility, and most chose the more generous provisions of customary law that gave the wife life interest in the tenement or control until the son reached the age of majority. Some other dower would be settled on her when she relinquished the land to their heir. The husband might also stipulate that the dower was hers only if she did not remarry. Other husbands left their widows clear title to some property that they could take with them if they married, but not the family land. Thus John Heywood provided his widow with £20, a number of animals, grain, and the household goods she had brought with her as dowry. These were to be given her "wit owt eny grugge . . . of my children."

The women of whom we have been speaking received sufficient property from fathers, husbands, or other kin to make them sought-after marriage partners. Society did not dictate a specific value for the dowry in order to marry; that was a matter of individual negotiations. But if family could not provide, how could a single woman hope to accumulate a dowry or supplement a meager one?

Servants received bequests from dying masters or mistresses in addition to wages. The typical bequests included items of clothing, sheep, a small sum of money, or malt. Occasionally, a favored servant would inherit a substantial bequest; Elizabeth Lamkyn was given 26s. 8d. "to her profeccion." Since servants were often the social equals of the masters, some of these gifts may have been part of a social network of village mutual support. Thus servants were rather like godchildren and received similar types of gifts in wills.

Female servants also converted wages into bits of land of an acre or two that they could add to their dowry, as indicated by the entrance fines they paid in manorial court. In the tight land market of preplague England even a woman with only an acre of land would be an attractive marriage partner. The living that such a small dowry could provide was not much and would probably be matched by a groom with equally meager resources, but five acres could support a couple in good years. Undoubtedly some young people even married without a cushion of land or savings, and had to rely on their labor for survival. When fathers or brothers did not provide dowries, the young women tended to choose their own husbands, as we shall see later. They had no need of parental consent, as they were not part of the family's economic strategy.

The dowry having been contributed to the new household, the bride settled into her other roles of providing her labor, reproductive capacity, and childrearing to the economy. The literature and folklore of the Middle Ages are decisive in dividing the men's sphere from the women's both in physical environment and types of work. John Ball's revolutionary jingle on class consciousness is well known: "When Adam delved and Eve span/Where then were all the gentlemen." It is instructive that Ball found nothing wrong with the sexual division of labor, only that in the beginning there were not class distinctions. Men and women were also distinguished by the symbols of their particular spheres of work, and these are common identifying characteristics in art and literature. The poem "The False Fox" provides a classic example:

> The good-wyfe came out in her smok,
> And at the fox she threw her rok [spindle].
>
> The good-man came out with his flayle,
> And smote the fox upon the tayle.

The accidental-death patterns in the coroners' inquests and manorial court evidence confirm the sex-specific division of labor in rural England.

Womens' work and their general round of daily activities was much less physically dangerous than men's; women comprised only 22 percent of the 2022 adults (over the age of fourteen) in the accidental-death cases in the coroners' inquests. Compared to the men, women's accidents indicate that they spent much more of their workday around the house and village: 29.5 percent of the women victims compared to 11.8 percent of the men died of accidents in their houses or closes. . . . Apparently they spent more time than men visiting and working with their neighbors: 5.8 percent of the women's fatal accidents were in a neighbor's home or close compared to 3.8 percent of the men. When women did venture from home, it was often in connection with their domestic duties. Thus 5.9 percent of the women victims drowned in a public well compared to a 1.6 percent of the men, and 9.7 percent of the women died in a village ditch or pond compared to 4.9 percent of the men. Men were much more likely than women to die in fields, forests, mills, construction sites, and marl pits. The place of death, therefore, confirms women's chief sphere of work as the home and men's as the fields and forests.

The time of accident was given very roughly in the inquests, but nonetheless a definite pattern of greater and less risks for men and women appears as they pursued their daily routines. Both rose at dawn, but women had only 4.2 percent of their accidents then, compared to 9.8 percent for men. The morning work was more risky for women, with 15.6 percent of their fatal accidents occurring at that time, compared to 9.8 percent of the men's. Noon was high-risk for both, as they tired of their labor and became hungry: 20.8 percent of the women's fatal accidents occurred then and 17.7 percent of men's. Women might have had a slightly higher number of accidents because they were involved with cooking at noon. For both sexes afternoon represented a lull in activities leading to fatal accidents (4.2 percent of female deaths and 7.5 percent of male deaths, and may indicate a postprandial nap. But evening saw another increase (15.6 and 18.9 percent for females and males, respectively). Night was truly hazardous for both sexes at 39.6 percent for women and 33.9 percent for men.

When one looks at the causes of women's accidental deaths and the places they occurred at these hours, the round of daily work becomes apparent. The morning, noon, and some evening deaths are connected with fetching water for washing and preparing meals. Working with large animals and brewing also appear in the morning and at noon. The afternoon deaths were from laundry or seasonal fieldwork. The high number of deaths at night resulted from dangers in the home, usually house fires or walls falling on unsuspecting sleepers, or from wandering about at night without candles. There were, as we have observed, many bodies of water and pits and wells that one could fall into and drown after nightfall.

The seasonal pattern of women's and men's deaths were parallel, except that women had a significantly higher percentage of fatal accidents in May (12.9 percent, compared to 7.7 percent). This is puzzling. The cause of death indicates that women were more prone to falls and drowning during May, but their work does not seem to be particularly seasonal. It is possible that more women were pregnant or recovering from pregnancy, but sixteenth-century data indicate that births were most frequent in February and March. The two high months for men's accidents, June and August, can be readily explained by harvest and other heavy fieldwork.

The division of labor by sex was set early in a child's life. As we shall see, by the age of two or three the accidental-death patterns of children reflected that of their respective parents.

Women's work in peasant households has been largely misrepresented by modern historians who tend to equate peasant women with pioneer women. Medieval peasant women did not spend much of their time producing from scratch the basic necessities for their families. Instead, most households availed themselves of specialists in weaving, tailoring, and even brewing and baking. A second misconception that must not be allowed to stand is that women's work involved fewer hours than men's or that, because women had fewer accidents, their work was not as strenuous.

Women's daily household routines are very well summed up in the "Ballad of the Tyrannical Husband." The goodwife of the poem had no servants and only small children, so that her day was a full one. She complained that her nights were not restful because she had to rise and nurse the babe in arms. She then milked the cows and took them to pasture and made butter and cheese while she watched the children and dried their tears. Next she fed the poultry and took the geese to the green. She baked and brewed every fortnight and worked on carding wool, spinning, and beating flax. She tells her husband that through her economy of weaving a bit of linsey woolsey during the year for the family clothes, they would be able to save money and not buy cloth from the market. Her husband insists that all this work is very easy and that she really spends her day at the neighbors' gossiping. But she retorts:

Soo I loke to our good withowt and withyn,
That there be none awey noder mor no myn,
Glade to pleas yow to pay, lest any bate begyn,
And for to chid thus with me, i-feyght you be in synne.

The housewife's first task in the morning was lighting the fire. She had to go into the close to get kindling or straw to light the embers and get the wood started. One woman, we are told in a coroner's inquest, went out early in the morning to get kindling, climbed into a tree leaning over the common way, and fell. A housewife who was over seventy went to her straw sack to get straw to start a fire, as she had done for many years, but fell from her ladder on this occasion. The fire started, the housewife heated the morning porridge and other food for breakfast.

Cleaning house occupied very little of a woman's time . . . the houses were small and furniture rudimentary and the peasants owned few pans and dishes. The floors were covered with straw, and chickens, pigs, cats, and dogs wandered in and out at will. But the primitive nature of housing should not lead one to conclude that the housewives were slovenly and cared nothing about cleanliness. As archaeological evidence has shown, floors were swept frequently enough that the brooms left U-shaped depressions on house sites.

Of the 237 women whose activity at the time of death is specified, the cause of death of 37 percent of them related directly to work around the house. The most dangerous task was drawing water from wells and pits (17 percent). The water was for cooking, washing, and drinking. Either the housewife or the children got water for the household. Doing the laundry was also a dangerous activity, with 3 percent of the women either drowning or being scalded. The earth around wells, ponds, and ditches became treacherously slippery with water splashed on them, so that it was easy to slip in. Thus one woman washing linen cloth by a ditch in December 1348 slid into the water and drowned. Other accidents involving work related to maintaining the house included cutting wood, baking, cooking, taking grain to the mill, and general housework.

Women's routine work for the household also included agricultural work. The women milked the cows and helped at calving time. They also kept the poultry: geese, hens, and maybe doves. The pig was in their charge, as was the garden in the close that produced vegetables and fruits. When their help was needed in the fields, they hoed, weeded, turned hay, tied sheaves, and even reaped. They gleaned when the harvest was over, a back-breaking task of picking up stray grain. One old woman was so tired after her day's gleaning that she fell asleep among her sheaves and failed to put her candle out.

In making our economic boundaries too rigid, we assume that peasants did not hunt and gather. Women picked nuts, wild fruits, herbs, and greens from the woods and roadways and if they lived near the shore, they also gathered shellfish. They collected firewood, carrying fagots of sticks from the woods on their backs. Although men usually did the heavy labor of cutting turves from peat pits, occasionally women did as well. One woman, over forty years of age, went to cut turves for the family fire when a piece fell on her.

One of the most significant contributions a wife could make to the household economy was the bearing and training of children. Children were an asset in the peasant economy; by the age of seven they could already be a help to the housewife in her daily round of chores. The early years were difficult, however, as the woman in the "Ballad of the Tyrannical Husband" pointed out. During that time the housewife added the burden of caring for young children to her other chores. But the production and training of the new work force was essential for a successful peasant household; otherwise one had to hire servants.

Women could also diversify their labor to bring more cash into the family economy. In addition to the usual egg, butter, and cheese production, some women engaged in fairly large-scale beer and bread making. Both these occupations required investment in large vessels or ovens. In Broughton the wealthier peasant families tended to be the chief producers of beer on a large scale. Brewing was an arduous and rather dangerous activity, since it involved carrying twelve-gallon vats of hot liquid and heating large tubs of water. Five percent of the women in the coroners' inquests lost their lives in brewing accidents, usually by falling into vats of boiling liquid or spilling the hot wort on themselves.

Spinning was the traditional supplemental economic activity for women. The spindle could be taken anywhere to occupy idle minutes. The woman may or may not have turned the thread into cloth. Most likely, she sold it to a weaver unless she was making rough material for daily wear and sheets.

Women could also work as wage laborers to aid the family economy. In a poor household supported by very little land, both the husband and wife would have to hire out their labor. We do not know yet if women received equal pay for equal work. The matter will require considerably more study because of the problems of assessing the nature and difficulty of tasks performed. For instance, a thatcher received 2d. a day in the thirteenth century, but his female assistant received only 1d. Her work was gathering the stubble and handing it up to him while he did the more skilled labor. In general, manors hired female laborers and boys for such unskilled agrarian tasks, and consequently their pay was low. The work of picking over seed grain, however, was a highly skilled occupation in which women excelled and, therefore, tended to be paid more. When men and women did the same work, they received equal pay. Thus, although women did not normally work for the lord by either hoeing or stacking hay, when they did so they received the same pay as men.

Some historians have maintained that with the decline of population after the Black Death women's wages became competitive with those of men. More systematic data will have to be accumulated to demonstrate this, however, for the statutory information indicates that women were supposed to be paid less than men. A statute of 1388 decreed that female laborers and dairymaids should earn 1s. less a year than the plowman. In 1444 women servants would receive 10s. annually for their work compared to 15s. for the men, and in 1495 women's labor was still to be reimbursed at only 10s. annually, but men's had climbed to 16s. 8d.

The village credit and land market as well as fairs and regional markets attracted women. A variety of sources show women aggressively engaged in market activities. For instance, Mabel the Merchant was charged in 1294 in Chalgrave court with taking ash trees. Women made loans to other villagers that are recorded in the court rolls. And there is even a case in the coroners' inquests of a woman who went out to negotiate a debt, leaving her nine-month-old baby alone in the house, so that it died of a fire in its cradle. Since women could inherit property and buy it as well, they played a fairly active role in the village land market even after marriage. Married women sometimes sold land they had brought with them to the marriage to help the family through a difficult time, or they might buy or inherit land that would eventually go to a child's marriage portion. Women were somewhat disadvantaged in the marketplace because, while they could bring suit on their own, they had no access to magisterial roles and seldom even used attorneys. Their pledges had to be men, although one woman tried to use all women in her case.

One can easily overlook the extralegal contributions women made to household ease and even survival. Olwen Hufton has emphasized the economy of makeshift that both peasant and urban women practiced in preindustrial France. These petty illegalities, or tolerated transgressions, were usually a source of additional food. In France the rioting for bread was the woman's provenance. In medieval England illegal gleaning was the most common way for a woman to get extra grain for her family. Gleaning after the main harvest, as observed earlier, was limited to the old and decrepit, but it was so profitable that wives of even prominent villagers did it. Reaping could pay only 1d. a day for women, but gleaning would bring in considerably more. Even being caught and fined was worth the risk because the fines were so low. The illegal gleaners appear in the coroners' inquests where they are caught in the act and a death ensued. Amicia, daughter of Hugh of Wygenale, died warding off an illegal gleaner. She had been hired by Agatha Gylemyn to guard her grain. During the night Cecilia, wife of Richard le Gardyner, came to steal the grain and threw Amicia to the ground when she tried to stop her. Three illegal gleaners got their punishment through an "act of God." They became frightened during a bad storm as they were gleaning illegally and hid in a haystack. Lightning struck them.

The only limit to these illegal, petty economic gains was the imagination. It was common to graze animals on other people's crops, to reap grass illegally, to dig turves and collect nuts and wood in prohibited areas. In Yorkshire Alice, daughter of Adam, the son of William, dug a pit for iron and another woman dug up the high road for coal. Occasionally women were even accused of bleeding a cow for blood sausage or clipping sheep in the pasture for their wool. Isabel of Abyndam came to the fields of the abbess and took three pounds of wool from four sheep there. When the shepherd found her, she fought him off so that he was forced to hit her in the legs with his staff in self-defense. She was taken into custody but was so frightened that she refused food and drink and died of hunger. Poultry theft and other petty thefts also appear frequently in manor courts.

In clearly felonious activities women also showed their concern for provisioning the family. They stole sheep and poultry rather than larger animals and stole proportionately more household goods and foodstuffs than did men. In the period of famine in the early fourteenth century, the number of females indicted for crimes increased to 12 percent and dropped to 9 percent after the period of dearth.

When the day was done, it was the woman of the house who tucked in the family and turned out the light. We know about this sex-specific role because of the times that a housewife forgot to blow out the candle and it fell onto the straw on the floor, setting the house afire. For instance:

> On Tuesday [April 24, 1322] a little before midnight the said Robert and Matilda, his wife, and William and John their sons lay asleep in the said solar, a lighted candle fixed on the wall by the said Matilda fell by accident on the bed of the said Robert and Matilda and set the whole house on fire; that the said Robert and William were immediately caught in the flames and burnt and Matilda and John with difficulty escaped with their lives.

We have argued that the woman's sphere of activity centered largely on production for the home, both in providing food and supplementary earnings for the household economy. She also reared the children and put them to work in the house and close at an early age. We have yet to investigate the value that the society placed on this contribution. Two historians, Joan Scott and Louise Tilly, have argued that "the separate spheres and separate roles did not, however, imply discrimination or hierarchy. It appears, on the contrary, that neither sphere was subordinate to the other."

But we must still ask who wore the breeches in the medieval peasant family. Were economic decisions joint ones, with both husband and wife participating, or did the husband take the role of economic planner? Was it only a shrew who could don the breeches and control family investments? Literary sources are not neutral on their opinion of women. The clergy did not have a monopoly on the antifemale traditions, and popular lyrics often fault women who gossip, cheat, and scold:

> Sum be mery and sum be sade,
> And sum be bosy, and sum be bade;
> Sum be wilde, by Seynt Chade;
>   Yet all be not so,
> For sum be lewed,
> And sum be shrewed;
>   Go, Shrew, wheresoeuer ye go.

Others praise women for their constancy and counsel and advise men to place their trust in their wives:

> ffor by women men be reconsiled,
> ffor by women was neyer man begiled,
> ffor they be of the condicion of curtes grysell [Griselda]
> ffor they be so meke and myled

Even the tyrannical husband indicated that the wife's work was half the productivity of the household and whatever the personal attributes of a wife, lazi-
ness would have been the most disastrous.

Sources other than literary are better for assessing appreciation of the
wife's contribution because the latter are so steeped in a misogynist tradition
that they are difficult to use. Wills are perhaps the best source. As a man lay on
his deathbed he often considered how he could ensure his family's well-being
and reward all for their contribution to the household economy. Wills showed
that the men entrusted their wives with considerable responsibilities and re-
warded them generously for their contributions during their lifetime. Most
men (65 percent) made their wives executors. Others indicated through specific
phrases the reliance they placed on their wives. One man left his son a bequest
if he would obey his mother; others made the wife responsible for choosing a
profession for a son; and one Yorkshire father went to great lengths in his
charge to his wife: "that my wiffe have a tendire and faithfull luffe and favour
in brynging uppe of hir childir and myne, as she will answer to God and me."
He went on to direct her to "reward them after her power for us both."

Most men leaving wills, therefore, trusted their wives to raise a family of
young children and run both the house and lands. The widow with young
children thus had an increased burden for maintaining the household. She
would either have to hire labor in the fields, rely on other family members for
aid, or remarry. It was not tradition alone that kept women from doing the
plowing themselves, but rather their already full work load. Although women
tended to outlive men and were more likely to be widowed, widowers were
also left in dire straits in managing the household economy. They also would
have to hire servants or rely on kin to rear young children and take care of
routine household chores. In the poll tax the great majority of cultivators were
married couples, because it was the most efficient unit. It is rare to find households composed of father/daughter or mother/son.

Although wills clearly establish the value and trust a man placed in his
wife on his deathbed, they do not indicate how or if he expressed these sentiments during his lifetime. The economic contributions may have been equal,
but decision making may not have been. The moralist writing "How the Good
Wife Taught her Daughter" recommended that women not gad about the
town or get drunk on the money they made from selling cloth, thereby implying that they had control over their butter and eggs money. The law protected
women's rights to their dowry and lands they inherited from their family, so
that a husband could not legally demise it without the wife's permission. But
more than one woman came into court complaining that she had not been consulted about the sale of land, because she feared to cross her husband. Joan,
wife of Hugh Forester, was typical. She demanded and won the rights to one
and a half acres that her husband demised without her permission because
she was "not able to gainsay it in his lifetime."

The argument for a partnership in the peasant marital economy, however,
is a persuasive one, even it some husbands were tyrants. Many of the decisions

that would have to be made during the course of the marriage would be ones in which mutual expectations or mutual needs would determine the course of action. Both partners shared the common assumption that children should receive a settlement from the accumulated family wealth. The couple would also share assumptions about investment in seed, tools, and household equipment. The needs of the economic unit were common to both. If the couple survived to retirement age, they would have a mutual interest in making arrangements for their support. Land transactions in manorial courts indicate a strong practice of mutual responsibility and decision making. When a villein couple married, it was common for the man to turn the land back to the lord, taking it again in both his name and that of his wife. Husband and wife also appear in manorial court purchasing or leasing pieces of land either for themselves or for their children or acting in concert in other business matters as well. While men appeared more frequently in economic transactions, they were not necessarily acting unilaterally. After all, a man would not leave his wife his executor if he had not gained some respect for her economic judgments during his lifetime.

The peasant family economy was based firmly on the contributions of both sexes with their separate skills and their separate domains. The initial goods and capital of the woman's dowry set up the household, and her labor and supplemental economic activities helped keep it going. The marriage was an economic partnership in which gender ordinarily determined the division of labor, but in which the goal of both partners was the survival and prosperity of the household unit. The mutual dependence of a couple on each other's economic contribution encouraged remarriage if one partner died and discouraged intrafamilial violence and homicide.

CHAPTER 20

Women and Children

Christiane Klapisch-Zuber

Engendering valid heirs was the great challenge that faced families in an epoch in which death struck hard and often. At the heart of the medieval house was the bedchamber. It was there that the woman lived—where she worked, conceived, gave birth, and died. We still know little about the biological life of the married woman or about the effects on her body and her behavior of the functions assigned to her. Documentary sources are heterogeneous, scattered, and often contradictory. We can at least see that everywhere her role in the reproduction of the group was what most frequently prompted discussions and admonitions, the greatest precautions and the highest praise.

The key to this role was thus marriage. During the early Middle Ages, barbaric law and synodal statutes, hagiographic tales and descriptions of great domains give the impression that young people at their first marriages (outside of the aristocracy, where girls were married at a very early age) married at roughly the same age and at a relatively mature age. In the central Middle Ages a clear change took place, and from one end of Europe to the other, barely adolescent girls were given to husbands markedly older than they. In Flanders, in England, in Italy, and in France in 1200 the aristocracy and the urban patriciate married their daughters when they were barely pubescent. An age of twelve or thirteen—the age at which canon law permitted engagement for marriage or the taking of religious vows—returns constantly in the lives of female saints (who, it is true, were in the very great majority born into good families). Information on marriages in the rural and popular classes before the fourteenth century is much more scarce. Still, the average age of girls at their first marriage in those milieus seldom seems greater than seventeen or eighteen in spite of demographic pressure for somewhat deferred marriage.

From the late twelfth century on, men seem to have entered into "the trammels of marriage" at a later age than had previously been the case. Scions of knightly families set the example by waiting to be installed in a fief, to have inherited, or to have found the heiress that would permit them a proper establishment. Information is just as scanty on customs among other classes of men before the fourteenth century, although the literature of the

From Christiane Klapisch-Zuber, "Women and the Family," in *Medieval Callings*, edited by Jacques Le Goff (Chicago: Chicago University Press, 1990), pp. 296–303. Reprinted by permission of The University of Chicago Press.

fabliaux widely exploits the theme of unequal ages in marriage between a graybeard and a tender young thing.

There is more information for the second half of the fourteenth century and for the fifteenth century, after the Black Death. More frequent censuses, although they too seldom display the wealth of data and the homogeneity of the Florentine *catasti* of the fifteenth century, nonetheless enable us to estimate the average age at marriage. For women it was under eighteen, with a tendency in the peasantry and the urban proletariat to delay marriage one or two years and among the rich to advance it to fifteen. A familial literature of journals, *livres de raison,* and *ricordanze* (especially in Tuscany) finally permit more accurate calculation of female age at marriage. In the Florentine bourgeoisie between 1340 and 1530 some 136 young brides were married at an average age of 17.2 years. Variations over this long period are slight, although there is a noticeable tendency to delay weddings somewhat, as around 1500 Florentine women married at an average of one year later than before 1400. The stability of the whole is nonetheless more noteworthy than this late rise.

Analogous calculations taken from a similar group of young men coming from the same families of the mercantile bourgeoisie show an average age of over twenty-seven at the celebration of their first marriages. This age shows stronger variation than the age at marriage for women, dropping, for example, after lethal epidemics; it declines discernibly during the latter third of the fifteenth century in a movement opposite to the rise in the curve for females. Still, the important fact is that ten years or so always separated male age at marriage from female.

A man nearing thirty, an adult, thus brought an adolescent into his house. This unsymmetrical situation in the later Middle Ages strangely recalls Roman customs of the classical age. Should we be astonished, then, that the resurgence of moralizing literature and treatises on domestic economy during the later Middle Ages included admonitions directly inspired by Aristotle's *Politics* or Xenophon's *Economics?* Rationalizing the practices of their own milieu and their times, men like Leon Battista Alberti (in his *Libri della famiglia*), or like Giovanni Morelli, took their model from real life: the man should wait to marry until he has reached the fullness of the "perfect age;" the woman to the contrary, should be given to a husband young—*fanciulla*—in order to avoid perversion before marriage, since women "become full of vices when they do not have what nature requires." Some writers deplored an evolution, which they judged recent, that led their contemporaries to give their daughters at an increasingly early age. All agreed that in order to establish his authority over the household and to engender the handsomest children, a man would do well to put off marriage. Late age at marriage—which was to continue to be characteristic of the population of Western Europe in the modern age—thus seems both the practice and the norm for the male partner alone from the thirteenth to the fifteenth centuries.

The nearly negligible proportion of first births in Florentine families occurring before the eighth month after the marriage is a good indication of the rigorous surveillance that their families exercised over these young women, who on occasion saw their intended husbands only on the day they received his nuptial ring. Similarly, the relatively large interval between marriage and the first birth shows that these adolescent girls certainly had not all attained the physiological maturity required for bearing a child immediately, although that did not stop their husbands from initiating them immediately into conjugal relations. After the first child, however, pregnancies and births followed one another at a rapid pace. In 1461, one burgher's wife from Arras became a widow at twenty-nine after having brought twelve children into the world in thirteen years of marriage. There is nothing extraordinary in this: the few French *livres de raison* and the many Italian *ricordanze* bring us many examples between the fourteenth and the fifteenth centuries of the high fertility rate characteristic at least of the women of wealthier urban milieux. A Florentine woman of good family who had married at seventeen and had not lost her husband before she reached the age of the menopause could hope to give birth to an average of ten children before she reached thirty-seven years of age, or one child more than French peasant women of the modern era, who married from seven to ten years later than Italian city women. Systematically marrying off daughters very young thus had a noticeable effect on the overall fertility rate and on the total number of births. By lowering female age at marriage, families sought, with varying degrees of awareness, to fill the terrible gaps made by the age's fearful death rate.

Their hopes were fragile, however, for even in families as protected as those of the bourgeoisie of one of the wealthiest cities of Europe, many unions ended prematurely, and the number of children they procreated was lower than the ten or so indicated for couples that enjoyed a long conjugal life. The total number of children brought into the world by all Florentine couples (whether their life together was interrupted by the premature death of one of the spouses or not) fell to an average of seven. This is still a considerable figure, but, as we shall see, few of this rapidly decimated progeny survived their parents.

For the moment, we might note that pregnancies occupied close to one-half of the lives of married women under the age of forty. In several families of notables from the French Limousin (also known by means of their journals), the average intergenetic interval was close to twenty-one months, which was also the average for seven hundred Florentine births occurring in families of comparable wealth. This figure even falls to less than eighteen months if we eliminate exceptional intervals evidently due to the husband's absence on business or if we restrict consideration to couples who remained united throughout their natural fertility span. In Florence, as near Limoges, conceptions followed one another more rapidly than two or three centuries later. In practical terms, this meant that a woman was pregnant or had just given birth and was newly "churched" for nine months out of every eighteen.

Another consequence of closely spaced pregnancies was that during half of their conjugal life a couple was theoretically supposed to abstain from marital relations for fear of "spoiling" the fetus, in particular after quickening. Infringing this prohibition was perhaps only a venial sin after the time of Albertus

Magnus, toward the middle of the thirteenth century, but it was sin all the same. The couple was also held to abstinence if the mother breast-fed her infant, for the birth of a younger child risked shortening the nursing period, hence the life, of its elder sibling. Did the couples in our French and Italian examples continue to respect these ancient prohibitions? It is difficult to tell. Contemporaries at times repeat the ancient taboos, which seem still in force, but which are more likely to concern the danger of sexual relations during the woman's menstrual period. The great preacher Bernardino da Siena told women, and the merchant Paolo da Certaldo reminded men, that "if children are generated at such a time, they will be born monstrous or leprous"; that one risks sick children or children with ringworm; and that "never is the creature generated at such a time born without some great and notable defect." Disgrace would fall on the father who had failed to respect the prohibition "and [the child] could also bring you enormous harm."

The degree to which people heeded submission to religious prohibitions is more obvious, and observance of "prohibited times"—Advent and Lent—when the church forbade the celebration of marriages and recommended continence (though without making it obligatory) is more directly measurable. It is a standard exercise to ascertain the effect of these prohibitions by checking the number of marriages and of conceptions. As it happens, in both the Limousin and in Tuscany, we can see significant dips in the marriage curve in December and in March and a lowering of conceptions during Lent. At least among city people, the preachers' target of choice, the church's injunctions were heeded.

Study of our French and Tuscan samplings suggests, finally, that couples did not seek to avoid conception by recourse to the various contraceptive means—abortive potions, salves, condoms, and charms—that their clients and their judges claimed were used by prostitutes and by women accused of magic and sorcery. All councils from the early Middle Ages to the twelfth century ceaselessly reiterated the prohibition and the punishment of actions aimed at preventing a birth or doing away with the infant. From the thirteenth century on, acquaintance with Arab medical treatises and the vogue for Ovid may have diffused contraceptive practices in certain milieux. In any event, discussion of them led the theologians to mitigate their prohibitions somewhat. Some of them no longer forbade copulation between barren partners or they allowed *coitus reservatus,* which meant that a couple could seek pleasure, not procreation. Others no longer equated contraception with infanticide. Up to the end of the period that concerns us, however, the preachers constantly returned to the mortal sin of a sexual union "against nature" that went against "the form of matrimony." Bernardino told his women listeners:

> Listen: every time that you use together in such a way as to prevent generation, every time it is a mortal sin. Have I told you clearly enough? . . . It is worse for a man to use in such a way than with his own mother in the usual way. . . . And yet—O Woman! learn this this morning, and tie it to your finger—if your husband asks of you something that is a sin against nature, do not ever consent to it.

The only occasion on which the woman could and must contravene her duty to obey her husband, even at peril of her life, was thus if he should impose upon her a position in sexual relations that "breaks the order of God," changes the woman "into a beast or into a male," and prevents conception.

Sodomitic or not, practices "against nature" between Christian spouses were combated by directors of conscience because they attributed contraceptive aims to them. It does not seem, however, that such procedures had any perceptible effect on the fertility rate of couples of the time. The average interval between births remained quite stable until the next to last birth, which shows that couples did not massively use any sort of artifice to avoid their duty to reproduce. It is true that Limousin notables and Florentine merchants had the means to provide for the upbringing of their progeny. Here again, we cannot generalize from their example to all provinces and all social milieus in medieval Europe.

There was one perfectly natural and legitimate way to slow the rhythm of births, which was to allow the mother to breast-feed her infant. The wet nurse, however, a familiar character in *chansons de geste* and courtly romances, was no longer the exclusive privilege of the nobility during the latter centuries of the Middle Ages. To cite Florence once more, in the fourteenth century patrician families frequently included a nurse in their households, and recourse to the services of a country woman was widespread throughout all the middle level of the bourgeoisie during the following century. This had two consequences: poor women, who nursed their own children for many months, rented out their milk if a child died, thus earning not only a wage but a chance to put off a new pregnancy. On the other hand, sending a child out to a wet nurse offered an opportunity for more closely spaced children, thus for more children, to wealthy families in search of heirs, who valued fertile women and large numbers of offspring. One can find the highest number of children per couple under the roofs of the wealthiest families listed by the census in Tuscany at the beginning of the fifteenth century. The bed of the poor was then less fecund than that of the powerful.

The childbearing life of an adult female married before she was eighteen years of age, as we have seen, was punctuated with births and ended some twenty years later. Few of all the children whom she had brought into the world were present at the same time under the paternal roof. Maternity was fitful in the Middle Ages. Mothers who gave their infants to a wet nurse outside the house immediately after baptism got them back—if they survived—only a year and a half or two years later. In the meantime some of the child's siblings might have succumbed to the diseases and plagues that periodically bled the population. This means that the enormous families of ten, even fifteen children remain theoretical, the result of a reconstitution on paper by historians of demography. In the everyday flux of births and deaths, medieval households included an average of barely more than two living children, as shown in the census documents, and the survivors mentioned in the father's or the mother's testaments rarely exceed this meager total.

Private journals show that in the merchant class at least one-fourth of the tiny Florentines sent out to nurse died there. Worse: 45 percent of the children born to wealthy families failed to reach the age of twenty. Death stalked the new life and lay in wait for its mother. Women died perhaps less often in childbirth than is said; nonetheless, even wealthy women went through one of the most perilous moments of their life. One out of three Florentine women who died before their husbands did so bringing a child into the world or as an immediate consequence of childbirth. To those who died we should add those who suffered for years from various postnatal disorders, like one unfortunate wife, who had borne her husband fifteen children in twenty-three years and was diagnosed by him in 1512 as having *mal della matricha*. Overall, one mother out of seven or eight in these otherwise well-protected families fell victim to her procreative duties. Obviously, she usually carried her newborn child to death as well.

The burden of pregnancies and childbirths thus meant that a child had only one chance out of two of reaching adulthood. We can understand the Christian resignation to which parents clung when once again they lost a child—a resignation that somewhat hastily leads us to tax them with insensitivity. Certainly, sending a newborn infant to a far-away nurse did little to favor the blossoming of maternal sentiments or paternal interest, and the news of the child's death did not provoke the rending anguish that follows daily observation of the child's development and that can be seen in expressions of the father's grief at the death of a child who lived at home. It is impossible not to believe in the sincerity of the father of Falchetta Rinuccini, who died at the age of three in 1509, when he writes "I am certain that she has flown to heaven" and prays that "this saintly little dove will pray Divine Goodness and his sweet Mother for us." Nor can we doubt Giovanni Morelli, who exclaims after his ten-year-old son's death in 1406, "I could never have thought that God having divided from me my said son, [and having him] pass from this life to another could have been for me and is such a grievous knife." Even the dryly conventional phrases that accompany notation of the death of a child at the wet nurse's do not completely veil the profound disappointment and frustration that parents so frequently experienced in their desire at least to perpetuate the family and the family name: "It pleased God to call to himself the said Lucha on the eleventh day of August 1390; let us hope he has received him with his blessing and with my own," and so forth. Another father notes, "And of the fourteenth day of the said month and year he was brought back dead from Pian di Ripoli by the nurse: We think she smothered him. He was buried in [the church of} San Jacopo tra le Fosse: may God bless him and our other dead."

CHAPTER 21

Fast, Feast, and Flesh: The Religious Significance of Food to Medieval Women

Caroline Walker Bynum

In reading the lives of the [ancients] our lukewarm blood curdles at the thought of their austerities, but we remain strangely unimpressed by the essential point, namely, their determination to do God's will in all things, painful or pleasant.

—Henry Suso
German mystic of the fourteenth century

Strange to say, the ability to live on the eucharist and to resist starvation by diabolical power died out in the Middle Ages and was replaced by "fasting girls" who still continue to amuse us with their vagaries.

—William Hammond
Nineteenth-century American physician and founder of the New York Neurological Society

Scholars have recently devoted much attention to the spirituality of the thirteenth, fourteenth, and fifteenth centuries. In studying late medieval spirituality they have concentrated on the ideals of chastity and poverty—that is, on the renunciation, for religious reasons, of sex and family, money and property. It may be, however, that modern scholarship has focused so tenaciously on sex and money because sex and money are such crucial symbols and sources of power in our own culture. Whatever the motives, modern scholars have ignored a religious symbol that had tremendous force in the lives of medieval Christians. They have ignored the religious significance of food. Yet, when we look at what medieval people themselves wrote, we find that they often spoke of gluttony as the major form of lust, of fasting as the most

From Caroline Walker Bynum, "Fast, Feast, and Flesh: The Religious Significance of Food to Medieval Women," © 1985 by The Regents of the University of California. Reprinted from *Representations*, Vol. 11. Summer of 1985, pp. 1–6, 8–16 by permission.

painful renunciation, and of eating as the most basic and literal way of encountering God. Theologians and spiritual directors from the early church to
the sixteenth century reminded penitents that sin had entered the world
when Eve ate the forbidden fruit and that salvation comes when Christians
eat their God in the ritual of the communion table.

In the Europe of the late thirteenth and fourteenth centuries, famine was
on the increase again, after several centuries of agricultural growth and relative plenty. Vicious stories of food hoarding, of cannibalism, of infanticide, or
of ill adolescents left to die when they could no longer do agricultural labor
sometimes survive in the sources, suggesting a world in which hunger and
even starvation were not uncommon experiences. The possibility of overeating
and of giving away food to the unfortunate was a mark of privilege, of aristocratic or patrician status—a particularly visible form of what we call conspicuous consumption, what medieval people called magnanimity or largesse.
Small wonder then that gorging and vomiting, luxuriating in food until food
and body were almost synonymous, became in folk literature an image of un-
bridled sensual pleasure; that magic vessels which forever brim over with
food and drink were staples of European folktales; that one of the most common charities enjoined on religious orders was to feed the poor and ill; or that
sharing one's own meager food with a stranger (who might turn out to be an
angel, a fairy, or Christ himself) was, in hagiography and folk story alike, a
standard indication of heroic or saintly generosity. Small wonder too that voluntary starvation, deliberate and extreme renunciation of food and drink,
seemed to medieval people the most basic asceticism, requiring the kind of
courage and holy foolishness that marked the saints.

Food was not only a fundamental material concern to medieval people;
food practices—fasting and feasting—were at the very heart of the Christian
tradition. A Christian in the thirteenth and fourteenth centuries was required
by church law to fast on certain days and to receive communion at least once a
year. Thus the behavior that defined a Christian was food-related behavior.
This point is clearly illustrated in a twelfth-century story of a young man (of
the house of Ardres) who returned from the crusades claiming that he had become a Saracen in the East; he was, however, accepted back by his family, and
no one paid much attention to his claim until he insisted on eating meat on
Friday. The full impact of his apostasy was then brought home, and his family
kicked him out.

Food was, moreover, a central metaphor and symbol in Christian poetry,
devotional literature, and theology because a meal (the eucharist) was the central Christian ritual, the most direct way of encountering God. And we should
note that this meal was a frugal repast, not a banquet but simply the two basic
foodstuffs of the Mediterranean world: bread and wine. Although older
Mediterranean traditions of religious feasting did come, in a peripheral way,
into Christianity, indeed lasting right through the Middle Ages in various
kinds of carnival, the central religious meal was reception of the two basic
supports of human life. Indeed Christians believed it *was* human life. Already
hundreds of years before transubstantiation was defined as doctrine, most

Christians thought that they quite literally ate Christ's body and blood in the sacrament. Medieval people themselves knew how strange this all might sound. A fourteenth-century preacher, Johann Tauler, wrote:

> St. Bernard compared this sacrament [the eucharist] with the human processes of eating when he used the similes of chewing, swallowing, assimilation and digestion. To some people this will seem crude, but let such refined persons beware of pride, which comes from the devil: a humble spirit will not take offense at simple things.

Thus food, as practice and as symbol, was crucial in medieval spirituality. But in the period from 1200 to 1500 it was more prominent in the piety of women than in that of men. Although it is difficult and risky to make any quantitative arguments about the Middle Ages, so much work has been done on saints' lives, miracle stories, and vision literature that certain conclusions are possible about the relative popularity of various practices and symbols. Recent work by André Vauchez, Richard Kieckhefer, Donald Weinstein, and Rudolph M. Bell demonstrates that, although women were only about 18 percent of those canonized or revered as saints between 1000 and 1700, they were 30 percent of those in whose lives extreme austerities were a central aspect of holiness and over 50 percent of those in whose lives illness (often brought on by fasting and other penitential practices) was the major factor in reputation for sanctity. In addition, Vauchez has shown that most males who were revered for fasting fit into one model of sanctity—the hermit saint (usually a layman)—and this was hardly the most popular male model, whereas fasting characterized female saints generally. Between late antiquity and the fifteenth century there are at least thirty cases of women who were reputed to eat nothing at all except the eucharist, but I have been able to find only one or possibly two male examples of such behavior before the well-publicized fifteenth-century case of the hermit Nicholas of Flüe. Moreover, miracles in which food is miraculously multiplied are told at least as frequently of women as of men, and giving away food is so common a theme in the lives of holy women that it is very difficult to find a story in which this particular charitable activity does not occur. The story of a woman's basket of bread for the poor turning into roses when her husband (or father) protests her almsgiving was attached by hagiographers to at least five different women saints.

If we look specifically at practices connected with Christianity's holy meal, we find that eucharistic visions and miracles occurred far more frequently to women, particularly certain types of miracles in which the quality of the eucharist as food is underlined. It is far more common, for example, for the wafer to turn into honey or meat in the mouth of a woman. Miracles in which an unconsecrated host is vomited out or in which the recipient can tell by tasting the wafer that the priest who consecrated it is immoral happen almost exclusively to women. Of fifty-five people from the later Middle Ages who supposedly received the holy food directly from Christ's hand in a vision, forty-five are women. In contrast, the only two types of eucharistic miracle that occur primarily to men are miracles that underline not the fact that the wafer is food but the power of the priest. Moreover, when we study medieval miracles, we note that miraculous abstinence and extravagant eucharistic visions tend to occur together and are frequently accompanied by miraculous bodily changes. Such changes are found almost exclusively in women. Miraculous elongation of parts of the body, the appearance on the body of marks imitating the various wounds of Christ (called stigmata), and the exuding of wondrous fluids (which smell sweet and heal and sometimes *are* food—for example, manna or milk) are usually female miracles.

If we consider a different kind of evidence—the *exempla* or moral tales that preachers used to educate their audiences, both monastic and lay—we find that, according to Frederic Tubach's index, only about 10 percent of such stories are about women. But when we look at those stories that treat specifically fasting, abstinence, and reception of the eucharist, 30 to 50 percent are about women. The only type of religious literature in which food is more frequently associated with men is the genre of satires on monastic life, in which there is some suggestion that monks are more prone to greed. But this pattern probably reflects the fact that monasteries for men were in general wealthier than women's houses and therefore more capable of mounting elaborate banquets and tempting palates with delicacies.

Taken together, this evidence demonstrates two things. First, food practices were more central in women's piety than in men's. Second, both men and women associated food—especially fasting and the eucharist—with women. There are, however, a number of problems with this sort of evidence. In addition to the obvious problems of the paucity of material and of the nature of hagiographical accounts—problems to which scholars since the seventeenth century have devoted much sophisticated discussion—there is the problem inherent in quantifying data. In order to count phenomena the historian must divide them up, put them into categories. Yet the most telling argument for the prominence of food in women's spirituality is the way in which food motifs interweave in women's lives and writings until even phenomena not normally thought of as eating, feeding, or fasting seem to become food-related. In other words, food becomes such a pervasive concern that it provides both a literary and a psychological unity to the woman's way of seeing the world. And this cannot be demonstrated by statistics. Let me therefore tell in some detail one of the many stories from the later Middle Ages in which food becomes a leitmotif of stunning complexity and power. It is the story of Lidwina of the town of Schiedam in the Netherlands, who died in 1433 at the age of 53.

Several hagiographical accounts of Lidwina exist, incorporating information provided by her confessors; moreover, the town officials of Schiedam, who had her watched for three months, promulgated a testimonial that suggests that Lidwina's miraculous abstinence attracted more public attention than any other aspect of her life. The document solemnly attests to her complete lack of food and sleep and to the sweet odor given off by the bits of skin she supposedly shed.

The accounts of Lidwina's life suggest that there may have been early conflict between mother and daughter. When her terrible illness put a burden on her family's resources and patience, it took a miracle to convince her mother of her sanctity. One of the few incidents that survives from her childhood shows her mother annoyed with her childish dawdling. Lidwina was required to carry food to her brothers at school, and on the way home she slipped into church to say a prayer to the Virgin. The incident shows how girlish piety could provide a respite from household tasks—in this case, as in so many cases, the task of feeding men. We also learn that Lidwina was upset to discover that she was pretty, that she threatened to pray for a deformity when plans were broached for her marriage, and that, after an illness at age fifteen, she grew weak and did not want to get up from her sickbed. The accounts thus suggest that she may have been cultivating illness—perhaps even rejecting food—before the skating accident some weeks later that produced severe internal injuries. In any event, Lidwina never recovered from her fall on the ice. Her hagiographers report that she was paralyzed except for her left hand. She burned with fever and vomited convulsively. Her body putrified so that great pieces fell off. From mouth, ears, and nose, she poured blood. And she stopped eating.

Lidwina's hagiographers go into considerable detail about her abstinence. At first she supposedly ate a little piece of apple each day, although bread dipped into liquid caused her much pain. Then she reduced her intake to a bit of date and watered wine flavored with spices and sugar; later she survived on watered wine alone—only half a pint a week—and she preferred it when the water came from the river and was contaminated with salt from the tides. When she ceased to take any solid food, she also ceased to sleep. And finally she ceased to swallow anything at all. Although Lidwina's biographers present her abstinence as evidence of saintliness, she was suspected by some during her lifetime of being possessed by a devil instead; she herself appears to have claimed that her fasting was natural. When people accused her of hypocrisy, she replied that it is no sin to eat and therefore no glory to be incapable of eating.

Fasting and illness were thus a single phenomenon to Lidwina. And since she perceived them as redemptive suffering, she urged both on others. We are told that a certain Gerard from Cologne, at her urging, became a hermit and lived in a tree, fed only on manna sent from God. We are also told that Lidwina prayed for her twelve-year-old nephew to be afflicted with an illness so that he would be reminded of God's mercy. Not surprisingly, the illness itself then came from miraculous feeding. The nephew became sick by drinking several drops from a pitcher of unnaturally sweet beer on a table by Lidwina's bedside.

Like the bodies of many other women saints, Lidwina's body was closed to ordinary intake and excreting but produced extraordinary effluvia. The authenticating document from the town officials of Schiedam testifies that her body shed skin, bones, and even portions of intestines, which her parents kept in a vase; and these gave off a sweet odor until Lidwina, worried by the gossip that they excited, insisted that her mother bury them. Moreover, Lidwina's effluvia cured others. A man in England sent for her wash water to cure his ill leg. The sweet smell from her left hand led one of her confessors to confess his own sins. And Lidwina actually nursed others in an act that she herself explicitly saw as a parallel to the Virgin's nursing of Christ.

• • •

Lidwina did not write herself, but some pious women did. And many of these women not only lived lives in which miraculous abstinence, charitable feeding of others, wondrous bodily changes, and eucharistic devotion were central; they also elaborated in prose and poetry a spirituality in which hungering, feeding, and eating were central metaphors for suffering, for service, and for encounter with God. For example, the great Italian theorist of purgatory, Catherine of Genoa (d. 1510)—whose extreme abstinence began in response to an unhappy marriage and who eventually persuaded her husband to join her in a life of continence and charitable feeding of the poor and sick— said that the annihilation of ordinary food by a devouring body is the best metaphor for the annihilation of the soul by God in mystical ecstasy. She also wrote that, although no simile can adequately convey the joy in God that is the goal of all souls, nonetheless the image that comes most readily to mind is to describe God as the only bread available in a world of the starving. Another Italian Catherine, Catherine of Siena (d. 1380), in whose saintly reputation fasting, food miracles, eucharistic devotion, and (invisible) stigmata were central, regularly chose to describe Christian duty as "eating at the table of the cross the food of the honor of God and the salvation of souls." To Catherine, "to eat" and "to hunger" have the same fundamental meaning, for one eats but is never full, desires but is never satiated. "Eating" and "hungering" are active, not passive, images. They stress pain more than joy. They mean most basically to suffer and to serve—to suffer because in hunger one joins with Christ's suffering on the cross; to serve because to hunger is to expiate the sins of the world. Catherine wrote:

> And then the soul becomes drunk. And after it . . . has reached the place [of the teaching of the crucified Christ] and drunk to the full, it tastes the food of patience, the odor of virtue, and such a desire to bear the cross that it does not seem that it could ever be satiated. . . . And then the soul becomes like a drunken man; the more he drinks the more he wants to drink; the more it bears the cross the more it wants to bear it. And the pains are its refreshment and the tears which it has shed for the memory of the blood are its drink. And the sighs are its food.

And again:

> Dearest mother and sisters in sweet Jesus Christ, I, Catherine, slave of the slaves of Jesus Christ, write to you in his precious blood, with the desire to see you confirmed in true and perfect charity so that you be true nurses of your souls. For we cannot nourish others if first we do not nourish our own souls with true and real virtues. . . . Do as the child does who, wanting to take milk, takes the mother's breast and places it in his mouth and draws to himself the

milk by means of the flesh. So . . . we must attach ourselves to the breast of the crucified Christ, in whom we find the mother of charity, and draw from there by means of his flesh (that is, the humanity) the milk that nourishes our soul. . . . For it is Christ's humanity that suffered, not his divinity; and, without suffering, we cannot nourish ourselves with this milk which we draw from charity.

To the stories and writings of Lidwina and the two Catherines—with their insistent and complex food motifs—I could add dozens of others. Among the most obvious examples would be the beguine Mary of Oignies (d. 1213) from the Low Countries, the princess Elisabeth of Hungary (d. 1231), the famous reformer of French and Flemish religious houses Colette of Corbie (d. 1447), and the thirteenth-century poets Hadewijch and Mechtild of Magdeburg. But if we look closely at the lives and writings of those men from the period whose spirituality is in general closest to women's and who were deeply influenced by women—for example, Francis of Assisi in Italy, Henry Suso and Johann Tauler in the Rhineland, Jan van Ruysbroeck of Flanders, or the English hermit Richard Rolle—we find that even to these men food asceticism is not the central ascetic practice. Nor are food metaphors central in their poetry and prose. Food then is much more important to women than to men as a religious symbol. The question is why?

Modern scholars who have noticed the phenomena I have just described have sometimes suggested in an offhand way that miraculous abstinence and eucharistic frenzy are simply "eating disorders." The implication of such remarks is usually that food disorders are characteristic of women rather than men, perhaps for biological reasons, and that these medieval eating disorders are different from nineteenth-and twentieth-century ones only because medieval people "theologized" what we today "medicalize." While I cannot deal here with all the implications of such analysis, I want to point to two problems with it. First, the evidence we have indicates that extended abstinence was almost exclusively a male phenomenon in early Christianity and a female phenomenon in the high Middle Ages. The cause of such a distribution of cases cannot be primarily biological. Second, medieval people did not treat all refusal to eat as a sign of holiness. They sometimes treated it as demonic possession, but they sometimes also treated it as illness. Interestingly enough, some of the holy women whose fasting was taken as miraculous (for example, Colette of Corbie) functioned as healers of ordinary individuals, both male and female, who could not eat. Thus, for most of the Middle Ages, it was only in the case of some unusually devout women that not-eating was both supposedly total and religiously significant. Such behavior must have a cultural explanation.

On one level, the cultural explanation is obvious. Food was important to women religiously because it was important socially. In medieval Europe (as in many countries today) women were associated with food preparation and distribution *rather than* food consumption. The culture suggested that women cook and serve, men eat. Chronicle accounts of medieval banquets, for example, indicate that the sexes were often segregated and that women were sometimes relegated to watching from the balconies while gorgeous foods were rolled out to please the eyes as well as the palates of men. Indeed men were rather afraid of women's control of food. Canon lawyers suggested, in the codes they drew up, that a major danger posed by women was their manipulation of male virility by charms and potions added to food. Moreover, food was not merely *a* resource women controlled; it was *the* resource women controlled. Economic resources were controlled by husbands, fathers, uncles, or brothers. In an obvious sense, therefore, fasting and charitable food distribution (and their miraculous counterparts) were natural religious activities for women. In fasting and charity women renounced and distributed the one resource that was theirs. Several scholars have pointed out that late twelfth- and early thirteenth-century women who wished to follow the new ideal of poverty and begging (for example, Clare of Assisi and Mary of Oignies) were simply not permitted either by their families or by religious authorities to do so. They substituted fasting for other ways of stripping the self of support. Indeed a thirteenth-century hagiographer commented explicitly that one holy woman gave up food because she had nothing else to give up. Between the thirteenth and fifteenth centuries, many devout laywomen who resided in the homes of fathers or spouses were able to renounce the world in the midst of abundance because they did not eat or drink the food that was paid for by family wealth. Moreover, women's almsgiving and abstinence appeared culturally acceptable forms of asceticism because what women ordinarily did, as housewives, mothers, or mistresses of great castles, was to prepare and serve food rather than to eat it.

The issue of control is, however, more basic than this analysis suggests. Food-related behavior was central to women socially and religiously not only because food was a resource women controlled but also because, by means of food, women controlled themselves and their world.

First and most obviously, women controlled their bodies by fasting. Although a negative or dualist concept of body does not seem to have been the most fundamental notion of body to either women or men, some sense that body was to be disciplined, defeated, occasionally even destroyed, in order to release or protect spirit is present in women's piety. Some holy women seem to have developed an extravagant fear of any bodily contact. Clare of Montefalco (d. 1308), for example, said she would rather spend days in hell than be touched by a man. Lutgard of Aywières panicked at an abbot's insistence on giving her the kiss of peace, and Jesus had to interpose his hand in a vision so that she was not reached by the abbot's lips. She even asked to have her own gift of healing by touch taken away. Christina of Stommeln (d. 1312), who fell into a latrine while in a trance, was furious at the laybrothers who rescued her because they touched her in order to do so.

Many women were profoundly fearful of the sensations of their bodies, especially hunger and thirst. Mary of Oignies, for example, was so afraid of taking pleasure in food that Christ had to make her unable to taste. From the late twelfth century comes a sad story of a dreadfully sick girl named Alpaïs who sent away the few morsels of pork given her to suck, because she feared that any enjoyment of eating might mushroom madly into gluttony or lust. Women like Ida of Louvain (d. perhaps 1300), Elsbeth Achler of Reute (d. 1420), Catherine of Genoa, or Columba of Rieti (d. 1501), who sometimes snatched up food and ate without knowing what they were doing, focused their hunger on the eucharist partly because it was an acceptable object of craving and partly because it was a self-limiting food. Some of women's asceticism was clearly directed toward destroying bodily needs, before which women felt vulnerable.

Some fasting may have had as a goal other sorts of bodily control. There is some suggestion in the accounts of hagiographers that fasting women were admired for suppressing excretory functions. Several biographers comment with approval that holy women who do not eat cease also to excrete, and several point out explicitly that the menstruation of saintly women ceases. Medieval theology—profoundly ambivalent about body as physicality—was ambivalent about menstruation also, seeing it both as the polluting "curse of Eve" and as a natural function that, like all natural functions, was redeemed in the humanity of Christ. Theologians even debated whether or not the Virgin Mary menstruated. But natural philosophers and theologians were aware that, in fact, fasting suppresses menstruation. Albert the Great noted that some holy women ceased to menstruate because of their fasts and austerities and commented that their health did not appear to suffer as a consequence.

Moreover, in controlling eating and hunger, medieval women were also explicitly controlling sexuality. Ever since Tertullian and Jerome, male writers had warned religious women that food was dangerous because it excited lust. Although there is reason to suspect that male biographers exaggerated women's sexual temptations, some women themselves connected food abstinence with chastity and greed with sexual desire.

Women's heightened reaction to food, however, controlled far more than their physicality. It also controlled their social environment. As the story of Lidwina of Schiedam makes clear, women often coerced both families and religious authorities through fasting and through feeding. To an aristocratic or rising merchant family of late medieval Europe, the self-starvation of a daughter or spouse could be deeply perplexing and humiliating. It could therefore be an effective means of manipulating, educating, or converting family members. In one of the most charming passages of Margery Kempe's autobiography, for example, Christ and Margery consult together about her asceticism and decide that, although she wishes to practice both food abstention and sexual continence, she should perhaps offer to trade one behavior for the other. Her husband, who had married Margery in an effort to rise socially in the town of Lynn and who was obviously ashamed of her queer penitential clothes and food practices, finally agreed to grant her sexual abstinence in private if she would return to normal cooking and eating in front of the neighbors. Catherine of Siena's sister, Bonaventura, and the Italian saint Rita of Cascia (d. 1456) both reacted to profligate young husbands by wasting away and managed thereby to tame disorderly male behavior. Columba of Rieti and Catherine of Siena expressed what was clearly adolescent conflict with their mothers and riveted family attention on their every move by their refusal to eat. Since fasting so successfully manipulated and embarrassed families, it is not surprising that self-starvation often originated or escalated at puberty, the moment at which families usually began negotiations for husbands for their daughters. Both Catherine and Columba, for example, established themselves as unpromising marital material by their extreme food and sleep deprivation, their frenetic giving away of paternal resources, and their compulsive service of family members in what were not necessarily welcome ways. (Catherine insisted on doing the family laundry in the middle of the night.)

Fasting was not only a useful weapon in the battle of adolescent girls to change their families' plans for them. It also provided for both wives and daughters an excuse for neglecting food preparation and family responsibilities. Dorothy of Montau, for example, made elementary mistakes of cookery (like forgetting to scale the fish before frying them) or forgot entirely to cook and shop while she was in ecstasy. Margaret of Cortona refused to cook for her illegitimate son (about whom she felt agonizing ambivalence) because, she said, it would distract her from prayer.

Moreover, women clearly both influenced and rejected their families' values by food distribution. Ida of Louvain, Catherine of Siena, and Elisabeth of Hungary, each in her own way, expressed distaste for family wealth and coopted the entire household into Christian charity by giving away family resources, sometimes surreptitiously or even at night. Elisabeth, who gave away her husband's property, refused to eat any food except that paid for by her own dowry because the wealth of her husband's family came, she said, from exploiting the poor.

Food-related behavior—charity, fasting, eucharistic devotion, and miracles—manipulated religious authorities as well. Women's eucharistic miracles—especially the ability to identify unconsecrated hosts or unchaste priests—functioned to expose and castigate clerical corruption. The Viennese woman Agnes Blannbekin, knowing that her priest was not chaste, prayed that he be deprived of the host, which then flew away from him and into her own mouth. Margaret of Cortona saw the hands of an unchaste priest turn black when he held the host. Saints' lives and chronicles contain many stories, like that told of Lidwina of Schiedam, of women who vomited out unconsecrated wafers, sometimes to the considerable discomfiture of local authorities.

The intimate and direct relationship that holy women claimed to the eucharist was often a way of bypassing ecclesiastical control. Late medieval confessors and theologians attempted to inculcate awe as well as craving for the eucharist; and women not only received ambiguous advice about frequent communion, they were also sometimes barred from receiving it at exactly the point at which their fasting and hunger reached fever pitch. In such circumstances many women simply received in vision what the celebrant or confessor withheld. Imelda Lambertini, denied communion because she was too young, and Ida of Léau, denied because she was subject to "fits," were given the host by Christ. And some women received, again in visions, either Christ's blood, which they were regularly denied because of their lay status, or the power to consecrate and distribute, which they were denied because of their gender. Angela of Foligno and Mechtild of Hackeborn were each, in a vision, given the chalice to distribute. Catherine of Siena received blood in her mouth when she ate the wafer.

It is thus apparent that women's concentration on food enabled them to control and manipulate both their bodies and their environment. We must not underestimate the effectiveness of such manipulation in a world where it was often extraordinarily difficult for women to avoid marriage or to choose a religious vocation. But such a conclusion concentrates on the function of fasting and feasting, and function is not meaning. Food did not "mean" to medieval women the control it provided. It is time, finally, to consider explicitly what it meant.

As the behavior of Lidwina of Schiedam or the theological insights of Catherine of Siena suggest, fasting, eating, and feeding all meant suffering, and suffering meant redemption. These complex meanings were embedded in and engendered by the theological doctrine of the Incarnation. Late medieval theology, as is well known, located the saving moment of Christian history less in Christ's resurrection than in his crucifixion. Although some ambivalence about physicality, some sharp and agonized dualism, was present, no other period in the history of Christian spirituality has placed so positive a value on Christ's humanity as physicality. Fasting was thus flight not so much *from* as *into* physicality. Communion was consuming—i.e., becoming—a God who saved the world through physical, human agony. Food to medieval women meant flesh and suffering and, through suffering, salvation: salvation of self and salvation of neighbor. Although all thirteenth and fourteenth-century Christians emphasized Christ as suffering and Christ's suffering body as food, women were especially drawn to such a devotional emphasis. The reason seems to lie in the way in which late medieval culture understood "the female."

Drawing on traditions that went back even before the origins of Christianity, both men and women in the later Middle Ages argued that "woman is to man as matter is to spirit." Thus "woman" or "the feminine" was seen as symbolizing the physical part of human nature, whereas man symbolized the spiritual or rational. Male theologians and biographers of women frequently used this idea to comment on female weakness. They also inverted the image and saw "woman" as not merely below but also above reason. Thus they somewhat sentimentally saw Mary's love for souls and her mercy toward even the wicked as an apotheosis of female unreason and weakness, and they frequently used female images to describe themselves in their dependence on God. Women writers, equally aware of the male/female dichotomy, saw it somewhat differently. They tended to use the notion of "the female" as "flesh" to associate Christ's humanity with "the female" and therefore to suggest that women imitate Christ through physicality.

Women theologians saw "woman" as the symbol of humanity, where humanity was understood as including bodiliness. To the twelfth-century prophet, Elisabeth of Schönau, the humanity of Christ appeared in a vision as a female virgin. To Hildegard of Bingen (d. 1179), "woman" was the symbol of humankind, fallen in Eve, restored in Mary and church. She stated explicitly: "Man signifies the divinity of the Son of God and woman his humanity." Moreover, to a number of women writers, Mary was the source and container of Christ's physicality; the flesh Christ put on was in some sense female, because it was his mother's. Indeed whatever physiological theory of reproduction a medieval theologian held, Christ (who had no human father) had to be seen as taking his physicality from his mother. Mechtild of Magdeburg went further and implied that Mary was a kind of preexistent humanity of Christ as the Logos was his preexistent divinity. Marguerite of Oingt, like Hildegard of Bingen, wrote that Mary was the *tunica humanitatis,* the clothing of humanity, that Christ puts on. And to Julian of Norwich, God himself was a mother exactly in that our humanity in its full physicality was not merely loved and saved but even given being by and from him. Julian wrote:

> For in the same time that God joined himself to our body in the maiden's womb, he took our soul, which is sensual, and in taking it, having enclosed us all in himself, he united it to our substance. . . . So our Lady is our mother, in whom we are all enclosed and born of her in Christ, for she who is mother of our saviour is mother of all who are saved in our saviour; and our saviour is our true mother, in whom we are endlessly born and out of whom we shall never come.

Although male writers were apt to see God's motherhood in his nursing and loving rather than in the fact of creation, they too associated the flesh of Christ with Mary and therefore with woman.

Not only did medieval people associate humanity as body with woman; they also associated woman's body with food. Woman was food because breast milk was the human being's first nourishment—the one food essential for survival. Late medieval culture was extraordinarily concerned with milk as symbol. Writers and artists were fond of the theme, borrowed from antiquity, of lactation offered to a father or other adult male as an act of filial piety. The cult of the Virgin's milk was one of the most extensive cults in late medieval Europe. A favorite motif in art was the lactating Virgin. Even the bodies of evil women were seen as food. Witches were supposed to have queer marks on their bodies (sort of supernumerary breasts) from which they nursed incubi.

Quite naturally, male and female writers used nursing imagery in somewhat different ways. Men were more likely to use images of being nursed, women metaphors of nursing. Thus when male writers spoke of God's motherhood, they focused more narrowly on the soul being nursed at Christ's breast, whereas women were apt to associate mothering with punishing, educating, or giving birth as well. Most visions of drinking from the breast of Mary were received by men. In contrast, women (like Lidwina) often identified with Mary as she nursed Jesus or received visions of taking the Christchild to their own breasts. Both men and women, however, drank from the breast of Christ, in vision and image. Both men and women wove together—from Pauline references to milk and meat and from the rich breast and food images of the Song of Songs—a complex sense of Christ's blood as the nourishment and intoxication of the soul. Both men and women therefore saw the body on the cross, which in dying fed the world, as in some sense female. Again, physiological theory reinforced image. For, to medieval natural philosophers, breast milk was transmuted blood, and a human mother (like the pelican that also symbolized Christ) fed her children from the fluid of life that coursed through her veins.

Since Christ's body itself was a body that nursed the hungry, both men and women naturally assimilated the ordinary female body to it. A number of stories are told of female saints who exuded holy fluid from breasts or fingertips, either during life or after death. These fluids often cured the sick. The union of mouth to mouth, which many women gained with Christ, became also a way of feeding. Lutgard's saliva cured the ill; Lukardis of Oberweimar (d. 1309) blew the eucharist into another nun's mouth; Colette of Corbie regularly cured others with crumbs she chewed. Indeed one suspects that stigmata—so overwhelmingly a female phenomenon—appeared on women's bodies because they (like the marks on the bodies of witches and the wounds in the body of Christ) were not merely wounds but also breasts.

Thus many assumptions in the theology and the culture of late medieval Europe associated woman with flesh and with food. But the same theology also taught that the redemption of all humanity lay in the fact that Christ was flesh and food. A God who fed his children from his own body, a God whose humanity *was* his children's humanity, was a God with whom women found it easy to identify. In mystical ecstasy as in communion, women ate and became a God who was food and flesh. And in eating a God whose flesh was holy food, women both transcended and became more fully the flesh and the food their own bodies were.

Eucharist and mystical union were, for women, both reversals and continuations of all the culture saw them to be. In one sense, the roles of priest and lay recipient reversed normal social roles. The priest became the food preparer, the generator and server of food. The woman recipient ate a holy food she did not exude or prepare. Woman's jubilant, vision-inducing, inebriated eating of God was the opposite of the ordinary female acts of food preparation or of bearing and nursing children. But in another and, I think, deeper sense, the eating was not a reversal at all. Women became, in mystical eating, a fuller version of the food and the flesh they were assumed by their culture to be. In union with Christ, woman became a fully fleshly and feeding self—at one with the generative suffering of God.

Symbol does not determine behavior. Women's imitation of Christ, their assimilation to the suffering and feeding body on the cross, was not uniform. Although most religious women seem to have understood their devotional practice as in some sense serving as well as suffering, they acted in very different ways. Some, like Catherine of Genoa and Elisabeth of Hungary, expressed their piety in feeding and caring for the poor. Some, like Alpaïs, lay rapt in mystical contemplation as their own bodies decayed in disease or in self-induced starvation that was offered for the salvation of others. Many, like Lidwina of Schiedam and Catherine of Siena, did both. Some of these women are, to our modern eyes, pathological and pathetic. Others seem to us, as they did to their contemporaries, magnificent. But they all dealt, in feast and fast, with certain fundamental realities for which all cultures must find symbols— the realities of suffering and the realities of service and generativity.

Spiritual and Temporal Power

During the Middle Ages the church was not regarded as a private association within the state. Medieval thinkers instead set out from the idea of one Christian people ruled over by two hierarchies of government. The ecclesiastical hierarchy directed spiritual and religious affairs; the temporal hierarchy directed secular and mundane affairs. There always existed a possibility that the two hierarchies might come into conflict with one another. In that case, which had the higher claim on a Christian's allegiance? The attempt to work out the right relationship between the two powers provides one of the main themes of medieval history.

In the eleventh century, kings were regarded as sacred figures. They controlled the appointment of bishops and regulated most aspects of church affairs. This system was radically challenged by Pope Gregory VII (1073–1085). Gregory claimed to be fighting for the "freedom of the church," but modern historians disagree about his aims and the scope of his claims for the papacy. According to one school of thought, Gregory and his great successors like Innocent III (1198–1216) asserted a doctrine of papal overlordship in all affairs, spiritual and temporal. An argument for this point of view is presented in the reading from Walter Ullmann below. Ullmann maintains that the high claims of the medieval popes were simply the overt expression of a permanent underlying theology, or ideology, of spiritual power. In a classic old history of medieval political theory, R. W. Carlyle and A. J. Carlyle presented a different interpretation that still commands support among historians who dissent from Ullmann's "hierocratic" thesis. The Carlyles argue that the medieval popes never lost sight of the essential duality of spiritual and temporal power, and they see the claims of Gregory VII as an understandable reaction to a particular historical situation, the "degradation" of the church in the eleventh century. (In evaluating these two positions, readers might want to compare the modern arguments with the medieval texts on church and state included in the book of *Sources* that accompanies this volume.)[1]

In a more recent study, Harold Berman argues that the policies of Gregory VII were not inspired by a permanent ideology of papal power or directed simply against existing abuses; rather, they were revolutionary in nature and they initiated one of the great revolutions in Western history. Says Berman, "at the start of the revolution—in the *Dictatus Papae* of 1075—the previous political and legal order was declared to be abolished. Emperors were to kiss the feet of popes." In the reading below, Berman discusses some consequences of the "revolution" and shows how, paradoxically, it led on to the birth of the secular state.

Note

1. *The Middle Ages. Vol. 1: Sources of Medieval History,* edited by Brian Tierney (Burr Ridge, Ill.: McGraw-Hill, 1998).

CHAPTER 22

The Hierocratic Doctrine

Walter Ullmann

It may be helpful to state here the essence of the hierocratic ideology, according to which the pope as successor of St. Peter was entitled and bound to lead the community of the faithful, the Church. The means for the pope to do so were the laws issued by him in his supreme jurisdictional function, which claimed universal validity, and concerned themselves with everything that affected the vital interests and structural fabric of the Christian community. Obviously, from this hierocratic point of view, the judge of what was in the interests of that community, what facts, circumstances, actions, or situations touched its vital concerns, was the pope. He was the "judge ordinary" and claimed to possess the specific knowledge of when legislation was required. The function of the pope was that of a true monarch, governing the community that was entrusted to him. A further essential feature of this theory was the hierarchical gradation of offices, which ensured what was called order and smooth working of the whole community. This order was said to be maintained if everyone remained within his functions which were assigned to him. Bishops had their special functions, and so had kings. If either king or bishop intervened in, or rather interfered with, the other's functions, order would suffer and disorder would follow. The limitation of functional action was the hallmark of the hierocratic thesis, or, in other words, the principle of division of labour was a vital structural element of the thesis. Supreme directive control, the supreme authority (sovereignty), remained with the pope, who, standing as he did outside and above the community of the faithful, issued his directions as a "steersman," as a *gubernator*.

While considering the theory, the allegorical manner of expressing the relationship between priesthood and laity deserves consideration. The metaphor constantly used was that of the soul and body. The *anima-corpus* allegory was adduced a hundredfold to show the inferiority of the laity and the superiority of the clergy, to show that, just as the soul ruled the body, in the same manner the clergy ruled the laity, with the consequence that, as for instance Cardinal Humbert in the mid-eleventh century stated, the kings were the strong arms of the clergy, for the clergy were the eyes of the whole Church who knew what was to be done. In interpreting this antithesis one should not be misled by pure allegory. What the metaphorical use of soul and body attempted to express was that, because faith in Christ was the cementing bond of the whole Church and the exposition of the faith the business of the clergy, the law itself as the external regulator of society was to be based upon the faith. Faith and law stood to each other in the relation of cause and effect. The "soul" in this allegory was no more and no less than the pure idea of right and law, the uncontaminated Christian idea of the right way of living. What legal or legislative action faith required could be discerned only by those who had the eyes to see, the clergy. Differently expressed, since every law was to embody the idea of justice, and since justice was an essential ingredient of the Christian faith, the "soul" in this allegory meant the Christian idea of justice. There can be little doubt that this thesis was the medieval idea of the "rule of law," manifested the idea of the supremacy of the law. For the body of the faithful could, so it was said, be held together only by the law based on (Christian) justice, which on the one hand externalized the faith and on the other hand reflected the teleological thesis, for the law was considered the appropriate vehicle by which the body of the faithful was enabled to achieve its end. In short, the law was the soul which ruled the body corporate of the Christians. The legalism of the Middle Ages and quite especially of the hierocratic form of government found its ready explanation. It was said often enough that only through the law could a public body live, develop, and reach its end. Within the hierocratic thesis the king was subjected to sacerdotal rulings, the basic idea being that the king was not qualified enough to lay down the law in those matters which touched the essential fabric of Christian society. Fundamentally, this thesis of soul and body expressed simply the idea of governing a body public and corporate by means of the law.

As a consequence, the hierocratic ideology which emerged in its full maturity from the pontificate of Gregory VII onwards (1073–85) also laid particular stress upon the law. In fact, this pope went so far as to state dogmatically that it was "legal discipline" that had led kings onto the path of salvation. After all, they were distinguished by divinity to be the trustees of their kingdoms and had therefore all the more grounds for showing themselves "lovers of justice" (*amatores justitiae*), and justice, as an ingredient of the Christian faith, could be expounded only by the Roman Church, which was consequently called the "seat of justice." The king's duty was obedience to papal commands: he was a subject of the pope, to whom all Christians in any case were subjects. The teleological argumentation received its precision, notably by reference to the accumulated body of knowledge and learning as well as to the interpretation of the coronation orders: the purpose of God granting power to the king in the public sphere was to repress evil. If there had been no evil, there would have been no need for the power of the physical sword. Hence the pope claimed to exercise a "universal government" (*regimen universale*) by means of the law which made no distinction between matters or persons. The Petrine powers were comprehensive, exempting no one and nothing from the pope's jurisdiction. With exemplary unambiguity for instance Gregory VII declared:

If the holy see has the right to judge spiritual things, why then not secular things as well?

On another occasion he stated:

For if the see of St. Peter decides and judges celestial things, how much more does it decide and judge the earthly and secular.

From the papal standpoint it was true to say that the pope bore a very heavy burden, not only of spiritual tasks, but also of secular business, for he considered himself responsible for the direction of the body of the faithful under his control and in his charge. Obviously, the governmental power of the popes referred specifically to kings, because they disposed of the means of executing papal orders and decrees. Moreover, the king, for the reason already stated, was an "ecclesiastical person," whose office concerned itself with the repression of evil. Both the kingdom and the king's soul were, as the popes repeatedly declared, in their power. But the developed hierocratic programme did make the qualification that the pope considered papal jurisdiction to come into play only when the basic and vital interests of the body of the faithful called for his intervention. None expressed this principle better than Innocent III (1198–1216) in his usual concise language. He stated that feudal matters as such were of no concern to the pope's jurisdiction, which came into full operation however when sin was involved. *Ratione peccati* (by reason of sin) was the technical expression to denote the overriding papal jurisdiction. Evidently, the judge of when sin was involved was the pope himself.

The process of monopolizing the Bible had meanwhile made great strides. The popes applied to themselves the passage in Jeremiah i, 10: "I have set thee over the nations and kingdoms . . . ," because this was, according to Innocent III, a "prerogative" (the term occurs here for the first time) of the pope: this was nothing but the explicit expression of the monarchic principle. The same Innocent III declared that he was less than God but more than man, a statement that brings into clearest possible relief the very essence of the papal thesis, namely the superior status of the pope, his sovereignty, standing outside and above the community of the faithful. And it was precisely by virtue of his "superior" status that the papal Ruler gave the law. The development in the twelfth century leading to the concept of the pope as the vicar of Christ only underlined this point of view. The papal vicariate of Christ in itself changed nothing in the papal function. It attributed no more powers to him than he already had. What the concept of the vicariate of Christ focused attention on were the vicarious powers which Peter was said to have been given by Christ: it was these which, by way of succession, came to be wielded by the pope. The concept considerably clarified the function of the pope, with the consequence that a number of biblical passages which referred to Christ were now directly applied to the pope, so, for instance, the Matthean passage: "All power is given unto me. . . ." The vicariate of Christ in the pope demonstrated the pope as the point of intersection between heaven and earth. Hence it was that Innocent III said that what he had decreed was decreed by

Christ Himself. And Innocent IV (1245–54) stated that the pope figured as Christ's "corporal presence." It was quite in keeping with this theory that the government of the pope was considered to be a true *monarchatus*, because, as the canon lawyers taught, in his hands the "keys of the kingdom of heaven" had changed into the "keys of the law." This monarchic theory was succinctly expressed by Gregory IX (1227–41) thus:

> When Christ ascended into heaven, He left one vicar on earth, and hence it was necessary that all who wished to be Christians were to be subjected to the government of the vicar.

By the virtue of the thesis that God was the creator of everything on earth, the claim was raised by Innocent IV that every human creature (and not merely Christians) were subjects of the pope (who in the doctrine of the canon lawyers was *de jure*, but not *de facto*, the universal monarch). Indeed, the pope possessed—or at least claimed to possess—supreme overlordship over both bodies and souls of all men, as the same Gregory IX asserted. And before him a similar theory was expressed by Innocent III who held that the princes of the world had power over the body only, whilst the priests had power on earth as well as in heaven and over the souls also.

Because the pope functioned as the monarch of the body of the faithful, he claimed that his laws had reference to anyone and anything. Wherever the line of distinction between spiritual and temporal matters might have been drawn, for papal governmental ideology the distinction had no operational value. Since the end of the body of the faithful governed by the pope lay in the other world, anything that might be called temporal was subjected to that spiritual end. St. Paul had often enough declared the superiority of the spiritual over and above the mundane, the visible, the corporeal, or the secular. And by the process of monopolization the papacy made these Pauline views its own. Some statements of Gregory VII have already been quoted, but there were dozens of similar views expressed by other popes in the twelfth and thirteenth centuries. There was also the actual government of the popes who intervened in what might well have appeared, to the less sophisticated contemporaries, purely temporal matters. In the final resort the papal standpoint was based on the view that Christianity seized the whole of man and the whole of his activities without splitting them up into different compartments, which view led to the "totalitarian" system of government. If, indeed—and as we shall see, it was the royal opposition which argued in this way—the temporal was to be exempt from papal jurisdiction, this would not only have contradicted the all-embracing character of the Petrine powers of binding and loosing, but also the very essence of Christianity, at least as the papacy saw it. Neither things temporal nor the temporal Ruler could have had an autonomous, independent, autogenous standing in the papal scheme of government. Each was a means to an end. The pope, as monarchic sovereign, stood indeed outside and above the body of the faithful, a body that was one—"we are one body in Christ" according to St. Paul—and which suffered no division. In brief, unity of the body demanded unity of government, which manifested itself in the monarchy of the pope as the "overseer" (*speculator*) over all matters of basic concern to the well-being of the body.

• • •

Innocent III's thesis owed a good deal to St. Bernard of Clairvaux who, a generation before, had introduced the hierocratically orientated Two-Sword theory into the discussion, a theory that was alleged to have had its origin in Luke xxii, 38, and which had been used in a different sense already by Charlemagne's adviser, Alcuin, as well as by Henry IV. But, according to the doctrine of St. Bernard the pope possessed both swords, that is, the spiritual and the temporal (material), the one signifying the pope's priestly coercive power, the other the regal coercive power. During the coronation the pope gave the latter to the emperor, who was then said to wield the sword at the bidding of the pope (*ad nutum*). This Two-Sword theory was to signify that the actual physical power the emperor possessed was derived from the pope, or rather from God through the mediating organ of the pope. The ancient Isidorian doctrine was given its allegorical clothing. Gregory IX explicitly stated that the Lord had given the pope both swords, one of which the pope retained and wielded, the other he gave away. Or, as his successor Innocent IV stressed, the power of the material sword belonged potentially to the pope, but actually to the emperor. This Two-Sword allegory had reference to the emperor only. What therefore at the end of the thirteenth century Boniface VIII asserted in his *Unam sanctam* could barely be squared with the actual development, for he applied the allegory also to the kings who had never been crowned, nor had ever expressed an intention to be crowned, as emperors: a characteristic extension of a suggestive allegory. What, however, is significant is that the relevant decrees of the popes, especially Innocent III and IV and Gregory IX, were appropriately enough incorporated in the official canon law books under the title "Of majority and obedience," which seems very important in view of the (medieval) meaning of "majority," that is, sovereignty and the corresponding obedience on the part of the subjects.

CHAPTER 23

The Duality of Medieval Society

R. W. Carlyle and A. J. Carlyle

The truth is that the most distinctive element in the traditional political theory of the Middle Ages lay in the theory of a dualism in the structure of human society, that dualism of the spiritual and the temporal aspects of life, which was clearly expressed in the words of St. Peter to the Jewish authorities, "We must obey God rather than men" (Acts v. 29). It is no doubt possible that there may have been a momentary hesitation when the Empire became Christian, but in the West at least, if there was any hesitation, it was only momentary, and the normal principle was apprehended and expressed, especially by St. Ambrose in the fourth century and by Gelasius I in the fifth—that is, the principle that human society is governed by two powers, not by one, by the Temporal and the Spiritual, and that these are embodied in two authorities, the secular and the ecclesiastical, two authorities which are each divine in their origin, and are, each within its own sphere, independent of the other. This principle is clearly and emphatically restated in the ninth century, and was always present to the minds of men in the eleventh and twelfth

That this was substantially a new principle in the Western world is not doubtful. We would, however, venture to suggest that the movement of thought and feeling, both in countries of the Hellenic and Roman civilisations, and among the Jews in the centuries immediately preceding the Christian era, deserves a more full and precise treatment than it has yet received. The importance of the new conception hardly requires any explanation, the importance that is of the conception that life on its spiritual side is not subject to the temporal authority, but independent of it. It is one aspect, and not the least important, of a new development of the significance of individual personality, of a new conception of liberty.

If, however, the conception was significant and its consequences far-reaching, the attempt to carry it out in the practical organisation of human society was, and is to this day, immensely difficult. It is easy to see, or to think

From R. W. Carlyle and A. J. Carlyle, *A History of Mediaeval Political Theory in the West* (Edinburgh: William Blackwood and Sons Ltd., 1922), Vol. 4, 384–395. Reprinted by permission of the publisher.

that we see, the distinction between the spiritual and the temporal, when we think of them in general terms or in abstraction from the concrete realities of life; but it is a very different thing when we endeavour to apply the distinction to these. We have endeavoured in the first volume to illustrate some aspects of this from the circumstances of the ninth century, and the practical difficulties were greatly increased in the course of the tenth and eleventh centuries by the feudalisation of the position of the bishops and abbots, and their growing political importance; but, apart from this, the question of the relative authority of the two powers presented immense difficulties, and the Middle Ages arrived at no final solution of them, nor, for that matter, have we achieved this today.

The subject which we have been considering in this volume is the question how far, in the eleventh and twelfth centuries, the dualistic conception was tending to be replaced by a theory of the unity of authority, of the supremacy of one power over the other. If we are to attempt to arrive at some conclusion we must be careful to distinguish three aspects of the question: first, how far in actual fact one power interfered with or exercised authority over the other; second, how far there was developed a theory or principle of this; and third, how far what may have happened, or the theories which men formed, had any real importance in the actual character of mediaeval political life and thought.

The first question is in our view of very great importance, for it seems to us clear that, whatever theoretical judgments may have been asserted in the period which we are considering, they were not for the most part the results of abstract speculation, or the expression of systematic thinking, but rather arose out of certain practical difficulties and demands. And the first thing that must be observed is that behind all the actions and theories with which we have dealt there lay that great movement of religious reform which grew up in the later part of the tenth century, the revolt against the degraded conditions of the Church and the Papacy, the movement of which the Cluniac reform was one expression, and of which for a time Cluny was the centre. It is clear that the great authority which the emperors, from Otto I to Henry III, exercised over the Papacy and the ecclesiastical organisation, was due in the first place to the fact that the whole system of the Church was disorganised and degraded, and in the second place to the political importance of the great ecclesiastical officers. It is no doubt impossible to distinguish clearly between the influence of political ambitions and of religious principles as determining the action of Otto I with regard to the Papacy, but it is true to say that the authority exercised by him and his immediate successors was justified by its results. And this is even more obviously true of the action of Henry III.

It is evident that so long as the imperial action coincided with and represented the reforming spirit, many of the most eminent and most zealous of the reforming Churchmen took little offence. This is, we think, clearly evident from the attitude of men like Peter Damian and Cardinal Humbert, though there were some who even then doubted or denied the propriety of the imperial action—men like Thietmar of Merseburg and Wazo of Liège, and the author of the tract "De Ordinando Pontifice,"—but they seem to have been exceptions. The justification of the action of the secular authority in the tenth and eleventh centuries rested then not so much upon theory as on the practical conditions, and it must be observed that the action of Frederick Barbarossa with respect to the disputed election of Alexander III was formally justified by similar considerations— that is, upon the contention that if the order of the ecclesiastical system was imperilled by its own officers, it was the duty of the head of the Temporal power to intervene, not to determine ecclesiastical matters by his own authority, but to set the proper ecclesiastical machinery in movement.

The authority claimed by kings and emperors in the appointment of bishops and abbots, while it may have been partly justified by similar conditions, was actually the result of the political position of the greater clergy, under the condition of that feudal system which had grown up in the tenth century; and, as it proved, it was impossible to set it aside entirely. Until the death of Henry III the reforming party, while asserting the rights of the electors, did not on the whole dispute the propriety of an important place in appointment belonging to the political head of the community.

If, then, it is the truth that the exercise of authority in ecclesiastical matters by the secular power had its reasonable justification in the actual circumstances of these centuries, it is also true that the revolt against this arose out of and was justified by new conditions, and these new conditions are on the whole clear. With the death of Henry III the Empire ceased to represent the movement of reform, and indeed soon appeared to be the very centre of degradation, and it was this which brought about the conflict against lay "investiture," that is, appointment by the secular authority. It was thus that the conflict presented itself to the reforming party as a conflict for the freedom of the Church. It is no doubt true that other considerations and other ambitions may have entered into it, but it seems to us quite unreasonable to suggest that the demand for freedom was unreal: freedom to the reforming Churchmen had become the necessary condition of reform. It is this which gives a real significance to the first serious attempt to find a solution—that is, the revolutionary proposal of Paschal II to surrender the "regalia" that is the political position and powers of the greater clergy. And when it proved impossible to persuade Churchmen to accept so radical a proposal, it became evident that the only possible solution lay in compromise, and that is the real nature of the settlement of Worms in 1122.

If we now look at the other side of the question, and ask how, and how far the ecclesiastical power came to claim and to exercise authority over the secular, it would seem that we are again dealing with objective facts and their results. It was the failure of the reforming spirit in the imperial authority which led to the demand for liberty, and it was the judgment of Gregory VII that the secular authority in the Empire and also in France was not only the enemy of reform but also the real centre of corruption, and especially of simony, which moved him to attack not merely ecclesiastical offenders, but the secular authorities themselves. No doubt this was a new policy, for here as in all history the originative or creative force of individual personality played an important or even determining part, but the policy itself was intelligible and relevant to the actual circumstances. It was no doubt, if not an entirely new thing, yet in that time an almost revolutionary action to excommunicate the king or emperor, but the action represented after all both the fundamental principles of ecclesiastical authority, and the actual circumstances of the time. The action was reasonable, but it involved consequences which went far beyond itself, for in the judgment of Gregory the right to excommunicate involved the right to depose.

There is no reason to think that in claiming the right to depose a king who had forfeited his place as a member of the Christian Church Gregory intended to assert any theoretical authority over the Temporal power in temporal matters; but in and through Gregory's action the Spiritual power was in fact claiming a vast and indeterminate authority over the Temporal; and while the Popes between Gregory VII and Innocent III, at any rate after the death of Henry IV, made no very serious attempt to assert it, the fact remained that the authority had been claimed and the claim had not been surrendered.

We have arrived at the point where we must clearly turn to our second question, the question how far in these times there did grow up a theory of the supremacy of the one power over the other. If we are to avoid falling into confusion we must here be careful to make some distinctions. It might be asserted that one power was superior in intrinsic dignity and importance to the other; or it might be meant that the nature of one power was so much superior to the other, that, if any question arose between them, the judgment of the superior authority must prevail; or it might be meant that one of the two powers was the source of the authority of the other, and continued in principle to possess a superior authority over it even in its own sphere.

Of these conceptions the first would have been generally admitted. It would generally have been assumed by mediaeval thinkers that the matters with which the spiritual authority was concerned were of greater significance than those which belonged to the temporal, and that the dignity of the ecclesiastical office was greater than that of the secular. This is the position represented by Hugh of Fleury, and in spite of some of the phrases used by writers like Gregory of Catino and the author of the York Tractates, would hardly have been disputed.

The second raises a much more difficult question, for the general assumption of the Middle Ages was that each authority had its separate sphere, and in principle the case could not arise. It is of course true that all secular as well as all ecclesiastical authority was thought of as being subject to the law of God and the law of nature, and that all laws, ecclesiastical or secular, contrary to these were null and void. But the law of God and nature must not be confused with the law of the Church, with ecclesiastical law. . . . There is little evidence that it was maintained that the ecclesiastical authority had a final judgment in cases of conflict between these laws.

The truth is no doubt that it is very difficult for us to interpret the mediaeval temper: we are still in a large measure under the influence of a conception of sovereignty as representing some absolute and even arbitrary authority in the State or the Church which was unknown to the Middle Ages. The only sovereignty they recognised was that of the law, and even that was subject to the law of God or nature. To them the question of a collision between the two systems of law was very different from what it is to us. A collision could only properly speaking occur if one authority intruded into the sphere of the other.

What are we then to say with regard to the third conception? It is in truth clear from the literature which we have examined, that if there was in the eleventh and twelfth centuries any theory of the supremacy of the Spiritual over the Temporal power in its own sphere, it can only be found in the claims set out in some of Gregory VII's letters, or in Honorius of Augsburg and John of Salisbury, and possible in the canonist Rufinus, for in no other of those writers whom we have examined can it be clearly found. We must therefore in the first place ask, Is a theory of this kind implied in Gregory VII's writings? On the whole we think not.

These claims were indeed in practice almost revolutionary; but we must, if we are to understand them, ask what they were in principle, and we think that the principle is sufficiently clear. Gregory claimed the same spiritual jurisdiction over kings and emperors as over any other laymen: for due cause he had the right to excommunicate them, that is, to cut them off from the society of the faithful. And he drew from this the conclusion that he had the right, for due spiritual cause, and for this alone, to declare them deposed as well as excommunicated, to pronounce the oaths of allegiance which had been taken to them null and void. It is true that he nowhere really discusses the rationale of this, and does little more than cite some doubtful precedents, but it would seem to be reasonable to think that in his view the position of an excommunicated ruler of a Christian society was an impossible one.

This is not the same theory as a claim that the Spiritual power, as represented by the Pope, had a supreme authority in temporal matters. Indeed it appears to us plain that his conduct from 1076 to 1080 is clear evidence that he made no such claim and held no such theory. For him the position of Henry and of Rudolph, once Henry had been absolved at Canossa, was a matter to be decided by the German people. If he proposed that he or his representative should take part in the decision, it was because he had been invited to do so. We do not mean that Gregory VII had quite such a clear view of the circumstances as that which we have tried to put into words, but we think that something of this kind is implied in his conduct. The action and the words of Gregory undoubtedly implied a theory, but it was the theory that the spiritual authority was as complete with regard to spiritual matters, over those who held temporal authority, as over all other men, and that excommunication rendered them incapable of holding authority; it was not the theory that temporal authority was derived from the spiritual, or was subject to it in temporal matters.

It is not till we come to Honorius of Augsburg that we find anything of this kind. Here at last we do find something of it. Here at last we seem to find a theory which was formally inconsistent with the Gelasian principle, with the dualistic theory. For he seems to assert that the ecclesiastical authority was the true and only representative of Christ, and that the authority of the secular power was derived from it. It is true that this conception is confused to a certain extent by his reference to the Donation of Constantine. Honorius and Placidus of Nonantula are the first writers of whom we can say with any confidence that they interpreted the Donation as meaning that Constantine handed over to the Pope the whole imperial authority in the West; later in the century the same interpretation was set out by the canonist Paucapalea, and Honorius even seems to interpret it as meaning that Constantine surrendered his whole authority in all parts of the empire. This conception was, however, not really quite consistent with Honorius's more revolutionary conception, that intrinsically all political as well as ecclesiastical authority belonged to the Spiritual power, and that the secular ruler derived his authority from it.

John of Salisbury seems to imply a similar theory, for he maintains that the two swords both belong to the Spiritual power, and that it is from it that the prince receives his sword, that the prince is the "minister" or servant of the "sacerdotium," and administers that part of the "sacred offices" which are unworthy to be discharged by the priest. This statement of John is, however, isolated in his work, and it must remain a little uncertain whether he really intended to assert all that it might imply.

The similar phrases of Bernard, which may have been in John of Salisbury's mind, are so incidental and casual that we cannot interpret them as meaning that he held this view, and the phrases of Hugh of St. Victor are too vague to enable us to form any judgment. There is, as far as we know, only one other writer of the twelfth century whose treatment of the relation of the two powers may seem to tend in this direction, and that is the canonist Rufinus in his work on Gratian's "Decretum." While he seems to interpret the phrase in Gratian's "Decretum," D. xxii. 1, "clavigero (i.e., Petro), terreni simul et celestis imperii iura commisit," as meaning that in some sense the Pope had authority in secular matters as well as spiritual, his words also suggest that he did not understand this to mean much more than that it was for the Pope to confirm the election of emperor, and to correct him and other secular rulers if they misused their authority.

These contentions of Honorius, of John of Salisbury, and of Rufinus are important, for they seem to mark the first appearance of a new theory, a theory which, in contradiction to the traditional view of the Church, would have reduced the conception of authority in the Church to one. There is no evidence that [this conception] had been put forward to any writer in the tenth or eleventh centuries; in the twelfth it appears in Honorius, perhaps in John of Salisbury and Rufinus, but, it should be carefully observed, in them alone.

It may possibly be suggested that we should connect with this the curious episode of the letter of Hadrian IV to Frederick Barbarossa, in which he was suspected of having intended to imply that the Empire was a fief of the Papacy, and the emperor the vassal of the Pope. If we are to think that Hadrian IV meant to assert this, it would no doubt be significant of the papal policy; but it must be remembered that Hadrian explicitly withdrew such a claim, or rather emphatically repudiated such a construction of his words. And, in any case, a claim to feudal superiority would have been a totally different thing from a claim to the intrinsic supremacy of the Spiritual over the Temporal power.

The theory therefore that the authority of the Temporal power was derived from and subject to the Spiritual, so far as it existed in the twelfth century, was a merely private opinion set out by one of perhaps three important writers; it must not be represented as having any official authority in the Church, and as being generally or widely held. It received no sanction from any Council or from any Pope.

We must finally ask how far the actions and theories which we have been considering had any really important place in the actual public life of the eleventh and twelfth centuries. In endeavouring to answer this question, we must distinguish rather sharply between the significance of the principles and actions of Gregory VII and that of the theories of those twelfth-century writers which we have just been considering.

The action of Gregory VIII contributed to produce a storm which raged at least till the death of Henry IV, and the principle that the Popes had authority not only to excommunicate but also to depose the secular ruler for spiritual offences continued to be held by the Popes for many centuries. That, however, is not the same as to say that the power of deposition was generally recognised; the power of excommunication was probably not seriously questioned, but the power of deposition was another matter, and it was emphatically denied by many, even in the time of Henry IV. The truth is that, except when there was discontent and revolt against a king or emperor for other reasons, it generally had little significance. As far as the twelfth century is concerned the matter had little importance.

The theories of Honorius, of John of Salisbury, and of Rufinus, as far as the twelfth century was concerned, were merely the theories of individuals, and had no relation to the actual facts and conditions of life; they did not themselves draw any practical conclusions from them, and there is no reason to think that they had any important place even in the thought of the time. It was indeed just at this time that in the hands of the great administrators of England and of France the powers and authority of the State were being organised and extended, and it is absurd to think that the great kings and ministers would have recognised that they held an authority delegated to them by the Pope. The truth is that the difficulty of distinguishing clearly the precise border-line of the authority of the two powers was great, but the distinction was still generally held, and assumed as part of the divine order.

The principle of the relation between the two authorities as it was generally accepted throughout the time of which we are speaking is nowhere better expressed than in the words of the canonist Stephen of Tournai, writing in the latter part of the twelfth century. In the one commonwealth and under the one king there are two peoples, two modes of life, two authorities, and a twofold jurisdiction. The commonwealth is the Church; the two peoples are the two orders in the Church—that is, the clergy and the laity; the two modes of life are the spiritual and the carnal; the two authorities are the priesthood and the kingship; the twofold jurisdiction is the divine law and the human. Give to each its due, and all things will be brought into agreement.

CHAPTER 24

The Papal Revolution

Harold J. Berman

The Papal Revolution was the first transgenerational movement of a program-matic character in Western history. It took almost a generation, from about 1050 to 1075, for the papal party to proclaim the program to be a reality. Then followed forty-seven years of struggle before another pope could reach an agreement with another emperor on the single question of papal versus impe-rial investiture of bishops and abbots. It took even longer for the respective criminal and civil jurisdictions of the ecclesiastical and secular powers within each of the major western European kingdoms to be defined. In England it was not until 1170, the year of Becket's martyrdom—ninety-five years after Gregory's *Dictatus* and sixty-three years after Henry I, the English king, had yielded on the investiture issue—that the Crown finally renounced its preten-sion to be the supreme ruler of the English clergy. Ultimately compromises were reached on a whole range of issues involving not only the interrelation-ship of church and state but also the interrelationship of communities within the secular order—the manorial system, the lord-vassal unit, the merchant guilds, the chartered cities and towns, the territorial duchies and kingdoms, the secularized empire. The children and grandchildren of the revolution en-acted its underlying principles into governmental and legal institutions. Only then was it more or less secure for succeeding centuries. Indeed, it was never wholly secure; there were always disputes at the boundaries of the ecclesiasti-cal and secular powers.

Social-Psychological Causes and Consequences of the Papal Revolution

Mention has been made of three aspects of the new social consciousness that emerged during the eleventh and twelfth centuries—a new sense of corporate identity on the part of the clergy, a new sense of the responsibility of the clergy for the reformation of the secular world, and a new sense of historical

From Harold J. Berman, *Law and Revolution* (Cambridge, Mass.: Harvard University Press, 1983), pp. 106–109, 112–115, 118–119.
Reprinted by permission of the publisher from *Law and Revolution* by Harold J. Berman, Cam-bridge, Mass.: Harvard University Press. Copyright © 1983 by the President and Fellows of Har-vard College.

time, including the concepts of modernity and progress. These all had a strong influence on the development of the Western legal tradition.

The first aspect, the corporate self-consciousness of the clergy (it would be called *class* consciousness today) was essential to the revolution, both as cause and as consequence. Of course, the clergy had always had some sense of their own group identity; yet it was at best a sense of spiritual unity, a unity of belief and of calling, and not a sense of political or legal unity. Politically and legally, the clergy prior to the eleventh century had been dispersed locally, with very few links to central ecclesiastical authorities. Even the sense of spiritual unity was flawed by the sharp division between the "regular" clergy and the "secular" clergy; the regular clergy were the "religious" ones, the monks and nuns, who having died to "this world," lived out their membership in the Eternal City; the secular clergy were the priests and bishops, who were almost wholly involved in the political, economic, and social life of the localities where they lived.

More than any other single factor, the Cluniac Reform laid the foundation for the new sense of corporate political unity among the clergy of Western Christendom. The zeal of the reformers helped to give a new consciousness of common historical destiny to both the regular and the secular clergy. In addition, Cluny provided a model for uniting the clergy in a single translocal organization, since all Cluniac houses were subject to the jurisdiction of the central abbey.

In adopting the principal aims of the Cluniac Reform, including the celibacy of the priesthood and the elimination of the purchase and sale of church offices, the papal party in the 1050s and 1060s appropriated the moral capital of the earlier movement, including the clerical class consciousness that it had helped to develop. To those older aims was joined the new cry for "the freedom of the church"—that is, its freedom from control by "the laity." This was both an appeal to clerical class consciousness and a stimulation of it. Moreover, by the very act of denouncing imperial control of the church, Gregory shattered the old Carolingian ideal. The clergy were confronted with a choice between political unity under the papacy and political disunity among new national churches, which would have inevitably arisen in the various polities of Europe if the papacy had lost the battle. The investiture struggle made that clear. Ultimately the question of investiture was settled by separate negotiations between each of the principal secular rulers, representing his secular polity, and the papacy, representing the entire clergy of Western Christendom. The Papal Revolution itself thus helped to establish the clerical class consciousness on which it was based.

The clergy became the first translocal, transtribal, transfeudal, transnational class in Europe to achieve political and legal unity. It became so by demonstrating that it was able to stand up against, and defeat, the one preexisting universal authority, the emperor. The emperor had no such universal class to support him. From the twelfth century to the sixteenth the unity of the clerical hierarchy in the West could only be broken by a few powerful kings. Even the Norman kings of Sicily, who in the twelfth and thirteenth centuries were able to exclude papal control over a clergy nominally subordinate to Rome, agreed to submit to the pope any disputed elections of bishops.

The term "class" has been used here to describe the clergy partly to emphasize that the Papal Revolution, like the German (Protestant) Revolution, the English Revolution, the French and American revolutions, and the Russian Revolution, involved the interactions not only of individuals or elites but also of large social groups that performed major functions in the society. The validity of the Marxian insight that a revolution involves class struggle, and the rise of a new ruling class, need not commit one to the narrow Marxian definition of class in terms of its relation to the means of production of economic wealth. The clergy in western Europe in the late eleventh and twelfth centuries did, in fact, play an important role in the production of economic wealth, since the church owned between one-fourth and one-third of the land; bishops and abbots were lords of manors with the same economic interests as their noneccle-siastical counterparts; the struggle against lay investiture was in part a struggle to wrest economic power from lay lords and to transfer it to the church. However, it was not primarily the economic interests of the clergy that gave them their class character. It was, rather, their role as producers of spiritual goods—as father confessors, as performers of marriage ceremonies, as baptizers of infants, as ministers of last rites, as preachers of sermons, and also as expounders not only of the theology of Western society but also of its basic political and legal doctrines.

The growth of the class consciousness of the clergy was associated with the second aspect of the new social consciousness of the eleventh and twelfth centuries—the development of a new sense of the clergy's mission to reform the secular world. On the one hand, the new tendency to identify the church primarily with the clergy, the "hierarchy," led to a sharp distinction between the clergy and the laity. On the other hand, this distinction carried the implication that the clergy were not only superior to, but also responsible for, the laity. In other words, the class consciousness of the clergy was at the same time a social consciousness in the modern sense, a conscientiousness with respect to the future of society.

· · ·

Closely related to both the clergy's sense of corporate identity and its sense of mission to reform the world was a third aspect of the new social consciousness that emerged in the eleventh and twelfth centuries, namely, a new sense of historical time, including the concepts of modernity and of progress. This, too, was both a cause and a consequence of the Papal Revolution.

A new sense of time was implicit in the shift in the meaning of *saeculum* and in the new sense of mission to reform the world. A relatively static view of political society was replaced by a more dynamic view; there was a new concern with the future of social institutions. But there was also a fundamental revaluation of history, a new orientation toward the past as well as the future, and a new sense of the relationship of the future to the past. The distinction between "ancient" and "modern" times, which had occasionally been made in previous centuries, became common in the literature of the papal party. In the twelfth century there appeared the first European historians who saw the history of the West as moving from the past, through stages, into a new future—men such as Hugo of St. Victor, Otto of Freising, Anselm of Havelberg, Joachim of Floris, and others. These men saw history as moving forward in stages, culminating in their own time, which some referred to as modern times or modernity (*modernitas*). Joachim of Floris and his disciples considered that a new age of the Holy Spirit was about to replace the age of the Son, which had come to an end. Otto of Freising wrote that secular history had entered into sacred history and was intertwined with it.

Like the English Revolution of the seventeenth century, the Papal Revolution pretended to be not a revolution but a restoration. Gregory VII, like Cromwell, claimed that he was not innovating, but restoring ancient freedoms that had been abrogated in the immediately preceding centuries. As the English Puritans and their successors found precedents in the common law of the thirteenth and fourteenth centuries, largely passing over the century or more of Tudor-Stuart absolutism, so the Gregorian reformers found precedents in the patristic writings of the early centuries of the church, largely passing over the Carolingian and post-Carolingian era in the West. The ideological emphasis was on tradition, but the tradition could only be established by suppressing the immediate past and returning to an earlier one. Writings of leading Frankish and German canonists and theologians of the ninth and tenth centuries were simply ignored. In addition, the patristic writings were interpreted to conform to the political program of the papal party, and when particular patristic texts stood in the way of that program they were rejected. Faced with an obnoxious custom, the Gregorian reformers would appeal over it to truth, quoting the aphorism of Tertullian and St. Cyprian, "Christ said, 'I am the truth.' He did not say 'I am the custom.' " Gregory VII quoted this against Emperor Henry IV. Becket quoted it against King Henry II. It had special force at a time when almost all the prevailing law was customary law.

It is the hallmark of the great revolutions of Western history, starting with the Papal Revolution, that they clothe their vision of the radically new in the garments of a remote past, whether those of ancient legal authorities (as in the case of the Papal Revolution), or of an ancient religious text, the Bible (as in the case of the German Reformation), or of an ancient civilization, classical Greece (as in the case of the French Revolution), or of a prehistoric classless society (as in the case of the Russian Revolution). In all of these great upheavals the idea of a restoration—a return, and in that sense a revolution, to an earlier starting point—was connected with a dynamic concept of the future.

It is easy enough to criticize the historiography of the revolutions as politically biased and, indeed, purely ideological. This, however, is to impose on revolutionaries the standards of objectivity asserted by modern historical scholarship, which is itself a product of its times and has its own biases. Moreover, it is important to recognize that the revolutionaries were perfectly aware that they were reinterpreting the past and adapting historical memories to new circumstances. What is significant is that at the most crucial turning points of Western history a projection into the distant past has been needed to match the projection into the distant future. Both the past and the future have been summoned, so to speak, to fight against the evils of the present.

The Rise of the Modern State

The Papal Revolution gave birth to the modern Western state—the first example of which, paradoxically, was the church itself.

As Maitland said a century ago, it is impossible to frame any acceptable definition of the state which would not include the medieval church. By that he meant the church after Pope Gregory VII, since before his reign the church had been merged with the secular society and had lacked the concepts of sovereignty and of independent lawmaking power which are fundamental to modern statehood. After Gregory VII, however, the church took on most of the distinctive characteristics of the modern state. It claimed to be an independent, hierarchical, public authority. Its head, the pope, had the right to legislate, and in fact Pope Gregory's successors issued a steady stream of new laws, sometimes by their own authority, sometimes with the aid of church councils summoned by them. The church also executed its laws through an administrative hierarchy, through which the pope ruled as a modern sovereign rules through his or her representatives. Further, the church interpreted its laws, and applied them, through a judicial hierarchy culminating in the papal curia in Rome. Thus the church exercised the legislative, administrative, and judicial powers of a modern state. In addition, it adhered to a rational system of jurisprudence, the canon law. It imposed taxes on its subjects in the form of tithes and other levies. Through baptismal and death certificates it kept what was in effect a kind of civil register. Baptism conferred a kind of citizenship, which was further maintained by the requirement—formalized in 1215—that every Christian confess his or her sins and take Holy Communion at least once a year at Easter. One could be deprived of citizenship, in effect, by excommunication. Occasionally, the church even raised armies.

Yet it is a paradox to call the church a modern state, since the principal feature by which the modern state is distinguished from the ancient state, as well as from the Germanic or Frankish state, is its secular character. The ancient state and the Germanic-Frankish state were religious states, in which the supreme political ruler was also responsible for maintaining the religious dogmas as well as the religious rites and was often himself considered to be a divine or semidivine figure. The elimination of the religious function and character of the supreme political authority was one of the principal objectives of the Papal Revolution. Thereafter, emperors and kings were considered—by those who followed Roman Catholic doctrine—to be laymen, and hence wholly without competence in spiritual matters. According to papal theory, only the clergy, headed by the pope, had competence in spiritual matters. Nevertheless, for several reasons this was not a "separation of church and state" in the modern sense.

First, the state in the full modern sense—that is, the secular state existing in a system of secular states—had not yet come into being, although a few countries (especially the Norman Kingdom of Sicily and Norman England) were beginning to create modern political and legal institutions. Instead, there were various types of secular power, including feudal lordships and autonomous municipal governments as well as emerging national territorial states, and their interrelationships were strongly affected by the fact that all of their members, including their rulers, were also subject in many respects to an overarching ecclesiastical state.

Second, although emperor, kings, and other lay rulers were deprived of their ecclesiastical authority, they nevertheless continued to play a very important part—through the dual system of investiture—in the appointment of bishops, abbots, and other clerics and, indeed, in church politics generally. And conversely, members of the clergy continued to play an important part in secular politics, serving as advisers to secular rulers and also often as high secular officials. The Chancellor of England, for example, who was second in importance to the King, was virtually always a high ecclesiastic—often the Archbishop of Canterbury or of York—until the sixteenth century.

Third, the church retained important secular powers. Bishops continued to be lords of their feudal vassals and serfs and to be managers of their estates. Beyond that, the papacy asserted its power to influence secular politics in all countries; indeed, the pope claimed the supremacy of the spiritual sword over the temporal, although he only claimed to exercise temporal supremacy indirectly, chiefly through secular rulers.

Thus the statement that the church was the first modern Western state must be qualified. The Papal Revolution did lay the foundation for the subsequent emergence of the modern secular state by withdrawing from emperors and kings the spiritual competence which they had previously exercised. Moreover, when the secular state did emerge, it had a constitution similar to that of the papal church—minus, however, the church's spiritual function as a community of souls concerned with eternal life. The church had the paradoxical character of a church-state, a *Kirchenstaat*: it was a spiritual community which also exercised temporal functions and whose constitution was in the form of a modern state. The secular state, on the other hand, had the paradoxical character of a state without ecclesiastical functions, a secular polity, all of whose subjects also constituted a spiritual community living under a separate spiritual authority.

• • •

The most important consequence of the Papal Revolution was that it introduced into Western history the experience of revolution itself. In contrast to the older view of secular history as a process of decay, there was introduced a dynamic quality, a sense of progress in time, a belief in the reformation of the world. No longer was it assumed that "temporal life" must inevitably deteriorate until the Last Judgment. On the contrary, it was now assumed—for the first time—that progress could be made in this world toward achieving some of the preconditions for salvation in the next.

Perhaps the most dramatic illustration of the new sense of time, and of the future, was provided by the new Gothic architecture. The great cathedrals expressed, in their soaring spires and flying buttresses and elongated vaulted arches, a dynamic spirit of movement upward, a sense of achieving, of incarnation of ultimate values. It is also noteworthy that they were often planned to be built over generations and centuries.

Less dramatic but even more significant as a symbol of the new belief in progress toward salvation were the great legal monuments that were built in the same period. In contrast not only to the earlier Western folklaw but also to Roman law both before and after Justinian, law in the West in the late eleventh and twelfth centuries, and thereafter, was conceived to be an organically developing system, an ongoing, growing body of principles and procedures, constructed—like the cathedrals—over generations and centuries.

The Medieval State: Sovereignty, Constitutionalism, Representation

One of the great contributions of the medieval era to the growth of Western civilization was the theory and practice of the constitutional state. In the earlier Middle Ages there was no conception of the state as we understand the term nowadays—as referring to a sovereign public authority supported by the allegiance of its citizens, endowed with a legitimate power to legislate and judge and tax. Before A.D. 1000, law was generally conceived of as the custom of the folk, not the decree of a legislative body. Allegiances were intensely personal—to one's family or to a feudal lord perhaps. Power was widely diffused.

Then, from the twelfth century onward, the revived study of Roman law and of Aristotelian philosophy reintroduced the classical idea of the state into medieval Europe. At the same time, more ordered, centralized monarchies were growing into existence. First in the church, then in the secular kingdoms, rulers promulgated substantial bodies of new law, often with the cooperation of representative assemblies and without any pretense that they were merely declaring ancient custom. The outcome of all this was something new. Entities were emerging that we can reasonably call states, but now they were states influenced by constitutional ideas concerning representation, consent, and rights of subjects that could be asserted against abuses of government. Specifically, it was asserted that subjects had a right of consent to legislation and taxation, and it was assumed that the consent of a whole people could be expressed through a representative assembly.

Historians have not found it easy to explain this whole phenomenon. Earlier explanations emphasized Germanic customary law with its implicit assumption that law should reflect the whole way of life of a society, not just the arbitrary will of a ruler. Alternatively, historians laid stress on the practice of feudal society that affirmed the rights of vassals against their lords. These things were important. They continued to influence medieval society. The difficulty is that neither customary law nor feudal practice contained in itself any conception of the state as an ordered, sovereign, public authority. Much modern research, therefore, has focused on Roman law and canon law as formative influences on the growth of the medieval state.

In the following readings, Gaines Post maintains that medieval jurists derived sophisticated concepts of sovereignty, public utility, and "reason of state" from their studies of Roman law. The next reading explores some constitutional ideas of the medieval canonists and their influence on the theory and practice of government. Antony Black illuminates the distinctive features of the medieval Western state by comparing them with Islamic patterns of government. Finally, the reading from G. L. Haskins complements these theoretical discussions with a vivid description of a fourteenth-century parliament in action.

CHAPTER 25

The Emergence of the State

Gaines Post

Almost forty years ago Charles Homer Haskins applied the word renaissance to the twelfth century. Whether or not it was a renaissance the twelfth century was in fact a period of great creative activity. The revival of political, economic, and social life, along with the appearance of new learning, new schools, and new literature and styles of art and architecture, signified the beginnings, in the West, of modern European civilization. In the thirteenth century what had begun in the twelfth arrived at such maturity that it is safe to say that early modern Europe was coming into being.

Among the institutions and fields of knowledge created by medieval men, the university and the State and the legal science that aided in the creation of both were, as much as the rise of an active economy and the organization of towns, important manifestations of the new age. While accepting and respecting tradition and believing in the unchanging higher law of nature that came from God, kings, statesmen, and men of learning confidently applied reason and skill to the work of introducing order into society and societies, into feudal kingdoms, Italian communes, and lesser communities of the clergy and laity. Long before the recovery of Aristotle's *Politics*, the naturalness of living in politically and legally organized communities of corporate guilds, chapters, towns, and States was recognized both in practice and in legal thought. Nature itself sanctioned the use of human reason and art to create new laws for the social and political life on earth—provided always, of course, that the new laws did not violate the will of God.

At the very time when merchants, artisans, townsmen, and schoolmen were forming their associations for mutual aid and protection, the study of the Roman and Canon law at Bologna introduced lawyers, jurists, and secular and ecclesiastical authorities to the legal thought of Rome on corporations. When kings were trying to overcome the anarchy of feudalism, the new legal science furnished those principles of public law that helped them convert their realms into States.

From Gaines Post, *Studies in Medieval Legal Thought* (Princeton, NJ: Princeton University Press, 1964), pp. 3–4, 7–9, 12–16, 23–24, 248–249. Reprinted by permission of Princeton University Press.

• • •

For the present purpose, it is sufficient to observe that Hans Kelsen, one of the greatest authorities on the modern State and the public law, defined the State as a juristic entity, a personification of the national legal order, a politically organized society, and a subject of rights and duties. Its rights are largely public rights, asserted in terms of the public welfare and the common utility. And the public law, let me add, is not only the law that deals with the public authority and the public welfare; it is at times the government, the constitutional order, without which the State is nothing. At any rate, we can understand that when the "public welfare clause" is invoked in connection with the building of highways or with necessary preparations for war, private rights inevitably must yield. The public interest, sometimes tyrannically, demands it. Evidently the "public welfare clause" is connected with the "right of State"; and the State, whatever it is, is thus superior to all individuals and individual rights. The State is above the law of the land which protects private rights. In times of grave crisis, of a national emergency, of necessity, it is certain that the government of the United States can do extraordinary things which normally the law of the land does not permit. And yet even then the public "right of State" must have some regard for the rights of private citizens.

In Germany and Italy we have seen the extreme logical application of the idea that the State is above the law—and normally rather than in emergencies. The State of Nazi Germany and Fascist Italy was the culmination of that amoral necessity or "reason of State" which, some historians claim, first appeared in the Italian Renaissance. In 1914 Bethmann-Hollweg asserted the principle in the words "Necessity knows no law" in order to justify the German violation of the neutrality of Belgium.

All of these expressions—"public" or "common utility" or "welfare," "emergency," "necessity," "necessity knows no law," and "reason of the *status* or public welfare"—are to be found in the twelfth and thirteenth centuries. The purpose of this study is to point to their origin in the Roman law, to show how the legists and canonists used them to develop the early modern theory of public law and the State; and to observe how kings, emperors, and popes were employing the new terminology to justify their claim to an authority that represented the public and common welfare and the *status* (state) of Realm or Church and was therefore above human if not natural law.

• • •

The legists started building their theories, naturally, on the foundation of Roman law, although Aristotle was of some influence by the end of the thirteenth century. They started with Ulpian's famous statement (D.1, 1, 1, 2; also *Inst.* 1, 1): "Public law pertains to the *status rei Romanae* [state of the Roman republic*]; private, to the utility of individuals. Public law relates to religion,

---

*The medieval word *status* was used in phrases like "state of the Church" and "state of the republic" to mean the general condition or public welfare of a community. Such usages led to the modern, more abstract concept of "the State."—Ed.

priests, and magistrates." On this, as early as 1228, a glossator even seemed to personify *status,* saying that public law exists "to preserve the state, lest it perish." But probably, like others, he meant the public welfare of the Empire. For Odofredo a little later asserted that the public law pertains chiefly to the *status* of the whole Empire, and the glossators in Accursius' *Glossa ordinaria* related *status* to the public utility. Like Azo, they held that if private law pertains primarily to the utility of individuals, it pertains secondarily to the public utility, since it interests the *Respublica* (the State) that no one should misuse his property. Contrariwise, what is primarily public, secondarily pertains to the utility of individuals. Accursius added that it is for the utility or welfare of individuals that the Republic be preserved unharmed—an approach to the frequently expressed idea that the common utility is essentially the safety of all collectively and individually. Odofredo said, in adding to the thought of the glossators, that one of the concerns of the Republic is that its subjects be rich, even though property belongs to private law.

The public law, then, dealt with the public or common utility and safety, with the *status* of the State. In the sense that the public utility was generally a higher good than private (this was also the opinion of the scholastic philosophers, particularly of St. Thomas Aquinas—the salvation of one's soul is the only private right that is superior to the public utility, except in the case of a bishop, who cannot, said Pope Innocent III, resign his office to save his own soul if he is needed to help others to salvation), in this sense the State, the true bearer of the public utility, was superior to its subjects considered individually and collectively.

It follows that public law must deal more specifically with the means of assuring the *status* of the *Respublica.* The concept of public law was attached to the public authority, the government, which existed to administer the State for the common utility, good, and safety of all, which interpreted the public law and the common welfare, and which therefore had a certain prerogative that made it superior, in an emergency or necessity, to the private law and private rights. Therefore, as Odofredo put it, summing up Azo and the glossators, it was of public interest to have *sacra,* churches and priests to save people from their sins, and to protect priests from injury; and to have magistrates, for laws would be of no value without men to administer justice. Public law, then, dealt with the Church and the clergy, and with the office of magistrates. The *Glossa ordinaria* added the *fiscus* and fiscal law to the realm of public law.

• • •

In their treatment of public law, therefore, the legists included the right of the public authority to tax for the *status* or public utility of the community. This power of taxation was not an outgrowth of the right of expropriation by the public authority, because it was not confiscation, and the consent of those taxed was more clearly involved. If the power to tax came under the scope of public law, so the power to legislate. This is not the place to discuss the medieval theory of legislation as law-finding rather than law-making. But in the thirteenth century the legists certainly held that the right to make statutes, general laws for the common utility, belonged to the public authority by public law, even though the consent of prelates and nobles (or, in the Italian republic, the consent of the leading citizens) was necessary. The power to legislate belonged to the ruler as the public authority, and general laws were made for the *status* or public utility of empire, kingdom, or city state. Moreover, the power of jurisdiction, as we have seen, was a part of the public law on magistracy, and jurisdiction in the Middle Ages was not clearly distinguished from legislation as law-finding. But all the same, there was a theory of law-making in the antique-modern sense. This theory derived in part from passages in *Code* and *Digest* on legislation by the Roman emperor for emergencies not covered by the old body of law, and on the making of new laws for new matters not decided by the old law, if "evident utility" exists. The legists interpreted "evident utility" as the common utility of all subjects and as a case of necessity. By doing so they showed that the public authority existed to meet emergencies, new situations, in order to maintain the common welfare or *status*, in the field of legislation as in that of taxation.

• • •

On the foundation of the two laws and of the rise of feudal monarchies, the theory, and some practice, of public law and the State thus arose in the twelfth and thirteenth centuries. Private rights and privileges remained powerful and enjoyed a recrudescence in localism and privileged orders in the fourteenth century and later. At times, in periods of war and civil dissension, they weakened the public authority of kings and threatened the very survival of the State. But the ideas and ideal of the State and public order, of a public and constitutional law, were constantly at hand to remind statesmen of their right to reconstitute the State. . . .

The objection is often raised, however, that medieval kingdoms were not States because (1) they accepted the spiritual authority of the pope and the universal Church, (2) king and realm were under God and the law of nature, and (3) the royal government was poorly centralized. As for the first argument, it might be raised against the use of the term "State" for Eire and Spain today. Yet we assume that these two countries are States even though they are essentially Catholic and in some fashion recognize the spiritual authority of the Roman Church. With respect to other ideals of universalism, the United States and Italy, not to mention other nations, are sovereign States, while belonging to the United Nations. As for the second argument, on subjection to God and a moral law, it must be replied that the official motto of the United States is "In God We Trust," and Americans take an oath of loyalty to "one nation indivisible under God." Furthermore, the sovereignty of the American people and their State is surely limited in fact by a moral law that belongs to the Judaeo-Christian tradition: it is not likely that the representatives of the people in Congress will ever think of making laws that violate the Ten Commandments, nor that the Supreme Court will approve them. It is therefore not absurd to call medieval kingdoms States despite limitations within which derived from the ideal of law and justice, and despite limitations from without (also within) from the universalism of Christianity and the Church. Papal arbitration of "international" disputes in the thirteenth century interfered with the sovereign right of kings to go to war (always the "just war" in defense of the *patria* and the *status regni*) no more and no less than international organizations do in the twentieth century. And "world opinion" was respected as much or as little.

In reply to the third argument, regarding the amount of centralization, one must ask, what degree of centralization is necessary for a State to exist? If the central government must be absolute in power, then the United States might not qualify, since a great many powers remain in the fifty states within. And did France become a State only with the more thorough centralization that resulted from the Revolution? Logically we might conclude that only a totalitarian State is a true State.

CHAPTER 26

Church Law and Constitutional Thought

Brian Tierney

The discussion of these problems can become extremely complex but the immediate point that I am concerned to make is not oversubtle. A modern institution of representative government like the American senate has no meaningful connection whatsoever with the ancient Roman senate. On the other hand its whole nature and mode of functioning are rooted in an antecedent tradition of parliamentary government—and parliament did not come into existence in ancient Greece or ancient Rome but in medieval England. The fact of the matter is that in 1200 there were no national representative assemblies anywhere and there never had been any, while by 1400 the whole Western Church was engaged in trying to replace papal monarchy with conciliar government, and almost every country from Scandinavia to Spain and from England to Hungary had produced constitutional documents stating that the ruler was under the law and had experimented with representative assemblies seeking to give effect to that principle. This is the phenomenon of medieval constitutionalism. It is, as I have emphasized, a rare, perhaps a unique phenomenon. There is no general work of synthesis that would explain the whole phenomenon satisfactorily. It is surely interesting enough to deserve an explanation.

Medievalists have always been aware of the importance of constitutional history. It has always been a central theme of our discipline. But they have not always approached it from the point of view that I have been suggesting. On the contrary, when the subject first began to be studied scientifically in the nineteenth century, there was a widespread assumption that a constitutional, representative system was a kind of natural norm of human government, which the English had come to exemplify first because of their innate Anglo-Saxon virtue, but toward which all societies could be expected to progress in due course given a little goodwill and a modicum of elementary education. With that preconception the whole task of explaining the origins of constitutionalism became one of merely documenting the stages by which medieval

From Brian Tierney, "Medieval Canon Law and Western Constitutionalism," *Catholic Historical Review*, Vol. 52 (1966), pp. 6–15.

men pursued this normal and natural course of development from Teutonic tribesmen to members of the House of Commons. This in itself presented some problems, and it is widely held nowadays that William Stubbs, the greatest of the early constitutional historians, presented the stages of development wrongly. Around 1900 revisionists like Maitland and McIlwain began to criticize him. The argument proliferated, and it is still going on. We now have a fantastically elaborate bibliography of hundreds of books and articles devoted to this one question and all the fascinating subsidiary issues that arise out of it—whether the English Parliament was already some kind of representative legislature in 1297 or whether we are so radically to modify our whole view of human progress as to suppose that this felicitous state of affairs did not begin to come about until, say, 1327. The material that has been unearthed in the course of the controversy is invaluable. If there is ever to be a satisfactory account of medieval constitutionalism as a whole the interpretation of English parliamentary records will play a major part in it. But this can hardly come about so long as parliamentary studies are conducted in an insular spirit and are dominated to such an extraordinary degree by the discussion of technical problems arising out of an academic dispute of sixty years ago. They need to be set in a broader perspective.

The study of the law of the universal Church can provide such a perspective. If we set out from the surely self-evident premise that constitutionalism is not a normal stage in the evolution of societies but extremely abnormal— its emergence improbable, its extension most difficult, its survival always precarious—then we must ask a new kind of question of the age that first produced it. The obvious question is this. What was abnormal about the Middle Ages? What elements of social organization or economic life were common to all the countries of Western Europe between 1200 and 1400 but peculiar to that medieval civilization as a whole compared to the others that we know of? This kind of question leads straight to the topics for which medieval canonists provide the primary source material. For there is nothing very out of the way about the medieval economy—a primitive agrarian basis diversified by a little commerce. Nor is the technology especially striking—more advanced than we used to think but not really remarkable. Nor is the basic social structure, with prestige accorded to a military aristocracy, highly unusual. It is only when we turn to the ecclesiastical aspects of medieval culture that we encounter situations that are indeed extremely abnormal by the standards of most other civilizations.

When students first come to consider the conflicts of popes and kings in the Middle Ages they are sometimes surprised at the pretensions of both sides. They find it remarkable that popes should claim to depose kings or kings to appoint bishops; but there is really nothing unusual in one ruler aspiring to exercise supreme spiritual and temporal power. That again is a normal pattern of human government. Innumerable societies have been ruled by a god-emperor, a divine king or a chieftain of magical potency. The unusual thing in the Middle Ages was not that certain emperors and popes aspired to a theocratic role but that such ambitions were never wholly fulfilled. There remained always two structures of government, ecclesiastical and secular, intricately interlinked but dedicated ultimately to different ends, often in conflict with one another, each constantly limiting the other's power. Evidently the very existence of such a situation would enhance the possibilities for a growth of human freedom by preventing medieval society from congealing into a rigid despotism, and Lord Acton pointed this out long ago. "To that conflict of four hundred years," he wrote, "we owe the rise of civil liberty."

But, although important, this is only part of the story. We have to deal with two societies that were not only frequently in conflict with each other but that were also in a state of constant interaction. Throughout the Middle Ages there was a very frequent interchange of personnel and also of ideas and institutional techniques between the spheres of ecclesiastical and secular government. Kings were anointed like bishops and bishops became feudal lords like kings. Secular laws relating to the ancient Senate were used to define the status of cardinals in the Roman church, and canonical rules regarding the choice of bishops were used to regulate the elections of emperors. The pope assumed the imperial tiara, and the emperor the episcopal miter. One could multiply such examples endlessly.

To understand the distinctive characteristics of medieval government, therefore, we have to consider two sets of problems—problems of conflict and problems of interaction between Church and State. On the whole the problems of interaction are more complex and more important, and these are the ones that I want particularly to consider. It is quite easy to see in the abstract that a very duality of Church and State in any society would produce a situation of exceptional flexibility. It is very difficult to explain in the concrete how that particular ecclesiastical organization interacted with that particular system of secular government to produce the new forms of constitutional organization whose origins we are trying to explore. Merely to mix ecclesiastical autocracy with feudal anarchy does not sound very promising, and it was widely assumed until recently that all canonical theories of papal authority were indeed starkly autocratic. But a major conclusion arising out of all the recent research is that medieval canon law was not merely, as it was once called, "a marvelous jurisprudence of spiritual despotism." On detailed investigation we find that the great canonistic glosses and *summae* of the age of Innocent III contain, not only the familiar and expected passages exalting papal authority, but also other sections that are filled with constitutional concepts, with sophisticated discussions on representation and consent and on the due limits to lawfully constituted authority, even papal authority.

Before we turn to this structure of ideas we ought to consider a preliminary question that inevitably presents itself. How could medieval canon lawyers, of all people, have been led to pioneer in the development of constitutional principles, of all things? To understand this we must consider one more way in which Western history has pursed an unusual course—I mean in the extraordinary convolutions of its chronological structure. Perhaps no other civilization, through the centuries of its existence, has enjoyed so many and such varied love affairs with its own past as those of the Western world, ranging as they do from the most prolific unions to the merest illicit flirtations.

From the twelfth century onward there were all those Renaissances of ancient culture that historians delight in multiplying until, the wheel coming full circle, the Middle Ages themselves became an object of flirtatious advances from the Romantics of the nineteenth century. To the historian, for whom time is the very raw material of his craft, the situation is one of intriguing complexity. For us the essential point is that, in the first great encounter of Western man with his past, the "Renaissance of the twelfth century," a revival of classical Roman law coincided precisely with a new systematic study of all the ancient-Christian sources assembled in Gratian's Decretum. Roman law re-introduced the ideas of sovereignty and the state into the Western world but the canonical texts had a distinctive contribution to make too. Early Christianity was not just a belief, but a body of believers, a communion, a community. The earliest references to Christian life are full of community meetings, community sharings, community participation in decisions, community election of officers. Something of this had persisted down to the twelfth century in that the Church was still a structure of elective offices, and the early tradition was reflected very strongly in many of the texts assembled by Gratian.

It would be tempting to assert simply that the first formulation of the basic concepts of Western constitutionalism was stimulated by an encounter between the Roman law idea of sovereign state and the patristic ideal of a corporate Christian community in the works of the medieval canonists. But this would not be quite the whole truth. After all there was classical law and Christian doctrine in the ancient world and they led on only to Byzantine absolutism. We have to deal with ancient law and early Christian institutions as they were perceived by the eyes of medieval men. The canonists had grown up in a world soaked in the preconceptions of feudalism and of Teutonic customary law, preconceptions that inevitably helped to shape their own personalities and temperaments. Moreover, men of the twelfth and thirteenth centuries did not have the advantage of knowing that they were living in the Middle Ages. They thought they were living in the latest age of the Roman Empire. They were hardly conscious of the great gulf between their own culture and that of the ancient world. This led them to assimilate classical ideas the more readily but almost inevitably to read into them new interpretations of their own. One finds the same pattern in many activities of medieval men. They read Vitruvius—and built Gothic cathedrals. They read Ovid—and wrote about courtly love. They read Justinian—and founded the constitutional state.

One of the most familiar platitudes of our textbooks is the assertion that Western culture was formed from a fusion of classical and Christian elements. It is true of course like most platitudes. But the textbooks do not always emphasize sufficiently that often the fusion took place in the Middle Ages, and still less that in the fields of law and government the works of the medieval canonists played a crucially important role in the whole process. Yet it could hardly have been otherwise. The canonists were the only group of intellectuals in Western history who were professionally concerned with classical law and with Christian doctrine to an equal degree. They delighted in applying to the papal office all the exalted language which Roman law used in describing the majesty of the emperor. They called the pope a supreme legislator whose very will was law, a supreme judge from whom there could be no appeal, a "lord of the world," "loosed from the laws." But these same canonists never forgot St. Paul's reminder that in the Church all power is given "for edification, not for destruction." Moreover, although they lacked the critical insights of a modern historian, there was a profoundly historical dimension to their thought. Gratian's Decretum depicted for the canonists all the ages of the Church's past—and depicted them "warts and all." The misdeeds of several popes who had sinned and erred in former times were recounted in the Decretum and such examples apparently had a sobering effect on the canonists. One of Gratian's texts (Dist. 40 c. 1) suggested that all popes were to be considered holy. The Ordinary Gloss, written about 1215, commented somewhat drily, "It does not say that they are holy but that they are to be presumed holy—until the contrary becomes apparent." The Decretists were fascinated by the potentialities for reform of a papacy wielding vast power but at the same time appalled by the dangers for the Church if all that power should fall into evil hands. They were up against the very nub of the problem of sovereignty. It is easy enough to avoid a despotism if one is content to tolerate an anarchy. The difficult task is to concede to a ruler all the very great powers needed for effective government while guarding against the dangers of arbitrary tyranny.

The canonists' approach to this problem was to seek in the consensus of the whole Christian community, in the indefectible Church guided by the Holy Spirit, norms of faith and order which could define the limits within which the pope's supreme legislative and judicial powers were to be exercised. (The English parliamentary leaders of a later age would set themselves an analogous task in relation to the political community and the limitations of secular kingship.) A juridical basis for the canonists was provided by a text of Pope Gregory the Great, incorporated in the Decretum at Dist. 15 c. 2, which declared that the canons of the first four General Councils were always to be preserved inviolate because they were established "by universal consent" or "by a universal consensus" (*universali consensu*). The canonists gave a precise meaning to Gregory's vague dictum by interpreting it in terms of their own categories of corporation law. They glossed it with phrases like these. "No man can withdraw from the common consent of his community," or "What touches all should be approved by all"—this latter text being used to defend the right of lay representatives to attend General Councils when matters of faith were to be discussed. In the years around 1200 it was commonly maintained that even the pope was bound by the canons of General Councils representing the whole Church, "in matters pertaining to the faith and the general state of the Church." Such a doctrine could be developed without any attack on the ancient principle of papal primacy because of course the pope himself was normally the presiding head of a General Council. Its canons could be regarded as manifestations of the papal will expressed in its highest, most sovereign form and so as binding on the pope himself considered as an isolated individual. The English canonist who, toward 1200, declared that "the authority of a pope with a council is greater than that of a pope without one" was expressing the same idea that King Henry VIII of England would apply to the secular sphere some three centuries later when he said, "We be informed by our judges that we at no time stand so highly in our estate royal as in time of Parliament wherein we as head and you as members are conjoined and knit together in one body politic."

There remained the possibility of an irreconcilable conflict between the pope and the representatives of the Christian community assembled in a General Council. The canonists of the early thirteenth century were deeply divided over this question but the more radical of them taught that a pope could be corrected and even deposed by a council if his conduct endangered the "state of the church." Fifty years later we find the barons of England claiming the right to oppose their king in defense of the "state of the realm." Long ago historians came to realize that the canonists influenced the history of Western political thought in that their theories of papal sovereignty provided an archetype for later theories of divine right monarchy. We are just beginning to understand the importance of their work for theories of representative government also.

It is a complicated task to reconstruct all the constitutionalist elements in the canonists' thought from their voluminous but scattered glosses, and still more complicated to explain in detail how their ideas influenced the growth of secular government. Basically there were two processes at work. Most obviously the canonists offered reflections on the constitutional law of the Church which could and did influence subsequent speculations on the right ordering of the State. But they also formulated a series of doctrines in the sphere of private law which eventually proved of the utmost importance in the growth of representative government although, at first, they had nothing to do with high matters of state. These private-law doctrines again reflected the collegial structure of the medieval Church. Much of the canonists' day-to-day business dealt with the affairs of ecclesiastical communities. They were therefore led to develop an elaborate jurisprudence concerning the representation of corporate groups, the prerogatives of the head of a juridical society in relation to its members, and the rights of individual members in relation to the whole community before such matters began to be discussed as overt issues of political theory.

Just as in some primitive economies there is a shortage of good currency, so too in the medieval polity there was a shortage of good law, especially of constitutional law. When the need for the more sophisticated structures of public law came to be urgently felt men naturally turned to the legal rules that were already available in the province of private law—especially in the well-developed canonical law of corporations—and applied them in the constitutional sphere also. A typical line of development was the assimilation of technical rules of Roman private law into canon law, the subsequent inflation of such rules into general principles of church government by the canonists, and the eventual transfer of those principles to the public law of the growing states by the usual medieval process of osmosis. For instance the already mentioned phrase, *Quod omnes tangit ab omnibus approbetur* (What touches all is to be approved by all), was developed from a mere technicality of the Roman law of cotutorship into a juristic theory about the right relationship between popes and General Councils in the works of the canonists who were writing around 1200. Then, moving from legal theory to real life, we find it in official documents convoking church councils and, finally, by the end of the thirteenth century, it occurs in writs of summons to secular representative assemblies.

This is not the occasion for a detailed exploration of all the maze of arguments that has grown up around the phrase *Quod omnes tangit* and around other terms that underwent a similar development—*plena potestas, status, necessitas.* Let me rather try to summarize the over-all effect of the quite exceptional interplay between all the diverse influences that were at work in thirteenth-century legal thought. The most striking result of their interaction was to produce a peculiar ambivalence in all the concepts commonly used in medieval political discourse. The ruler's power was conceived of as flowing from both God *and* the people. It was held to be in some ways above the law and in some ways below it. The medieval term *status,* the origin of our "state," was used to extend the authority of rulers by justifying extraordinary or extra-legal actions undertaken by them for the defense of the community, but it also served to define a condition of public welfare that the ruler himself was not permitted to disrupt. Representation could mean either the symbolizing of a community in its head, with absolutist implications, or a delegation of authority from the subjects, with constitutionalist implications. The doctrine of natural law provided both a stimulus to new legislation and a criterion for judging its value. It is not that we find popes and princes, intent on building up centralized power, using one set of concepts, and subjects, intent on limiting that power, using another. The very concepts that all had in common were ambivalent; every building block of sovereignty had a constitutional face; Western political thought was already beginning to revolve around the central problem, or paradox, that has fascinated its greatest exponents ever since, the problem of reconciling the idea of sovereignty with the ideal of limited government, of government "under the law."

Some scholars will think that ideas and ideals have little enough to do with the growth of governmental institutions. One young expert has recently observed that, "It did not matter too much what one or another theorist said. . . ." And, certainly, we could all agree that, when medieval kings summoned representative assemblies, they were not normally inspired to do so by protracted meditations on the subtleties of canonical jurisprudence. Kings needed help or counsel or money. They wanted assent to their policies and political support for them. These obvious facts should indeed receive due emphasis in any institutional history of the Middle Ages, but it is a delusion to suppose that, by merely calling attention to them, we are providing a sufficient explanation for the rise of medieval constitutionalism. The problem of maximizing assent to governmental policies arises for all rulers in all societies. It is not normally solved by the development of representative assemblies. Our argument is not that hard-headed medieval statesmen behaved in such-and-such a way because some theorist in a university had invented a theory saying that they ought to do so. The argument is rather that all men behave in certain ways in part at least because they adhere to certain ways of thinking. No doubt the ideas that are most influential in shaping actions are ones that the agent is hardly conscious of at all—he takes them so much for granted. But the historian has to make himself conscious of those ideas if he is to understand the men of a past age and the institutions that they created. The works of the medieval canonists provide invaluable source material for the constitutional historian precisely because they can help him to become aware of the implicit presuppositions about men and society that lay below the surface of medieval political thought and political action.

CHAPTER 27

Medieval Institutions: Islam and the West

Antony Black

It is with trepidation that I have undertaken to compare two whole political traditions, especially since I am far more familiar with medieval Europe than with classical Islam. The task of understanding a different political context and 'language' is obviously immense. The only reason for taking it up is that it ought to be done, first, because if, as commonly occurs, Islam (or any other major tradition) is omitted from the study of the history of political ideas, that study is necessarily incomplete. Secondly, as in any group of phenomena, understanding requires classification and classification requires comparison. Still more, it is only by comparison that we can fully grasp the essentials and nature of any particular tradition; by perceiving, inter alia, what it is not. Lastly, it ought eventually to be possible to contribute something to the discussion about what makes 'the west' different (Weber's topic), by examining in what ways its political philosophy and culture are *sui generis*.

It is often alleged that pre-modern cultures have certain features in common. In the case of Christendom and Islam, people sometimes assume that each was more like the other in earlier times than by, say, the seventeenth century. It may be said that the one became 'modern,' while the other remained 'medieval' and 'feudal,' for example. We are indeed faced with two societies which both believed in one God, whose nature, works and promises were known through a historic revelation and a sacred, immutable text, and in a divinely inspired world wide religious community; one might even compare pope or emperor with caliph or sultan. Such assumptions and appearances are, as I hope to show, wholly wrong.

Three points strike anyone who looks at these two civilizations side by side: the difference in the conception of the religious community, of the reli-

From Antony Black, "Classical Islam and Medieval Europe: A Comparison of Political Philosophies and Cultures," as appeared in *Political Studies*, Vol. 41 (1993), pp. 58–69, 1993 Copyright 1993 Political Studies Association. Reprinted by permission.

I would like to thank Patricia Crone for her most helpful comments on an earlier draft, Jean-Philippe Genet for stimulating this paper for a meeting of the European Science Foundation study group on the origins of the modern State at Istanbul in November 1991, and the participants there, especially Halil Bergtay and Selim Deringil for their heartening response.

gious law, and the difference in the mode of political reasoning. Both Christianity and Islam preached a message of salvation that was personal and social, aimed at improving the way human beings treated each other but the contrast between the ethos of early Christianity and early Islam could hardly be greater. They had radically different conceptions of what religion was about. Muhammad preached the religion of Abraham to his own Arab people, giving them a sense of their salvation, their election by God and their uniqueness as a channel of divine power in the world. To do this, he appropriated the promises of the Jewish scriptures and prophecy to himself and his followers. His vision meant converting and directing the whole life of the people, in its social and economic as much as its religious and ritual aspects, as another Moses. The Christians, on the other hand, far from setting out to conquer the world, expected it to come to a speedy end; in the meantime, the dominant ideal was fearless preaching, non-resistance to violence and martyrdom.

Each of these religions in turn created a new type of religious community: the church (*ekklesia, universitas fidelium*) and the *umma* of believers. One only has to read these words to be aware of a fundamental difference in the type of community. The Christian community (generalising drastically) was initially designed as a gathering-together or assembly (*ekklesia*: literally, calling out) of those who were to be saved from the world. It consisted at first of small groups meeting together for prayer and the Eucharist, dedicated to proclaiming the Gospel. Within a few generations, it transformed itself into a cosmopolitan structure of cells linked by 'bishops' (overseers) who collaborated world wide to define, defend and proclaim the faith. By the fourth century AD it was developing a patriarchal character and becoming a mass society.

The *umma* of Islam, on the other hand, was designed by Muhammad and his followers to overcome blood feud and tribalism among the Arabs by submitting them all to a single set of moral and legal rules and to a unified political and military leadership. It was of the essence of the *umma* to be a new total society; Muhammad conceived no separation between 'spiritual' and 'secular' aspects of society; his prophecy and leadership were spiritual, judicial, fiscal and military. The *umma* should and did undertake war to vindicate the supremacy of its faith. After Muhammad, the Caliph stood as 'the defender of the faith, the dispenser of justice, the leader in prayer and war, all in one.' In Islamic thought and Islamic society at all levels, religion, the religious law (*shari'a*) and religious government (the Caliphate) were concerned both with this world and with the next; this was a powerful source of social discipline. For the early Muslims, conquest, political power and a conspicuously flourishing economy were a mark of their true religion. The jurist, Ibn Taymiyya (1262–1328), remarked that 'Religion without *sultan* (power) *jihad* (holy war) and wealth is as bad as *sultan,* wealth and *harb* (war) without religion.' For Christians, the essential function of the religious community was, rather, to provide them with safe passage through the perils of the present life.

Integral to this first difference was the difference in conceptions of religious law. The early Christians preached the supercession of the Mosaic and any other religious law by what they called grace, faith and liberty of spirit; in the main, regulation and ritual gave way to a few very general principles. The Sermon on the Mount was not a new set of rules but a new conception of morality and of the kind of 'law' to which a spiritually minded person could be subject; this was an aspect of the 'other-worldliness' of Christianity. The Christian community simply did not have a religious law in the Judaic or Islamic sense. What mattered was inner disposition, 'faith' and the world to come. St. Paul and others were quick to add that this did not sanction immorality or illegality; yet even 'morality' appears in much of the New Testament as a kind of afterthought. Political and economic matters were left virtually unregulated; Christian 'social teaching' was wide open to outside influences. There was space for the adoption of forms of social and political organisation undreamt of in the original deposit of faith. This may not have been clear in Muhammad's day, when eastern Christianity was yoked to Byzantine institutions but in the long run St. Augustine proved quite right: the fall of Rome was of little consequence to the Christian people.

Islamic law (the *shari'a*) on the other hand aspired to cover every aspect of life from conception to burial. It specified social relationships of many kinds, including political ones, adjudication, property, social welfare as well as ritual matters. In principle, it was supposed to be applicable to everything. To say even this does not quite capture the meaning of *shari'a*; it embodies at once the religious, ritual, moral and social ideal; to practice or restore, it is the primary aim of all believers, alongside worship of God. To be practised, it has to be implemented in social as well as individual life; hence the problem for pluralism in the Muslim tradition. Much of what we call 'political thought,' including constitutional theory, was covered, or supposed to be covered, in the *shari'a*. The first purpose of any government is to establish the *shari'a* and the ruler is bound by it. There was little space for manoeuvre without a fundamental redefinition of the religious premises.

In the Islamic religio-juristic system there was no place for legislation. While until the tenth century religious scholars could interpret and apply law by independent reasoning (*ijtihad*), this practice was thereafter regarded as fulfilled. On the other hand, from the Abbasids onwards, laws other than the *shari'a* were laid down to deal with matters not covered by the *shari'a* on an *ad hoc* basis. The status of such 'secular' laws (*qanun*) and their relationship with the *shari'a* remained unspecified. This, as we shall see, made it more difficult to determine any moral criteria for non-*shari'a* laws and led to the attitude that one non-sacred law was as good as another.

In medieval Europe, on the other hand, the validity of secular laws was always fully recognised; indeed Roman law was sometimes accorded almost scriptural respect. Further, the papacy set an example as a legislative authority entitled to revise old laws and promulgate new ones in the light of new needs. European states, from about the twelfth century, adopted procedures for lawmaking. The most striking and perhaps in the long term most important contrast lay in the rationale behind such acts, namely the concept of natural justice. This referred to moral criteria which must be observed in any legal system (such as *pacta sunt servanda*) but which can be implemented in different ways by particular peoples and rulers. This gave flexibility, the capacity for legitimate change and at the same time a moral basis. It was connected, as we shall see, with the prevailing mode of moral discourse.

Probably the most important result of what has been observed so far was that a distinction between 'church' and 'state' (in medieval language, spiritual-ecclesiastical and temporal-secular power) was accepted, canonised and institutionlised in the Christian world, at least of the Latin west, in a manner and to an extent it could never be in Islam. True, this could develop in remarkably different ways, and was sometimes obscured, as in the 'caesaro-papist' policies of Byzantium. But the important point was that it was sanctioned throughout the New Testament (especially in Matthew 22:21, 'Render unto Caesar. . . .'). Christian leaders and constituents had gratefully accepted the 'conversion' of the Roman emperors and acknowledged their authority in 'mundane' matters. The definition of this boundary was endlessly problematic but in Europe the high Middle Ages saw broadly speaking an emerging consensus, despite occasionally bitter disputes over such matters as property rights and taxation. The clergy were to control religious doctrine and the sacraments. Secular rulers kept the peace and, as time went on, handled the great bulk of fiscal and judicial questions. The question was complicated and yet simplified by the fact that in any dispute secular rulers could engage their own clergy to argue their case. What emerged was a distinction of functions, a separation of powers, in fact an underlying pluralism of authorities.

Following the decline of the Caliphate by the mid-tenth century, a working relationship developed in Islamic society between those who de facto held political might (*sultans, emirs*) and the religious leaders (*ulama*) but this was never regarded as the norm, only as a second-best accommodation to bad times. The norm remained, for Sunnis, the Medinan Caliphate and for the Shia, the just authority of the righteous imam, to be finally vindicated with the return of the twelfth or 'hidden' imam in the fullness of time. In both cases, truly legitimate authority was both spiritual and secular. The separate authorities of Christian clergy and rulers, on the other hand, were in place from the start. Certainly, concerted attempts were made to subordinate one wholly to the other; in the West, popes made a bid for political leadership of a united, almost *umma*-like 'Christian commonwealth (*respublica christiana*)' but this failed. What strikes one is the precarious nature of any fusion of the two powers in a seriously Christian milieu and of their separation in any seriously Muslim milieu. In Islam, the distinction was purely conceptual, as reflected in a saying of Persian origin, 'religion and secular power (*dawlat*) are twins.' For European Christians, at least after c. 1300, it was institutional.

The mode of political discourse and reasoning was also fundamentally different in Islam and in Europe. This difference was not, however, so apparent early on. It emerges quite clearly, nonetheless, if we compare the vast bulk of Islamic political thought from the tenth century onwards with that of Europe from the twelfth century onwards. Political reasoning in classical Islam came to take the form of complicated juristic interpretation and discussion of the *Qur'an*, the *hadith* (sayings and acts ascribed to Muhammad) and the whole tradition (*sunna*) broadly embodied, in differing interpretations, in the *shari'a* (law, way of life). It was a question, partly, of who was believed to have said what and ultimately to have heard it from Muhammad or one of his close companions; and partly of explaining or justifying new political experiences as they arose in the light of established notions, such as Caliph, *sultan*, *hisba* (the right to criticise). Within the juristic system, the scope for independent reasoning (*ijtihad*) was progressively narrowed until by the tenth century it had been virtually eliminated. There was thus no notion of justice as something human beings might arrive at by their own 'natural' or 'rational' judgement (to use western terms) but only as the order laid down by God through his prophet (whom Islamic philosophers not unreasonably referred to as the 'legislator' in the Greek sense). In this way Islamic political thought became almost exclusively religious-juristic. It was not, for the most part, about politics in an ancient-Greek or a medieval and modern European sense. There were plenty of manuals on statecraft and advice books for princes; yet systematic moral philosophy was absent. What counted was not principles in the (Greco–Roman–European) sense of general moral rules (such as 'give to each his due [*ius suum cuique reddere*]') or inductions from human experience (such as the need to avoid strife), though Muslim thinkers were doubtless well aware of such things, but rather particular precepts derived by traditional methods from an authoritative source. Given the ascendancy of the religious scholars (*ulama*) in the social system, the effect of all this on mental attitudes generally must have been enormous.

A certain proportion of European political thought, up to and also beyond the twelfth century, was not dissimilar but Latin-Christian political culture and philosophy were at no time based exclusively upon religious tradition. Christian thought in general, as noted, was (and due to the happy limitations in its own sources was virtually bound to be), open to, indeed dependent upon, other sources, notably neoplatonic metaphysics, Stoic ethics and Aristotelian logic. Indeed the transmission of some Ciceronian and other Roman writings on ethics and politics to the courts of Europe took place virtually alongside the transmission of Christian texts themselves.

The crux came when, from c. 1150 to c. 1350, logical reasoning and empirical evidence became accepted as a valid way of knowing what exists and what ought to be. The Christian-European trick, learned by the time of Aquinas, was to say that such 'natural' principles were discoverable by 'natural reason' as well as by divine revelation, while insisting that they were still identical, or compatible, with the latter. The original Christian conception of law and grace made it possible to say that many of the prescriptions of the Old Testament, and indeed aspects of church tradition, might have been valid once but were not necessarily valid now. The rediscovery of Aristotle's *Nicomachaean Ethics* and *Politics* put what was henceforth called 'political science' or 'prudence' on a fully respectable academic basis as a discipline of systematic argument and discovery. Political discourse was conducted in ethical, analytical and, to a limited degree, empirical terms, both by philosophers and by jurists. It was enriched by a plurality of approaches: theological, legal, natural-philosophical (based on Aristotle) and, by the fifteenth century, historical.

Much could be said about the irony that this development took place in Europe and not in the Islamic countries where, from the seventh till the twelfth centuries, much more attention had been paid to the methods and ideas of Greek philosophy. Indeed one may wonder whether the work of Ibn Khaldun (1332–1406) in history and social science was equalled in the West before the eighteenth century. The major Arabic-speaking philosophers (*falasifa*) produced the kind of synthesis between their (Muslim) religious faith and the philosophical and political language of Neoplatonism and Aristotelianism for which Westerners like Aquinas later became famous. But, whereas Aquinas' approach heralded a new orthodoxy in Europe, the approach of the *falasifa* was effectively suppressed by the rising social power of the *ulama*.

Something similar might have happened in Europe but for whatever reason (and the respective social status of *ulama* and of the European universities is part of the explanation) not only the ideas but the spirit of intellectual enquiry initiated by the ancient Greeks became established. Commitment to the pursuit of truth by intellectual methods acquired an almost religious standing (in Ockham, for example) and must be seen as linking the thought-world of Aquinas to that of Wittgenstein. Behind this stood Abelard's 'by doubting we perceive truth' and Anselm's 'I believe in order to understand.' The institutionalised debate in the universities opened the door to the reception of Aristotle and to the possibility of alternative ways of interpreting the world. This European 'rationality' had a social and legal basis in, for example, jury trial: truth emerges from the presentation of alternative views. Like the boundary between clerical and lay power, the demarcation of 'faith' and 'reason,' fundamental to European theology, philosophy, law and political science, was not entertained in the Islamic world.

By far the most crucial difference between classical Islam and medieval Europe was the emergence in Europe, of what we know as the idea of the state, of fully legitimate secular political authority. We have looked at some of the reasons why it did not emerge in Islamic society. Indeed the kind of state which emerged in Europe between the twelfth and the seventeenth centuries, often referred to as 'the modern state,' was *sui generis* and may not have appeared in any other civilisation. What requires explanation, therefore, is above all its genesis in Europe at this time.

We have already seen how the perceived nature of religious community and of law, and the mode of political discourse prevailing, were at least facilitating factors in the development of the state idea. The New Testament left a space for independent political authority; Christian theologians had always regarded the secular power as ordained by God. The discourse of 'natural' political philosophy meant that the *raison d'être* and responsibility of the state could be found in the needs and aspirations of ordinary mortals, regardless of their religious belief and independently of divine intervention. Indeed, the idea of the European state itself did not come from within Christian teaching itself, any more than it arose within Islamic teaching. Rather, it came, for Europeans, first from Rome and then, from about AD 1250 onwards, from ancient Greece. Here, within the conflation of *Christianitas* and *Romanitas* that was European culture, it was the latter that was the driving force. It was the ancient Greeks who had developed the most far-reaching ideology of self-governing territorial communities (*poleis*) largely under secular control, dependent for their success upon the skill and initiative of the free male population ('the men make the city'), under a variety of constitutions. There, rather than in Rome, was the precedent for a plurality of such states, a states system. Rome contributed the ideal of patriotism, of glory and self-sacrifice for the political community, of the supremacy of the public good and *respublica* over personal or factional interests. On the other hand, by the thirteenth century the attempt to introduce Greek philosophy into the Islamic thought-world had failed completely, so that the prospects for a philosophy or culture of the state were practically nullified. In medieval Europe the *civitas* became accepted as an entity in its own right and to some extent with its own norms. From the twelfth century onwards, it became more and more part of the social consciousness of peoples. Crucially, here was a society, and the idea of a society, that had ethical content and meaning but was not a church.

It is true that, just as the Middle Ages did not evolve any term exactly corresponding to our 'state' (if indeed we are agreed as to what that means), so it is not easy for us to recapture exactly what they understood by words like *civitas* and *respublica*. Yet it is clear that these words connoted not only what we call legitimacy but glory, devotion and self-sacrifice; and that was true before as well as after the Italian Renaissance. Indeed, as Nederman has shown, this did not require any 'Aristotelian revolution' connected with the translation of the *Politics* (c. 1260), for people already knew of and recited sympathetically Cicero's account of the origin of political authority in the human need for a reliable means of settling disputes, protection of property, promotion of justice and the institutionalisation of sociability. What acquaintance with Aristotle's *Politics* did, was to enshrine all this in regular philosophical discourse. From then on the secular state advanced steadily as a power base and as an ideology. The progressive development of this state concept forms the backbone of what we know as medieval and early modern political thought, from Aquinas, through Marsiglio, Machiavelli and Bodin, to Hobbes and beyond.

The core idea, never wholly lost since the Carolingian renaissance, was that in the state—it is above all Cicero and through him, ancient Rome and the Greek *polis* speaking—men devote themselves to the higher good of the *patria*, whose claims can override all private interests, even family bonds. The transition in basic loyalties from clan to state or nation was painful, long and very uneven, as the history of the Italian republics demonstrates. In fact, this did have a theological aspect, in that the Gospels themselves taught that family obligations were secondary to those of Christ (Matthew 10:21, 35; 12:46–50; 19:29). A good example of how sentiment could run was the analogy made by Remigio de'Girolami, a Dominican preacher in Florence in the early 1300s, between devotion to the community of the state and courtly love.

This state idea was not, as in late-antique Rome, tied to a single worldwide *patria communis* but to a multiplicity of territorial allegiances, including feudal monarchies, dukedoms and city-states. This too was not merely a *de facto* arrangement but was justified in theory as well as finding varying degrees of support in popular mentalities. Some, like Nicole Oresme in the fourteenth century, were already arguing that different peoples could and should have different governments because power was territorially limited in practice and also because peoples' character varied due to climate and language. Others argued on the basis of a right to self-determination. Among these, it was symptomatic of the European intelligence that Bartolus of Sassoferrato (1314–57) could meet the objection to such plurality contained throughout the authoritative texts of Roman law in a manner partially reminiscent of the Islamic jurists. That is, he reinterpreted the meaning of accepted concepts: for example, *princeps* can refer not only to the emperor but to any de facto sovereign political community. However he and numerous others went further, reinterpreting the existing law in a prodigal way, often using it as a starting-point for an independent discussion: this was the fruit of the application of the dialectical method to jurisprudence. The Islamic intellectual authorities, on the other hand, while acknowledging since al-Ghazali (1058–1111) that a plurality of rulers existed in reality, never seem to have regarded this as a natural or really valid order of things. The people themselves for the most part saw their allegiance and membership in terms of family, the entire *umma*, and particular religious cells, sects or schools, but not in terms of separate territorial states or nations.

In Islamic society, then, the space that could have been available for the state was occupied by these other groupings. A principal characteristic was that, from the tenth century onwards, a particular kind of 'communalism' developed consisting notably of 'Shi'i sects, Sunni schools of law, and Sufi brotherhoods,' which helped to make 'Islamic religious leaders and organizations the basis of organized community life' throughout the Middle East. These provided the kind of social networks which in European society consisted of, for example, urban, professional and courtly élites. However, such 'communal' groups also occupied the organisational space which in Europe nurtured the growth of town and village communities and of city-states. These were in many regions the essential organs for the development of political participation and what we now call the civic culture. Islamic cities, on the contrary, were never self-governing and seldom acquired any organisational coherence for the territorial unit as a whole. Perhaps the prophetic prohibition of (secular, tribal) communalism (*asabiya*) was a factor here but in any case their place was effectively taken by groupings based upon religious adherence, nonterritorial and often fairly factious in nature.

Political leadership in Islamic society, whether by a *sultan* and his dynasty or by the religious *ulama*, was intensely personal. This too may have stood in the way of a development of the impersonal kind of authority which we associate with the state, which was already in place during the Middle Ages, in such concepts as the crown, the *respublica* and the *universitas* (the whole of a society as a legal corporation).

We can also see how the different approaches to, in particular, sacred law and political rationality, meant that the problem of relating theory and practice to one another arose in quite different ways in Islamic and European society. The Islamic programme of a divinely revealed code and set of institutions to cater for the needs of this world *and* the next, of itself posed a unique problem. For not only the broad principles of justice but their detailed application and highly specific rules came to be regarded as unchangeable. This imposed a static grid on political thought and culture. The various emirs and sultans, holders of *de facto* power based on military support, often of slave armies, were legitimised either by the fiction that they were really delegates of the Caliph or, alternatively, by saying that any *de facto* holder of power is entitled to obedience from the faithful. Practical adaptation to circumstances did of course take place but it was regarded by the intellectual authorities, notably the *ulama*, with suspicion, as at best provisional.

European Christendom could have had a similar problem if the early sanctification of empire and kingship had become accepted as authoritative church teaching but in fact it was contested. Much of the responsibility for this lay with the papacy itself which, under pope Gregory VII (1073–85) and his fellow reformers, launched a frontal assault on the ideology of sacred kingship. While it was commonly stated, in Aristotelian language, that monarchy was the 'best' constitution, oligarchies prevailed in many city-states. Many held that 'popular government' (*regimen ad populum*), for example partially representative government by guild leaders, was quite legitimate. 'Monarchy' itself could mean many things, including some constitutional checks and a role for parliament. Indeed Europe in the high and late Middle Ages was characterised by a relatively widespread belief that the condition of people could be ameliorated: serfs could be liberated, urban communities could acquire charters of liberties, grievances could be redressed and laws brought into line with natural right. The kind of Christian humanism which developed from the twelfth century onwards included the belief that political arrangements were subject to human design and could therefore be improved. Eventually, belief in the adaptability of institutions was applied to the church hierarchy itself.

The whole question of the rightful *form* of government, of absolute versus constitutional monarchy, received much less attention in classical Islam than in medieval Europe. Yet on this subject the starting-points of the two cultures were in some respects not dissimilar. Each had inherited a theory of monarchical beneficence, the west from Rome, the Caliphate from Persia. Each at first incorporated a tradition of consultation of leading members of the community, such as tribal elders (sanctified in the *Qur'an* itself as *shura*: 3:150). Indeed Christianity had started out with a prevalent ethos of political quietism and non-resistance where as early Islam was politically turbulent with groups vehemently contesting, on religious and moral grounds, the authority of particular Caliphs. Belief in the obligation to criticise and to resist unjust government was initially widespread but as the west became less quietist, Islamic society became more so. The Sunni *ulama* qualified the duty or right of resistance by saying that resistance should only be offered if there was a good chance of success. The problem here was that the method of resistance was never specified by those religious scholars and jurists who alone were capable of gaining general approval for such measures. Restraints upon rulers remained moral and were not translated into legally binding obligations. The ideology and theatre of Persian monarchy were taken over by the Caliphs, together with a thorough system of secret policing; there was no doubt where power actually lay.

Al-Ghazali summed up what became the final juristic position when he stated that:

> An evil-doing and barbarous sultan, so long as he is supported by military force, so that he can only with difficulty be deposed and that the attempt to depose him would create unendurable civil strife, must of necessity be left in possession and obedience must be rendered to him.

The Koranic injunction to obey 'those who exercise authority' (4:62) was applied to all those capable of exercising political and military might; in other words, no consistent guidance other than that of the sword was offered. The Shi'ite tradition became equally quietist. Since all power other than that of the Caliph or hidden Imam is intrinsically unjust, it did not much matter to Sunnis or Shi'ites who held it or how it was acquired. The only proviso was that one must not obey a command contrary to the *shari'a*.

In the case of both the Sunni and the Shi'ite traditions, one may see a possible connection between this absence of interest in constitutional restraints and the weak legitimacy of existing regimes, as well as the absence of a general moral theory (such as natural law), of a moral discourse apart from the one stemming from divine revelation. One may also find examples in medieval European thought of a connection between weak legitimacy, or lack of interest in worldly governments generally, and disregard for constitutional restrains together with quietism. In the Augustinian tradition, all human government was a mere suppression of disorder by whoever is most powerful. This echoed the classical Islamic view but was not the dominant belief in Europe, at least not from the later eleventh century. Indeed church leaders themselves, notably the Gregorian papacy, sanctioned and stimulated the right of resistance on the grounds, for instance, that some rulers were more willing to promote divine justice. Thereafter constitutionalism developed in many parts of feudal Europe, most obviously in England and Aragon; while in the cities and city-states very elaborate constitutions were etched out among oligarchical elites and guild-dominated regimes *a popolo*. As regards theory, Aquinas' partially prudential view of resistance, that it is justified if in a just cause, for the public good and with a good chance of success, nicely echoed the view of pre-twelfth century Muslim scholars. The theory of resistance was fully developed during the religious controversies of the sixteenth and seventeenth centuries. While it is interesting to note that Hobbes' statement of virtual non-resistance is in exact agreement with al-Ghazali, neo-Thomists and neo-Calvinists worked out striking alternatives to the tradition of political quietism.

It is clear, then, even from such a necessarily incomplete survey as this, in how many ways the political philosophies and cultures of the Occident and of Islam differed from each other in the period up to about 1500. These differences were neither superficial nor transient. They reached to the very roots of social consciousness in the minds of ordinary people as well as to the peaks of intellectual endeavour by philosophers, jurists and theologians. They covered practical constitutional matters as well as fundamental *Gestalt*. What is more, as the two cultures proceeded through time, these contrasts increased. Far from converging towards some kind of modernity, each culture was becoming more and more itself. I have barely taken the story into the sixteenth century; ahead lies the whole development of modern European political thought and what look like centuries of philosophical stagnation and political conservatism in the Middle East. Eventually, the Ottomans became all too aware of what was lacking.

What I hope this discussion has also done is to open up the question of the contrasting developments of political thought in different cultures and their separate 'languages.' By comparing these, the historian of the 'Western' canon can comprehend far more clearly what developments were most remarkable or unique and what it is that most needs to be explained. By noting what it was not, one can have a far clearer view of the character and contours of a tradition as well as its limitations.

CHAPTER 28

A Fourteenth-Century Parliament

George L. Haskins

Most people, when they think of parliament or the house of commons, conjure up to the mind's eye the spectacle of the stately neo-Gothic Houses of Parliament on the Embankment of the Thames. But it is not with buildings such as these that the medieval parliament was associated, for they date only from the second quarter of the nineteenth century. Shadowed by those Houses, and by the towering Abbey of Westminster, lies the long bulk of gray-black stone known as Westminster Hall. No one edifice typifies so well the continuity of the English government; few places have been so intimately associated with its history. Its dark roof has rung with the acclamations that hailed many an heir to the throne; its somber flags have known the tread of throngs who sought to pay last homage to a sovereign king. It was here that the royal courts of justice had their first beginnings. Here the king's High Court of Parliament was convened; here, until the eighteenth century, the great trials for high treason were held. "The Great Hall of William Rufus," exclaims Macaulay in his famed description of the trial of Warren Hastings.[1] A great hall it is, and a masterpiece of early English architecture—in length all of two hundred and forty feet, in height nearly one hundred. In the proud boast of its builder, the Red King, son and heir of William the Conqueror, it was but a bedchamber in comparison with the building he intended to put up.[2]

Could we turn back the centuries in the glass of time, it would be a very different spectacle we should see at Westminster on a winter's morning in the opening years of the fourteenth century. No more the tapering pinnacles and crockets of neo-Gothic, nor the massive grays of Whitehall: instead, low-lying marshes and pasture land, flooded by a swollen Thames, sullenly resenting the massive walls and bulwarks of the royal palace on the Isle of Thorns. It is a wide and muddy Thames that runs with the salt tide by the palace, by the long staple of the wool merchants, and by the gleaming white of the sumptuous Abbey church hard by. A slow river, with many a small fishing craft and much river traffic, running by the orchards of the Strand, past the river Fleet

From George L. Haskins, *The Growth of English Representative Government* (Philadelphia: University of Pennsylvania Press, 1948), pp. 4–17. Reprinted by permission.

down to London City, with its red roofs, its lead-clad steeples, its hostels, its monasteries, its great cathedral church of St. Paul.

It is not to London City that we shall look on this early morning, but to the bustle and activity about the royal palace and the Great Hall at Westminster. It is Sunday, and the bells and chimes cannot be stilled; for King Edward I has returned from the North to consult with his magnates and the princes of the Church from all England, summoned by royal writ to attend his parliament at Westminster.

> Edward, by the Grace of God, King of England, Lord of Ireland and Duke of Aquitaine, Greeting. Inasmuch as we wish to hold a special consultation with you and the other lords of this realm, touching certain establishments to be made concerning our land of Scotland, we strictly enjoin you, by the love and fidelity by which you are bound to us, and command that you shall put aside all other business and appear before us at our palace of Westminster on the Sunday after the Feast of St. Matthew the Apostle next ensuing, personally there to treat with us on these matters, in order that we may weigh your counsel.[3]

Parliament is a very solemn affair to which all the great of the kingdom must come. It is the great council of the realm, wherein appointments must be made, difficult cases discussed, and important matters of policy considered. For more than two hundred years now the kings of England have been following a practice, current throughout the kingdoms of Europe, of summoning to their courts at the great festivals of the Christian year their vassals, tenants-in-chief, and the princes of the Church, in order that they may hold "deep speech" with them. Yet the English kings are more than feudal lords. Of late, now, King Edward has stretched out his powerful administrative arm into the private feudal jurisdictions of the kingdom, questioning closely by what warrant they are held. His royal courts have multiplied, and his enemies declare that the land is wearied by excess of justice, by the constant questioning of royal justices, as they move from county to county, enquiring into the misdeeds of local officers and all manner of crime and malfeasance. King Edward is a powerful king, the "English Justinian" he will be called in time to come. He has opened his courts to the poorest and humblest subject, and step by step he is destroying local franchises and customs and building up a great body of uniform, national law. His parliament has thus become a great court of justice, wherein, as a contemporary lawyer describes it, "judicial doubts are determined, and new remedies are established for new wrongs, and justice is done to every one according to his deserts."[4] In his parliaments, held usually three times a year, the king is surrounded by lawyers from the courts, by jurists from the great Universities of Paris and Bologna, experts in the civil and canon law. Parliament is indeed a very solemn affair.

Besides counsel and justice, the king has found still another use for his parliaments. His elaborate administration requires many servants who must be paid; and he cannot give away his justice for nothing. His ordinary revenues do not suffice, for there is as yet no general taxation. He can ask a gracious aid from his barons and from the Church; but that again will not suffice.

And so, following a precedent of recent years, writs have gone out to the sheriffs of every county in England, phrased in these words:

> To the sheriff, greeting:
>
> We firmly enjoin you to see to it that from your county two knights are elected without delay; and from each town or city in your county, two of the more discreet burgesses or citizens, capable of work. And they are to be made to appear before us at Westminster on the Sunday following the Feast of St. Matthew next ensuing. And these knights, citizens and burgesses are to have full and sufficient power for themselves and their respective communities to do and consent to those things which in our parliament shall be ordained, lest for lack of this power these matters should remain unaccomplished.[5]

It has become clear that there are many persons of property and wealth who are not actually among the magnates of the realm, particularly that there are many rich merchants in the towns and cities. And so two hundred of the townsfolk of England and seventy-four knights of the shire will respond to the summons; they have no choice. Altogether the numbers attending the king's parliament will be very nearly seven hundred: upwards of one hundred great prelates of the Church, one hundred and fifty representatives or proctors of the lower clergy, more than one hundred barons and earls, besides fifty or so of the king's official staff.

Such is the parliament the king has summoned. Of late it has been to the royal palace of Westminster that he has called his assembly, although there is no prescription by law or custom that he may not call it elsewhere. Although but a straggling village among the marshes, many sentiments of the people are crystallized about Westminster. Since before the coming of the Normans, it has been the recognized home of the king. The Conqueror was wont to hold his summer courts here, and for long the work of government and justice has centered about the royal palace. The pious Edward the Confessor, last of the Saxon kings, lived here and died here, and the Abbey church has in the course of time become the scene of royal coronations. "The crown, the grave, the palace, the festival . . . all illustrate the perpetuity of a national sentiment typifying the continuity of the national life."[6]

It is easy to understand that the summoning of a parliament means an enormous increase of activity about Westminster. Some days before this parliament was to meet, orders went out to the sheriffs of Surrey, Sussex, Kent, and London to purchase some three thousand bushels of wheat, much livestock, and over one hundred tuns of ale; wooden dishes, brazen pots, and copper in mass were to be supplied.[7] There were to be many mouths to feed, for the king's household is large. And a week before, a grave and important-looking personage, called Master in Chancery, had stood forth in the Great Hall and silenced the noisy courts of law there assembled. Scroll in hand, he had read out his "crye," that the king was to gather his great council of the realm on the Sunday next ensuing. Continuing, he pronounced:

> All who wish to bring forward petitions at this next parliament should deliver them day by day between now and the first Sunday in Lent, at the latest, to Sir

John Kirkby, and Master John Bush, or to one of these. And they are assigned to receive them between now and the first Sunday in Lent.[8]

The same proclamation he had read publicly in the West Cheap, by St. Paul's in London, and also in the ancient Guildhall close by. And everywhere it had been greeted with applause, as the king thus proffered his readiness to hear any complaint. People had come to associate the relief of private grievances with the meeting of the king's parliament; and somewhere in their minds would echo the famed promise in the Great Charter of nearly a century ago, "to no one will we sell, to no one will we deny or delay right or justice."[9]

To others the holding of this parliament meant something very different. To most of the great tenants-in-chief, to most, that is, who were not perpetually attendant on the king's person, it meant a long and wearisome journey in the flood season from some remote corner of England, restless nights in smoke-clouded inns, with the dreary creaking of a loose blind outside, and the splash of rain in the mire-filled roads. It meant leaving the hunting, the comfort of the castle or the big manor house; it meant a dreary three weeks in London at one's own expense, with a wearying attention to details of the king's affairs with Philip of France, or his dispute about the investiture of the new archbishop. The king would ask for money; and he would have new statutes to enact, currently described as amendments to the customary law, but in reality a fresh and insolent excuse to invade some local immunity or prerogative. Undoubtedly, the baron reflects, one of his own men will have the face to bring up some trifling case of injustice to the king's highest tribunal, and he, the lord, will be amerced or fined. The tedious journey to Westminster would entail little pleasure. Yet if he disobeys the summons, one of the ubiquitous royal officers will carry off a part of his goods until a fine has been paid.

To the lesser nobility, if we may use this term of the knights of the shire, the king's summons is equally irksome. Though closely connected by blood ties and other interests with the earls and barons, the elected knights are made to feel distinctly unimportant at the king's parliament. True, the knight senses he is vastly superior to the uncouth burgess representative from the town; and he has been elected to parliament because he is a prominent man in county affairs. The king may want official information as to the doings of royal officers, the bailiffs and sheriffs; the allegations of a petitioner may want corroboration. Unofficial testimony may be wanted, as to "what men are saying in remote parts of England, . . . and the possibilities of future taxation have to be considered."[10] None the less it is no privilege to come to Westminster, and the wages which his county will pay him, four shillings a day, will hardly balance his disbursements. He has had to find pledges, men who will guarantee his appearance in parliament, or perhaps four of his best oxen have been "bound over" by the sheriff, lest he try to escape the duty imposed by the king's summons.

Many of the elected knights have been before to the king's parliament.[11] They know what to expect. If, like John de Pabenham, knight of the shire for Bedford County in this parliament, there are any who were at the Michaelmas

Parliament in 1297, they will recall the king's wrath when the knights and nobles in one body refused the king a grant of money until he had redressed their grievances about the forest laws.[12] Then, of an earlier day, one or two may recall that the knights and lords had promised the king a levy of a fifteenth on all their movable property, on condition that he would expel every Jew from England.[13] That was, they could reflect, a masterful stroke of genius. Oh yes, it was money the old king wanted, and when it had been promised he would bid them all go quietly and quickly, prepared to come again when they were needed. Why else had he thought to summon the vulgar townspeople, who spent their days dicing and drinking in an unsavory room at the Sign of the Rose, listening to vagrant student songs on an untuned lute?

After this fashion the baron or the knight might well be thinking as he crowds into the king's Great Hall beside the palace. Close on seven hundred persons are there, and the morning mists hang heavy about the old roof. Bay upon bay the stout chestnut of Normandy and the black oak of Ireland stretch on into the gloom to where at the end, surrounded by torches, sits King Edward I. His lined face and graying beard bear witness to relentless campaigns against the Scot and the turbulent Welsh, to ceaseless energies in building up his great administrative machine in the face of the tyranny of feudal franchises. Now he sits in his capacity as lawgiver, the English Justinian, holding his full court before the communities of the realm.

On his right is the Archbishop of Canterbury; on his left the Chancellor, William de Hamilton; below, some thirty members of the king's small council—his ministers and permanent official advisers. For reasons of comfort as well as in token of their dignity they sit upon great wool-sacks, brought in from the neighboring Woolstaple. Close at hand are the justices of the Common Pleas, the Exchequer, and the King's Bench; their advice will be needed during the session to frame any statutes the king may propose. Among them are the great lawyers of the day, Bereford and Ralph Hengham, whose learning and common sense have forged powerful links in the relentless chain of the king's justice.

Sitting apart are the ninety-five prelates of the realm, together with all manner of archdeacons and deans from the cathedral chapters. The king's business is not their business, they feel; even though they are ranked as an estate of the realm. But they know that if they do not attend parliament, in all likelihood there will be little left of their lands and property, which the barons and earls will almost certainly vote to tax. And at this moment there is grave fear that the king means to take action against the exporting of gold and other tribute to the Holy See in Rome.

Beyond stand the barons, earls, and other magnates of the realm, clothed in stamped velvets of blue, red, or yellow, with cloaks of silk and cloth of Tars. Their arms and weapons they have been forbidden to bear in time of parliament by an ordinance of the king, whose special peace, protecting all coming to parliament, he means to enforce.[14] It is not so long since the treasurer and other retainers of the Earl of Cornwall were murdered in the streets in broad daylight when on their way to parliament at Westminster.[15] And some can still remember how a jealous Archbishop of Canterbury set armed men upon the retainers of the Archbishop of York, broke his cross, and committed other outrages upon the prelate as he was making his way to parliament.[16]

Toward the back of the hall, mingled with the barons, are the knights of the shire, clad in velvet doublets, well lined with rich furs; and beyond, awkward and uncertain in a group of nearly two hundred, the citizens and burgesses elected by the towns. Two or three, like Gilbert de Rokesle, the great wool merchant and master of the exchange, seem to know their business and form the center of groups who talk about the grant of money that the king is sure to demand.

Suddenly the Bishop of London, clad in purple and scarlet, arises, and the talking ceases as he opens with a prayer. The Archbishop of Canterbury follows with a sermon on the text, "How shall a court correct the ills of the whole realm, unless it shall first be itself corrected." What is in store is now clear enough to many; and there are mutterings as the sermon comes to a close. How, they think, can the king reform his realm when his subjects in parliament are reluctant to grant him money? This is the plain meaning of what the Archbishop has been saying. Enough of this reform, it is in the mouths of many to cry. Let the king live of his own; let him mind his own affairs and leave other people alone to mind theirs. And many will instinctively pluck their purses from their sleeves and draw the strings together more closely.

Then silence again, as the Chancellor, the dignified Dean of York, William de Hamilton, addresses the assembled parliament. The purport of the summons to parliament is reiterated: the Archbishop, bishops, earls, barons, knights, and burgesses elected by the communities of the shires and towns have been called together in the king's parliament to discuss certain weighty affairs touching the safety of the realm and in particular the land of Scotland. The king wishes to urge that those who have petitions to present or grievances to be redressed are to bring their complaints to those of the king's council commissioned to receive them. Lastly he emphasizes that the king has incurred heavy expenses in connection with his wars, and especially because of the rebellion of Robert Bruce and others in the North. It is therefore of the utmost importance that the assembled communities should grant a gracious aid to the king for the better ordering of peace and quiet in the kingdom. He earnestly requests that the several estates should deliberate on the matter among themselves and report their decision to the council. Meanwhile, the hour being late—toward ten in the morning—the assembly is adjourned for the day.

The king, followed by his ministers and his council, leaves by the upper end of the hall into St. Stephen's Chapel; the clergy, the lay lords, and the knights remain to discuss the subsidy; the town representatives move off in disorderly groups across the Palace Yard and Dirty Lane toward the refectory of the Abbey, there to deliberate the share which they will grant the king. When these various orders have decided on the grant, as they will do very shortly, their work at the king's parliament is nearly ended.

It is, however, elsewhere than at the Great Hall that the main business of parliament will be accomplished; and it is by others than the great barons, the clergy, the elected knights and burgesses that that work will be done. Should we follow the day-by-day activities of the parliament after the opening of the session, it would be to the council chamber on the south side of the Old Palace Yard that we should repair.[17] Here we should soon understand that the king's parliament in the opening days of the fourteenth century is more in the nature of a high court of justice than a deliberative or legislative assembly. For it is the council, with the king as presiding officer, which is the heart and core of the medieval parliament—a council of ministers, judges, and experts in the law. In the great chamber beyond St. Stephen's Chapel, its roof thickly sown with golden stars on a background of azure, the council has its meeting place. In time to come this room will be known as the Star Chamber, and a mighty and powerful tribunal will take its name from the room. Now it is the center of all the work of consultation of a medieval parliament. Here, from early morning until nearly noon, the council will sit. Their work is confined to the early hours of the day, for, as Sir Henry Spelman shrewdly observes, "Our Ancestours and other the Northern Nations being more prone to distemper and excess of diet used the Forenoon only, lest repletion [in food and drink] should bring upon them drowsiness and oppression of spirit. . . . To confess the truth, our Saxons were immeasurably given to drunkenness."[18]

Before the council knights of the shire will be called and appointed to administrative posts in their shires, and prominent burgesses will be summoned to find out what future customs can be imposed on the wool export. Before the council a deputation of prelates, barons, and knights will come at this parliament we have been describing to offer the king an aid of one-thirtieth to be assessed on their movable property. Before the council the burgesses will decide on a tax of one-twentieth to be levied on their goods. Finally, it is before the council that petitions for the redress of grievances will be presented, and before the council that the petitioner must appear, if he is wanted, to prosecute his case.

Before the representatives at this parliament return home, a group of townsfolk, representing their constituencies and perhaps feeling they should not return empty handed, will essay to make complaint that juries are corrupted by the rich and that ecclesiastical judges are meddling in temporal suits.[19] But the king and council will decide that the complaint has not sufficient foundation, and the petition will be dismissed. To this extent will the future house of commons attempt to participate in the king's parliament. It is not very difficult to see that the king and council are all-powerful, that the burgesses, even the knights of the shire, are no very essential part of parliament. There is something not a little ironical in the phrase of the summons which enjoins them to come to do what shall be ordained.

For when they have made their grant, when they have been given such instructions as the king sees fit, there will be another speech in the Great Hall to the assembled parliament of seven hundred. The king then addresses the estates in words preserved for us in a contemporary record:

Bishops and other prelates, counts, barons, knights of the counties, citizens and burgesses and other people of the community who have come to this parliament at the bidding of the lord king: greatly the king thanks you for your coming and wishes that you will return at once again to your home, so that you may come again quickly and without delay at whatever hour you shall be needed. But the bishops, counts, barons, judges, justices and other members of the lord king's council shall not go without special leave of the king. Those, too, who have business to transact before the council may remain and pursue their business.

And the knights of the shire who have come on behalf of the counties, and the others who have come on behalf of the cities and towns, are to go to Sir John Kirkby, who will make out writs for the payment of the expenses of their coming.[20]

The purpose for which the lessor barons the elected knights and burgesses have been summoned is answered. The seventy councilors, together with their clerks and assistants, will remain; and the high court of parliament will still be considered in full session, even though the representatives and many magnates have gone home. It will remain in session for as much as three or four weeks, transacting the important business which has waited to come before the king's parliament.

There is much business. Nicholas Segrave has been accused of high treason in the Scottish campaign and must be indicted before the king in council. Now that the war is over, a settled form of government must be provided for Scotland—a task that will demand long debates. The Bishop of Glasgow, the Earl of Carrick, and John Mowbray will be called before the council to say how Scotland should be represented at the king's Midsummer parliament in the same year.[21] There will be discussion of policy to be pursued in the lately recovered province of Aquitaine; vast quantities of writs will have to be issued for payments in arrears, and there will be important appointments to be made there, from the seneschal downwards.[22]

The greatest activity of the king and council involves the despatching of hundreds of petitions which have come in from all over the kingdom, as well as from Scotland, Ireland, and Gascony. Four-fifths of the records which this parliament will leave behind are concerned with those petitions and the action consequent upon them. Committees will have been appointed to deal with them, and no suitor will be turned away. The citizens of Lincoln will protest against the abuse of a local franchise in prejudice to their rights.[23] The University of Cambridge will ask leave to found a college.[24] The citizens of Norwich will ask for the grant of a special aid for murage for the safety of the city.[25] Simon le Parker will plead by petition that he has not received justice before the king's judges and is being held on suspicion of murder in the gaol at Canterbury.[26]

Oftentimes the courts of common law, even though sufficiently honest, were not sufficiently strong to do justice in cases where a powerful magnate interfered. The power of granting relief lay in the king, and extraordinary jurisdiction could be, and was, exerted in behalf of an otherwise helpless suitor.[27] And so the idea of relief of private grievances fast became an essential characteristic of the king's parliament. It came to be a court placed over all other courts, for the purpose, as the contemporary lawyer reminds us, of re-solving doubtful judgments, providing new remedial measures for newly emergent wrongs and meting out justice to all according to their deserving.[28]

Notes

1. T. B. Macaulay, "Warren Hastings," *Literary and Historical Essays* (Oxford, 1923), p. 618.
2. J. Stow, *A Survey of the Cities of London and Westminster* (ed. Kingford: Oxford, 1908), ii. 113.
3. Cf. *The Parliamentary Writs and Writs of Military Summons* (ed. Palgrave: London, 1827), i. 138.
4. *Fleta* (London, 1647), p. 66.
5. Cf. *Parliamentary Writs*, i. 115, 140.
6. W. Stubbs, *The Constitutional History of England* (Oxford, 1896), iii. 395.
7. *Parliamentary Writs*, i. 407.
8. Ibid., i. 155.
9. C. 40.
10. *Records of the Parliament Holden at Westminster, 1305* (ed. Maitland, Rolls Series: London, 1893), lxxv.
11. Figures on the number of knights who were re-elected to Parliament at this time may be found in J. G. Edwards, "Personnel of the Commons in the Parliaments of Edward I and Edward II," *Essays in Medieval History Presented to T. F. Tout* (Manchester, 1925).
12. *Chronicon Walteri de Hemingburgh* (ed. Hamilton: London, 1848–1849), ii. 148.
13. *Annales Monastici* (ed. Luard, Rolls Series: London, 1866), iii. 362.
14. Cf. *Statutes of the Realm* (Record Commissioners: London, 1810), i. 170.
15. *Calendar of the Patent Rolls, 1281–1292*, pp. 489, 517.
16. *Historical Papers and Letters from the Northern Registers* (ed. Raine, Rolls Series: London, 1873), pp. 59–63.
17. In 1293 and in 1305 the council was assembled in the house of the Archbishop of York, which stood where the White Hall of later years was to stand. See *Rotuli Parliamentorum*, i. 91, 178.
18. H. Spelman, *Posthumous Works* (Oxford, 1698), p. 89.
19. *Records of the Parliament of 1305*, p. 305, number 472.
20. *Parliamentary Writs*, i. 155.
21. *Records of the Parliament of 1305*, pp. 14–16.
22. Ibid., pp. 328–38.
23. Ibid., pp. 305–6, number 473.
24. Ibid., p. 33, number 50.
25. Ibid., p. 11, number 10.
26. Ibid., p. 11, number 10.
27. *The Collected Historical Works of Sir Francis Palgrave* (ed. Thompson: Cambridge, 1922), viii, 114.
28. Above, note 4.

God, Nature, and Art

One aspect of the rise of medieval civilization in the twelfth and thirteenth centuries was the growth of a more confident attitude concerning man's relationship with the natural world. In combating the Cathar heresy—which held that material creation was intrinsically evil—medieval Christians remembered the teaching of Genesis that, in the beginning, God made the whole universe and "saw that it was good." On a practical level, the extension of agricultural land around existing villages and the planting of new settlements in former wasteland brought more and more of the natural environment under human control. The intellectual life of the universities in the thirteenth century was characterized by an enormous confidence in natural human reason; theologians thought that they could combine all the natural science of Aristotle with the sacred truths of Christian revelation into great, new works of synthesis.

The following readings suggest that ways of perceiving nature could influence spheres as diverse as the practice of agriculture, the art of the great cathedrals, and the speculations of leading theologians. Lynn White offers a provocative thesis on the relationship between traditional Christianity and modern ecological problems. Emile Mâle discusses the medieval view of the universe as a symbol of divine wisdom and power in relation to Gothic art. Etienne Gilson explains how Thomas Aquinas transformed the remote, impersonal "first cause" of Aristotle's natural philosophy into the living, active God of Jewish and Christian revelation. And, finally, Robert Fossier takes us into a different world of religious culture—the faith of the simple, unlettered peasants who lived close to nature and far from the schools of theology.

CHAPTER 29

The Historical Roots of Our Ecological Crisis

Lynn White, Jr.

A conversation with Aldous Huxley not infrequently puts one at the receiving end of an unforgettable monologue. About a year before his lamented death he was discoursing on a favorite topic: Man's unnatural treatment of nature and its sad results. To illustrate his point he told how, during the previous summer, he had returned to a little valley in England where he had spent many happy months as a child. Once it had been composed of delightful grassy glades; now it was becoming overgrown with unsightly brush because the rabbits that formerly kept such growth under control had largely succumbed to a disease, myxomatosis, that was deliberately introduced by the local farmers to reduce the rabbits' destruction of crops. Being something of a Philistine, I could be silent no longer, even in the interests of great rhetoric. I interrupted to point out that the rabbit itself had been brought as a domestic animal to England in 1176, presumably to improve the protein diet of the peasantry.

All forms of life modify their contexts. The most spectacular and benign instance is doubtless the coral polyp. By serving its own ends, it has created a vast undersea world favorable to thousands of other kinds of animals and plants. Ever since man became a numerous species he has affected his environment notably. The hypothesis that his fire-drive method of hunting created the world's great grasslands and helped to exterminate the monster mammals of the Pleistocene from much of the globe is plausible, if not proved. For 6 millennia at least, the banks of the lower Nile have been a human artifact rather than the swampy African jungle which nature, apart from man, would have made it. The Aswan Dam, flooding 5000 square miles, is only the latest stage in a long process. In many regions terracing or irrigation, overgrazing, the cutting of forests by Romans to build ships to fight Carthaginians or by Crusaders to solve the logistics problems of their expeditions, have profoundly changed some ecologies. Observations that the French landscape falls into two basic types, the open fields of the north and the *bocage* of the south and west, inspired Marc Bloch to undertake his classic study of medieval agricultural methods. Quite unintentionally, changes in human ways often affect nonhuman nature. It has been noted, for example, that the advent of the automobile eliminated huge flocks of sparrows that once fed on the horse manure littering every street.

The history of ecologic change is still so rudimentary that we know little about what really happened, or what the results were. The extinction of the European aurochs as late as 1627 would seem to have been a simple case of overenthusiastic hunting. On more intricate matters it often is impossible to find solid information. For a thousand years or more the Frisians and Hollanders have been pushing back the North Sea, and the process is culminating in our own time in the reclamation of the Zuider Zee. What, if any, species of animals, birds, fish, shore life, or plants have died out in the process? In their epic combat with Neptune have the Netherlanders overlooked ecological values in such a way that the quality of human life in the Netherlands has suffered? I cannot discover that the questions have ever been asked, much less answered.

People, then, have often been a dynamic element in their own environment, but in the present state of historical scholarship we usually do not know exactly when, where, or with what effects man-induced changes came. As we enter the last third of the 20th century, however, concern for the problem of ecologic backlash is mounting feverishly. Natural science, conceived as the effort to understand the nature of things, had flourished in several eras and among several peoples. Similarly there had been an age-old accumulation of technological skills, sometimes growing rapidly, sometimes slowly. But it was not until about four generations ago that Western Europe and North America arranged a marriage between science and technology, a union of the theoretical and the empirical approaches to our natural environment. The emergence in widespread practice of the Baconian creed that scientific knowledge means technological power over nature can scarcely be dated before about 1850, save in the chemical industries, where it is anticipated in the 18th century. Its acceptance as a normal pattern of action may mark the greatest event in human history since the invention of agriculture, and perhaps in nonhuman terrestrial history as well.

Almost at once the new situation forced the crystallization of the novel concept of ecology; indeed, the word *ecology* first appeared in the English language in 1871. Today, less than a century later, the impact of our race upon the environment has so increased in force that it has changed in essence. When the first cannons were fired, in the early 14th century, they affected ecology by sending workers scrambling to the forests and mountains for more potash, sulfur, iron ore, and charcoal, with some resulting erosion and deforestation. Hydrogen bombs are of a different order: a war fought with them might alter the genetics of all life on this planet. By 1285 London had a smog problem arising from the burning of soft coal, but our present combustion of fossil fuels threatens to change the chemistry of the globe's atmosphere as a whole, with consequences which we are only beginning to guess. With the population explosion, the carcinoma of planless urbanism, the now geological deposits of sewage and garbage, surely no creature other than man has ever managed to foul its nest in such short order.

There are many calls to action, but specific proposals, however worthy as individual items, seem too partial, palliative, negative: ban the bomb, tear down the billboards, give the Hindus contraceptives and tell them to eat their sacred cows. The simplest solution to any suspect change is, of course, to stop it, or, better yet, to revert to a romanticized past: make those ugly gasoline stations look like Anne Hathaway's cottage or (in the Far West) like ghost-town saloons. The "wilderness area" mentality invariably advocates deep-freezing an ecology, whether San Gimignano or the High Sierra, as it was before the first Kleenex was dropped. But neither atavism nor prettification will cope with the ecologic crisis of our time.

What shall we do? No one yet knows. Unless we think about fundamentals, our specific measures may produce new backlashes more serious than those they are designed to remedy.

As a beginning we should try to clarify our thinking by looking, in some historical depth, at the presuppositions that underlie modern technology and science. Science was traditionally aristocratic, speculative, intellectual in intent; technology was lower-class, empirical, action-oriented. The quite sudden fusion of these two, towards the middle of the 19th century, is surely related to the slightly prior and contemporary democratic revolutions which, by reducing social barriers, tended to assert a functional unity of brain and hand. Our ecologic crisis is the product of an emerging, entirely novel, democratic culture. The issue is whether a democratized world can survive its own implications. Presumably we cannot unless we rethink our axioms.

The Western Traditions of Technology and Science

One thing is so certain that it seems stupid to verbalize it: both modern technology and modern science are distinctly *Occidental*. Our technology has absorbed elements from all over the world, notably from China; yet everywhere today, whether in Japan or in Nigeria, successful technology is Western. Our science is the heir to all the sciences of the past, especially perhaps to the work of the great Islamic scientists of the Middle Ages, who so often outdid the ancient Greeks in skill and perspicacity: al-Rāzi in medicine, for example; or ibn-al-Haytham in optics; or Omar Khay-yám in mathematics. Indeed, not a few works of such geniuses seem to have vanished in the original Arabic and to survive only in medieval Latin translations that helped to lay the foundations for later Western developments. Today, around the globe, all significant science is Western in style and method, whatever the pigmentation or language of the scientists.

A second pair of facts is less well recognized because they result from quite recent historical scholarship. The leadership of the West, both in technology and in science, is far older than the so-called Scientific Revolution of the 17th century or the so-called Industrial Revolution of the 18th century. These terms are in fact outmoded and obscure the true nature of what they try to describe—significant stages in two long and separate developments. By A.D. 1000 at the latest—and perhaps, feebly, as much as 200 years earlier—the West began to apply water power to industrial processes other than milling grain. This was followed in the late 12th century by the harnessing of wind power. From simple beginnings, but with remarkable consistency of style, the West rapidly expanded its skills in the development of power machinery, labor-saving devices, and automation. Those who doubt should contemplate that most monumental achievement in the history of automation: the weight-driven mechanical clock, which appeared in two forms in the early 14th century. Not in craftsmanship but in basic technological capacity, the Latin West of the later Middle Ages far outstripped its elaborate, sophisticated, and esthetically magnificent sister cultures, Byzantium and Islam. In 1444 a great Greek ecclesiastic, Bessarion, who had gone to Italy, wrote a letter to a prince in Greece. He is amazed by the superiority of Western ships, arms, textiles, glass. But above all he is astonished by the spectacle of waterwheels sawing timbers and pumping the bellows of blast furnaces. Clearly, he had seen nothing of the sort in the Near East.

By the end of the 15th century the technological superiority of Europe was such that its small, mutually hostile nations could spill out over all the rest of the world, conquering, looting, and colonizing. The symbol of this technological superiority is the fact that Portugal, one of the weakest states of the Occident, was able to become, and to remain for a century, mistress of the East Indies. And we must remember that the technology of Vasco da Gama and Albuquerque was built by pure empiricism, drawing remarkably little support or inspiration from science.

In the present-day vernacular understanding, modern science is supposed to have begun in 1543, when both Copernicus and Vesalius published their great works. It is no derogation of their accomplishments, however, to point out that such structures as the *Fabrica* and the *De revolutionibus* do not appear overnight. The distinctive Western tradition of science, in fact, began in the late 11th century with a massive movement of translation of Arabic and Greek scientific works into Latin. A few notable books—Theophrastus, for example—escaped the West's avid new appetite for science, but within less than 200 years effectively the entire corpus of Greek and Muslim science was available in Latin, and was being eagerly read and criticized in the new European universities. Out of criticism arose new observation, speculation, and increasing distrust of ancient authorities. By the late 13th century Europe had seized global scientific leadership from the faltering hands of Islam. It would be as absurd to deny the profound originality of Newton, Galileo, or Copernicus as to deny that of the 14th century scholastic scientists like Buridan or Oresme on whose work they built. Before the 11th century, science scarcely existed in the Latin West, even in Roman times. From the 11th century onward, the scientific sector of Occidental culture has increased in a steady crescendo.

Since both our technological and our scientific movements got their start, acquired their character, and achieved world dominance in the Middle Ages, it would seem that we cannot understand their nature or their present impact upon ecology without examining fundamental medieval assumptions and developments.

Medieval View of Man and Nature

Until recently, agriculture has been the chief occupation even in "advanced" societies; hence, any change in methods of tillage has much importance. Early plows, drawn by two oxen, did not normally turn the sod but merely scratched it. Thus, cross-plowing was needed and fields tended to be squarish. In the fairly light soils and semiarid climates of the Near East and Mediterranean, this worked well. But such a plow was inappropriate to the wet climate and often sticky soils of northern Europe. By the latter part of the 7th century after Christ, however, following obscure beginnings, certain northern peasants were using an entirely new kind of plow, equipped with a vertical knife to cut the line of the furrow, a horizontal share to slice under the sod, and a moldboard to turn it over. The friction of this plow with the soil was so great that it normally required not two but eight oxen. It attacked the land with such violence that cross-plowing was not needed, and fields tended to be shaped in long strips.

In the days of the scratch-plow, fields were distributed generally in units capable of supporting a single family. Subsistence farming was the presupposition. But no peasant owned eight oxen: to use the new and more efficient plow, peasants pooled their oxen to form large plow-teams, originally receiving (it would appear) plowed strips in proportion to their contribution. Thus, distribution of land was based no longer on the needs of a family but, rather, on the capacity of a power machine to till the earth. Man's relation to the soil was profoundly changed. Formerly man had been part of nature; now he was the exploiter of nature. Nowhere else in the world did farmers develop any analogous agricultural implement. Is it coincidence that modern technology, with its ruthlessness toward nature, has so largely been produced by descendants of these peasants of northern Europe?

This same exploitive attitude appears slightly before A.D. 830 in Western illustrated calendars. In older calendars the months were shown as passive personifications. The new Frankish calendars, which set the style for the Middle Ages, are very different: they show men coercing the world around them— plowing, harvesting, chopping trees, butchering pigs. Man and nature are two things, and man is master.

These novelties seem to be in harmony with larger intellectual patterns. What people do about their ecology depends on what they think about themselves in relation to things around them. Human ecology is deeply conditioned by beliefs about our nature and destiny—that is by religion. To Western eyes this is very evident in, say, India or Ceylon. It is equally true of ourselves and of our medieval ancestors.

The victory of Christianity over paganism was the greatest psychic revolution in the history of our culture. It has become fashionable today to say that, for better or worse, we live in "the post-Christian age." Certainly the forms of our thinking and language have largely ceased to be Christian, but to my eye the substance often remains amazingly akin to that of the past. Our daily habits of action, for example, are dominated by an implicit faith in perpetual progress which was unknown either to Greco-Roman antiquity or to the Orient. It is rooted in, and is indefensible apart from, Judeo-Christian teleology. The fact that Communists share it merely helps to show what can be demonstrated on many other grounds: that Marxism, like Islam, is a Judeo-Christian heresy. We continue today to live, as we have lived for about 1700 years, very largely in a context of Christian axioms.

What did Christianity tell people about their relations with the environment?

While many of the world's mythologies provide stories of creation, Greco-Roman mythology was singularly incoherent in this respect. Like Aristotle, the intellectuals of the ancient West denied that the visible world had had a beginning. Indeed, the idea of a beginning was impossible in the framework of their cyclical notion of time. In sharp contrast, Christianity inherited from Judaism not only a concept of time as nonrepetitive and linear but also a striking story of creation. By gradual stages a loving and all-powerful God had created light and darkness, the heavenly bodies, the earth and all its plants, animals, birds, and fishes. Finally, God had created Adam and, as an after-thought, Eve to keep man from being lonely. Man named all the animals, thus establishing his dominance over them. God planned all of this explicitly for man's benefit and rule: no item in the physical creation had any purpose save to serve man's purposes. And, although man's body is made of clay, he is not simply part of nature: he is made in God's image.

Especially in its Western form, Christianity is the most anthropocentric religion the world has seen. As early as the 2nd century both Tertullian and Saint Irenaeus of Lyons were insisting that when God shaped Adam he was foreshadowing the image of the incarnate Christ, the Second Adam. Man shares, in great measure, God's transcendence of nature. Christianity, in absolute contrast to ancient paganism and Asia's religions (except, perhaps, Zoroastrianism), not only established a dualism of man and nature but also insisted that it is God's will that man exploit nature for his proper ends.

At the level of the common people this worked out in an interesting way. In Antiquity every tree, every spring, every stream, every hill had its own *genius loci*, its guardian spirit. These spirits were accessible to men, but were very unlike men; centaurs, fauns, and mermaids show their ambivalence. Before one cut a tree, mined a mountain, or dammed a brook, it was important to placate the spirit in charge of that particular situation, and to keep it placated. By destroying pagan animism, Christianity made it possible to exploit nature in a mood of indifference to the feelings of natural objects.

It is often said that for animism the Church substituted the cult of saints. True: but the cult of saints is functionally quite different from animism. The saint is not *in* natural objects: he may have special shrines, but his citizenship is in heaven. Moreover, a saint is entirely a man: he can be approached in human terms. In addition to saints, Christianity of course also had angels and demons inherited from Judaism and perhaps, at one remove, from Zoroastrianism. But these were all as mobile as the saints themselves. The spirits *in* natural objects, which formerly had protected nature from man, evaporated. Man's effective monopoly on spirit in this world was confirmed, and the old inhibitions to the exploitation of nature crumbled.

When one speaks in such sweeping terms, a note of caution is in order. Christianity is a complex faith, and its consequences differ in differing contexts. What I have said may well apply to the medieval West, where in fact technology made spectacular advances. But the Greek East, a highly civilized realm of equal Christian devotion, seems to have produced no marked technological innovation after the late 7th century, when Greek fire was invented. The key to the contrast may perhaps be found in a difference in the tonality of piety and thought which students of comparative theology find between the Greek and the Latin Churches. The Greeks believed that sin was intellectual blindness, and that salvation was found in illumination, orthodoxy—that is, clear thinking. The Latins, on the other hand, felt that sin was moral evil, and that salvation was to be found in right conduct.

Eastern theology has been intellectualist. Western theology has been voluntarist. The Greek saint contemplates; the Western saint acts. The implications of Christianity for the conquest of nature would emerge more easily in the Western atmosphere.

The Christian dogma of creation, which is found in the first clause of all the Creeds, has another meaning for our comprehension of today's ecologic crisis. By revelation, God had given man the Bible, the Book of Scripture. But since God had made nature, nature also must reveal the divine mentality. The religious study of nature for the better understanding of God was known as natural theology. In the early Church, and always in the Greek East, nature was conceived primarily as a symbolic system through which God speaks to men: the ant is a sermon to sluggards; rising flames are the symbol of the soul's aspiration. This view of nature was essentially artistic rather than scientific. While Byzantium preserved and copied great numbers of ancient Greek scientific texts, science as we conceive it could scarcely flourish in such an ambience.

However, in the Latin West by the early 13th century natural theology was following a very different bent. It was ceasing to be the decoding of the physical symbols of God's communication with man and was becoming the effort to understand God's mind by discovering how his creation operates. The rainbow was no longer simply a symbol of hope first sent to Noah after the Deluge: Robert Grosseteste, Friar Roger Bacon, and Theodoric of Freiberg produced startlingly sophisticated work on the optics of the rainbow, but they did it as a venture in religious understanding. From the 13th century onward, up to and including Leibnitz and Newton, every major scientist, in effect, explained his motivations in religious terms. Indeed, if Galileo had not been so expert an amateur theologian he would have got into far less trouble: the professionals resented his intrusion. And Newton seems to have regarded himself more as a theologian than as a scientist. It was not until the late 18th century that the hypothesis of God became unnecessary to many scientists.

It is often hard for the historian to judge, when men explain why they are doing what they want to do, whether they are offering real reasons or merely culturally acceptable reasons. The consistency with which scientists during the long formative centuries of Western science said that the task and the reward of the scientist was "to think God's thoughts after him" leads one to believe that this was their real motivation. If so, then modern Western science was cast in a matrix of Christian theology. The dynamism of religious devotion, shaped by the Judeo-Christian dogma of creation, gave it impetus.

An Alternative Christian View

We would seem to be headed toward conclusions unpalatable to many Christians. Since both *science* and *technology* are blessed words in our contemporary vocabulary, some may be happy at the notions, first, that, viewed historically, modern science is an extrapolation of natural theology and, second, that modern technology is at least partly to be explained as an Occidental, voluntarist realization of the Christian dogma of man's transcendence of, and rightful mastery over, nature. But, as we now recognize, somewhat over a century ago science and technology—hitherto quite separate activities—joined to give mankind powers which, to judge by many of the ecologic effects, are out of control. If so, Christianity bears a huge burden of guilt.

I personally doubt that disastrous ecologic backlash can be avoided simply by applying to our problems more science and more technology. Our science and technology have grown out of Christian attitudes toward man's relation to nature which are almost universally held not only by Christians and neo-Christians but also by those who fondly regard themselves as post-Christians. Despite Copernicus, all the cosmos rotates around our little globe. Despite Darwin, we are *not*, in our hearts, part of the natural process. We are superior to nature, contemptuous of it, willing to use it for our slightest whim. The newly elected Governor of California, like myself a churchman but less troubled than I, spoke for the Christian tradition when he said (as alleged), "when you've seen one redwood tree, you've seen them all." To a Christian a tree can be no more than a physical fact. The whole concept of the sacred grove is alien to Christianity and to the ethos of the West. For nearly 2 millennia Christian missionaries have been chopping down sacred groves, which are idolatrous because they assume spirit in nature.

What we do about ecology depends on our ideas of the man-nature relationship. More science and more technology are not going to get us out of the present ecologic crisis until we find a new religion, or rethink our old one. The beatniks, who are the basic revolutionaries of our time, show a sound instinct in their affinity for Zen Buddhism, which conceives of the man-nature relationship as very nearly the mirror image of the Christian view. Zen, however, is as deeply conditioned by Asian history as Christianity is by the experience of the West, and I am dubious of its viability among us.

Possibly we should ponder the greatest radical in Christian history since Christ: Saint Francis of Assisi. The prime miracle of Saint Francis is the fact that he did not end at the stake, as many of his left-wing followers did. He was so clearly heretical that a General of the Franciscan Order, Saint Bonaventura, a great and perceptive Christian, tried to suppress the early account of Franciscanism. The key to an understanding of Francis is his belief in the virtue of humility—not merely for the individual but for man as a species. Francis tried to depose man from his monarchy over creation and set up a democracy of all God's creatures. With him the ant is no longer simply a homily for the lazy, flames a sign of the thrust of the soul toward union with God; now they are Brother Ant and Sister Fire, praising the Creator in their own ways as Brother Man does in his.

Later commentators have said that Francis preached to the birds as a rebuke to men who would not listen. The records do not read so: he urged the little birds to praise God, and in spiritual ecstasy they flapped their wings and chirped rejoicing. Legends of saints, especially the Irish saints, had long told of their dealings with animals but always, I believe, to show their human dominance over creatures. With Francis it is different. The land around Gubbio in the Apennines was being ravaged by a fierce wolf. Saint Francis, says the legend, talked to the wolf and persuaded him of the error of his ways. The wolf repented, died in the odor of sanctity, and was buried in consecrated ground.

What Sir Steven Runciman calls "the Franciscan doctrine of the animal soul" was quickly stamped out. Quite possibly it was in part inspired, consciously or unconsciously, by the belief in reincarnation held by the Cathar heretics who at that time teemed in Italy and southern France, and who presumably had got it originally from India. It is significant that at just the same moment, about 1200, traces of metempsychosis are found also in western Judaism, in the Provençal *Cabbala*. But Francis held neither to transmigration of souls nor to pantheism. His view of nature and of man rested on a unique sort of pan-psychism of all things animate and inanimate, designed for the glorification of their transcendent Creator, who, in the ultimate gesture of cosmic humility, assumed flesh, lay helpless in a manger, and hung dying on a scaffold.

I am not suggesting that many contemporary Americans who are concerned about our ecologic crisis will be either able or willing to counsel with wolves or exhort birds. However, the present increasing disruption of the global environment is the product of a dynamic technology and science which were originating in the Western medieval world against which Saint Francis was rebelling in so original a way. Their growth cannot be understood historically apart from distinctive attitudes toward nature which are deeply grounded in Christian dogma. The fact that most people do not think of these attitudes as Christian is irrelevant. No new set of basic values has been accepted in our society to displace those of Christianity. Hence we shall continue to have a worsening ecologic crisis until we reject the Christian axiom that nature has no reason for existence save to serve man.

The greatest spiritual revolutionary in Western history, Saint Francis, proposed what he thought was an alternative Christian view of nature and man's relation to it: he tried to substitute the idea of the equality of all creatures, including man, for the idea of man's limitless rule of creation. He failed. Both our present science and our present technology are so tinctured with orthodox Christian arrogance toward nature that no solution for our ecologic crisis can be expected from them alone. Since the roots of our trouble are so largely religious, the remedy must also be essentially religious, whether we call it that or not. We must rethink and refeel our nature and destiny. The profoundly religious, but heretical, sense of the primitive Franciscans for the spiritual autonomy of all parts of nature may point a direction. I propose Francis as a patron saint for ecologists.*

*On April 6, 1980, Pope John Paul II named Francis patron saint of ecology.—Ed.

CHAPTER 30

The Mirror of Nature

Emile Mâle

The Mirror of Nature is carved in brief on the façades of most of the French cathedrals. We find it at Chartres, at Laon, at Auxerre, Bourges and Lyons, treated in a restrained and conventional way. At Chartres a lion, a sheep, a goat and a heifer stand for the animal world, a fig tree and three plants of indeterminate character represent the vegetable kingdom; there is an element of greatness in this summing up of the universe in some five or six bas-reliefs. Some naïve details are full of charm. In the representation at Laon the Creator sits in deep reflection before dividing the darkness from the light, and counts on His fingers the number of days needed to finish His work. Later in the series, when His task is accomplished, He sits down to rest like a good workman at the end of a well-spent day, and leaning on His staff he falls asleep.

One might well feel that these few typical forms were inadequate representations of the wealth of the universe, and might accuse the thirteenth-century craftsmen of timidity and want of power, did the animal and vegetable worlds really occupy no further place in the cathedral scheme. But a glance upward shows us vines, raspberries heavy with fruit and long trails of the wild rose clinging to the archivolts, birds singing among the oak leaves or perching on the pillars. Beasts from far-off lands side by side with homely creatures of the countryside—lions, elephants and camels, squirrels, hens and rabbits—enliven the basement of the porch, while monsters securely fastened by their heavy stone wings bark fiercely at us from above. How little do these old masters with their unequalled, if naive love of nature deserve the reproach of lack of power or invention. Their cathedrals are all life and movement. The Church to them was the ark to which every creature was made welcome, and then—as if the works of God were not sufficient for them—they invented a whole world more of terrible beings, creatures so real that they surely must have lived in the childhood of the world.

In this way the chapters of the Mirror of Nature are inscribed everywhere—on pinnacle and balustrade as on the smallest capital. What is the meaning of all the plants, animals, monsters? Are they due to caprice or have they significance, and do they teach some great and mysterious truth? May one not suppose that they too are symbols, clothing some thought like the statues and bas-reliefs which we shall have occasion to study later?

In order to answer such questions some attempt must be made to understand the mediaeval view of the world and of nature. What is the visible world? What is the meaning of the myriad forms of life? What did the monk dreaming in his cell, or the doctor meditating in the cathedral cloister before the hour of his lecture think of it all? Is it merely appearance or is it reality? The Middle Ages were unanimous in their reply—the world is a symbol. As the idea of his work is in the mind of the artist, so the universe was in the thought of God from the beginning. God created, but He created through His Word, that is, through His Son. The thought of the Father was realised in the Son through whom it passed from potentiality to act, and thus the Son is the true creator. The artists of the Middle Ages, imbued with his doctrine, almost invariably represent the Creator in the likeness of Jesus Christ. The absence in the churches of any likeness of God the Father filled Didron with needless amazement and Michelet with mistaken indignation. For, according to the theologians, God the Father created *in principio,* which is to say *in verbo,* that is by His Son. Jesus Christ is at once Creator and Redeemer.

The world therefore may be defined as "a thought of God realised through the Word." If this be so then in each being is hidden a divine thought; the world is a book written by the hand of God in which every creature is a word charged with meaning. The ignorant see the forms—the mysterious letters—understanding nothing of their meaning, but the wise pass from the visible to the invisible, and in reading nature read the thoughts of God. True knowledge, then, consists not in the study of things in themselves—the outward forms—but in penetrating to the inner meaning intended by God for our instruction, for in the words of Honorius of Autun, "every creature is a shadow of truth and life." All being holds in its depths the reflection of the sacrifice of Christ, an image of the Church and of the virtues and vices. The material and the spiritual worlds are one.

How mystical were the thoughts which arose in the minds of the mediaeval doctors in the presence of nature. We read how in the refectory of the monastery Adam of St. Victor, holding a nut in his hand, reflects—"What is a nut if not the image of Jesus Christ? The green and fleshy sheath is His flesh, His humanity. The wood of the shell is the wood of the Cross on which that flesh suffered. But the kernel of the nut from which men gain nourishment is His hidden divinity."

Peter of Mora, cardinal and bishop of Capua, contemplates the roses in his garden. Their natural beauty does not move him, for he is intent on thoughts which are unfolding within. "The rose," he says, "is the choir of martyrs, or yet again the choir of virgins. When red it is the blood of those who died for the faith, when white it is spotless purity. It opens among thorns as the martyr grows up in the midst of heretics and persecutors, or as the pure virgin blooms radiant in the midst of iniquity."

Hugh of St. Victor looking at a dove thinks of the Church. "The dove has two wings even as the Christian has two ways of life, the active and the contemplative. The blue feathers of the wings are thoughts of heaven; the uncertain shades of the body, the changing colours that recall an unquiet sea, symbolise the ocean of human passions in which the Church is sailing. Why are the dove's eyes this beautiful golden colour? Because yellow, the colour of ripe fruit, is the colour too of experience and maturity, and the yellow eyes of the dove are the looks full of wisdom which the Church casts on the future. The dove, moreover, has red feet, for the Church moves through the world with her feet in the blood of the martyrs."

Marbodus, bishop of Rennes, ponders on precious stones and discovers a mystic consonance between their colours and things of the spirit. The beryl shines like sunlit water and warms the hand that holds it. Is this not an image of the Christian life warmed and illuminated to its depths by Christ the sun? The red amethyst seems to send out fire. Here is an image of the martyrs, who as their blood is shed send up ardent prayers for their persecutors.

The whole world is a symbol. The sun, the stars, the seasons, day and night, all speak in solemn accents. Of what were the Middle Ages thinking in the winter time when the days were shortening sadly and the darkness seemed to be triumphing for ever over the light? They thought of the long centuries of twilight that preceded the coming of Christ, and they understood that in the divine drama both light and darkness have their place. They gave the name of Advent (*Adventus*) to those weeks of December, when by means of the liturgy and lessons from Scripture they expressed the long waiting of the ancient world. It was at the winter solstice, at the time when light begins to reappear and the days to lengthen, that the Son of God was born. Even the round of the year shadows forth man's course upon earth, and recounts the drama of life and death. Spring, which gives new life to the world, is the symbol of baptism which renews the spirit of man at his entrance into life. Summer too is a type, for its burning heat and light are reminders of the light of another world and of the ardent love of the eternal life. Autumn, season of harvest and vintage, is the dread symbol of the last Judgment—that great Day on which men will reap as they have sown. Winter is a shadow of that death which awaits mankind and the universe. Thus the thinker moved in a world of symbols, thronged by forms pregnant with spiritual meaning.

Are these the interpretations of individuals, mystical fancies born of the exaltation of cloistered life, or are we in the presence of an ordered system, an ancient tradition? The answer is found in the most cursory reading of the works of the Fathers and the mediaeval doctors. Never was doctrine more closely knit or more universally accepted. It dates back to the beginning of the Church, and is founded on the words of the Bible itself. In the Scriptures, indeed, as interpreted by the Fathers, the material world is a constant image of the spiritual world. In each word of God both the visible and the invisible are contained. The flowers whose scent overpowered the lover in the Song of Songs, the jewels which adorned the breastplate of the high priest, the beasts of the desert which passed before Job are at once realities and symbols. The juniper tree, the terebinth, and the snowy peaks of Lebanon are alike thoughts of God. To interpret the Bible is to apprehend the harmony which God has established between the soul and the universe, and the key to the scriptures is the key to the two worlds.

CHAPTER 31

Thomas Aquinas: Reason and Revelation

Etienne Gilson

. . . [Thomas's] intention was not to make theology still more learned than Albert the Great had already made it. It was first to eliminate from it all learning irrelevant to the exposition and intellection of the saving truth, then to integrate in theology the relevant learning even if, in order to do so, it was necessary to reform certain commonly held positions and to reinterpret certain philosophical principles. Insofar as Christian faith itself was concerned, Thomas Aquinas never intended to touch it. The magnificent elaboration of Christian dogma left by Augustine to his successors was likewise taken up by Thomas Aquinas and integrated by him in his new synthesis. On the contrary, always with a pious respect for his great predecessor, yet fearlessly, Thomas felt free to reinterpret and, wherever it was necessary, to replace with a truer philosophy the purely philosophical elements integrated by Augustine in his own theological synthesis. His reason for doing so was simple. Philosophy is not necessary for human salvation; it is not even necessary for theology to resort to philosophy, but, if it does, the philosophy it uses should be the true philosophy. When a theologian has good reasons to think that Augustine did not make use of the best possible philosophy, he should not hesitate to change it.

Because Thomas Aquinas did so, his reformation of theology entailed a reformation of philosophy. There is no reason not to call it an Aristotelian reformation, for indeed, on many points, Thomas Aquinas substituted for the doctrines borrowed from Plotinus by Augustine, other doctrines which he himself was borrowing from Aristotle. Two points, however, should be kept in mind. First, the philosophical reformation achieved by Thomas Aquinas is a moment in the history of theology before being one in the history of metaphysics. Secondly, even on the level of pure philosophy, his doctrine cannot be understood as a further stage in the progressive discovery of Aristotle by the Latins. Thomism was not the upshot of a better understanding of Aristotle. It did not come out of Aristotelianism by way of evolution, but of revolution. Thomas uses the language of Aristotle everywhere to make the Philosopher say that there is only one God, the pure Act of Being, Creator of the world, infinite and omnipotent, a providence for all that which is, intimately present to every one of his creatures, especially to men, every one of whom is endowed with a personally immortal soul naturally able to survive the death of its body. The best way to make Aristotle say so many things he never said was not to show that, had he understood himself better than he did, he could have said them. For indeed Aristotle seems to have understood himself pretty well. He has said what he had to say, given the meaning which he himself attributed to the principles of his own philosophy. Even the dialectical acumen of Saint Thomas Aquinas could not have extracted from the principles of Aristotle more than what they could possibly yield. The true reason why his conclusions were different from those of Aristotle was that his own principles themselves were different. As will be seen, in order to metamorphose the doctrine of Aristotle, Thomas has ascribed a new meaning to the principles of Aristotle. As a philosophy, Thomasism is essentially a metaphysics. It is a evolution in the history of the metaphysical interpretation of the first principle, which is "being."

We are living in times so different from those of Thomas Aquinas that it is difficult for us to understand how philosophy can become theology and yet gain in rationality. This, however, is exactly what happened to philosophy in the *Summa Theologiae*, when Thomas changed the water of philosophy to the wine of theology. Thomas always considered himself a theologian. Up to the last years of his life he kept faith with the teaching of Augustine forcefully restated in the injunction of Gregory IX to the theologians of the University of Paris. In his own view, he was not only a theologian, but a monk who had no right to indulge in philosophical activities except in the spirit of his religious vocation. "The philosophers," Thomas says, "made profession of studying Letters in view of acquiring secular learning, but what chiefly befits a religious is to study those Letters that pertain to the learning that is *according to godliness*, as is written in the Epistle to Titus, i, I. As to the other branches of learning, they are not suitable objects of study for a religious whose whole life is dedicated to the divine service, except insofar as their study is related to sacred learning." Whereupon Thomas immediately quotes Augustine in support of his assertion. Thomas intended to do exactly the same thing as all the other theologians of his time, only he did it differently. Then, naturally, the question arises: since he was a theologian, and such a strict one, how could he have anything to do with philosophy? His own notion of the nature of theology will be the answer to this difficulty.

• • •

The true nature of the distinction there is between philosophy and theology is a matter to be settled between philosophers and theologians. All that a historian can say is that, in the mind of Thomas Aquinas himself, their distinction was not as simple as it is sometimes supposed to be. With all theologians, Thomas affirms that, supposing the free will of God to save mankind as a whole, it was necessary that the knowledge required for human salvation should be revealed to men. This is evident in the case of those saving truths which escape the grasp of natural human reason. But even when it was within the grasp of natural human reason, saving truth had to be revealed because, otherwise, most men would have remained ignorant of it. Few men are gifted for metaphysical or ethical studies; even those who have the necessary gifts have to wait up to the later part of their life before reaching conclusions in these lofty matters, and who knows at what age he will die? Above all, even those philosophers who live long enough to reach these conclusions, never or seldom do it without some admixture of error.

A first consequence follows from these facts. To the extent that it pertains to the sacred teaching imparted to man through revelation (*sacra doctrina*) theology must deal with some philosophically knowable truths, namely, those whose knowledge is required for the salvation of any man; for instance, God exists, he is one, he is incorporeal, etc. Since they have been in fact revealed to men, these truths were revealable, but the formal reason of the "revealable" extends even beyond the limits of the actually revealed; it includes the whole body of human natural knowledge inasmuch as it can be considered by the theologian in the light of revelation and used by him in view of its end, which is the salvation of man in general. This leaves intact, within theology, the formal distinction between natural knowledge and supernatural knowledge, but it includes them both under a still wider formal reason since "revealables" comprise the whole body of natural cognitions considered as being at the disposal of the theologian in view of his own theological end which is the salvation of man.

If this be true, the unity of theology is that of an organic whole whose parts are united under one single formal reason. Naturally, it first includes what God has actually revealed (whether it be naturally knowable or not). It also includes what the theologian deduces, as a necessary consequence, from the actually revealed truth (theologians often call this the "virtually" revealed). Moreover, it includes all the material provided by logic, the sciences of nature and metaphysics, to the extent that it is taken up by the theologian and incorporated by him into his work. He alone is judge of this extent. Just as it is the soul that builds itself a body, so also theology builds itself the philosophical body which it needs in order to promote the saving work of the sacred teaching.

• • •

Like all theologies the doctrine of Saint Thomas is dominated by his own notion of God. Like all Christian theologians, he knew that the proper name of God was I AM WHO AM, or HE WHO IS (Exod. 3, 14), but even for men who agreed on the truth of this divine name, there remained a problem of interpretation. Modern philology has a right to investigate the question; naturally, it will find in this text what can be found in any text by means of grammars and dictionaries alone. This is not negligible but, philosophically speaking, it seldom amounts to much. Even with such a limited aim in mind, the grammarians have already achieved amazingly different results. What we are concerned with is very different. Our own problem is to know what meaning the Christian masters have attributed to this famous text. Most of them agreed that it meant: I am Being. But what is being? To Augustine, "who was imbued with the doctrines of the Platonists," being was eternal immutability. To John Damascene, absolute being was an "infinite ocean of entity." To Saint Anselm, it was that whose very nature it is to be: *natura essendi*. In all these cases, the dominating notion was that of "entity" (*essentia*). In the mind of Thomas Aquinas, the notion of being underwent a remarkable transformation; from now on, and so long as we will be dealing with Thomas Aquinas, the deepest meaning of the word "being" will be the act pointed out by the verb "to be." Since, in common human experience, to be is to exist, it can be said that, in the doctrine of Thomas Aquinas, being has received the fullness of its existential meaning. In order to avoid all possible confusions with some modern uses of the word "existence," let us add that, in every being, "to be," or *esse*, is not to become; it is not any kind of projection from the present into the future. On the contrary, because it is act, "to be" is something fixed and at rest in being: *esse est aliquid fixum et quietum in ente*. In short, this act is the very core of all that is, inasmuch precisely as what is, is a being.

As Thomas Aquinas understands him, God is the being whose whole nature it is to be such an existential act. This is the reason why his most proper name is, HE IS. After saying this, any addition would be a subtraction. To say that God "is this," or that he "is that," would be to restrict his being to the essence of what "this" and "that" are. God "is," absolutely. Because "what" a thing is usually receives the name of "essence," or of "quiddity"(its "whatness"), some say that since he is "being only" (*essetantum*), God has no essence or quiddity. Thomas Aquinas does not seem to have favored this way of expressing the purity of the divine act of being. He prefers to say that the essence of God is his *esse*. In other words, God is the being of which it can be said that, what in other beings is their essence, is in it what we call "to be." All the attributes of God are either deducible from this true meaning of his name, or qualified by it.

In our human experience, a "being" is "something that is," or exists. Since, in God, there is no something to which existence could be attributed, his own *esse* is precisely that which God is. To us, such a being is strictly beyond all possible representation. We can establish *that* God is, we cannot know *what* he is because, in him, there is no what; and since our whole experience is about things that *have* existence, we cannot figure out what it is to be a being whose only essence is "to be." For this reason, we can prove the truth of the proposition "God is," but, in this unique case, we cannot know the meaning of the verb "is." Such is the Thomistic meaning of the classical doctrine of the ineffability of God.

Unknowable in himself, at least to us and in this life, God can be known by man imperfectly, from the consideration of his creatures. Two things at least are known of him in this way: first, that he is entirely unlike any one of his creatures; secondly, that he is in himself at least what he has to be in order to be their cause. For this reason, our knowledge of God is said to be "analogical"; we know that God is, with respect to the universe, in a relation similar to that which obtains, in our human experience, between causes and their effects. Such a cognition is not purely negative, since it enables us to say something true about God; it is not wholly positive, and far from it, since not a single one of our concepts, not even that of existence, properly applies to God; we call it "analogical" precisely because it bears upon resemblances between relations, that is, upon proportions.

This notion of God as the absolute act of being flows from the demonstrations of his existence. To demonstrate it is both possible and necessary. It is necessary because the existence of God is not immediately evident; self-evidence would only be possible in this matter if we had an adequate notion of the divine essence; the essence of God would then appear to be one with his existence. But God is an infinite being and, as it has no concept of him, our finite mind cannot see existence as necessarily implied in his infinity; we therefore have to conclude, by way of reasoning, that existence which we cannot intuit. Thus the direct way apparently opened by Saint Anselm's ontological argument is closed to us; but the indirect way which Aristotle has pointed out remains open. Let us therefore seek in sensible things, whose nature is proportioned to our intellect, the starting point of our way to God.

All the Thomistic proofs bring two distinct elements into play: (1) the existence of a sensible reality whose existence requires a cause; (2) the demonstration of the fact that its existence requires a finite series of causes, and consequently a Prime Cause, which is what we call God. Because movement is immediately perceptible to sense knowledge, let us start from the fact that movement exists. The only superiority of this "way" with respect to the other ones, is that its point of departure is the easiest to grasp. All movement has a cause, and that cause must be other than the very being that is in motion; when a thing seems to be self-moving, a certain part of it is moving the rest. Now, whatever it is, the mover itself must be moved by another, and that other by still another. It must therefore be admitted, either that the series of causes is infinite and has no origin, but then nothing explains that there is movement, or else that the series is finite and that there is a primary cause, and this primary cause is precisely what everyone understands to be God.

Just as there is motion in sensible things, there are causes and effects. Now what has just been said of the causes of movement can also be said of causes in general. Nothing can be its own efficient cause, for in order to produce itself, it would have to be anterior, as cause, to itself as effect. Every efficient cause therefore presupposes another, which in turn presupposes another. Now, in this order of causes, in which each higher one is the cause of the lower, it is impossible to go on to infinity, otherwise, there would be neither a first efficient cause, nor intermediate causes, and the effects whose existence we perceive could not possibly exist. There must therefore be a first efficient cause of the series, in order that there may be a middle and a last one, and that first efficient cause is what everyone calls God.

Now let us consider beings themselves. As we know them, they are cease-lessly becoming. Since some of them are being generated, while others are passing away, it is possible for them to be or not to be. Their existence then is not necessary. Now the necessary needs no cause in order to exist; precisely because it is necessary, it exists of itself. But the possible cannot account for its own existence, and if there were absolutely nothing but possibility in things, there would be nothing. This is to say that, since there is something, there must be some being whose existence is necessary. If there are several neces-sary beings, their series must be finite for the same reason as above. There is therefore a first necessary being, to whose necessity all possible beings owe their existence, and this is what all men call God.

A fourth way goes through the hierarchical degrees of perfection observed in things. There are degrees in goodness, truth, nobility and other perfections of being. Now, more or less are always said with reference to a term of com-parison which is absolute. There is therefore a true and a good in itself, that is to say, in the last resort, a being in itself which is the cause of all the other be-ings and this we call God.

The fifth way rests upon the order of things. All natural bodies, even those which lack knowledge, act for an end. The regularity with which, by and large, they achieve their end, is a safe indication that they do not arrive at it by chance and that this regularity can only be intentional and willed. Since they themselves are without knowledge, someone has to know for them. This pri-mary Intelligent Being, cause of the purpose there is in natural things, is the being we call God.

Since God is first from all points of view and with respect to all the rest, he cannot enter into composition with anything else. The cause of all other beings can enter into composition with none of them. Consequently, God is simple. His simplicity itself has many consequences. Because corporeal bodies are in potency with respect to both motion and being, they are not simple; hence God cannot be corporeal. For the same reason, since he is pure act, God is not composed of matter and form. He is not even a subject endowed with its own form, essence or nature. Divinity is something that God *is*, not that he *has*. But what is such a being which *is* all that he can be said to be, and *has* nothing? He is WHO IS. Since God *is* what other beings only *have*, there is in him no distinct essence to unite with the act of being. This unique being, the only one whose whole essence it is "to be," is so perfectly simple that it is its own being.

If this direct argument seems too abstract to satisfy the intellect, let us re-member the conclusions of each one of the five "ways." All particular beings owe their existence to the Prime Cause. Consequently, they receive existence. In other words, what they are (i.e., their essence) receives from God the exis-tence which it has. On the contrary, since the Prime Efficient Cause does not receive its own existence (otherwise it would not be prime) there is no sense in which it can be said to be distinct from it. If there were such a thing as a pure and absolute "fire," it would not *have* the nature of fire, it would *be* it. Simi-larly, God is not really "being"; he is the very act of what we call "to be." He does not share in it, he is it. Naturally, since we have no experience of this unique being, our mind is unable to conceive it and our language has no perfectly fitting words to express it. From the very first moment we attempt to say what God is, we must content ourselves with saying that he is not in the same way as other things are. As has already been said, we do not know what it is for God "to be"; we only know that it is true to say that God is.

The metaphysician thus joins, by reason alone, the philosophical truth hidden in the name that God himself has revealed to man: I AM WHO AM (Exod. 3, 14). God is the pure act of existing, that is, not some essence or other, such as the One, or the Good, or Thought, to which might be attributed existence in addition; not even a certain eminent way of existing, like Eternity, Immutability or Necessity, that could be attributed to his being as characteristic of the divine reality; but Existing itself (*ipsum esse*) in itself and without any addition whatever, since all that could be added to it would limit it in determining it. If he is pure Existing, God is by that very fact the absolute Plenitude of being; he is therefore infinite. If he is infinite Being, he can lack nothing that he should acquire; no change is conceivable in him; he is therefore sovereignly immutable and eternal, and so with other perfections that can be fittingly attributed to him. Now, it is fitting to attribute all of them to him, for, if the absolute act of existing is infinite, it is so in the order of being; it is therefore perfect.

Such is the cause of the many deficiencies of the language in which we express him. This God whose existence we affirm, does not allow us to fathom what he is; he is infinite, and our minds are finite; we must therefore take as many exterior views of him as we can, without ever claiming to exhaust the subject. A first way of proceeding consists in denying everything about the divine essence that could not belong to it. By successively removing from the idea of God movement, change, passivity, composition, we end by positing him as an immobile, immovable being, perfectly in act and absolutely simple; this is the way of negation. But one can take a second way and try to name God according to the analogies obtaining between him and things. There is necessarily a connection, and consequently a resemblance, between cause and effect. When the cause is infinite and the effect finite, it obviously cannot be said that the properties of the effect are found in it such as they are in the cause, but what exists in effects must also be pre-existent in their cause, whatever its manner of existing. In this sense, we attribute to God all the perfections of which we have found some shadow in the creature, but we carry them to the infinite. Thus we say that God is perfect, supremely good, unique, intelligent, omniscient, voluntary, free, and all-powerful, each of these attributes being reduced, in the last analysis, to an aspect of the infinite and perfectly single perfection of the pure act that God is.

CHAPTER 32

Peasant Families

Robert Fossier

Knowledge and Belief

This is an ambitious title to which we all know it is impossible to give a satisfactory answer. Even in the modern period any understanding of rural attitudes is hampered by irrelevant assumptions. These people could not write
and they speak to us only through clerics and nobles who presented them as
absurd caricatures. Iconography continued, unperturbed, to reproduce the
classical and Carolingian *topoi* of men working the land. As we shall see, it is
only their fantasies which have reached us untouched, because the Church
tracked them down in its fight against witchcraft and heresy and they are
sometimes illuminated by accusations in trial proceedings. But for the anonymous poets of *Aucassin et Nicolette* and *Le Charroi de Nîmes* and for Chrétien de
Troyes these deformed beings, dressed in rags with squashed features and
filthy mops of hair, black hands and yellow teeth, verged on the bestial.
Thought was beyond them!

Beliefs Rather Than a Faith

All preachers were unanimous and all the conciliar canons in agreement on
one issue: that peasant worship was irregular, their knowledge and understanding of dogma scanty in the extreme. St. Bernard in the twelfth century
and Jacques de Vitry 100 years later both deplored the misconceptions on
which heresy thrived; Dominicans like Hugues de Romans or Etienne de
Bourbon, prelates like Eudes Rigaut, archbishop of Rouen, who scoured their
dioceses, documented poor attendance at mass, ignorance of the Creed and
even the Lord's Prayer, the infrequent practice of confession and even more of
communion; the men were in the tavern, the women doing their laundry together: behind the lord and his household at mass there was a handful of children, widows and spinsters. Moreover, they had no knowledge of Latin, an ignorance sometimes shared by their priest, and there was no question of
learning to write. At first sight, although the church dominated the village
with its sheer size and served as a meeting-place and defensive retreat, it was
little more than a communal building whose bells marked the hours of work

From Robert Fossier, "Families and Popular Religion," *Peasant Life in the Medieval West* (Oxford:
Basil Blackwell Ltd., 1988), pp. 39–43. Reprinted by permission of Basil Blackwell Ltd.

and rest. It made little difference if the fields and houses were owned by a monastery, or whether they were one of the restitutions of patronage usurped by the laity and very, very slowly surrendered to the monasteries between 1050 and 1225–50.

This miserable picture, a little brighter in the thirteenth than in the eleventh century, distressed Rome at the time and affects too many historians of the Church today. This is undoubtedly to misunderstand peasant spirituality; in our largely urban and mechanized world we take too little account of the effect on the peasant soul of the forest encircling the village, the heath or marsh covered by sudden mists, thunderstorms and capricious rains. Where were God and the Incarnation to be found in these experiences? This was why the practice of the Christian faith remained at the level of what was useful, visible and probable, mingling the Christian message with the phantasms of protohistory. Of the sacraments proclaimed by the hierarchy of the Church only baptism was universal, for that was a rite of passage, a ceremony of introduction to the world in which they were to find their place and there were difficulties in persuading the villagers to proceed with it at the earliest opportunity. In their eyes this rite should accompany the dawn of the child's full consciousness when he was six or seven years old. The Last Rites were also in demand, but bore a strange resemblance to the pagan departure for the other world. Moreover, well into the thirteenth century there are descriptions of strange ceremonies performed by women in which new-born children were exposed on the edge of the forest, immersed in water, passed nine times between the branches of a tree or lighted tapers: "Puerile superstition!" exclaimed Etienne de Bourbon, who knew nothing of anthropology and had no comprehension of the rites of separation, purification and retrieval which freed the new-born child from the powers of evil and made him truly his mother's son. For supreme power was seen to reside in Nature who was to be flattered and entreated. This was why women were intermediaries with the irrational: preachers saw this as the consequence of the Fall from grace in Eden, also brought about by a woman, without realizing that Earth, Moon and Water were also female. Only women could avert or precipitate sterility by the enchantments they practised at night in the *escrennes* in the wood or the land round the hut where they spun and wove. Only they could concoct philtres of mandrake, deadly nightshade or mint which served as contraceptives or abortifacients; only they could turn into witches and fairies to mislead credulous males or spoil the crops. Think of Yvain, Perceval or Tristan, ridiculed by wandering Melusines, goddesses of death and misfortune. The forest remained the favoured place for manifestations of this kind and of beings, good or evil, like elves, or the werewolves that have since metamorphosed into the child-eating wolves of fairytales.

Throughout this period the Church did not attempt to forbid—although little inclined to indulgence, like St. Bernard, many priests made a real effort to understand—but it did attempt to regain control of these agrarian, sexual or initiation rites. When fertile rains had to be induced in late spring, the village priest placed himself at the head of the Rogationtide procession (on the Sunday before Ascension Day) and sprinkled the fields with holy water; after the harvest, when the earth had set an example of fecundity, boys and girls danced or coupled on the threshing floor to beat the grain; afterwards purificatory fires were organized in the name of St. John, who could do nothing whatever about it; similarly, in May, the priests led torch-lit processions to plant a new tree or decked the girls who were to be married with garlands. Lent, too, was happily placed at the moment when the granaries were empty, transforming grudging penury into voluntary sacrifice; there was the sacrificial Paschal lamb of the Bible from whose blood the God was reborn and also the sacrifice of the pig fattened during the autumn and killed at Christmas, not—as once upon a time—to celebrate the winter solstice, but the presumed birth of Jesus.

Our list will stop there. The "conversion" of the European peasantry was not complete at the beginning of the fourteenth century; it could be maintained that the process was not finished until after the Council of Trent. But this distorted faith was based on essential beliefs rooted in centuries of agrarian life: the bonds between the living and the dead, the belief in salvation, the concept of good and evil and the certainty that there would be a Judgement when the indistinct Godhead who ruled the world willed it. This Godhead was so indistinct that the workers in the fields required an intermediary to make themselves understood: if men did not consult a wizard or a hermit in the forest, it would be the Virgin or a patron saint—a terribly human Virgin with a child in her arms, a saint still more so, because they kept a relic such as a piece of bone or clothing.

Overall during this period the peasant gave the Church all his not inconsiderable tokens of acceptance and obedience: the "Hail Mary" was easily introduced and became widespread at the time when statues of the mother of God were also appearing in church portals; the priest was virtually everywhere and it was he, even more than the blacksmith, who went up to the castle and talked to the lord of the manor; the wealthier man was prepared to make a bequest to the neighbouring monastery on his deathbed; peasants were willing to fast and to receive the body and blood of Christ once a year. The peasant accepted the Christian faith because in it he found the roots of simple belief—rustic in the full sense of the word—which gave a regular pattern to his daily earthly life. As for the future of the world and eschatological hopes and fears, if he gave way to moments of exaltation and terror, it was always because an impassioned preacher had led him to join a wandering band searching for a better existence. There were feverish outbursts of millenarianism at intervals throughout this period: around the years 1000, 1033 (millennium of the passion of Christ), 1095 (when the fall of Jerusalem was believed to have defiled the city), but it also broke out around 1107 and 1120, then again in 1170–80, in the middle of the thirteenth century and at its close. But in each case religious desire for purification was mingled with a specific upheaval of a different kind—oppression by the lord, famine, the threat of an epidemic, a desire to re-establish peace or to save the king.

ON THE MARGIN:
VAGABONDS, OUTCASTS,
AND JEWS

We cannot fully understand the life of the medieval world by considering only the great constructive achievements of medieval men and women. Then—as now—there were marginal classes of people, existing on the fringes of society, excluded from full participation in the social and economic life of the time. Moreover, it seems that attitudes toward such persons grew harsher in the later Middle Ages. In the following readings Bronislaw Geremek discusses the roles of these marginal people—vagabonds, habitual criminals, lepers, heretics, Jews, members of "degrading professions." Jeremy Cohen considers especially the position of the Jews. After a period of relative toleration in the early Middle Ages, savage outbreaks of anti-Jewish violence occurred from the twelfth century onward. To explain why this happened is a major problem for historians. Was it because of the church's teachings or in spite of them? Was the underlying cause religious animosity? economic grievances? dawning nationalism? Jeremy Cohen's review of some of the modern literature illustrates the complexity of the theme. Finally, Philip Ziegler shows how the catastrophe of the Black Death provoked a wave of anti-Jewish hysteria in the fourteenth century.

CHAPTER 33

Marginal People

Bronislaw Geremek

Marginal figures have left few traces in historical documentation. They established few relations, inherited no property, acted as the protagonists of no great enterprises that could be passed on to history. When they do appear it is above all in the archives of repression, thus in a reflected image that shows the anxiety and the hatred of organized society as well as its justice. For this reason, the data available regard society itself, and only on a second level the objects of society's repression. Furthermore, our information refers more to legal norms than to persons. For many centuries of the Middle Ages, the best we can do is ask what customary law considered punishable and how social groups executed its orders. Thus everything took place within local societies, which could stigmatize offenders (with branding, for example) but rarely did so. More often they were directly excluded by being banished from the community. No written traces remain of such procedures; custom had no need for documents. Even when written reports on judicial procedures had become a fairly widespread practice and court registers had begun to be used, a good many disputes were resolved by extrajudicial means, leaving no records. From the twelfth century on, the archives of repression made their appearance in medieval Europe, and in the late Middle Ages they became the general rule. They furnish both an overall picture of delinquency in the Middle Ages and existential portraits of marginal individuals. . . .

. . . Marginality and criminality were of a different essence. Only criminal behavior that involved class demotion and desocialization thrust a person, a family, or a group beyond the limits of society. Observation of these processes requires examination of individual biographies, furnished, of course, by criminal archives, albeit in sketchy form.

The Bedfordshire coroners' rolls note the case of a violent quarrel that took place on 28 April 1272 in Dunton. Some vagabonds freshly arrived in town—two men and two women—first attempted (unsuccessfully) to sell an animal skin, then, also in vain, to obtain hospitality. A fight broke out between the two male vagabonds and one of them dropped dead of knife wounds. One of the women took refuge in the church, claiming right of asylum, and later admitted to the coroner that she had committed a good many thefts and declared that

From Bronislaw Geremek, "The Marginal Man," in *Medieval Callings* edited by Jacques Le Goff (Chicago: University of Chicago Press, 1990), pp. 353–371. Reprinted by permission of The University of Chicago Press.

her companions were thieves as well. The murderer, sentenced to be hanged, was defined in the verdict as "a vagabond and a person belonging to no tithing."

We know nothing of the earlier history of this group. I might add, though, that they came from different parts of England, which bolstered the opinion that they were indeed vagabonds. They had managed to live, moving from one place to another, by robbing, begging, hunting when they had the chance, or working sporadically. The group had formed after a chance meeting on the road when they had eaten together in a tavern. After, they had occasionally organized thefts together. More often they acted independently, at times as "married" couples. One of the men, who came from Berwick-upon-Tweed, and one of the women, from Stratford, were referred to as a married couple, perhaps in a "marriage" resulting from their travels. The phraseology of the sentence characterizing the vagabond murderer as of no tithing is telling, as it reveals the important fact that he belonged to no local group and was thus cut off from social ties. This was considered an argument for hanging.

One portrait of a vagabond *sui generis* comes from a Tuscan judicial register for the year 1375. Sandro di Vanni, called Pescione, who came from near Florence, is identified as a robber, a forger, a man of evil reputation, and a vagabond without fixed domicile either in or around Florence or elsewhere. Furthermore, he had been banned from Florence and its surroundings. The list of his offenses includes several dozen court cases, for the most part for thefts of linens and sacks, often involving deceit when he presented himself as a buyer's agent or a collector for charity. Such petty thievery and fraud required continual changes of place, but Pescione operated within a fairly limited area, never leaving Tuscany and selling his goods and spending the winter in Florence or in Pisa.

Judicial records normally furnish a distorted image in that they center attention, obviously, on the unlawful acts that led to the suspect's arrest. Still, on occasion court procedures called for biographical information. The woman who confessed her thefts to the coroner of Bedfordshire in 1272 did so knowing that the laws covering the right of asylum stipulated that a person who confessed to crimes in that manner might avoid punishment for them, the judge pronouncing by which port the banished criminal would leave the kingdom, making his or her way carrying a cross. The *lettres de rémission* in France usually give not only a description of the crime for which the person mentioned in the letter was imprisoned or sentenced, but also a detailed list of wrongdoings committed throughout his or her lifetime. According to the king's law, the letter of remission lost all its value if any offense committed by the person involved did not figure in the list, so it was in the suspect's interest to confess to all crimes committed to that date. The biographical information that comes to light in this manner is sparse: place of birth, the profession of the person's father and his or her own profession; changes of residence. At times court records show malefactors of a clearly asocial profile who come from criminal milieus and whose life was one of unwavering delinquency. More often, however, marginality for these people seems to be instable, accidental, one might say, close to normal life.

The people we find in criminal archives are basically common men and women from the organized working world, set in contexts of family and good neighborly relations, but who broke with those structures at some point, suddenly or gradually. In Paris in 1416 a cleric who had for a while even been a Carmelite monk but had left the monastery was brought to justice, accused of theft and homicide. We know the particulars of his life through the exchange of arguments between ecclesiastical and secular jurisdictions contending for the right to judge him. Of illegitimate birth, he had loved gaming from childhood. After leaving the Carmelites he had enrolled in a military company. He had also worked as a lackey in the court of a noblewoman and, before his arrest, had appeared in the Paris marketplace in "public farces." This, at least, is how this malefactor and vagabond was presented by the king's prosecutor, who argued that the accused did not have the right to the benefits of the *privilegium fori*. The representative of the ecclesiastical jurisdiction affirmed that the cleric had obtained a dispensation from the church because of his illegitimate birth, and had participated in public spectacles for amusement and not for gain. Thus "il n'est buffo ne gouliart ne jongleur ou basteleur" (he was neither a buffoon nor a player nor a juggler nor a tumbler), so the objections to his right to enjoy clerical privilege did not pertain. Arguments aside, there was a fundamental conflict in his curriculum vitae: he was a cleric, a soldier, a vagabond, and an actor. Every now and again he had committed a robbery, and he had ended up in prison on at least four occasions. We can suppose that this "jack of all trades," a medieval precursor of the *picaro*, had had long periods of law-abiding life, at least in the sense that he had earned his living and had had a master over him. Were his violations of the law then only accidental situations that did not define his life in general? Only one thing is certain; organized society, of which the police and the courts were institutionalized expressions and which in turn protected that society, treated him as a vagabond, an unstable individual, and an outcast.

In the case narrated here, we can see that even a noncriminal life led to marginality when it lacked professional stabilization or when the trades that were exercised touched the limits of social acceptance or were considered degrading. The same could be said of a Parisian musician who ended up on the gallows in 1392. When he grew too old to support himself with his trade in Paris, he went from place to place in Normandy, committing petty thefts (stealing tin basins from houses). Here the reason for his marginality was old age, but we can find roots of it in his earlier mode of life, as he had already been imprisoned for theft. Urban delinquency was most commonly due to the presence of a number of workers carrying out a great variety of activities, often outside the purview of the guilds. In the unstable way of life of this sort of people day-work alternated or coexisted with robbery and begging. One day-worker and mason's helper (*homme de labour et varlet à maçon*) sometimes worked in the city, but at other times did seasonal work in the country. His wife remained in Paris, where she sold cheese. Work or no work, this man committed a number of thefts, both in Paris and its suburbs. In some of his undertakings he was helped by a companion, a roast-meat seller by profession, who had been crippled in military service (which explained his nickname, *Court-Bras*) and who later worked as a stevedore. When Court-Bras no longer could find work, he begged, then turned to robbery, operating alone or with an accomplice. In 1390 another day-laborer was imprisoned in Paris for stealing the tools furnished to him. During his interrogation he declared that he had worked for many years as a carter, transporting wine to Bourges, Flanders, Picardy, and Germany. Under torture he admitted to various other thefts, so he mounted the gallows. The judges had no doubts that he was a vagabond. One might say that this was how day workers were treated, since for the most part they were immigrants, which means that they were far from local and familial ties and were excluded from the guilds. Although they were only sporadically accused of crimes, still they were treated with suspicion and considered a burden on society. The few who fell into the clutches of the law were severely punished, even though the lives of this large group of workers, as we have seen, combined honest earnings and crime. This milieu, which was to increase in numbers in the late Middle Ages, continued to occupy an intermediate zone of its own, a liminality between city and country, between work and delinquency, between free vagabondage and corporative stability.

A category of persons who could be defined as "professional delinquents"—persons who more or less permanently based their existence on crime without pursuing any other sort of work—also existed in the Middle Ages. It is difficult to delimit this category with any precision, since on certain levels the confines between delinquency and labor tended to disappear. Labor in these cases was unskilled, unable to satisfy the requirements of artisanal specialization, and lacking corporative organization. Furthermore, even though participation in an organized criminal band could be considered proof of professional delinquency, this sort of life could not be pursued for more than a limited time. In Amiens in 1460, for example, a band of vagabonds was arrested and accused of having a committed a number of thefts and robberies during fairs and festivities and of running houses of prostitution, (They were sentenced only to banishment, for insufficient proof of the charges.) We know little about the members of the band: one was a bastard twenty-six years old who came from Lens in the Artois; another, thirty years old, came from near Grammont in Flanders; a third, thirty-two, was a barber from Louvain; a fourth, a laborer from near Tournai (*pyonnier, piqueur et manouvrier*) was twenty-eight; a fifth, sixteen years old, declared himself a serge worker from Valenciennes. Some of these men were defined by their trade, some not. All were foreigners or immigrants in Amiens.

Marginality in the late Middle Ages was greatly accelerated by war, which created possibilities for existence outside the normal life experience of peasants and artisans, first in regularly commanded companies and then in autonomous bands. The difference was not great between normal military service and brigandage, between an army company and a robber band. A letter of remission of the king of France dated 1418 describes the case of one poor wretch between twenty and twenty-two years of age, a carter's helper by profession (*varlet charretier*), who, when he failed to find work, enrolled in the army on the side of the "Burgundians" and against the "Armagnacs." He and some other soldiers were making their way one day from Provins to Meaux, when they met a monk who asked them for directions, showing by his speech that he was a foreigner. They forthwith robbed him. This is certainly typical of the life of soldiers of the time. Another document of this sort speaks of a young blacksmith from Amiens who, after practicing his craft for two years, left in 1415 with some fifteen companions to go to Paris to sign up as soldiers, "as young people have been wont to do in the last two or three years." On their way, however, the band attacked two livestock merchants. On another occasion in 1420 two armed young men were involved in a simple skirmish that ended up in a homicide. The first, a barber by trade, was the illegitimate son of a noble; the other was an ex-vintner who led a brigand's life and gave his name as "Coiner," which might have been a family name or might refer to counterfeiting. The reason for their quarrel is less important than the question of whether the first man could really have been a nobleman if he was a barber. Even more important, war and the military profession were enough to cancel previous professional descriptions. To cite one more example: three soldiers who had fought in various regions of France were unable to find work on their return from Guienne in 1407. Since they were "poor companions without means," they set out for Beauce in search of ready money through robberies.

• • •

Court records often use such phrases as "of bad fame" or "marked with infamy" when they speak of malefactors or vagabonds. Ill fame resulted from knowledge of previous criminal activities, but at the same time it was an essential argument in judicial proceedings, since it demonstrated that the matter at hand was not an isolated lawbreaking act but part of a life-style counter to the norms of social cohabitation. During the Middle ages, the concept of "infamy" functioned in another context as well. It was associated with the performance of certain occupations that by law and in social consciousness were considered "dishonest" or "unworthy" and that stamped with infamy the people who exercised them (and sometimes their descendants as well). In this case, infamy was a mechanism of social exclusion very similar to the situation in caste societies—that is, to the creation of the pariahs in India or the *eta* in Japan. Or at least it was an analogous civilizational tendency.

In the ideological discourse of the Middle Ages, the problem of value judgments concerning occupations arose in the context of praise of the "three orders" of society (the "division of labor" between those who prayed, those who fought, and those who worked the land), in celebrations of the virtue of rural occupations, and in the condemnation of certain trades. Tertullian, for example, demonstrated that from the moral viewpoint trades like those of artists who painted divine images, astrologers, teachers, and merchants were suspect or even unacceptable to Christian culture. He holds merchants and others in the luxury trades responsible for the spread of wealth. The occupational categories held to be morally blameworthy changed in the works of the Fathers of the church and in theological writings, with usury, prostitution, and the dramatic arts henceforth leading the list. It should be noted that not only were occupations subject to moral evaluation; some were branded as contemptible, thus justifying the widespread exclusion of those who practiced them from Christian society. This is explicit in canon law and clear in municipal practices.

Canon law used the terms *mercimonia inhonesta* or *vilia officia* in connection with a certain number of occupations held to be irreconcilable with membership in a corporate association and in order to deprive a person *via facti* of the enjoyment of clerical privilege. The latter concerned not only priests but many who, once their schooling had ended, had obtained minor orders and could even marry without losing their rights as clergy. Lists of occupations prohibited to the clergy vary in form, and from the great compilations of canon law to the individual synodal statutes they gradually grow shorter. A cleric could not be a jongleur or an actor; he could not pursue activities associated with prostitution or a trade that had anything to do with blood, animal carcasses, waste or rubbish, or usury. The earliest documents even forbade all commerce. Synodal statutes and the articles of customary law often also mention as *personnes diffamez* by reason of their trade innkeepers, wizards and magicians of various sorts (*enchanteurs, sorciers*), and people responsible for city hygienic services (who cleaned the latrines, for example). The "infamy" connected with such trades not only barred the way to an ecclesiastical career but, in some cities, disqualified a candidate for city office.

Statutes regulating the crafts in German cities show ample proof of the concept of a degrading profession affecting a person's descendants. Where guild statutes specified the registration of "worthy birth" as a prerequisite to the acquisition of corporate rights and privileges, they excluded not only persons born out of wedlock or of unfree parentage but also the offspring of persons in certain professional categories. The long list includes executioners, jailers, executioners' assistants and lesser law-enforcement officials, gravediggers, butchers, custodians of public baths, barbers, prostitutes and their protectors, musicians, acrobats or buffoons, canvas weavers, fullers, and shepherds. (In German folklore, the maxim *Schäfer und Schinder, Geschwisterkinder*—shepherd and jailer are like two cousins—is eloquent proof of the persistence of this attitude.) The exclusion of people of "degrading occupations" outlived the Middle Ages, if it is true that even in the seventeenth and eighteenth centuries the laws of the German states felt it necessary to take up the question, and ethnographic studies have demonstrated that even today the problem is not completely dead.

A certain discrepancy existed between the norms—in canon law, municipal law, or juridical custom concerning trades and professions—and the actual social situation, and in time some of the occupations considered dishonorable obtained full rights to dignified social status. The area of operation of such norms, in terms of both time and space, has as yet been little studied. The importance of the phenomenon is nonetheless beyond doubt, and its documentation in canon law had a certain effect in an epoch in which the church provided models for the principal ideological structures and social behavior patterns. The strictures of Roman law concerning "infamy" undoubtedly influenced medieval norms regarding degrading occupations, as did barbarian law concerning persons deprived of rights. Clearly these were deeply rooted traditions touching on the violation of taboo as well as cultural attitudes toward certain professional occupations valued according to criteria of "pure" and "filthy." These traditions and these attitudes imposed marginality on some persons because of the trades they exercised. We need to examine some of these occupations in greater detail.

Professional entertainers figured prominently among the disapproved categories. Roman law regarded those who earned a living as actors as persons without dignity; Germanic customary law treated the *Spielleute* and their associates as *unrecht* through their occupation, by analogy to those who were *unrecht* by birth. In the tradition of the first Christians, *histriones* were treated the same way as prostitutes, and St. Augustine even denies them the sacraments. Actors and musicians were held to spread evil and were considered allies of the Devil. Synods and councils expressed themselves on the subject with clear hostility. As the centuries passed, the terms defining the various artistic activities changed, but the condemnation of players and entertainers remained in force in articles of the law, in theological treaties, and in religious oratory. "Jongleurs" and "histrions" were thrust into the lowest social categories, along with beggars, vagabonds, and cripples. Admittedly, however, greater moral value was gradually attached to the players' art in the ideological context of the thirteenth century.

Thomas Aquinas was persuaded that acrobats, minstrels, actors, and players of all sorts of musical instruments were equally reprehensible. Thomas excludes from his list the *ioculatores* who recounted the lives of the saints and the heroic actions of rulers to the accompaniment of musical instruments: they had a chance of saving their souls. Francis of Assisi went a good deal further, even calling himself "God's fool" (*ioculatore Dei*). Still, condemnation of these occupations remained. In countries of Orthodox Christianity, direct persecution of the players called *skomoroch* followed moral condemnation of them. The climate of moral ambiguity that surrounded the acting profession in early modern societies doubtless derived from this long tradition of condemnation.

Was it true, though, that medieval jongleurs and minstrels were people who existed at the fringes of society? That depended on how they actually lived. Organized corporations of minstrels who performed during the city festivities and played at weddings existed within the structures of communal life. In the courts, days passed according to a special rhythm, and professional entertainers were a permanent and often a stable part of court activities. Nonetheless, there continued to be groups of players who, by their nomadic life, resembled vagabonds or were considered equivalent to them. Such occupations often recur in the biographies of the accused criminals discussed above, together with other activities typical of vagabonds. The church's ideological mistrust of a profession that threatened its cultural monopoly, combined with the traditional disrepute attached to these occupations, found justification in the unstable, and therefore asocial, lives of a professional category that had no place in the organized structures of society, in the distribution of social roles, or in the division of labor.

John of Salisbury maintained that jongleurs and prostitutes were generally to be considered monsters with human bodies, thus should be exterminated. One of the arguments for the condemnation and exclusion of players was their involvement with prostitution and licentious living in general, though the condemnation of prostitution was much more evident than that of players. Even in this case, however, scholasticism to some extent revised its positions, indicating that prostitution had a certain utility. This did not mean that it was any less degrading; only that a basis for its reintegration into organized life, more precisely into urban life, could be created.

Prostitution took may forms in the Middle Ages. It was by no means confined to the city, as judicial archives show it to have been widespread in country areas. Prostitutes were present wherever the rural population met, at markets and fairs, near mills, and in taverns. Prostitutes went from one village to another, accompanying groups of harvesters, workers, or merchants. They were permanent fixtures in the cities, and venal love was one of the products offered on city markets. The municipal authorities permitted "houses of toleration" to remain open, and some cities used city funds to organize their own *postribulum publicum*, leasing it out to a manager. Even the public baths functioned as bordellos. Some cities had ghettos of prostitution—*la rue aux putains* of the French cities.

The moral and religious condemnation that struck prostitutes and their consequent social exclusion were commonly accepted facts. Here again, however, the prostitute's actual way of living was the determining factor, and there was a remarkable heterogeneity among prostitutes, both of category and in their standard of living. Some Venetian and Florentine courtesans lived sumptuously, became famous, and played an important role in the evolution of culture, even to claiming a social prestige beyond the wildest dreams of the pensioners of the city brothels. The city's prostitutes also enjoyed a measure of stability, but a good part of the category was made up on itinerant prostitutes at the mercy of go-betweens and "protectors." Often prostitution was a "second job" for women day workers and, more generally, for plebeian women. A common destiny, a similar way of life, and personal acquaintance linked them to vagabonds and criminals.

Despite the various forms of stabilization associated with them, prostitutes were in fundamental opposition to the reigning social order since they remained outside the family, not having the right to have a family of their own. Even when medieval literature presents a miraculous change in the life of a prostitute, the "happy ending" could only be a trip to heaven for the repentant sinner or her entry into a convent. In one French story of the twelfth century, a prostitute called Richeut decides to have a child, but only as a way to increase her earnings by attributing paternity to a series of gullible men. When the child is born, she participates in the usual religious rites, she makes an offering to the priest, the baby has godparents, and other representatives of her "craft" take part in the baptismal ceremonies. When the son grows up, he takes on the craft of *lescherie*—that is, he becomes a pimp, drawing on his mother's knowledge. The mother, for her part, takes the trouble to introduce him into her circle, but she treats him as an outsider when he shows signs of attempting to outwit her. Connubial ties in the world of prostitution, established by a "promise of love," were a negative reflection of the matrimonial relation, since they sealed the professional bond between the prostitute and her protector. When we encounter a couple or a family connected with this profession, there is usually a loss of caste involved that has led to prostitution as an occasional or stable source of earnings.

On occasions prostitutes were under the rule of a *roi des ribauds*, a *podestá dei ribaldi*, a *podestas meretricium*, or a *roi des filles amoureuses*—functionaries who had little authority outside the world of prostitution. The leaseholders of city brothels—usually communal appointees, on occasion the executioner, thus also of an "ignoble occupation"—had no prestige but were tolerated by both the church and the law. Public opinion and the judicial machinery for repression unanimously condemned anyone who organized prostitution outside "houses of toleration." To be a pimp or protector, an occupation that usually accompanied other activities associated with delinquency, was considered evident proof of an asocial life.

Detailed analysis of the professional activities that led to social exclusion reveals various instances of the violation of taboos. Marginalization nonetheless depended upon economic conditions and upon the sort of life such people led. Credit operations did not lead to marginality, even when they were truly usurious, hence open to moral condemnation. This was true even independently of the evolution of the canonical doctrine of the church, which, through the idea of restitution and the prospect of Purgatory, gave usurers hope of saving their souls and even made a place for them in Christian society. Marginality depended primarily upon position in society. Shepherds worked within the agrarian world—which usually came in for praise during the Middle Ages—and theirs was a seasonal activity universally practiced. Nonetheless, the shepherds' world prompted profound mistrust. Sheepherding required a migratory life; it meant living far from permanent settlements and spending long periods in solitude, and migrations and solitude were two elements in marginality. Furthermore, the shepherd was also a butcher, so he had contact with blood; he acted as a veterinarian and even as a physician for the country people—all of which quite naturally aroused suspicion and fear at the time. Living alone with animals for long periods, far from home and from collective society, the shepherd attracted suspicions of various sorts, among them, of bestiality and sodomy. In Germany shepherds were much scorned; indeed, many among them were simpleminded. It is not known, however, whether this negative attitude, amply documented in Germanic lands, was common throughout medieval Europe.

Problems concerning the body cannot be left out of any consideration of the condemnations, the infamy, and the marginalization connected with certain occupations. Such problems were determinant in the alienating effects of sickness and in the social condition of the ill and the infirm. Charity toward the sick went hand in hand with fear of contagion and with aversion and contempt for the crippled.

Leprosy provides a classic example of the connection between marginalization and contagious disease. The church and public institutions acted together to effect a total separation of lepers from the rest of society. The person struck by that terrible disease underwent a sort of civil death that included a spectacular ceremony—almost a funeral service—to accompany him or her beyond the confines of the inhabited area. In the *Congés* of Arras two leprous troubadours describe their leave-taking of their friends before going to the lepers' hospital. When the gangrene of the sinful soul passed into the body there was hope for eternal salvation, but in this world the leper was obliged to live apart from healthy people, hence separate from society. Still, the leprous enjoyed society's aid: they were provided for copiously enough to arouse envy, and collections were continually taken for them. They had to remain outside inhabited areas, however, they could not touch anything touched by healthy people, and they had to announce their presence by sounding a rattle (as if their horrendous aspect were not enough of a warning). Public opinion observed them fearfully, perhaps also with hatred. They were thought to practice unrestrained sexuality (as seen in the story of Tristan and Isolde), and were suspected of hatching villainous schemes against the society of the healthy. These attitudes extended to the offspring of lepers, who were obligated to live in ghettos and limited to the practice of trades held to be dishonorable or dirty. The marginalization of lepers in medieval society was so evident that in German they were called *Aussätzige*, or *die Üszetzigen*—the excluded. Furthermore, they were excluded forever. When Hartmann von Aue, in his *Der Arme Heinrich*, portrays first the protagonist's loss of caste through divine castigation (considered the cause of leprosy) and then his miraculous cure and consequent return to society, he is presenting a quite unusual case. This simply did not happen in real life. Although they were excluded and forced into a sort of ghetto, lepers nonetheless remained part of the social scene, and every time they appeared among people, in the city or the countryside, it reinforced their differentness.

Leprosy was clearly a quite special illness, but in the Middle Ages we find a certain ambivalence toward sick people in general and an attitude of mixed compassion and marginalization. Much depended on the social status of the sick person. If he (or she) belonged to a wealthy family, he could remain at home and could count on assistance. Even in the case of leprosy, a well-to-do person could avoid social exclusion. Among the lower classes, on the contrary, where existence depended upon physical labor, sickness meant marginalization. The sick were objects of charity. They were beggars, and they had to live on alms and try to find a shelter in an institution. The Christian doctrine of charity accorded cripples and sick persons the right to live by begging. Some writers, Guilelmus de Sancto Amore in the thirteenth century, for example, cited St. Augustine and enlarged on the notion of weakness to authorize extending aid even to those who by their upbringing and because of their traditional social status were not used to doing physical labor but who had fallen onto evil days. Although these *pauperes verecundi* still enjoyed a certain social consideration, the rest of the poor had to force recognition of their right to be aided by a public display of their infirmity, their weakness, or their penury. Infirmity had a socially degrading effect, at least in the sense that sickness was identified with destitution.

If we note that the process of marginalization was based on an exclusion that moved people outside social bonds, on their voluntary abandonment of those bonds, or on their loss of a place in society's division of labor or in the allotment of social roles, it becomes difficult to consider beggars marginal. Beggars were needed because they gave others the opportunity to demonstrate charity. They were organized and established; they respected the norms of social coexistence. An ambivalent attitude toward beggars and poverty ranging from disapproval of their way of life to praise of the virtue of renunciation can be traced as early as the writings of the Fathers of the church. In medieval society acceptance of the beggar's functional role prevailed as long as beggars did not compromise the work ethos or the equilibrium of the labor market. The dramatic social crises that led to seasonal or permanent pauperization prompted a change of attitude with respect to beggars. The change that took place in the doctrine of poverty during the thirteenth century was an expression of precisely the sort of situation that caused a spread of repressive and exclusionary attitudes toward beggars.

Mechanisms for degradation were inherent in the beggars' condition, however. In the last analysis, begging was an occupation that relied on techniques for arousing people's pity, Not only did beggars display their real physical defects; they used subterfuge to simulate infirmity or illness. Tales from Arabian literature of the early Middle Ages paint a picture much like the one presented in fifteenth-century France in the *balades* of Eustache Deschamps, in the Italian *Speculum cerretanorum,* and the German *Liber vagatorum.* The stabilization of beggars affected only a part of this world, and in reality wandering brought better earnings. Trades and professions could mix in an errant life and the vagabond could work, beg, or rob. Confusion in occupations meant marginalization in the Middle Ages.

Groups that remained outside organized society for sociocultural reasons also deserve a place in our panorama of marginality. It is difficult, however, to distinguish cultural from other criteria in the processes of marginalization, although a cultural element was clearly at work in "dishonorable" trades and in the marginalization of lepers. For this reason, I shall use the notion *sensu largo* to include religious and ideological factors. It was the heretics and the infidels—that is, people of a different faith and pagans—who were excluded from the Christian community, hence from the fundamental structures of medieval Europe. The simple fact of not accepting the truths of Christian orthodoxy was sufficient reason for a sense of difference and for exclusion. Other elements contributed to the stereotyped judgments concerning such groups to empha-size their difference: the Saracens of the *Chanson de Roland* were reproached for failing to fulfill their obligations as vassals; the records of the Inquisition and polemical writings charged heretics with deviance from established sexual norms and refusal of authority and social obligations; the Jews were accused of plotting to exterminate Christians, of spreading epidemics, and of practic-ing usury. Since they had no part in the dominant religion and the dominant culture, these groups were considered a danger to the very bases of social order. Furthermore, more than any other marginal group, they were conscious of their own difference.

I have used various criteria in this description of marginality in an attempt to throw light on the determinant social and cultural processes of separating individuals and groups from society. I have also spoken of phenomena of vol-untary marginality resulting from a radical rejection of the dominant system, from a search for internal spiritual perfection, or even from a combination of the two. It is clear that we need to reach beyond these specific social processes to discern sociopsychological processes. For the marginal, these would be an awareness of the differentness of their situation; for society, they would be an internalization of collective norms and of the principles governing the social status quo, realized through condemnation of those who failed to conform to those norms. On the one hand, then, people were to some extent conscious of their own individual destiny, though this was less true of groups; on the other hand, there was the sense of community precisely in relation to those who were different.

Social condition was fixed in medieval culture, and this was one aspect of the semiotic nature of this culture. This was true for the marginal as well. Cer-tain categories stood out clearly: difference in skin color or language set apart ethnic minorities; a certain type of work could function just like external signs of disease or an obvious infirmity. Dress was the most frequent form of "dis-tinction." Vagabonds and felons did not dress substantially differently from others from the lower social strata, but we can suppose that they were defined by the rags they wore and the staff in their hand—the classic image in prints from later centuries. A missing ear denoted a thief. For beggars, rags over a naked body—effective in eliciting alms—were obvious signs of social condi-tion. Jews could be recognized by their dress: in German regions they wore a characteristic pointed hat, but the Fourth Lateran Council of 1215 also intro-duced the wearing of a distinguishing sign, a practice that became common throughout Christendom and stamped the Jews with infamy. In many coun-tries prostitutes had to conform to strict norms regarding their dress, and they too were often obliged to wear a distinguishing sign. As for heretics, one mark of their penitence might be a cross on their clothing, front and back, and heretics were often sentenced to exposure in public wearing or bearing some defamatory sign such as a mitre, a letter H, and so forth.

These objective signs of marginal condition were thus instruments of in-famy, exclusion, or repression more often than they were natural symptoms. We know nothing (or next to nothing) about marginal people's consciousness of their own situation. We can occasionally make an inference about it thanks to some personal note in reported testimony, and occasionally through literary discussion, as in the work of the goliards, Rutebeuf, or Villon.

The infamy of marginal groups was not only exploited instrumentally but actualized in the life of society. Jews were obligated to participate in royal entries in ways that degraded them and, according to later testimony (in Kraków such matters were recorded in the seventeenth century), the tradition continued in a repressive and segregationist manner in Corpus Christi processions. One analysis of collective acts of humiliation and degradation encountered in the context of armed conflicts between Italian cities in the fourteenth century reveals that races between prostitutes or lackeys (*ribaldi, barattieri*) were major aggressive events. Festive contests in which "ignoble" people took part were held in Périgueux as early as 1273; they developed into such institutions as the *palio* of the cities of Italy, which surely go back to the early fourteenth century. Vagabonds and men and women of the underclasses took part in foot races and horse or mule races. Their marginality, which was based on their social condition, had a function, since it reinforced the honor of the community organizing the exhibition and served to humiliate the community that the city considered its enemy.

Naturally, there were essential and, on occasion, capital differences between the various categories that made up the marginal world in the Middle Ages. There were gradations of exclusion and segregation, and demotion in class did not mean the same thing for the knight and for the peasant. Nor did social marginalization always involve exclusion and segregation. Boundaries were rarely as rigid as they were in the case of lepers. All of these categories of persons, however, were characterized by the difference of their way of life, by their not being subjected to established norms and life models, and by their refusal to work or to play the social role assigned to them. The marginal were also united in the aversion, sense of alienation, fear, and on occasion, hatred, that society displayed toward them.

CHAPTER 34

The Decline of Medieval Jewry

Jeremy Cohen

The Catholic church in western Europe first took official note of the Jewish community in its midst at one of its earliest episcopal synods, the Council of Elvira held at the beginning of the fourth century. Even before the Roman Empire had chosen to tolerate Christianity, Spanish prelates must have viewed the Jews as a sufficiently significant element in society to warrant legislation against excessive social intercourse with them.[1] Throughout the Middle Ages, the Jews constituted the only nonbelieving group consistently allowed to live in Latin Christendom on any regular and prosperous basis. Nevertheless, by the middle of the sixteenth century few Jews remained in western Europe. Expelled from England in 1290, France in 1394, Spain and Sicily in 1492, Portugal in 1497, and the Kingdom of Naples in 1541, European Jews could then live only in portions of Germany and Italy. Most of those who remained found themselves subject to increasingly harsh and humiliating forms of discrimination, ranging from ghettoization and exclusion from respectable occupations to excessive taxation and the public degradation of their religion.

How ought one to account for the dramatic downfall of European Jewry— a community which had once stood at the forefront of Jewish economic and cultural productivity—during the closing centuries of the medieval period? Historians have grappled incessantly with this question since the rise of critical Judaic scholarship in nineteenth-century Germany, and the subject has still not been exhausted. Virtually every authority on the period has had something new to add to the discussion, so that the pertinent historiography now abounds and itself demands recognition as a primary source for more recent intellectual history. . . .

The church's role in the decline of medieval European Jewry constitutes a complex question, whose difficulty is underscored by the decisiveness with which some historians have discounted it. The church did not contribute to the downfall of the medieval Jewish community, Gavin Langmuir and Kenneth Stow have argued, because medieval popes themselves never abandoned the patristic doctrine, first formulated as an institutional policy by Pope Gregory the Great, that the Jews had a rightful place in Christian society. *Sicut Iudeis*, the title of the papal edict of protection for the Jews issued repeatedly during the High Middle Ages, faithfully captured the spirit of ecclesiastical Jewish policy: "Just as license ought not to be granted the Jews to presume to do . . . more than the law permits them, just so ought they not to suffer curtailment in those [privileges] which have been conceded them."[2] Christian theology, to be sure, generated often virulent anti-Judaism in medieval society, but, in Kenneth Stow's words, "as the formal executive and legislative—and theological—center of the Church, it was the papacy which established what, for want of a better word, may be called the official policy toward the Jews. And it was to the papacy that Jews, from all the countries of Latin Europe, turned in time of crisis and tried to secure guarantees against attacks."[3]

Ought our discussion to end here? Should we reformulate our concern as the *religious component* in (rather than the ecclesiastical causes of) late medieval anti-Judaism, or may we recall that the medieval church viewed itself as embodying not only the papacy but all of Christian society? Semantic considerations aside, distinctions between the upper echelons of the ecclesiastical hierarchy, particular clerics or clerical factions, and the masses of the European laity acting on religious impulse deserve mention in any treatment of the church and the Jews.[4] And just as expressions of popular Christian piety often failed to comport with "official" church policy, so too did that policy at times develop for reasons having little to do with theology and doctrine, the anti-Jewish legislation of late medieval popes, for example, was seldom enforced thoroughly in the Papal States.[5] Moreover, since most would agree that medieval Jewry declined for a variety of interrelated reasons, how ought one to isolate and calculate the responsibility of the church? If anti-Jewish teachings permeated Christian theology when the Jews prospered as well as when they suffered, can one fairly deem them the cause of Jewish misfortune? Lacking extensive physical control over the life of the late medieval layman, does the church deserve blame for his actions undertaken in the name of its God? These and other questions have moved scholars to differentiate between "origins" and "causes" in evaluating the responsibility of the church for medieval anti-Judaism.[6] . . .

Against this background, we may proceed to classify the noteworthy scholarly literature, characterized by two opposing schools of thought. On the one hand stand those interpretations which ascribe a major role in the decline and virtual disappearance of medieval Jewry to theological factors—reflected in official church policy or popular piety and belief, expressed in a substantive shift in Christian ideology, or manifested simply in the diligent application of hitherto unenforced doctrinal principles. The most popular tendency among such opinions, first evidenced clearly over a century ago by Otto Stobbe, views 1096 and the anti-Jewish violence which accompanied the Crusades as a decisive turning point, after which the status of the Jew declined steadily. The massacres of Franco-German Jewish communities in the name of Catholic piety revealed the inadequacy of existing legal safeguards for the person and property of the Jews. . . . The blood of the Jews had, as it were, been made free for the Christian masses. In respect to legal formulations, security and possibilities of livelihood, the First Crusade inaugurated a new and harsh epoch for Jews in Christian lands."[12] This outlook is reflected in the periodization which under-lies major works of recent Judaic scholarship, despite a disinclination to view the crusading period as a "watershed" in general or Christian historiography.[13] Insightful variations on this theme include the argument of Hans Liebeschütz, that the ideas of Cluniac and Gregorian reform turned Christendom against the Jews even before the Council of Clermont in 1095. Amos Funkenstein has noted a new conception of medieval Jews as irrational and even heretical in the polemical writings of twelfth-century theologians. Lester Little, moreover, has argued that in the wake of the Crusades, European society first projected onto the Jews, who had played a dominant role in early medieval trade and com-merce, the guilt derived from its own emergent "profit" economy. Christen-dom subsequently dispensed with the Jews altogether once new types of spiri-tuality had mollified such pangs of conscience, and the presence of the Jews with their investment capital was no longer essential.[14] Nevertheless, the con-tinuing prosperity of the western European Jewish community during the 150 years after 1096 has led other writers to discern religious causes for its decline only after the early Crusades. Heinrich Graetz, Moritz Güdemann, George Caro, and above all Solomon Grayzel have located such developments in the anti-Jewish legislation of Innocent III and his papal successors.[15] . . . And I have stressed the ideas and activities of the new mendicant friars, who called for the exclusion of the Jews from Europe on theological grounds, just as the thirteenth-century *Ecclesia* was attempting to regiment all of Western society into a perfectly integrated Christian commonwealth, often conceived organi-cally as the mystical body of Christ. Scrutinizing the Talmud and other works of postbiblical Judaism, Dominican and Franciscan friars claimed that medieval Jews had forsaken their Old Testament heritage for a heretical, rabbinic perver-sion thereof and had thereby forfeited their privilege of inclusion in a properly ordered Christendom. Instead of the blind witnesses to the Christological truth of biblical prophecy whom church fathers like Augustine had perceived in the Jews, the friars now depicted them as deliberate unbelievers, ones who had killed the divine messiah intentionally and whose books and traditions could serve the church no constructive purpose.[16]

On the other hand, various scholars minimize the significance of religious factors in explaining the changing plight of medieval European Jewry. "Ex-pansion and contraction of West-European Jewry," Salo Baron asserts categor-ically, "coincided with the great rise and decline in the temporal power of the Roman Church."[17] Only as the power and political influence of the papacy waned did the rulers of Europe expel their Jews. To explain this, Wilhelm Roscher contended in 1875 that the commercial jealousies of a nascent Christ-ian bourgeoisie turned late medieval rulers against the Jewish community, which had virtually monopolized European commerce before the Crusades but by the thirteenth and fourteenth centuries could no longer be deemed in-dispensable. . . .

Despite the probable affinity between Roscher's views and German anti-Semitism of the late nineteenth century which Toni Oelsner has identified and vehemently condemned, many scholars, Jewish as well as Christian, have accepted this idea at face value and assumed it to be valid.[18] Others have suggested that the socioeconomic impact of Jewish moneylending, or perhaps even the emptiness of royal treasuries, caused the downfall of Jewish communities and the confiscation of their assets.[19] True to his theory that the Jews throughout history have fared worst in Gentile states of single nationalities, Baron himself explains that incipient medieval nationalism underlay the expulsions from England, France, Spain, and Portugal. Baron thus accounts for the survival of Jews in portions of early modern Italy and Germany, which failed to coalesce into national polities before the nineteenth century.[20] Yet another school of thought has stressed the changing configurations of political alliances involving king, aristocracy, and bourgeoisie, in which the Jews were not directly involved but from whose volatility they often had most to lose.[21]

From this spectrum of interpretations, three stand out as especially helpful in illuminating and clarifying the complexities of our subject. In a lengthy article titled "The Jews and the Archives of Angevin England: Reflections on Medieval Anti-Semitism," Gavin Langmuir grapples with the question through his analysis of H. G. Richardson's *English Jewry under the Angevin Kings* and exemplifies the tendency to disregard almost completely the role of the church in the decline of medieval Jewry. Criticizing "an archival perspective in medieval studies . . . whose horizon is limited by a concern to establish as much detailed information on a given topic as the state of the archives will permit . . . but the level of [whose] insight into the implication of the facts so discovered tends to be low,"[22] Langmuir demonstrates the extensive ramifications of medieval anti-Judaism as a historical and historiographical problem. Popular prejudices both medieval and modern join with the complex legal, socioeconomic, and theological status of the Jews so as to require of the historian an imaginative and discerning disposition as well as a scientific one. As for the church's contribution to the persecution and eventual expulsion of English Jews in the thirteenth century, assumed by Richardson to be significant, Langmuir proceeds to the opposite extreme. Not only must one distinguish between ecclesiastical policies properly implemented by clerical authorities and unlicensed actions of individual churchmen, but one must also look beyond the reason why the Jews in particular suffered during the Middle Ages and consider European society's need for a scapegoat in the first place. Although the church had always condemned Judaism, it consistently called for toleration; and "what is remarkable in the Middle Ages is not that the doctrine on the Jews was emphasized, but that it underwent so little change."[23] Such constancy in Christian doctrine was hardly duplicated in the actual treatment of the Jews— hence "the existence of the doctrine is a very insufficient explanation" for their downfall, especially in view of the simultaneously waning influence of the church over European kings. Instead, Langmuir calls for further research into the effects "of a new social, political, and economic order" on late medieval Jewry, and into the changing nature of irrational popular attitudes toward the Jews between 1096 and 1400.[24]

Writing only two years after Langmuir, Lea Dasberg presents a sound case that religious ideas did contribute heavily to the anti-Jewish persecutions of the High and late Middle Ages, beginning with the massacres accompanying the Crusades.[25] Dasberg argues effectively against attributing these hostilities to commercial rivalries, still a popular scholarly tendency. The Jews did not dominate European commerce to the extent that many have assumed, nor was it the Christian merchant who typically turned against them.[26] Although sympathetic with Kisch's view of 1236 as the commencement of Jewish serfdom in Germanic law, Dasberg's argument demonstrates the gap so characteristic of the relationship between imperial policy and lawbook. In this case, "Jewry law" lagged far behind important changes in "Jewish policy," which in turn emerged from a new religious orientation two centuries in its development. For the changing conceptions of the Jews evident in the massacres of 1096 derived from the spirit of Cluniac reform in the tenth century, a new idealism vis-à-vis worldly issues which within several generations had influenced the policies of the papacy. While the church endeavored to raise the esteem of the simple man and transformed basically economic issues into religious-ethical ones, it also began to pose itself against the established political-economic power held responsible for such social injustice—the secular princes and, by extension, the Jews under their protection. Dasberg treats the Investiture Controversy and the anti-Jewish violence of the Crusades as two stages of the same conflict, that of reformers versus the simoniacal establishment, and even classifies the respective reactions of burghers, princes, and bishops to the violence according to their stance in the papal-imperial conflict. Coupled with a surge of apocalyptic fervor calling for the conversion of the infidel, the piety which sustained the Crusade understandably precipitated the persecution of the Jews.

In a brief but penetrating essay published [in 1978], Israeli historian Maurice Kriegel proposes a qualitatively new "organic" model to account for the expulsion of Jews from England, France, and Spain (and even from portions of Germany)—a theory which in many ways balances the opposing viewpoints of Langmuir and Dasberg.[27] This interpretation properly considers each of the traditional explanations—theological, socioeconomic, or political—unsatisfactory on its own, either because it fails to account for the complexity of the process which culminated in the expulsions or because the events of the specific expulsions simply fail to substantiate it. Instead, Kriegel argues, decrees of banishment in fact derived from royal attempts to integrate and mobilize previously fragmented societies, through the consolidation of territorial domains, the strengthening of urban power centers, the institution of a governmental bureaucracy—in a word, through the construction of a state. Realization of these goals depended in large measure on the successful manipulation of public opinion to engender a unity of spirit among diverse elements of the population. Here Kriegel's thesis departs from the nationalistic interpretation of Salo Baron. For the goal of unity induced Edward I of England, Philip IV of France,

and Ferdinand and Isabella of Spain to exploit the traditional religious sentiments of their subjects, seeking to characterize their monarchies as sacred,
heavenly kingdoms. Appeal to popular religious belief and custom allowed
these monarchs to rally their constituencies around policies which often lacked
theological derivation, without impinging upon their ability to generate and
pursue such policies autocratically. . . . Desire for political and economic gain
did not preclude the sincerity of their piety; such was "le paradoxe de la double
présence de la religiosité et de la convoitise."[28] Sociopolitical mobilization and
modernization built upon age-old Christian beliefs and institutions, and the
need for valuable unanimity in religious ideology outweighed any benefits
which accrued from the Jewish presence. Curiously, concludes Kriegel, the
emergence of the modern state united with traditional religious fervor to in-
duce the expulsion of the Jews, *ad maiorem Dei gloriam.*

Each of the three scholars mentioned here signals progress achieved in recent historiography as well as directions in which research into this question
must still advance. The problematic relationship between popular piety and
official ecclesiastical doctrine notwithstanding, the teachings and policies of
the medieval church clearly played a part in the downfall of the European
Jewish community together with numerous other factors. These require careful identification and definition, while their interaction with Christian theology and popular prejudice demands analysis. We need to know precisely how
religious ideas were brought to bear upon political policy and socioeconomic
reality. The arguments of Langmuir, Dasberg, and Kriegel have shown that
the answer is far from simple. Any convincing interpretation of the demise of
medieval Jewry must consider factors which ultimately had little to do with
the Jews and Judaism—Cluniac or Gregorian reform, the development of popular superstition and prejudice, and the drive toward sociopolitical integration
on a national scale. In much the same way as John Boswell has shown how the
general penchant for order and uniformity in twelfth-century Christendom
triggered the persecution of homosexuals, who previously had enjoyed toleration, historians of the Jews must integrate their particular concerns with the
larger tendencies and processes of medieval European history in general.[29]
Moving in this direction, Langmuir, Dasberg, and Kriegel succeed in discredit-
ing traditional and simplistic interpretations of earlier historians, but the full
value of their respective theories has not yet been appreciated. Their speculative suggestions have yet to be tested thoroughly, and the applicability of their
explanatory models must be shown to transcend medieval political boundaries, in order to do justice to our historical puzzle.

Notes

1. Mansi, 2:8 (16), 14 (49–50), 18 (78). See also my "Roman Imperial Policy toward the Jews from Constantine until the End of the Palestinian Patriar-
   chate (ca. 429)," *Byzantine Studies* 3 (1976): 3ff.
2. Kenneth R. Stow, *Catholic Thought and Papal Jewry Policy, 1555–1593,* More-
   shet: Studies in Jewish History, Literature and Thought 5 (New York,

1977), pp. xi–xxviii; Gavin I. Langmuir, "The Jews and the Archives of Angevin England: Reflections on Medieval Anti-Semitism," *Traditio* 19 (1963): 183–244. The text and a translation of *Sicut Iudeis* appear in Solomon Grayzel, *The Church and the Jews in the XIIIth Century* (1933; reprint New York, 1966), pp. 92–95. See also Solomon Katz, "Pope Gregory the Great and the Jews," *Jewish Quarterly Review*, n.s. 24 (1933–34): 113–36; and Grayzel, "The Papal Bull *Sicut Judaeis*," in *Studies and Essays in Honor of Abraham A. Neuman*, ed. Meir Ben-Horin et al. (Leiden, 1962), pp. 243–80.

3. Stow, *Catholic Thought*, p. xix. Stow has since developed, refined, and strengthened his thesis in "Hatred of the Jews, or Love of the Church: Papal Policy toward the Jews [in Hebrew]," in *Antisemitism through the Ages*, ed. S. Almog (Jerusalem, 1980), pp. 91–111; and in *The "1007 Anonymous" and Papal Sovereignty: Jewish Perceptions of the Papacy and Papal Policy in the High Middle Ages*, Hebrew Union College Annual Supplements 4 (Cincinnati, 1984).

4. Among many others, see in this regard Peter Browe, "Die Judenbekämpfung im Mittelalter," *Zeitschrift für katholische Theologie* 62 (1938): 197–231, 349–84, "Die religiöse Duldung der Juden im Mittelalter," *Archiv für katholisches Kirchenrecht* 118 (1938): 3–76, and *Die Judenmission im Mittelalter und die Päpste*, Miscellanca historiae pontificiae 6 (Rome, 1942); and Joshua Trachtenberg, *The Devil and the Jews: The Medieval Conception of the Jew in Its Relation to Modern Antisemitism* (New Haven, 1943), esp. chaps. 11ff.

5. Moritz Güdemann, *Geschichte des Erziehungswesens und der Cultur des abendländischen Juden während des Mittelalters und der neueren Zeit*, 3 vols. (1880–88; reprint Amsterdam, 1966); 2:74ff.; Solomon Grayzel, "The Avignon Popes and the Jews," *Historia Judaica* 2 (1940): 1–12; and Salo Wittmayer Baron, *A Social and Religious History of the Jews*, 2d ed., 17 vols. (New York, 1952–80), 9:44–50—among others.

6. Langmuir, "Jews," p. 230.

• • •

12. Otto Stobbe, *Die Juden in Deutschland während des Mittelalters in politischer, socialer and rechtlicher Beziehung* (1866, reprint Amsterdam, 1966), pp. 15, 103ff., 163–93; Haim Hillel Ben-Sasson et al., *A History of the Jewish People*, trans. George Weidenfeld (Cambridge, Mass., 1976), p. 414. Cf. also Simon Dubnow, *Weltgeschichte des jüdischen Volkes*, 10 vols. (Berlin, 1925–30), 4:269ff.; Browe, "Judenbekämpfung im Mittelalter," pp. 198, 211–23; Parkes, *Jew*, pp. 81ff.; George LaPiana, "The Church and the Jews," *Historia Judaica* 11 (1949): 117–44; Trachtenberg, *Devil*, p. 167; and Leon Poliakov, *The History of Anti-Semitism*, vol. 1, trans. Richard Howard and Natalie Gerardi (New York, 1965), pt. 2.

13. For examples of the tendency in Jewish historiography, see Benzion Dinur, *Israel in the Diaspora, II: From the Persecutions of 1096 until the Black*

Death (in Hebrew), 2d ed., vol. 1 (Tel Aviv, 1965), esp. pp. 1–6; Blu-
menkranz, *Juifs et Chrétiens*; Cecil Roth, ed., *The Dark Ages: Jews in Christian
Europe, 711–1096,* World History of the Jewish People 11 (New Brunswick,
N.J., 1966); and the original Hebrew of Ben-Sasson, *History of the Jewish
People,* vol. 2, *The Middle Ages* (in Hebrew) (Tel Aviv, 1969), pp. 21, 83.
Robert Chazan's *European Jewry and the First Crusade* (Berkeley, 1986) did
not appear in time for consideration in this essay.

14. Hans Liebeschütz, "The Crusading Movement in Its Bearing on the Christian Attitude towards Jewry," *Journal of Jewish Studies* 10 (1959): 97–111;
Amos Funkenstein, "Changes in the Patterns of Christian Anti-Jewish
Polemic in the Twelfth Century" (in Hebrew), *Zion,* n.s. 33 (1968): 125–44,
and idem, "Basic Types of Christian Anti-Jewish Polemics in the Later
Middle Ages," *Viator* 2 (1971): 373–82; Lester K. Little, *Religious Poverty and
the Profit Economy in Medieval Europe* (Ithaca, N.Y., 1978), pp. 42–57, 216.

15. Graetz, *Geschichte,* 6:226f., and ibid., vol. 7, 3d ed. (Leipzig, 1894), pp. 3–18;
Güdemann, *Geschichte,* 2:84ff.; Georg Caro, *Sozial- und Wirtschaftsgeschichte
der Juden im Mittelalter und der Neuzeit* (1908–18; reprint Hildesheim, 1964),
1:228–453; and of the many works of Solomon Grayzel, see, above all,
Church and the Jews, esp. pp. 1–82; "The Beginning of Exclusion," *Jewish
Quarterly Review,* n.s. 61 (1970); 15–26 (quotation on p. 15), and "Popes,
Jews, and the Inquisition from 'Sicut' to 'Turbato,' " in *Essays on the Occa-
sion of the Seventieth Anniversary of Dropsie University,* ed. Abraham I.
Katsch and Leon Nemoy (Philadelphia, 1979), pp. 151–88. Cf. also Louis I.
Rabinowitz, *The Social Life of the Jews of Northern France in the XII–XIV Cen-
turies as Reflected in the Rabbinical Literature of the Period* (1938; reprint New
York, 1972), p. 18.

16. See my *The Friars and the Jews: The Evolution of Medieval Anti-Judaism*
(Ithaca, N.Y., 1982), "The Jews as the Killers of Christ in the Latin Tradition, from Augustine to the Friars," *Traditio* 39 (1983): 1–27, and "Scholarship and Intolerance in the Medieval Academy: The Study and Valuation
of Judaism in European Christendom," *American Historical Review* 91
(1986): 592–613.

17. Baron, *History,* 9:3, 5.

18. Wilhelm Roscher, "Die Stellung der Juden im Mittelalter, betrachtet vom
Standpunkte der allgemeinen Handelspolitik," *Zeitschrift für die gesamte
Staatswissenschaft* 31 (1875): 503–26, the relevant portion of which has been
translated by Solomon Grayzel as "The Status of the Jews in the Middle
Ages Considered from the Standpoint of Commercial Policy," *Historia Judaica* 6 (1944): 13–26 (quotation on p. 20). The nature and influence of
Roscher's views have been discussed by Guido Kisch, "The Jews' Function
in the Medieval Evolution of Economic Life," *Historia Judaica* 6 (1944): 1–12;
and Toni Oelsner, "Wilhelm Roscher's Theory and the Economic and Social Position of the Jews in the Middle Ages: A Critical Examination," *Yivo
Annual of Jewish Social Science* 12 (1958–59): 176–95, and idem "The Place of
the Jews in Economic History as Viewed by German Scholars," *Yearbook of
the Leo Baeck Institute* 7 (1962): 188–91. Subsequent advocates of Roscher's

approach to our question have included Karl Gottfried Hugelmann, "Studien zum Recht der Nationalitäten im deutschen Mittelalter," *Historisches Jahrbuch* 48 (1928): 578–81; Raphael Straus, "The Jews in the Economic Evolution of Central Europe," *Jewish Social Studies* 3 (1941): 15–40; Karl W. Deutsch, "Anti-Semitic Ideas in the Middle Ages," *Journal of the History of Ideas* 6 (1945): 248, 250; and Abraham Leon, *The Jewish Question: A Marxist Interpretation* (New York, 1970).

19. P. Elman, "The Economic Causes of the Expulsion of the Jews in 1290," *Economic History Review*, 1st ser. 7 (1936–37): 145–54; Parkes, *Jew*, chap. 10; Trachtenberg, *Devil*, chap. 13; Simon Schwarzfuchs, "The Expulsion of the Jews from France (1306)," in *Seventy-fifth Anniversary Volume of the Jewish Quarterly Review*, ed. Abraham A. Neuman and Solomon Zeitlin (Philadelphia, 1967), pp. 482–89.

20. Salo Wittmayer Baron, "Nationalism and Intolerance," *Menorah Journal* 16 (1929): 503–15 (quotation on p. 504), 17 (1929): 148–58; idem, *History* 10:116–17, 11:118–283, 12:3–4.

21. Benzion Netanyahu, *Don Isaac Abravanel, Statesman and Philosopher*, 3d ed. (Philadelphia, 1972), chaps. 1–2, passim; Barnett D. Ovrut, "Edward I and the Expulsion of the Jews," *Jewish Quarterly Review*, n.s. 67 (1977): 24–35.

22. Langmuir, "Jews," p. 185; H. G. Richardson, *English Jewry under the Angevin Kings* (London, 1960).

23. Langmuir, "Jews," p. 235. On attitudes to Jewish history in modern historiography, see also idem, "Majority History and Post-Biblical Jews," *Journal of the History of Ideas* 27 (1966): 343–64.

24. Langmuir, "Jews," pp. 235–44. In "L'absence d'accusation de meurtre rituel à l'ouest du Rhône," in *Juifs et judaisme de Languedoc: XIIIe siècle- début XIVe siècle*, ed. Marie-Humbert Vicaire and Bernhard Blumenkranz, Collection Franco-Judaica 6/Cahiers de Fanjeaux 12 (Toulouse, 1977), pp. 235–49, Langmuir subsequently applied his perspective to the popularity of the ritual murder accusation in northern Europe of the later Middle Ages and its virtual absence in southern Europe. Socioeconomic and psychological factors, not the doctrine of the church, underlay the realia of anti-Jewish persecutions. In the south, Langmuir explains (pp. 245–46), "l'hostilité populaire existait, bien sûr, mais elle fut bien moindre qu'en Europe du Nord, peut-être parce que, en Europe du Sud, le developpement précoce du commerce et du crédit chrétien avait rendu les Juifs moins distincts; y contribuaient également le pluralisme culturel, l'instruction générale, et la complexité de l'organisation sociale. De plus, 'il semble que les croyances religieuses aient joué un rôle plus circonscrit dans cette vielle société bien romanisée."

25. Lea Dasberg, *Untersuchungen über die Entwertung des Judenstatus im 11. Jahrhundert* (Paris, 1965).

26. See also Oelsner, "Roscher's Theory."

27. Maurice Kriegel, "Mobilisation politique et modernisation organique: Les expulsions de Juifs au bas Moyen Age," *Archives de sciences sociales des religions* 46 (1978): 5–20. Kriegel has developed his interpretation of the expulsion from Spain more extensively in "La prise d'une décision: L'expulsion des Juifs d'Espagne en 1492," *Revue historique* 260 (1978): 49–90. Cf. also his *Les Juifs à la fin due Moyen Age dans l'Europe.*

28. Kriegel, "Mobilisation," p. 17.

29. John Boswell, *Christianity, Social Tolerance, and Homosexuality: Gay People in Europe from the Beginning of the Christian Era to the Fourteenth Century* (Chicago, 1980), pt. 4. See also my *Friars*, esp. chap. 10, which seeks to establish a similar basis for the anti-Judaism of thirteenth- and fourteenth-century Dominicans and Franciscans.

CHAPTER 35

The Black Death and the Jews

Philip Ziegler

When ignorant men are overwhelmed by forces totally beyond their control and their understanding it is inevitable that they will search for some explanation within their grasp. When they are frightened and badly hurt then they will seek someone on whom they can be revenged. Few doubted that the Black Death was God's will but, by a curious quirk of reasoning, medieval man also concluded that His instruments were to be found on earth and that, if only they could be identified, it was legitimate to destroy them. What was needed, therefore, was a suitable target for the indignation of the people, preferably a minority group, easily identifiable, already unpopular, widely scattered and lacking any powerful protector.

The Jews were not the only candidates as victims. In large areas of Spain the Arabs were suspected of playing some part in the propagation of the plague. All over Europe pilgrims were viewed with the gravest doubts; in June, 1348, a party of Portuguese pilgrims were said to be poisoning wells in Aragon and had to be given a safe conduct to get them home. In Narbonne it was the English who were at one time accused. But it was the leper who most nearly rivalled the Jew as popular scapegoat. The malign intentions of the leper had long been suspected by his more fortunate fellows. In 1346, Edward III decreed that lepers were no longer to enter the City of London since:

> . . . some of them, endeavouring to contaminate others with that abominable blemish (that so, to their own wretched solace, they may have the more fellows in suffering) as well in the way of mutual communication, and by the contagion of their polluted breath, as by carnal intercourse with women in stews and other secret places, detestably frequenting the same, do so taint persons who are sound, both male and female, to the great injury of the people dwelling in the city. . . .

But it is one thing to try to infect others with one's own disease for the sake of the extra companionship, another to spread the plague out of sheer devilry. When in Languedoc, in 1321, all the lepers were burnt on suspicion of poisoning wells, it was claimed that they had been bribed to do so by the Jews

From Philip Ziegler, *The Black Death* (London, HarperCollins, 1969), pp. 97–109. Copyright 1969 by Philip Ziegler. Reprinted by permission of HarperCollins Ltd.

who, in their turn, were in the pay of the King of Granada. There were one or two cases, notably in Spain, where lepers suffered during the Black Death on suspicion of complicity but there do not seem to be any where the Jews were not accorded the leading role and the lepers cast as the mere instruments of their wickedness.

One reason for this was that nobody had cause for envying the lepers or economic reason for wishing them out of the way. It was very different with the Jews whose popular image was that of the Prioress's Tale:

> . . . sustened by a lord of that contree
> For foule usure and lucre of vileynye,
> Hateful to Christ and to his compaignye.*

In Germany, and to some extent also in France and Spain, the Jews provided the money-lending class in virtually every city—not so much by their own volition as because they had been progressively barred from all civil and military functions, from owning land or working as artisans. Usury was the only field of economic activity left open to them; an open field, in theory at least, since it was forbidden to the Christian by Canon Law. In cities such as Strasbourg they flourished exceedingly and profited more than most during the economic expansion of the thirteenth century. But the recession of the fourteenth century reduced their prosperity and the increasing role played by the Christian financiers, in particular the Italian bankers, took away from them the cream of the market. In much of Europe the Jew dwindled to a small money-lender and pawnbroker. He acquired a large clientele of petty debtors so that every day more people had cause to wish him out of the way. "It can be taken for granted," wrote Dr. Cohn, "that the Jewish money lenders often reacted to insecurity and persecution by deploying a ruthlessness of their own." It is fair to criticise the medieval Jews for exacting exorbitant rates of interest from their victims but it is also only fair to remember the extreme precariousness of their business, dependent on the uncertain protection of the local ruler and with virtually no sanctions at their disposal to enable them to recover their money from a reluctant debtor. To ensure their own safety the luckless Jews were forced to pay ever larger bribes to the authorities and, to raise the money for the bribes, they had to charge higher interest and press their clients still more harshly. Animosity built up and, by the middle of the fourteenth century, Shylock had been born. The Jew had become a figure so hated in European society that almost anything might have served to provoke catastrophe.

But though the economic causes for the persecution of the Jews were certainly important it would be wrong to present them as the only, or even as the principal reason for what now happened. The Jew's role as money-lender predisposed many people to believe any evil which they might hear of him but

---

*. . . . . supported by the Crown
For the foul lucre of their usury,
Hateful to Christ and all his company.

the belief itself was sincere and had far deeper roots. The image of the Jew as Antichrist was common currency in the Middle Ages. It seems to have gained force at the time of the First Crusade and the Catholic Church must accept much of the responsibility for its propagation. The vague enormity of such a concept was quickly translated into terms more comprehensible to the masses. In particular the more irresponsible priests spread rumours that the Jews kidnapped and tortured Christian children and desecrated the host. They were represented as demons attendant on Satan, portrayed in drama or in pictures as devils with the beards and horns of a goat, passing their time with pigs, frogs, worms, snakes, scorpions and the horned beasts of the field. Even the lay authorities seemed intent on fostering public belief in the malevolence of the Jews; in 1267, for instance, the Council of Vienna forbade purchases of meat from Jews on the ground that it was likely to be poisoned.

Today such fantasies seem ludicrous. It is hard to believe that sane men can have accepted them. And yet Dr. Norman Cohn has drawn a revealing parallel between anti-Semitism in the fourteenth century and under the Third Reich. On 1 May, 1934, *Der Stürmer* devoted a whole issue to alleged murders of Christian children by the Jews; illustrating its text with pictures of rabbis sucking blood from an Aryan child. Most Germans were no doubt revolted by such vicious propaganda but Buchenwald, Auschwitz and Belsen live vividly enough in the memory to save this generation from any offensive sense of superiority to its ancestors. Nor do the still more recent Chinese accusations that American airmen, in 1952, showered the countryside around Kan-Nan Hsien with voles infected with *Pasteurella Pestis*, the bacillus of bubonic plague, suggest that man's infinite capacity for thinking ill of man is in any way on the wane.

The Black Death concentrated this latent fear and hatred of the Jews into one burning grievance which not only demanded vengeance but offered the tempting extra dividend that, if the Jews could only be eliminated, then the plague for which they were responsible might vanish too. There was really only one charge levelled against the Jews; that, by poisoning the wells of Christian communities, they infected the inhabitants with the plague. The Polish historian, Dlugoss, claimed that they also poisoned the air but this view does not seem to have been at all widely shared. Some of the more fanciful reports alleged that the Jews were working under the orders of a conspiratorial network with its headquarters in Toledo; that the poison, in powdered form, was imported in bulk from the Orient, and that the same organisation also occupied itself in forging currencies and murdering Christian children. But these were decorative frills, the attack on the sources of drinking water was the central issue.

The emphasis on this accusation is surprising. With the exception of the Faculty of Medicine at Paris, which suggested that a minor contributory cause of the epidemic might be the pollution of the wells as a result of earthquakes, none of the contemporary experts seem to have tried to link infection with the drinking of tainted water. There were other ways of spreading the plague which must have seemed at least as plausible to medieval man. Alfonso of Cordova's vision of the infection of air by the release of a "certain confection" into a "strong, slow wind" has already been mentioned and in subsequent epidemics Jews were accused of passing around clothes taken from the dead or smearing walls and windows with an ointment made from the buboes of plague victims.

A partial explanation may be that many wells in built-up areas were polluted by seepage from nearby sewage pits. The Jews, with their greater understanding of elementary hygiene, preferred to draw their drinking water from open streams, even though these might often be farther from their homes. Such a habit, barely noticed in normal times, would seem intensely suspicious in the event of plague. Why should the Jews shun the wells unless they knew them to be poisoned and how could they have such knowledge unless they had done the poisoning themselves? This theory is supported by Tschudi who, in the *Helvetian Chronicle,* records not only that the Jews knew the wells to be contaminated by "bad, noxious moistures and vapours" but also that, in many places "they warned the people against them." If they did, the warnings seem to have gone unheeded and certainly those who received them were little disposed to feel gratitude to the Jews for their consideration.

There can be little doubt that the majority of those who turned on the Jews believed in the literal truth of the accusations against them. It might be thought that this certainty would have been shaken by the fact that Jews died as fast as Christians; probably faster, indeed, in their crowded and unhealthy ghettoes. But the Christians seem simply to have closed their eyes to reality. Since the Jews caused the Black Death it was ridiculous to suppose that they could also suffer from it. Any appearance to the contrary was merely further evidence of their consummate cunning. . . . But though such crude suspicions might have been acceptable to the mob, they can hardly have been taken seriously by the intelligent and better educated. Dr. Guerchberg has analysed the attitude of the leading plague tractators. The most remarkable feature is how few references there are to the guilt or innocence of the Jews. Konrade of Megenberg brusquely dismissed the accusations: "Some say that this was brought about by the Jewish people, but this point of view is untenable." In his *Buch der Natur* he cites as evidence Jewish mortality in Vienna which was so high that a new cemetery had to be constructed. Gui de Chauliac was equally categoric. Alfonso of Cordova considered that, by all the rules of planetary action, the Black Death should only have lasted a year and that any subsequent extension must be the result of a wicked plot. But he did not specifically accuse the Jews of being responsible. The "Five Strasbourg Physicians" warned against poisoned food and water but it is doubtful whether they believed that the poisoning was done deliberately by man. No other tractator paid any attention to the possibility that some human agency was involved in the spread of the plague, still less that such villains must be identified as the Jews.

On the whole, this reticence on the part of the tractators must be taken to indicate that they did not believe the accusations. It is impossible that they did not know what had been suggested and, if they had really thought that a principal cause of the plague was the poisoning of the wells by Jews, then they could hardly have failed to say so in their examination of the subject. Their silence might imply that they thought the idea too ridiculous to mention but it is more likely that they shrank from expressing publicly an unpopular view on an issue over which people were dangerously disturbed.

For it took considerable moral courage to stand up for the Jews in 1348 and 1349 and not many people were prepared to take the risk. The first cases of persecution seem to have taken place in the South of France in the spring of 1348, and, in May, there was a massacre in Provence. Narbonne and Carcassone exterminated their communities with especial thoroughness. But it is possible that the madness might never have spread across Europe if it had not been for the trial at Chillon in September 1348 of Jews said to have poisoned certain wells at Neustadt and the disastrous confessions of guilt which torture tore from the accused. Balavignus, a Jewish physician, was the first to be racked. "After much hesitation," he confessed that the Rabbi Jacob of Toledo had sent him, by hand of a Jewish boy, a leather pouch filled with red and black powder and concealed in the mummy of an egg. This powder he was ordered, on pain of excommunication, to throw into the larger wells of Thonon. He did so, having previously warned his friends and relations not to drink the water. "He also declared that none of his community could exculpate themselves from this accusation, as the plot was communicated to all and all were guilty of the above charges." Odd scraps of "evidence" were produced, such as a rag found in a well in which it was alleged that the powder, composed largely of ground-up portions of a basilisk, had been concealed. Ten similar confessions were racked from other unfortunates and the resulting dossier sent to neighbouring cities for their information and appropriate action.

So incriminating a confession settled the doubts or perhaps quietened the consciences of many who might otherwise have felt bound to protect the Jews. On 21 September, 1348, the municipality of Zurich voted never to admit Jews to the city again. In Basle all the Jews were penned up in wooden buildings and burned alive. "In the month of November began the persecution of the Jews," wrote a German chronicler. Henry of Diessenhoven has recorded the movement of the fever across his country. In November, 1348, the Jews were burnt at Solothurn, Zofingen and Stuttgart; in December at Landsberg, Burren, Memmingen, Lindau; in January, Freiburg, Ulm and Speyer. At Speyer the bodies of the murdered were piled in great wine-casks and sent floating down the Rhine. In February it was the turn of the Jews at Gotha, Eisenach and Dresden; in March, Worms, Baden and Erfurt.

In most cities the massacres took place when the Black Death was already raging but in some places the mere news that the plague was approaching was enough to inflame the populace. On 14 February, 1349, several weeks before the first cases of infection were reported, two thousand Jews were murdered in Strasbourg; the mob tore the clothes from the backs of the victims on their way to execution in the hope of finding gold concealed in the lining. In part at least because of the anti-Semitism of the Bishop, the Jews of Strasbourg seem to have suffered exceptionally harshly. A contemporary chronicle puts the grand total of the slaughtered at sixteen thousand—half this would be more probable but the Jewish colony was one of the largest of Europe and the higher figure is not totally inconceivable.

From March until July, there was a lull in the persecution. Then the massacre was renewed at Frankfurt-am-Main and, in August, spread to Mainz and Cologne. In Mainz, records one chronicler, the Jews took the initiative, attacked the Christians and slew two hundred of them. The Christian revenge was terrible—no less than twelve thousand Jews, "or thereabouts," in their turn perished. In the North of Germany, Jewish colonies were relatively small, but their significance was no protection when the Black Death kindled the hatred of the Christians. In the spring of 1350, those Jews of the Hansa towns who had escaped burning were walled up alive in their houses and left to die of suffocation or starvation. In some cases they were offered the chance to save themselves by renouncing their faith but few availed themselves of the invitation. On the contrary, there were many instances of Jews setting fire to their houses and destroying themselves and their families so as to rob the Christians of their prey.

Why the persecutions died down temporarily in March, 1349, is uncertain. It could be that the heavy losses which the Black Death inflicted on the Jews began to convince all those still capable of objectivity that some other explanation must be found for the spread of the infection. If so, their enlightenment did not last long. But the blame for the renewal of violence must rest predominantly with the Flagellants. It is difficult to be sure whether this was the work of a few fanatics among the leaders or merely another illustration of the fact that mass-hysteria, however generated, is always likely to breed the ugliest forms of violence. In July, 1349, when the Flagellants arrived in procession at Frankfurt, they rushed directly to the Jewish quarter and led the local population in wholesale slaughter. At Brussels the mere news that the Flagellants were approaching was enough to set off a massacre in which, in spite of the efforts of the Duke of Brabant, some six hundred Jews were killed. The Pope condemned the Flagellants for their conduct and the Jews, with good reason, came to regard them as their most dangerous enemies.

On the whole the rulers of Europe did their best, though often ineffectively, to protect their Jewish subjects. Pope Clement VI in particular behaved with determination and responsibility. Both before and after the trials at Chillon he published Bulls condemning the massacres and calling on Christians to behave with tolerance and restraint. Those who joined in persecution of the Jews were threatened with excommunication. The town-councillors of Cologne were also active in the cause of humanity, but they did no more than incur a snub when they wrote to their colleagues at Strasbourg urging moderation in their dealings with the Jews. The Emperor Charles IV and Duke Albert of Austria both did their somewhat inadequate best and Ruprecht von der Pfalz took the Jews under his personal protection, though only on receipt of a handsome bribe. His reward was to be called "Jew-master" by his people and to provoke something close to a revolution.

Not all the magnates were so enlightened. In May, 1349, Landgrave Frederic of Thuringia wrote to the Council of the City of Nordhausen telling them how he had burnt his Jews for the honour of God and advising them to do the same. He seems to have been unique in wholeheartedly supporting the murderers but other great rulers, while virtuously deploring the excesses of their subjects, could not resist the temptation to extract advantage from what was going on. Charles IV offered the Archbishop of Trier the goods of those Jews in Alsace "who have already been killed or may still be killed" and gave the Margrave of Brandenburg his choice of the best three Jewish houses in Nuremberg, "when there is next a massacre of the Jews." A more irresponsible incitement to violence it would be hard to find.

Nor were those rulers who sought to protect the Jews often in a position to do much about it. The patrician rulers of Strasbourg, when they tried to intervene, were overthrown by a combination of mob and rabble-rousing Bishop. The town-council of Erfurt did little better while the city fathers of Trier, when they offered the Jews the chance to return to the city, warned them quite frankly that they could not guarantee their lives or property in case of further rioting. Only Casimir of Poland, said to have been under the influence of his Jewish mistress Esther, seems to have been completely successful in preventing persecution.

An illustration of the good will of the rulers and the limitations on their effective power comes from Spain. Pedro IV of Aragon had a high opinion of his Jewish subjects. He was therefore outraged when the inhabitants of Barcelona, demoralised by the Black Death and deprived, through the high mortality and the flight from the city of the nobles and the rich, of almost any kind of civic authority, turned on the Jews and sacked the ghetto. On 22 May, 1348, he sent a new Governor to the city and gave orders that the guilty were to be punished and no further incidents allowed. A week later he circularised his authorities throughout the Kingdom ordering them to protect the Jews and prevent disturbances. By February, 1349, the new Governor of Barcelona had made no progress in his search for those responsible. King Pedro grew impatient and demanded immediate action. In a flurry of zeal a few arrests were made, including Bernal Ferrer, a public hangman. But the prosecution in its turn was extremely dilatory. Six months later no judgement had been passed and, in the end, it seems that Ferrer and the other prisoners were quietly released.

Meanwhile, in spite of the King's injunctions, anti-Jewish rioting went on in other cities of Aragon. There was a particularly ugly incident in Tarragona where more than three hundred Jews were killed. Here again Pedro demanded vengeance and sent a commission to investigate. The resulting welter of accusation and counter accusation became so embittered that virtual civil war ensued. In the end this prosecution too was tacitly abandoned. But the King did at least ensure that a new ghetto was built and intervened personally on behalf of several leading Jews who had been ruined by the loss of their houses and documents. When the next epidemic came in 1361 the Jews appealed to the King for protection and an armed guard was placed at the gates of the ghetto.

Flanders was bitten by the bug at about the same time as the Bavarian towns. "Anno domini 1349 sloeg men de Joden dood" is the chronicler's brutally laconic reference to massacres that seem to have been on a scale as hideous as those in Germany. In England there were said to be isolated prosecutions of Jews on suspicion of spreading the plague but no serious persecution took place. It would be pleasant to attribute this to superior humanity and good-sense. The substantial reason, however, was rather less honourable. In 1290, King Edward I had expelled the Jews from England. Such few as remained had little money and were too unobtrusive to present a tempting target. Some small credit is due for leaving them in peace but certainly it cannot be held up as a particularly shining example of racial tolerance.

PROBLEMS OF LATE MEDIEVAL SOCIETY

The apparently serene, harmonious civilization of the thirteenth century did not endure for long. The history of the fourteenth century is a catalogue of disasters. In the later Middle Ages European society had to endure famine, plague, war, rebellions in many lands, and schism in the church. Some of the troubles of the age arose from fortuitous natural disasters, e.g., a series of bad harvests in 1315–1317 and the devastating Black Death in the middle years of the century. But many of them grew out of tensions inherent in earlier medieval civilization.

The problems that emerged concerned both economic and religious life. All the achievements of the twelfth and thirteenth centuries had been based on a steady increase of population and of real wealth. By 1300 the growing population was beginning to press on the available economic resources. In the first group of readings below, Emmanuel Le Roy Ladurie discusses the rearing of children as a way of maintaining family prosperity in a peasant society; M. M. Postan deals with the overall economic impact of population growth; A. R. Lewis considers the strains and stresses of overpopulation in terms of the familiar "frontier thesis"; and Edith Ennen describes some aspects of urban social life in the century after the onset of the plague.

In the realm of religious life the Black Death produced some pathological results, including the renewed persecution of the Jews discussed above in Chapter 35. Within the Christian church, dissident apocalyptic movements grew up which looked forward to a revolutionary transformation of society in a coming new age. In the final reading Norman Cohn compares such movements with the totalitarian ideologies of the twentieth century.

One has to add finally that these problems did not lead to a general collapse of civilization comparable to the "fall of the Roman empire." The Black Death produced new kinds of economic dislocation, but it ended for centuries the pressure of overpopulation in Europe. The fifteenth and sixteenth centuries brought further change and new problems, but there was no sharp break in the continuity of Western civilization.

CHAPTER 36

Family and Population

A. PARENTS AND CHILDREN

*Emmanuel Le Roy Ladurie**

As was normal under the *ancien régime*, the peasant family in Montaillou was a large one. Mengarde and Pons Clergue had four sons and at least two daughters known to us. Guillemette Belot had four sons and two daughters. Guillaume and Guillemette Benet had at least two sons and three daughters. Raymond Baille had four sons, but no daughter is mentioned. Pierre and Mengarde Maurs had four sons and one daughter. There were four Marty brothers. Alazaïs and Raymond Maury had six sons and at least two daughters.

There were smaller families. Bernard and Gauzia Clergue had only two known children, a son and a daughter. Two couples, Guillemette and Raymond Maurs and Bernard and Guillemette Maurs, had two sons each, as well, probably, as daughters unknown to us in name or number. From the information available, eighteen couples emerge who were in the process of completing, or had completed, their family in the demographic period 1280–1324, the time roughly covered by the Fournier Register. These eighteen families, complete and incomplete, gave birth to a minimum of forty-two boys and twenty girls. The number of girls is clearly under-estimated or under-recorded. The figure for boys certainly does not take into account losses from infant mortality, the deaths which occurred between birth and the end of the first year of life. It also leaves out an indeterminable fraction of juvenile mortality, especially between one and five years of age. Even so, this gives us a mean of 2.3 boys per couple. So, taking into account various imponderables, it is reasonable to assume 4.5 legitimate births, including boys and girls, per family, complete or incomplete,[1] a fertility rate equal to that of

From Emmanuel Le Roy Ladurie, *Montaillou* (New York: George Braziller, Inc., 1978), pp. 204, 207, 210–213. Reprinted by permission.
*Between 1318 and 1325 Bishop Jacques Fournier investigated the whole population of the little village of Montaillou in southern France on suspicion of heresy. The detailed records of the interrogations survive, and from them Emmanuel Le Roy Ladurie was able to construct a brilliant picture of the social and religious life of the village. The pages given here are a fragment of this account. Figures interpolated in the text refer to Fournier's register.—Ed.

the prolific inhabitants of Beauvaisis in modern times. The illegitimacy rate in Montaillou was higher.

One explanation of the size of Montaillou families is the early age at which girls married. Moreover our figures are chiefly concerned with the Cathar and endogamous group of big farming families, allied among themselves, which dominated Montaillou around 1300. For reasons which are perhaps fortuitous, the few Catholic families in the village, for example the Azémas, recorded fewer children and fewer marriages than the heretics.

There were limits to this fecundity. The richest family, the Clergues, in Pierre and Bernard's generation, seem to have practised certain kinds of birth control (magical herbs, or perhaps *coitus interruptus*). Pons Clergue's many sons left several bastards but no legitimate child, though there were other Clergues in the village to carry on the name. As for the lower ranks, the shepherds tended not to get married. More generally, the last generation with which we are concerned, that which married between the round-up of 1308 and the interrogations of 1320–25, was greatly disturbed. Many people were put in prison and the circumstances may have led some couples to practise abstinence or contraception. At all levels, during the decade beginning in 1310, which was also economically unpropitious, fertility in Montaillou seems to have declined.

Between 1280 and 1305, however, there was in Montaillou, as elsewhere, a baby boom. Large groups of two brothers or even four all living together were very common (i.193, 203). A high birth rate was taken for granted. If you lost one child and were not too old, it was very likely that you would have more and these, according to a farfetched Cathar interpretation of metempsychosis, might be the means of restoring to a mother the souls of her previously lost children (i.203).

My fellow-sponsor, Alazaïs Munier, says Guillaume Austatz, *bayle* of Ornolac, *was sad; in a short time she had lost all her four sons. Seeing her desolate, I asked her the cause.*

'How could I be other than unhappy,' she asked, *'after having lost four fine children in so short a time?'*

'Don't be upset,' I said to her, *'you will get them back again.'*

'Yes, in Paradise!'

'No, you will get them back again in this world. For you are still young. You will be pregnant again. The soul of one of your dead children will enter into the new foetus. And so on!'

We see that Guillaume Austatz did not think it strange that a woman should have eight pregnancies in all.

The countrymen of this period were well aware of the population pressure of the 1300s, resulting from, among other things, the high fertility rates discussed above. *Where,* it was asked (i.191), *would there be room to put all the souls of all the men who are dead and of all those who are still alive? At that rate the world would be full of souls! The entire space between the city of Toulouse and the Merens Pass would not be enough to hold them all!* Fortunately, explained Guillaume Austatz, God had found a simple remedy. Every soul was used several times.

It emerged from a human body which had just died, and entered almost immediately into another. And so on.

In theory, the Cathar dogma professed by many of the people of Montaillou, though little known to them in detail, was hostile to marriage and procreation. The most sophisticated Cathar peasants, and *parfaits* or pseudo-*parfaits* like Bélibaste, were acquainted with this point. Bélibaste himself (ii.48), who wanted *through virginity to transport the seed of this world into the next,* would not have *any man join himself carnally to a woman; nor would I have sons or daughters born of them. For if people would hold to barrenness, all God's creatures would soon be gathered together* [in heaven]. *That is what I should like.* Similarly, we have seen Pierre Clergue of Montaillou making use of contraception, perhaps magical. But how many people in the village of the yellow cross were capable of such refinements? In any case, the duty of barrenness was incumbent only on the goodmen, not on mere 'believers.' So the peasants of Montaillou, even when they were sympathetic to heresy, continued to produce numerous children. There was enough land, especially pasture, to provide them with employment when they grew up. Moreover, Catalonia, which as Bélibaste said (ii.42) *lacked neither pastures nor mountains for the sheep,* welcomed surplus youth from Montaillou with open arms. They easily found jobs there as shepherds and muleteers. In these circumstances, why worry? A *domus* rich in children was a *domus* rich in manpower; in other words, rich, pure and simple. This explains the large number of sons produced by the big farming families of Montaillou—the Belots, the Maurys, the Martys and so on. Only the last generation of Clergues, wealthy enough not to have to descend to manual labour, were not interested in producing a large number of workers. So, both in theory and in practice, they could afford views favourable to contraception and hostile to marriage.

There are many examples in upper Ariège of the sorrow of country parents at the death of their offspring. It is true that within the framework of the *domus* system, love for children was not, in the last resort, entirely disinterested. Bélibaste suggested as much when exhorting Pierre Maury against remaining a bachelor (iii.188). Alazaïs Azéma was more precise still, reporting on the feelings of Guillaume Benet, a farmer of Montaillou, on the loss of his son (i.321). *When Raymond Benet, son of Guillaume Benet, died, I went after a fortnight to Guillaume Benet's house. I found him in tears.*

'Alazaïs,' he said, 'I have lost all I had through the death of my son Raymond. I have no one left to work for me.'

All Alazaïs could say was: 'Cheer up; there's nothing we can do about it.'

But if a male child meant a strong right arm to Guillaume Benet, he also meant much more. Guillaume loved Raymond for himself. And he was somewhat consoled to think that Guillaume Authié had hereticated his son before he died. So the son was in fact happier than his father, left behind in this vale of tears: 'I hope,' said Guillaume, 'that my son is in a better place than I am now.'

When Guillemette Benet of Montaillou lost a daughter and was weeping for her, Alazaïs Azéma tried to console her (i.320). 'Cheer up, you still have some daughters left; and anyhow you can't get the one that is dead back again.'

To which Guillemette replied: '*I would mourn even more than I do for the death of my daughter; but,* Deo gratias, *I have had the consolation of seeing her hereticated on the night before her death by Guillaume Authié, who hurried here in a blizzard.*'

Sincere as all this affection was, it was also ritualized, socialized and shared. So were the condolences offered to a bereaved parent by friends and neighbours. The difference there might be between a father's and a mother's love is shown in the story of the Pierre family, an episode which has the additional interest of dealing with a little girl less than one year old. Despite the infant's extreme youth, it was undoubtedly the object of emotion. Raymond Pierre was a sheep-farmer in the village of Arques, a terminus on the migration route used by the people of Montaillou. He had one daughter, Jacotte, by Sybille his wife (iii.414–15). Jacotte, not yet a year old, was seriously ill, and her parents decided, so much did they love the child, against all the rules of heresy, to have her hereticated before she died. In theory it was not right to hereticate anyone so young: Jacotte *did not have the understanding of good.* But Prades Tavernier, the *parfait* who undertook the ceremony, was laxer than the Authiés and thought there was nothing to be lost by it.[2] So he started to administer the *consolamentum: He performed a lot of bows and elevations,* and placed that rare object, a book, on the child's head. Once these rites were accomplished, Raymond Pierre could say to his wife, '*If Jacotte dies, she will be an angel of God. Neither you nor I, wife, could give our daughter as much as this heretic has given.*'

Full of joy and disinterested love, Raymond Pierre left the house to see Prades Tavernier on his way. Before going, the *parfait* told Sybille not to give the baby any milk or meat. If Jacotte lived, all she was to have was fish and vegetables (ii.414). For a child of that age, and in the dietetic conditions of the period, this was risky. In fact, what it amounted to was that after the father and the *parfait* left, Jacotte would be doomed to imminent death by a process similar to the *endura*, or final fast.

But there was a hitch. Sybille Pierre's love for her little girl was essentially warm and physical, not spiritual and sublime like that of Raymond. So, relates Sybille, *when my husband and Prades Tavernier had left the house, I could not bear it any longer. I couldn't let my daughter die before my very eyes. So I put her to the breast. When my husband came back, I told him I had fed my daughter. He was very grieved and troubled, and lamented. Pierre Maury* [Raymond Pierre's shepherd] *tried to console his master. He said to my husband, 'It is not your fault.'*

And Pierre said to my baby, 'You have a wicked mother.'

And he said to me, 'You are a wicked mother. Women are demons.'

My husband wept. He insulted and threatened me. After this scene, he stopped loving [diligere] *the child; and he also stopped loving me for a long while, until later, when he admitted that he had been wrong.* (Raymond Pierre's change of heart occurred at the same time as all the inhabitants of Arques decided collectively to renounce Catharism.) *My daughter Jacotte,* Sybille concluded (ii.415), *survived this episode for a year; and then she died.*

All this shows that there was not such an enormous gap, as has sometimes been claimed, between our attitude to children and the attitude of the people in fourteenth-century Montaillou and upper Ariège. Another example is the case of Raymond Benet's new-born son, who was not expected to live. Perhaps his mother was already dead. Guillemette Benet, who lived in the same village as her brother, tells the story (i.264). *Raymond Benet of Ornalac had a new-born son who was dying. He sent for me when I was going to the woods to gather firewood, so that I could hold the dying child in my arms. So I did hold it from morning until evening, when it died.*

There are, of course, some differences between our attitude to our children and the affection felt by the peasants and especially the women of Montaillou towards their offspring. But they probably loved their children just as intensely as we do, and perhaps even spoiled them too.[3] Of course, parental love had to be divided up among a greater number of children than today. It also had to adapt itself to a higher rate of infant mortality. Lastly, many couples seemed to be comparatively indifferent to very young infants.[4] But this indifference was less marked than has recently been claimed.[5]

Notes

1. The couples in question here are: Pons Clergue and Mengarde (four boys, two girls: Guillaume, Bernard, Pierre, Raymond, Esclarmonde, Guillemette); a couple whose head, unreferred to elsewhere, was called Bar (three sons and two daughters: Pierre, Raymond, Guillaume, Mengarde, Guillemette; see i.418); Bernard Rives and Alazaïs (one son, two daughters: Pons, Raymonde and Guillemette, who married one of the Clergues); Pons Azéma and Alazaïs (one son: Raymond); Pierre Azèma and Guillemette (one son: Raymond); Bernard Clergue (the *bayle's* namesake) and Gauzia (one boy, one girl: Raymond, Esclarmonde); Bernad Clergue, *bayle* of Montaillou, and Raymonde (no children); Belot senior (Christian name unknown) and Guillemette (four sons, two daughters: Raymond, Guillaume, Bernad, Arnaud, Raymonde and, according to i.371, Alazaïs); Guillaume Benet and Guillemette (two sons, four daughters: Raymond, Bernard, Alazaïs, Montagne; and, according to i.400, Gaillarde and Esclarmonde); Raymond Baille and X (four sons: Pierre, Jacques, Raymond, Arnaud); Vital Baille and Esclarmonde (one son: Jacques); Pierre Maurs and Mengarde (four sons and one daughter: Arnaud, Guillaume, Raymond, Pierre, Guillemette); Raymond Maurs and Guillemette (two sons: Pierre and Bernard); Bernard Maurs and Guillemette (two sons: Raymond and Pierre); the four Marty brothers, the name of whose mother and father are unknown: Guillaume, Arnaud, Bernard and Jean; X Testanière and Alazaïs (one son and one daughter: Prades and Vuissane); Raymond Maury and Alazaïs (six sons and two daughters: Guillaume, Pierre, Jean, Arnaud, Raymond, Bernard, Guillemette and Raymonde); Jean Guilhabert and Allemande (one son and three daughters: Guillaume,

Alazaïs, Sybille and Guillemette, according to i.403, ii.256 and ii.482 and 484). I have left out the very old groups, like those of Pons and Guillaume Clergue, which were already decimated by death, not only among infants and children but also among adults and elderly people. I have also left out very young couples only a small part of whose procreative life fell within the last years of the Fournier Register; moreover, these were greatly disturbed by the Inquisition. Finally, I have left out the wives who were widowed early and took refuge in Catalonia. It goes without saying that the records we are dealing with have only a very indirect and unintended demographic value.

2. iii.144. In fact, Prades Tavernier, a villager by origin, not a bourgeois like the Authiés, was influenced by the pressure of Catholic behaviour, and administered the *consolamentum* to a baby in just the same way as a Roman priest would administer baptism in the same circumstances.

3. I think I have said enough to counter the point of view expounded by Madame B. Vourzay, who writes that 'children were of little account' for the people of Montaillou. (Vourzay (1969), p. 91). It is true, as she rightly says, that grown-ups in upper Ariège were afraid that children might betray them to the Inquisition. But in my view this did not affect the general feeling towards children.

4. There is little mention of the death of infants in Montaillou itself, though such losses must have been frequent.

5. There is not enough information available for us to go into the question of the attitude of grandparents. But to take a few examples, Beatrice de Planissoles was an attentive grandmother (i.249) and a dead grandmother came back as a ghost to embrace her grandchildren in bed (i.135). The Fournier Register tells us nothing about grandfathers: men were much less likely to live long enough to become grandparents. But see iii.305 for the interest taken by Raymond Authié (namesake of the *parfait*) in a suggestion of marriage concerning his granddaughter, Guillemette Cortil.

B. LAND AND POPULATION

M. M. Postan

. . . The most obvious even if indirect sign of continued population growth will be found in the continuous expansion of land settlement and reclamation throughout the seven or eight centuries separating the Anglo-Saxon conquest from the beginning of the fourteenth century. We have seen that, to begin with, the area occupied by agricultural settlers was very small, not much greater than it had been under Roman occupation, and that the greater part of the English plain was reclaimed in later centuries. It is of course impossible to assign a precise enumerator to the total additions made to the occupied land before 1300, but we can be certain that it had grown manifold.

Our demographic deduction from this fact is that population must also have grown by at least the same rate. In theory it is possible to assume that an agricultural population, even a wholly settled one, would try to expand the acreage of its land and continue to do so indefinitely merely in response to the insatiable desire of individual peasants to add and to go on adding to their holdings. This is not, however, what in fact took place in most of the rural societies in the past, and it is certainly not what happened in medieval England. On the contrary, such evidence as we possess—and it will be recalled again later—makes it quite clear that the average size of family holdings between the eleventh century and the fourteenth declined. If so, the population must have increased at a rate even faster than the areas reclaimed for arable and improved pasture. . . .

By the end of the thirteenth century the land hunger revealed itself in innumerable ways. One of its signs was the long and lengthening queues of men seeking land. In some places the queues had become so long as to disrupt the traditional routine of succession from father to son on the former's death. So valuable was the land, and so numerous were the men willing to take it up, that sitting holders were frequently tempted to sell long before they died. Purchase was becoming a common method of acquiring land. On the Glastonbury estates in the second half of the thirteenth century more than a third of the sitting tenants had acquired their holdings by various forms of open or disguised purchase, and sometimes over the heads of the legal heirs whom they frequently bought out. Another, and increasingly common, means of acquiring land was to marry well-endowed women, more especially widows with land. What made widows especially attractive was that in most villages the spouses of customary holders were allowed to keep the whole of their deceased husbands' tenements. On some manors, such as Taunton, men marrying widows with land could retain the land on the wives' death and were thus able to contract second marriages destined to produce later a further crop of marriageable widows.

The transmission of land by purchase or by marriage, and the declining proportion of transmission by ordinary inheritance, was merely one of the signs of the increasing land hunger. This hunger was the most obvious consequence of an overgrown population, and its principal economic penalty. Society was paying for its growing numbers by moving ever nearer to the margin of subsistence. It is because the margin was so close and getting closer that the death rates were high and may have been getting higher.

Needless to say, in some years the high death rate resulted from severe epidemics or bouts of severe weather. But it is highly revealing to find how frequently death rates rose in years of bad harvest. The bad harvests themselves may have become more frequent because the quality of the land was declining. But even if we make full allowances for possible deterioration of the weather (the catastrophically bad harvests of 1290 and 1315–17 were obviously due to unusually wet seasons), the high mortality in years when crops failed would not have been as high as it was had not the population been especially sensitive to bad harvests. Its sensitivity manifests itself in our documents in various ways. In years of very bad harvests we find manorial bailiffs pleading an inability to carry out this or that operation, or justifying the high cost of the operation by the dearth of labourers (*caristia operariorum*) caused by bad crops. In other words, when harvests were very bad labourers died off and were scarce. In a more general way the steeply increasing death rates in years of bad harvest are revealed by the upsurge in heriots, the manorial death duties. Moreover, on the estates on which these records of heriots are abundant and are capable of being correlated with the total number of tenants, they frequently bring out not only the connection between harvests and deaths, but also that between death rates from starvation and impoverishment. For on these estates poorer sections of the population were the ones to succumb most frequently to privations following the failures of crops. It is obvious that large and growing sections of the population had been reduced to a condition in which they could keep body and soul together only in years of moderately good harvests.

The dynamics of medieval population before the first half of the fourteenth century is thus unmistakable. Population grew but could not have gone on growing forever. By the beginning of the fourteenth century, and perhaps even earlier, the relative overpopulation was so great as to push the death rates to a punishing height. In theory over-population could also have brought the birth rates down, by reducing the ability of the young men to set up households and to marry. Our sources being what they are, this theoretical possibility cannot be convincingly demonstrated; but even if, for lack of evidence, the changes in marriage rates and ages of marriage were disregarded, the behaviour of the death rates would by itself have been sufficient sooner or later to prevent the population from continuing its growth.

CHAPTER 37

The Closing of the Medieval Frontier

Archibald R. Lewis

Historians whose field of study is American history have long found the concept of the frontier useful and meaningful in explaining the American past. In a recent important book an American historian, Walter Prescott Webb, has extended this concept to include the entire Western European world during the period from 1500 to the present. On the whole, however, historians whose interest is the Middle Ages have made little use of a frontier thesis to explain developments in Europe during the mediaeval period, except in regard to the German advance into Slavic Europe beyond the Elbe. This is a surprising fact, for few periods can be better understood in the light of a frontier concept than Western Europe between 800 and 1500 A.D. This article is then an attempt to open up what appears to be a fruitful field for historical speculation by examining a crucial period of Western European history in the light of a frontier thesis.

We must begin this examination by briefly noting that from the eleventh to the mid-thirteenth century Western Europe followed an almost classical frontier development. Indeed in some respects one might carry the beginnings of this development back to the Carolingian era of the ninth century. For our purposes, however, this is not necessary. We can begin our survey with that impetus to expansion and growth which started again after the stimulus of the Carolingian Empire and Viking expansion had ended and a new growth had begun about the year 1000 A.D. Starting about this period then what were the frontier bases of the newly emerging Western Europe for the next two and half centuries?

First let us examine Western Europe's frontiers themselves. Early in the eleventh century Western Europeans began to advance their frontiers South into the Mediterranean into regions where Carolingian and Ottonian efforts had been unsuccessful. In the next two centuries this resulted in most of Spain being successfully wrested from Moorish control, in an occupation of the Balearics, Sardinia, Corsica, and in a Norman conquest of Southern Italy and

From Archibald R. Lewis, "The Closing of the Medieval Frontier, 1250–1350." *Speculum*, Vol. 33 (1958), pp. 475–483. Reprinted by permission of the Mediaeval Academy of America.

Sicily, which were lost by Byzantium and Islam. Nor did this advance stop there. The early Crusades added Cyprus, Palestine, and Syria to Western European control, and after 1204, Crete, the Aegean Islands and much of the Byzantine Empire had been conquered too. By the first years of the thirteenth century economic and maritime control of most of the Mediterranean and its coasts had passed into Western European hands.

During the same period Norman-Northern French expansion had brought first England and then most of Wales, Scotland, and Ireland within the compass of this new Western European continental civilization. Nor was this all, for Scandinavia, the Baltic, and much of Eastern Europe up to Russia were also being firmly integrated in a religious, economic, and political sense into the continental Western European world. By the time of Innocent III, then, one can note that Europe's frontier in the broad sense of the word had been extended North, South, East, and West from its Carolingian heartland to include many areas which had previously either been somewhat remote from continental Europe or, as in parts of the Mediterranean, had actually earlier been part of the very different Byzantine and Moslem civilizations.

Now as Western Europe's frontiers expanded this resulted in much new land being thrown open to settlement or colonization. Behind the moving frontiers of the Reconquista in the Iberian Peninsula, during the eleventh, twelfth, and early thirteenth centuries, historians are beginning to appreciate the role of a peasantry who settled much of the newly conquered land in Aragon, Castile, and Portugal and made the reconquest permanent for the future. Similarly, as the German nobility moved east of the Elbe to conquer pagan Slavs and Balts the lands they seized were frequently settled by German peasants from the West. Norman-French conquest of England had as a sequel a similar movement of peasant cultivators into parts of Southern Wales, into Scotland below the Highland line, and into the Irish Pale, as Anglo-Norman nobles extended their influence into these remoter parts of the British Isles.

In some areas like Southern Italy, Sicily, and the Byzantine and Moslem East there was little mass colonization by Westerners, and the native peoples were not displaced. But even here thousands of Western European nobles, soldiers of fortune, and merchants settled as a governing and commercial exploiting class who drew riches from their control of such areas. . . . The Italian and Provençal merchants who settled in Constantinople and the seaport cities of Syria, like the French, Provençal, German, and Italian nobles who set up their feudal principalities in the East and in Southern Italy and Sicily show the extent of Western European penetration of areas which had previously been closed to them.

These new frontier conquests, whether they were fully settled colonial areas or regions dominated by a Western European governing and commercial minority were not Europe's most important frontiers, important though they were. The important frontier was an internal one of forest, swamp, marsh, moor, and fen. It was this waste land which Europe's peasants settled and largely put into cultivation between the years 1000 and 1250. Due to their efforts the primeval forest which had covered a large part of Britain, Northern

France, Belgium, Germany, Scandinavia, and Slavic Europe was hacked down and divided into assarts. Polders rescued maritime Flanders, Holland, and much of Northern Germany and Eastern England from the sea. A vast new area of virgin soil capable of sustaining a growing population was put to the plough or made available for pasturing increased flocks of sheep and cattle.

Nor was this all. Historical research in recent years has revealed an increased tempo of exploitation of mineral resources such as salt, silver, lead, zinc, copper, tin, and iron in Britain, France, Italy, Germany, and Scandinavia. New mining methods and other technological advances increased mineral production everywhere. The abundant timber and naval stores of Britain, Scandinavia, and the Baltic became more important commercially than ever before. The sea was exploited more systematically for its fisheries, especially the cod of Iceland and the Norwegian coasts and the herring of the Baltic caught in great numbers in this period off Swedish Skåne.

Can we wonder, in the light of this expanding internal and external frontier, that these years saw a steady growth of trade, of manufacturing, of urbanization. This was largely the result of new lands inside Europe's heartland and on the frontier being put into production, of greater exploitation of mineral and maritime resources, of the tribute which Islamic, Byzantine, and border peoples paid to enterprising Western merchants and conquerors. Western Europe lost its earlier isolation during these years and entered into the full stream of world commerce and trade.

Nor need we be surprised that these same centuries saw the development of a great Western European civilization, with its romanesque and Gothic art and architecture, its troubadour, chivalric, and fabliaux literature, its schools and universities which studied Roman law, medicine, and subtle scholastic philosophy. All were in part the by-products of an expanding prosperous Western European economy.

If one examines government, one notes similar progress. Feudalism in many areas during these years gave way to more advanced centralized government. The papacy established itself as a great international administrative system. Towns arising as new political entities developed urban institutions to fit the needs of their middle-class inhabitants. Even in the conservative countryside the manorial system, where it had existed, began to disappear, and Western Europe's peasant population by 1250 was everywhere rising from serfdom towards the greater freedom of tenant status. In the economic, the political, and the social and the cultural spheres these years were ones which saw steady advances for almost all the people of Western Europe.

In some ways, then, it is all the more surprising to note the changes which one finds in the following century, from 1250 to 1350, in most of Western Europe. These changes are beginning to engage the interest of a growing number of historians and have already given rise to a number of controversies. Let us briefly catalogue the nature of these new developments.

First and most noticeable, one finds during this century an end of the expansion and growth of Europe's urban communities. This is not true of Florence and perhaps Venice and some other parts of Italy, Barcelona in the Iberian

Peninsula, and some towns in Southern and Northern Germany. But these are but exceptions to the general rule that these years saw a halt to the earlier trend towards increasing Western European urbanization.

Second, one can note within almost every town which has been carefully examined a growing separation of the burgesses into two distinct classes—one an urban patriciate of merchants and professional groups, the other an artisan proletariat. Venice in 1298 enshrined this difference in a Golden Book. Flanders reveals it in the struggle a little later centering around the personalities of the Van Artevelde family. Florence developed these differences into two recognized political parties, the *Popolo Grosso* and the *Popolo Minuto*, replacing to some degree the old Guelf-Ghibelline division. Study of thirteenth-century Montpellier or the cities of Germany reveals the same fundamental split in the urban population, which now leads to new discord and friction in the towns of Western Europe.

In the countryside a somewhat similar series of changes is apparent. The trend towards freedom stopped and in some places was reversed. Some peasants, taking advantage of their freedom and the new money economy, began to rent additional land from their landlords and rise to the level of a yeoman class. Others, however, were less fortunate. They kept their freedom in most areas but without resources they sank to a cottar-bordar level as a rural proletariat of agricultural laborers. As one authority has said, the problem in the countryside in the fourteenth century was no longer peasant freedom, but the price of agricultural labor. Soon we enter an era of peasant revolts, a symbol of a malaise and social discontent unknown to agrarian regions prior to 1250.

In political life one notes similar friction and basic instability. Germany and Italy after 1254 relapsed into political anarchy and disunity. The rulers of the Iberian Peninsula, who had collaborated in winning victories over the Moors in the twelfth and early thirteenth centuries wasted their resources in family and dynastic internecine squabbles. In France, the enlightened monarchy of St. Louis gave way to the growing despotism of Philip the Fair and his ministers. Even in England, best governed of all during these years, the strong rule of Edward I gave place to the weaker rule of Edward II and the Despensers. Scandinavia, Slavic Europe, and Hungary were wracked by disorders in contrast to the relative stability in the late twelfth and earlier thirteenth centuries. The Avignon papacy with all its limitations succeeded to the strong Roman pontificate of the previous century. Politically as well as economically Europe moved from strength and stability to weakness and disorder.

One notices the same thing in the field of culture. The Gothic lost its originality and special strength, except in England, and a new naturalism modified the mediaeval sculptural styles of Northern Europe. In Italy one leaves the mediaeval world of ideals exemplified by Dante to move into the more uncertain secularism and questioning of Petrarch. North of the Alps chivalric literature lost its *raison d'être* as the practical, cynical Jean de Meun completed Guillaume de Lorris' idealistic *Roman de la Rose* on a new bourgeois note. Scholasticism lost its unifying intellectual role as the syntheses of Albertus Magnus, Aquinas, and Bonaventura were destroyed by the nominalistic logic of Ockham and Duns Scotus. New disturbing ideas of conciliarism were voiced by Marsilio of Padua and John of Jandum. The older mediaeval cultural pattern, like its economy and political life, was threatened with dissolution and decay.

It would be unwise not to recognize that the causes of these changes were infinitely varied and complex in nature. No single cause suffices to explain them. For instance, the nascent capitalism arising in important cities in Flanders, Southern France, and Italy was one factor which helped provoke class struggles between urban patriciates and proletariats everywhere and helped cause the dissolution of guild organizations. One cannot view the disintegration of Germany and Italy without recognizing how much this was due to the thirteenth-century struggles between popes and Hohenstaufens. Likewise one must note the importance of the national monarchies of France and England and their victory over Boniface as a cause of the ineffectiveness of the Avignon papacy. And there can be little doubt that the Black Death and Hundred Years' War lie behind many fourteenth- and fifteenth-century troubles which affected Europe.

Nevertheless, it seems probable that there was a more underlying reason than any of the foregoing—namely, the ending or closing of Europe's internal or external frontiers between the years 1250 and 1350, which influenced all segments of life in this period.

One can see this change best in examining Europe's external frontiers. By 1250 Western Europe had ceased to expand its influence in the Mediterranean. After losing control of most of Spain in the early thirteenth century, for instance, the Moors rallied to hold their mountain kingdom of Granada secure behind the mountain ramparts of the Sierra Nevada. On the other side of the Mediterranean the Moslem world recovered the Syrian coast from Crusading families who had clung to certain footholds there for many decades. In the Byzantine East Michael Paleologus by 1261 had regained Constantinople from the Latins and reconstituted the Byzantine Empire.

Many Western European footholds remained in the Orient. Cyprus, Crete, the Aegean Islands, and principalities in Southern Greece, protected by Italian sea power, remained Western. Activities like those carried on by the Catalan Companies show that opportunities still existed in this area for Western soldier adventurers to exploit. Also, there can be little doubt that Italian merchants were still the dominant economic power in both Mediterranean and Black Sea regions. One need only examine the careers of Marco Polo and other Italian traders who penetrated as far as China and the Indian Ocean during this century to be convinced of this fact. But it is equally true that after 1250 Western Europe increasingly found itself on the defensive in the Orient. It was not to it but to the rising power of the Ottoman Turks that the immediate future was to belong.

In Eastern Europe after 1250 one notices a similar contraction of Western European influence. Continued Mongol control of Russia restricted Western influence to Novgorod, while disorder in Germany helped to stall the Teutonic *Drang Nach Osten* for many decades. Not until the second quarter of the fourteenth century was it resumed with the growing power of the Hanseatic League and Teutonic Knights in the Baltic and the beginning of Luxembourg hegemony in Bohemia. In Eastern Europe, as in the Mediterranean, Western Europe found its influence waning, as Byzantines, Moslems, Slavs, and Balts resisted more successfully the pressures of Western European peoples. Even in the British Isles the story of the Bruces in Scotland and Ireland seems to show a resistance to Anglo-Norman influence, which had been all but irresistible earlier.

More serious, however, was the end of another frontier expansion—the internal one between the years 1250 and 1350. During this century in area after area of Western Europe unused land ceased to exist. In some places this was true by 1250. In others, like Southern France, it was a more gradual process not complete until well into the first years of the fourteenth century. As unused land was exhausted, however, Western Europe's peasantry (particularly in areas north of the Alps) lost the possibility of taking up vacant lands and raising their status. Forest, fen, marsh, and moor had at last been tamed and brought under cultivation and opportunities no longer existed for the hardy peasant to hack out an assart or drain low-lying swamp on terms more favorable than those available to him in his own village. No longer could the unearned increment of virgin land enrich monastic proprietor, noble landlord, and peasant cultivator alike. The boom in the countryside, which had lasted more than two centuries, came to an end. Few *villes neuves* or *bastides* remained to be founded. Instead, one finds emphasis upon forest laws, which were often conservation measures, necessary to protect what remained of the forests of France and England. Much research still remains to be done on agrarian population patterns, but some partial studies of Northern France suggest that by the fourteenth century there were probably as many people living in the countryside as were to be found there in the nineteenth century. A recent study of the villages of late mediaeval England also seems to show that in certain areas the population in this period was even greater than it is today. In Ireland and Scotland and Wales it seems clear that there was no increase in the area under cultivation after 1350 until the eighteenth century, when the arable area was increased at the expense of nearby pastoral clan societies.

Equally interesting is a fact which study of glaciers in Greenland, Iceland, and Norway has made clear. From about the year 1300 on for several centuries the climate of Northern Europe grew more severe. As it did, expansion of agricultural land toward the north ceased and the cultivated area even contracted in Norway, Sweden, and Finland.

We can sum up our conclusions as follows. After 1250 the external frontiers of Western Europe contracted and the internal frontier all but disappeared, except perhaps during the early fourteenth century along the borders of Eastern Germany and in Bohemia, where expansion continued to take place. With the end of the internal frontier ended the unearned increment of land which had enriched Western European society. With the contraction of the external frontier the riches which rulers, exploiters, and merchants (particularly those of Northern Europe) had drawn from Byzantine, Moslem and other peoples decreased as well. A Western European world which had been steadily expanding internally and externally down to 1250 saw its expansion halted and come to a stop as its frontiers closed.

It seem probable that the crisis produced by this fact lies at the root of the many changes that took place between 1250 and 1350. As free land gave out inside Western Europe, the peasants had no place to go now—few *villes neuves* or assarts beckoned the dissatisfied and the enterprising. Naturally the movement towards greater freedom came to an end. Instead, the peasantry had to face restrictions on their freedom, especially in parts of Germany, and their discontent began to be translated into a dissatisfaction with their lot which caused those peasant risings which were such a feature of fourteenth- and fifteenth-century Europe.

At the same time, the urban communities were equally affected by the end of this rural real estate boom which had fed their prosperity and expansion. Their growth ended and the crisis was made worse by the fact that smaller gains flowed into Europe from foreign areas, particularly Europe beyond the Alps. A Florence or a Venice or even a Barcelona might be prosperous, but other communities like Montpellier or Marseilles or Pisa were not. One can, as a matter of fact, see this urban depression by examining the building of cathedrals during this century. If one does, one notes an interesting fact. Between 1150 and 1250 in almost every community new cathedrals were built and older ones enlarged. Between 1250 and 1350, except in parts of Germany, this ceased to be so. Evidently Western European towns could no longer afford the building activity which seemed easy and natural a century earlier.

Now this end of urban growth and prosperity had a number of serious results which, in many cases, extended beyond the towns themselves. It ended a second safety-valve for Western Europe's rural population, already restricted by the ending of the internal frontier. Now dissatisfied peasants could not hope, except for a rare Dick Whittington, to find employment in a growing town labor force. Nor could peasant villages near towns count, as they had earlier, on a growing demand for their surplus agricultural produce to bring life-giving cash into their exchequers. There was now little escape available to the cottars and bordars who more and more became a depressed agricultural proletariat. Even a cursory examination of Piers Plowman reveals how bitter their lot often was.

These facts also help to explain why, in so many towns in Flanders, France, and Italy, there was friction and discord between the merchant patriciate and artisan proletariat during this period. It was no longer possible, as it had been earlier, for merchants to dispose of the goods which the town artisan guilds produced in increasing amounts except at a loss. There was no built-in expanding market for such production after 1250. Hence discord grew between producer and middleman which often took the form of civic disorder. At the same time in artisan guilds themselves it ceased to be always possible for journeymen to rise to the position of masters, as had generally been the case earlier. There was simply no market for goods produced by more than a few shops. Hence discontent within guilds, restrictive practices enforced more rigidly everywhere and that phenomenon of the late Middle Ages, the jour-neyman's guild. In the town as in the countryside opportunity for advance-ment had ended for many who had not been troubled by this problem earlier.

Even the nobility were adversely affected. Earlier new lands put into pro-duction had enriched noble landlords. Or younger sons had had the safety-valve of careers of adventures and the possibility of carving out estates for themselves in Spain, the Near East, Slavic Europe, or the troubled border lands of Scotland and Ireland. Now this became less possible. No wonder such nobles in increasing numbers thronged the courts of rulers in the fourteenth and fifteenth century looking for preferment and position as their only hope of maintaining their place in society. Those idle nobles, whom we meet in Frois-sart or who formed the political machine manipulated by John of Gaunt, were created by the changed conditions of the period. Noble, burgher, and peasant alike were caught by the crisis of a society which had ceased expanding as the external frontier contracted and the internal frontier ended for most of West-ern Europe.

When one examines the papacy and royal governments of Europe during these years one sees the results of the closing of the mediaeval frontier with particular clarity. Up to the year 1250 or thereabouts the problems faced by the mediaeval papacy were essentially moral, religious, and political. Take, for in-stance, the Investiture Controversy, the Crusades, the struggle with German emperors over control of the Italian peninsula, or the problems of heresy in Southern France. After 1250 papal problems became increasingly financial, es-pecially for the Avignon popes. At the same time we note a growing tide of criticism of the Church and papacy as corrupt, rapacious, and interested only in money. Such complaints had been made earlier, but not with the same force and unanimity. Now we find a rising tide of criticism, led by the Spiritual Franciscans, against papal annates, expectancies and the like, which were reit-erated later in the century by monarchs like the kings of England and move-ments like those led by Wycliff and Hus.

Now careful examination of papal administration seems to show that the Avignon papacy with all its faults was much better organized than its Roman predecessor, so that, despite corruption, there was less waste in the collection of papal revenues. Why the outcry then? The answer seems obvious. A less prosperous Europe was less able to pay the costs of church government than had been the case earlier, and in the face of this fact the Avignon popes were forced to increase their pressure to collect the sums they felt necessary to run their papal Curia and their Church—a situation which was eventually to lead directly to the Reformation.

Nor were the popes alone in facing the dilemma of lowered revenues. The same problem faced the monarchs of Western Europe. This was no new prob-lem, as all who have studied the financial difficulties that beset a Frederick Barbarossa or a John or Henry III of England well know. But after 1250 it be-came more acute. Rulers could no longer live on their own. They could not count on the appreciation in value of their royal estates or customs levies or court fines and the like to meet the expenses of their growing administrations.

All of these had increased earlier as the result of an expanding Europe with expanding frontiers. This was now no longer so. Thus, a Philip the Fair of France tried to meet the crisis in part by reaching out for the rich Flanders towns or manipulating the coinage, that classic answer of a financially distressed government. Such expedients were, however, but temporary palliatives. The more general response to this problem was the development all over Europe of a new type of national taxation—whether it be in the Spanish monarchies, in Britain, in France, in Scandinavia or even in remote Bohemia. Rulers called on their nobles, middle class, and peasantry to help pay the cost of their growing administrations, until by 1350, this new type of taxation affected every segment of Western European society, although not always equally.

In the modern world Webb has pointed out a very similar phenomenon as the frontier has given out. When, as he has said, the sovereign has given out all the free land and none remains, it is necessary for him to begin to tax—taking back in another form the wealth he earlier showered out upon his people. This vertical movement of wealth, as he calls it, he regards as one of the results of the closing of the modern great frontier. Certainly exactly the same thing happened in mediaeval Europe, where new national taxation began at the very moment when the frontier ended there too. With this new taxation there arose all over Europe that late mediaeval phenomenon of representative institutions. This was caused in part by the need of the rulers to have the various classes of society vote them taxes and assist them in their collections until such time as the rulers felt powerful enough to dispense with such assistance. National taxation in late mediaeval Europe, then, and even representative governments, were in no small measure the result of the closing of the mediaeval frontier.

We might sum up the situation in Western Europe between 1250 and 1350 as follows. The crisis which Europe faced in this century was largely the result of the end of the mediaeval frontier. It was the crisis of a suddenly frontierless society. The results were serious indeed: the end of growing peasant freedom and tension in the countryside; a political, economic, and social crisis in cities which had ceased to expand; a church which had to concern itself so much with finances that it neglected its spiritual and moral leadership; and governments which had to meet this crisis by inaugurating large-scale taxation buttressed by representative institutions. That this was followed by that first of modern great wars, the Hundred Years' War, and that first of modern great plagues, the Black Death, simply compounded the difficulties Europe faced. We who, if we may believe Webb, face a somewhat similar frontierless existence may well reflect on how our European forebears met such a situation in the late thirteenth and fourteenth centuries and what the results were for the society and culture of Western Europe.

CHAPTER 38

Cities and Social Classes

Edith Ennen

The population curve altered in the fourteenth century. The frequency of abandoned settlements in the countryside, the pause in the colonization movement eastwards of the peasantry, the abandonment of new town foundations and the arrested growth of many existing towns even to the extent of a considerable decline in urban populations are all indisputable signs of this negative trend. The plague was neither the original nor the sole cause of the crisis. In many individual cases the decline in population can be shown to have set in before the Black Death of 1348. With the high medieval mortality rate, only a small fall-back in births sufficed to bring a population reduction. Here we find a phenomenon which reflects human vitality and which requires biological investigation and proof. The plague accentuated the existing negative tendencies. There were famines on top of plague, notably that of 1315–1317 which affected the whole of northern Europe and may have contributed to the high death rate in the first great plague of 1348 by weakening the population.

Whether or not one is dealing with a general and century-long crisis in the later Middle Ages is a matter for dispute. The situation varied from one economic region to another. One must contrast signs of depression in Flanders and Provence with indications of progress in other regions, in south Germany, especially in Nürnberg, as well as in the Saar and Moselle regions and in Holland and England. In France non-economic factors were at work, notably the Hundred Years' War. The chronology of the crises varied. In Barcelona its high-point was between 1431 and 1443 and was caused as much by the military ventures of King Alfonso as by the economic stagnation in Genoa. The meagre nature of the statistical work which has been done still makes a closer definition of "up and down" tendencies impossible. The question, in any case, cannot be solely answered by studying the towns. Thus, a conclusive answer to the question of whether there was a cyclical or a structural crisis, and whether the change in the agrarian economy was decisive, still cannot be given.

In north-western Europe, the late-medieval economic crisis expressed itself in the sharp rise and decline of different regions, in bitter competition for markets, and in the powerful reaction of the towns to advances in rural indus-

From Edith Ennen, *The Medieval Town* (Amsterdam: Elsevier Science Publishing, 1979), pp. 190–197. Reprinted by permission from Elsevier Science Publishing B. V., Amsterdam.

tries. Within the towns considerable social tensions accompanied the creation of an urban proletariat from displaced master-craftsmen and from apprentices who had lost all hope of ever becoming masters. There were sharp distinctions of wealth and ossification and stagnation in the economic sector.

• • •

Credit was essential for the smooth conduct of trade and production. Its use was a natural part of the chain of transactions from the purchase of raw materials to the sale of the finished article to the consumer. Industrial production for export was largely based on credit, either in the form of supplying craftsmen in their homes or of collective purchases by the guild. Credit linked one merchant with another. Creditworthiness was an essential prerequisite for a merchant's success. Interest was a natural accompaniment to it. Here we are faced with the teaching of the Church, and the Church had to come to terms with the prevailing situation. The doctrine that the existence of risk justified profit must be attributed to the scholastic theologians of the later Middle Ages. They began an extension of the theory of interest. The public sector also intervened in credit transactions: the favourite urban form of borrowing was the sale of rents.

A striking feature of the last part of the fourteenth century was the amount of social unrest. In Cologne in 1369–1370 the weavers brought about the overthrow of patrician control, and in 1396, after an embittered family feud between the Greifen and Freunden, they brought about a change in the constitution. The *Richerzeche* disappeared and the *Verbundbrief* formed the basis of the constitution until the imperial towns disappeared altogether as a concept. In the last years of the fifteenth century, unresolved differences brought about a renewed outbreak of trouble in the rising of 1482. In 1513 another insurrection led to the *Transfixbrief* which enlarged the clauses of the *Verbundbrief.* All the towns producing textiles for export suffered revolts by weavers in the fourteenth century: Constance and Augsburg in the south, Stendal in north Germany, and other towns from Flanders to Florence. There was unrest in the Hanseatic area, in the *Knochenhauer* (butchers) Revolt in Lübeck, in Danzig, Brunswick, in Nürnberg, Liège and Metz. The cliché "guild wars" does not sufficiently explain this phenomenon. Its antecedents are more complex. The movements led by the Parisian merchant, Étienne Marcel and the Jacquerie in France reflected the political crisis of a land at war as well as its serious social problems. Steinbach and Maschke have rightly warned against misunderstanding these movements. They were not the beginning of modern democracy. The political equality of corporations and not of individuals was in question. The work of Steinbach and Herborn for Cologne shows how quickly a closed society of the privileged reformed itself after 1396. Van Werveke has shown the same for Ghent. Here too, while the guilds were successful in controlling some or the majority of seats on the town council, they did not really rule the towns. In Ulm, Esslingen and other Swabian towns, the office of town mayor was still always held by a patrician although the constitution permitted a craftsman to be chosen. The cause lies in the operation of the principle of indispensability already recognized by Weber and more fully marked out by Maschke.

In many towns in which the guilds took control, in Strasbourg, Constance, Basel, and Augsburg, the patricians cut themselves off and formed an exclusive group. The result was that they declined in numbers. Urban society was organized according to occupation, and status symbols consisted in ways of dressing and in invitations to festivals and dances which were limited to chosen people. The dress permitted to each class was laid down by the town council. Patricians met in drinking societies. Their control of the town continued unweakened in trading towns without large export industries, for instance in Metz. Genoa too recognized only *nobili* and *populari* but no distinction between the *popolo grasso* and *popolo minuto* which was such a marked feature of Florentine society. Genoa also had the *albergo* which served as a social meeting place of the *nobili* and which corresponded to the German *Trinkstube* and from the fourteenth century there was also a popular equivalent to the *alberghi* of the nobility.

In central Europe egoism and conservation dominated guild life. The many apprentices with no hope of ever becoming masters also became an element likely to cause unrest and rebellion. They formed bands, and wandering apprentices became an ever-increasing phenomenon. The master craftsmen also combined, often on a regional basis in common cause against their apprentices. For example, in 1352 the bakers of Mainz, Worms, Speyer, Oppenheim, Frankfurt, Bingen, Bacharach and Boppard formed a super-guild to prevent an apprentice who had been dismissed by his master in one town from being able to find lodging and work elsewhere. The inter-town guild also turned against married apprentices: if the wife of a baker's apprentice came to market and sold flour and cereal, no master in any of the eight towns might employ her husband. The practice of masters and their apprentices living together in the same house became less frequent. Solidarity among the apprentices themselves increased and had its outward manifestation in the uniform which they wore. The masters continued their opposition nevertheless. In 1442, for example, the furriers of Bavaria and Austria met to deny their apprentices every corporative right. In Strasbourg in 1404 forty-eight apprentice furriers from Bohemia and the Tyrol combined to form a separate brotherhood; in this very capital intensive business the chance of ever becoming a master was particularly remote. The master-craftsmen maintained that the urban authorities alone were empowered to settle conflicts between masters and apprentices. In 1465 this association of masters broadened when it acquired further links in Franconia, Swabia and the Rhineland. Unrest, strikes, and strife between master and apprentice filled the whole of the fourteenth and fifteenth centuries.

In Florence in 1378 disturbances turned into the revolt of the *ciompi* or woolcarders. This rising was of great interest to Renaissance historical writers and has been also to modern neo-Marxist researchers, although it has been correctly interpreted by neither group. This was no "proletarian revolution" with social revolutionary aims. In the July revolt, which resulted in a new political regime, people from all classes of Florentine society took part including patrician leaders from famous families like the Strozzi, Alberti and Medici; members of the industrial and mercantile middle classes and a great mass of wage earners. The revolt took its name from the woolcarders or *ciompi*, but every class of worker from the lower orders was represented—cloth dyers, fullers, finishers and small entrepreneurs who were not members of the Arte della Lana but their subordinate employees, namely *sottoposti*. Characteristically, three new guilds were formed to include them and these were added to the seven upper guilds and the fourteen lower ones. The aims and wishes of the *sottoposti* and *ciompi* were very mixed. Disappointment of the *ciompi* with the new conservative regime brought a further outbreak of trouble in August which produced no clear programme. As Brucker says:

> It was a characteristic Florentine *imbroglio,* neither very bloody nor very destructive and as strongly influenced by personal hatreds and loyalties as by any spirit or sense of class. The historical significance of the Ciompi episode was its utilization by the Florentine patriciate to justify the increasingly narrow social base of politics and the progressive exclusion of the lower class from office.

In 1382 "order was restored."

At the same time the craftsmen of Ghent, supported by those of Bruges and Ypres, rose against the count, but he, with his allies the French knights, defeated them at West-Roosebeke in 1382. The overwhelmingly political character of the Ghent revolts in the fourteenth century is unmistakeable. In Liège the patricians were excluded from the town council. The corps of craftsmen who now wielded power had already begun to exclude apprentices and aliens. The entry fee for becoming a master was increased. This was a widespread development. The rule of the patricians was replaced by control by small artisan entrepreneurs. A proletariat grew up below them in the fifteenth century.

. . . The relatively greater prosperity of the major towns is revealed through statistics of poverty. The Brabantine accounts also provide evidence here. While the number of poor in Antwerp decreased between 1437 and 1480 from 13.5 percent to 10.5 percent, the proportion in Louvain increased from 7.6 percent to 18.3 percent, in Brussels between 1437 and 1496 from 10.5 percent to 17.1 percent. In smaller towns the number of poor rose as high as 36 percent. These poor came from declining industries or were made up of unskilled workers and immigrants from the countryside.

The time of most severe misery for the mass of workers coincided with the high-point of bourgeois luxury in the Low Countries. The most splendid buildings were erected by the prosperous upper class. In the meantime, the gulf between the moneyed aristocracy and the proletarian masses widened. The urban magistracy was no longer able to cope with the problems arising from poverty and the government had to intervene. In the fifteenth century, princes like Philip the Good intervened actively, if not systematically, against begging.

Poverty also had a place in the medieval social hierarchy: it gave the rich the possibility of doing acts of charity. The rich man was dependent on the intercession of the poor so that the poor man had prayers to offer in return for alms. The poor also formed their own associations. In 1454 a Brotherhood of Beggars was formed in Zülpich and was joined by cripples, the blind and other poor people. It raised fees from members and cared for the sick. The fierce struggle against the poor and beggars is an expression of early modern feeling and a product of the situation in early modern times. The beggar was still integrated into medieval society. Even if the lower classes in the Middle Ages were politically without rights and economically weak, frequent movement into the upper classes took place. Possibilities of saving and thereby advancement existed, especially for servants and apprentices. In Basel servants and craftsmen's assistants accounted for 17 percent of the population and 29 percent of all those who had to pay taxes. In general they formed what was the upper working class while among the wage earners, merchants' apprentices formed a lower middle class. Beneath the apprentices and servants were the day workers, unskilled workers, single women and, beneath them again, the beggars.

CHAPTER 39

Religion and Revolution

Norman Cohn

Between the close of the eleventh century and the first half of the sixteenth it repeatedly happened in Europe that the desire of the poor to improve the material conditions of their lives became transfused with phantasies of a new Paradise on earth, a world purged of suffering and sin, a Kingdom of the Saints.

The history of those centuries was of course sprinkled with innumerable struggles between the privileged and the less privileged, risings of towns against their overlords, of artisans against merchant capitalists, of peasants against nobles. Usually those risings had strictly limited aims—the securing of specific rights, the removal of specific grievances—or else (like the famous *Jacquerie*) were mere outbreaks of destructive rage provoked by sheer misery. But risings could also occur which had quite a different scope. The Middle Ages had inherited from Antiquity—from the Jews and the early Christians—a tradition of prophecy which during those same centuries took on a fresh and exuberant vitality. In the language of theology—which seems here the most appropriate language—there existed an eschatology, or body of doctrine concerning the final state of the world, which was chiliastic in the most general sense of the term—meaning that it foretold a Millennium, not necessarily limited to a thousand years and indeed not necessarily limited at all, in which the world would be inhabited by a humanity at once perfectly good and perfectly happy. Offering so much solace of a kind which the official teaching of the medieval Church withheld, this eschatology came to exercise a powerful and enduring fascination. Generation after generation was seized at least intermittently by a tense expectation of some sudden, miraculous event in which the world would be utterly transformed, some prodigious final struggle between the hosts of Christ and the hosts of Antichrist through which history would attain its fulfilment and justification. Although it would be a gross over-simplification to identify the world of chiliastic exaltation with the world of social unrest, there were many times when needy and discontented masses were captured by some millennial prophet. And when that happened movements were apt to arise which, though relatively small and short-lived, can be seen in retrospect to bear a startling resemblance to the great totalitarian movements of our own day.

• • •

. . . *Prophetae* would construct their apocalyptic lore out of the most varied materials—the Book of Daniel, the Book of Revelation, the Sibylline Oracles, the speculations of Joachim of Fiore, the doctrine of the Egalitarian State of Nature—all of them elaborated and reinterpreted and vulgarised. That lore would be purveyed to the masses—and the result would be something which was at once a revolutionary movement and an outburst of quasi-religious salvationism.

This salvationism, too, is of a peculiar kind, in that the salvation promised is terrestrial and collective. The Heavenly City is to appear on this earth; and its joys are to crown not the peregrinations of individual souls but the epic exploits of a "chosen people." And such a revolutionary movement is of a peculiar kind, in that its aims and promises are boundless. A social struggle is imagined as uniquely important, different in kind from all other struggles known to history, a cataclysm from which the world is to emerge totally transformed and redeemed. But this, again, is the very thing that in our time has most clearly characterised the two great totalitarian movements, Communist and Nazi, especially in their early, revolutionary stages. What has set these latter-day movements so utterly apart from the ordinary run of political parties in Europe—whether conservative or reformist—is precisely their way of endowing social conflicts and aspirations with a transcendental significance—in fact with all the mystery and majesty of the final, eschatological drama. In this sense the story unfolded in *The Pursuit of the Millennium* can be regarded as a prologue to the vast revolutionary upheavals of the present century.

Some suspicion of this has occurred to Communist and Nazi ideologists themselves. An enthusiastic if fanciful exposition of the heterodox German mysticism of the fourteenth century, with appropriate tributes to Beghards, Beguines and Brethren of the Free Spirit, fills a long chapter of Rosenberg's *Myth of the Twentieth Century*; while a Nazi historian devoted a whole volume to interpreting the message of the Revolutionary of the Upper Rhine. As for the Communists, they continue to elaborate, in volume after volume, that cult of Thomas Müntzer which was inaugurated already by Engels.* But whereas in these works the *prophetae* of a vanished world are shown as men born centuries before their time, it is perfectly possible to draw the opposite moral—that, for all their exploitation of the most modern technology, Communism and Nazism have been inspired by phantasies which are downright archaic. And such is in fact the case. It can be shown (though to do so in detail would require another volume) that the ideologies of Communism and Nazism, dissimilar though they are in many respects, are both heavily endebted to that very ancient body of beliefs which constituted the popular apocalyptic lore of Europe.

That peculiar faith which is of the very essence not indeed of chiliasm as such but of militant, revolutionary chiliasm—the tense expectation of a final,

---

*Thomas Müntzer was a religious visionary and a leader of the German Peasants' Rebellion (1325)—Ed.

decisive struggle in which a world tyranny will be overthrown by a "chosen people" and through which the world will be renewed and history brought to its consummation—this did not disappear with the fall of the New Jerusalem at Münster. It continued a dim, subterranean existence down the centuries, flaring up briefly in the margins of the English Civil War and the French Revolution, until in the course of the nineteenth century it began to take on a new, explosive vigour, now in France, now in Germany, now in Russia. It is true that in the nineteenth century a naïve and explicit super-naturalism was gradually replaced by an orientation which was secular and which even claimed to be scientific, so that what had once been demanded by "the will of God" was now demanded by the "purposes of History." But the demand itself remained unchanged: to purify the world by destroying the agents of corruption. What is more, the agents of corruption were still identified with social groups which had been so regarded already in the Middle Ages: sometimes "the great ones" (now called "the bourgeoisie") and sometimes the Jews—with the clergy inevitably less prominent than they were, yet not wholly forgotten either. And as for the coming society itself—that too was still pictured much as it had been in the Middle Ages: as a state of total community, a society wholly unanimous in its beliefs and wholly free from inner conflicts. Such was the tradition of apocalyptic fanaticism which—secularised and revivified—was inherited by Lenin and by Hitler.

• • •

In the Middle Ages the people for whom revolutionary chiliasm had most appeal were neither peasants firmly integrated in the life of village and manor nor artisans firmly integrated in their guilds. The lot of such people might at times be one of poverty and oppression, and at other times be one of relative prosperity and independence; they might revolt or they might accept their situation; but they were not, on the whole, prone to follow some inspired *propheta* in a hectic pursuit of the Millennium. These *prophetae* found their following, rather, where there existed a surplus population, rural or urban or both. This was as true of Flanders and northern France in the twelfth and thirteenth centuries as of Holland and Westphalia in the sixteenth; and recent researches have shown it to have been equally true of the Bohemia of the early fifteenth century. Revolutionary chiliasm drew its strength from the surplus population living on the margin of society—peasants without land or with too little land even for subsistence; journeymen and unskilled workers living under the continuous threat of unemployment; beggars and vagabonds—in fact from that amorphous mass of people who were not simply poor but who could find no assured and recognised place in society at all. These people lacked the material and emotional support afforded by traditional social groups; their kinship-groups had disintegrated and they were not effectively organised in village communities or in guilds; for them there existed no regular, institutionalised methods of voicing their grievances or pressing their claims. Instead they waited for a *propheta* to bind them together in a group of their own—which would then emerge as a movement of a peculiar kind, driven on by a wild enthusiasm born of desperation.

Because these people found themselves in such an exposed and defenceless position they were liable to react very sharply to any disruption of the normal, familiar, pattern of life. Again and again one finds that a particular outbreak of revolutionary chiliasm took place against a background of disaster: the plagues that preluded the First Crusade and the flagellant movements of 1260, 1348–1349, 1391 and 1400; the famines that preluded the First and Second Crusades and the popular crusading movements of 1309–1320, the flagellant movement of 1296, the movements around Eudes de l'Étoile and the pseudo-Baldwin; the spectacular rise in prices that preluded the revolution at Münster. The greatest wave of chiliastic excitement, one which swept through the whole of society, was precipitated by the most universal natural disaster of the Middle Ages, the Black Death; and here again it was in the lower social strata that the excitement lasted longest and that it expressed itself in violence and massacre.

But the rootless masses of the poor were not only shaken by those specific calamities or upheavals that directly affected their material lot—they were also peculiarly sensitive to the less dramatic but equally relentless processes which, generation after generation, gradually disrupted the framework of authority within which medieval life had for a time been contained. The one authority which was universal, embracing with its prescriptions and demands the lives of all individuals, was that of the Church. And by canalising the emotional energies of the laity, by directing their yearnings firmly towards an after-life in another world, the Church did indeed do much to impede the spread of revolutionary chiliasm. But the authority of the Church was not unquestioned. A civilisation which regarded asceticism as the surest sign of grace was bound to doubt the value and validity of a Church which was manifestly infected with *Luxuria* and *Avaritia*. Again and again during the second half of the Middle Ages worldliness amongst the clergy resulted in disaffection amongst the laity—and always that disaffection was most complete amongst the poor. It was inevitable that many of those whose own lives were condemned to hardship and insecurity should doubt whether ostentatious prelates and easy-going priests could really help them towards salvation. But if these people were alienated from the Church, they also suffered from their alienation. How much they needed the Church is shown by the enthusiasm with which they welcomed every sign of ascetic reform and the eagerness with which they would accept, even adore, any genuine ascetic. To be uncertain of the consolation and guidance and mediation of the Church aggravated their sense of helplessness and increased their desperation. It is because of these emotional needs of the poor that the militant social movements we have considered were at the same time surrogates for the Church—salvationist groups led by miracle-working ascetics.

Almost as much as to the Church, supernatural authority pertained to the national monarchy. Medieval kingship was still to a large extent a sacred kingship; the monarch was the representative of the powers that govern the cosmos, an incarnation of the moral law and the divine intention, a guarantor of the order and rightness of the world. And here again it was the poor who most needed such a figure. When we first meet the *pauperes*, in the First Crusade, they are already creating prodigious monarchs out of their own imagination: a resurrected Charlemagne, an Emico of Leiningen made emperor, a King Tafur. And to the poor any prolonged interruption or manifest failure of the royal power brought intense anguish from which they struggled to escape. It was "the poor, weavers and fullers" of Flanders who refused to accept the death in captivity of Count Baldwin IX and who became the most devoted followers of the pseudo-Baldwin, Emperor of Constantinople. The first horde of *Pastoureaux*, in 1251, were inspired by the prospect of rescuing Louis IX from Saracen captivity. And later, whereas in France revolutionary chiliasm waned as the prestige of the monarchy increased, in Germany the long decline of the imperial office fostered the cult of the saviour of the poor in the Last Days, the resurrected or future Frederick. The last emperor to possess all the aura of sacred kingship was Frederick II; and with his death and the fatal disruption known as the Great Interregnum there appeared amongst the common people in Germany an anxiety that was to persist for centuries. The career of the pseudo-Frederick of Neuss in the thirteenth century, the imperial lore that grew up around the flagellant leader Konrad Schmid in the fourteenth and fifteenth centuries, the prophecies and pretensions of the Revolutionary of the Upper Rhine in the sixteenth century—these things bear witness both to an enduring disarray and to the wild chiliasm that throve upon it.

When, finally, one comes to consider the anarcho-communistic millenarian groups which flourished around the close of the Middle Ages, one fact is immediately obvious: it was always in the midst of some great revolt or revolution that a group of this kind emerged into daylight. This is equally the case with John Ball and his followers in the English peasants' revolt of 1381; with the extremists during the early stages of the Hussite revolution in Bohemia in 1419–1421; and with Thomas Müntzer and his "league of the elect" in the German peasants' revolt of 1525. And it is true, also, of the radical Anabaptists at Münster—for the establishment of their New Jerusalem came at the end of a whole series of revolts, not only at Münster but throughout the ecclesiastical states of north-west Germany. In each of these instances the mass insurrection itself was directed towards limited and realistic aims—yet in each instance the climate of mass insurrection fostered a special kind of millenarian group. As social tensions mounted and the revolt became nation-wide, there would appear, somewhere on the radical fringe, a *propheta* with his following of paupers, intent on turning this one particular upheaval into the apocalyptic battle, the final purification of the world. . . .

A boundless, millennial promise made with boundless, prophet-like conviction to a number of rootless and desperate men in the midst of a society where traditional norms and relationships are disintegrating—here, it would seem, lay the source of that peculiar subterranean fanaticism which subsisted as a perpetual menace to the structure of medieval society. It may be suggested that here, too, lies the source of the giant fanaticisms which in our day have convulsed the world.